A PAPER
The Ending of Yugoslavia

Mark Thompson was born in Sheffield in 1959. Educated in London and Cambridge, he has worked as an editor of *END Journal* and a translator of Italian and French fiction. He is currently the London correspondent of *Mladina* magazine in Slovenia.

Mark Thompson

A PAPER HOUSE

The Ending of Yugoslavia

VINTAGE

To my mother, and in memory of my father

VINTAGE

20 Vauxhall Bridge Road, London SW1V 2SA

London Melbourne Sydney Auckland Johannesburg
and agencies throughout the world

First published by Hutchinson/Radius, 1992
Vintage edition 1992

1 3 5 7 9 10 8 6 4 2

© Mark Thompson 1992

Printed and bound in Great Britain by
Cox & Wyman Ltd, Reading

ISBN 0 09 921211 0

Contents

Pronunciation

In the Serbo-Croatian and Slovenian languages,

c   is pronounced "ts" as in flats
č   is "ch" as in church
ć   is "tj", or "tu" as in tune
dj   is approximately a crisp "j" as in jeans
dž   is approximately a soft "g" as in gentle
j   is "y" as in yes
lj   is "liyuh", like the middle sound of "million"
nj   is "ny" as in canyon
š   is "sh" as in shot
ž   is a "zh" sound, as in plea*sure*

Other letters are pronounced much as in English.

List of Maps

The moon is eating its heart out
On the downhill stretch of June: last quarter.
And the century is waning fast, making for
The delta, headlong down the slope.

> *Ivan V. Lalić*

It was a time at the limits of two epochs in human history, when one could more easily see the end of that epoch which was closing than the beginning of that new one which was opening.

> *Ivo Andrić*

We too are Europe, but in our own way.

> *Milovan Djilas*

Who are we? Where are we from? Where are we going?

> *Danilo Kiš*

Note for this edition

Nothing in this edition has been changed except a few literals and factual errors, and a scattering of clumsy expressions. I was tempted to amend the cautiously but blindly optimistic closing pages of the Bosnian chapter. "After all, it wouldn't be cheating," I argued feebly to myself. "The book's analysis surely shows that Serbia and the federal army were bound to carry the war into Bosnia-Hercegovina once the military deadlock in Croatia had been stabilized in their favour by the United Nations' intervention. If hope made me briefly lose my nerve, so what?"

But sense prevailed. My stupidity at that point (it was mid March when I revised the proofs) was shared by observers much better informed than myself; it, too, belongs to the ending of Yugoslavia, and to censor it now would be worse than futile. Besides, it would hardly be fair to suppress this plain proof of my own susceptibility to the Yugoslav affliction of wishful thinking (see Preface).

Instead there is an Afterword, principally to describe the horrors in BiH and explain how they came to happen, who perpetrates them, and why the outside world lets them keep happening for month after month.

I also take the chance to include an Appendix which had to be omitted in the first edition for reasons of space.

London, September 1992

Preface

A foreign mercenary in Yugoslavia in 1991 told a journalist that "We have our own reasons for being here. I wanted to understand why this war was happening." The man's method of research was extreme, but anyone can sympathize with his bafflement. This book is not a war report, though I hope it explains why the war reportage presented such a confusing picture. Nowhere in Europe, as the Cold War ended, was it trickier for outsiders to tell the needful from the needless destruction, than in federal Yugoslavia. This book attempts that distinction. More personally, it records a kind of passion to understand a place; to experience something as it vanished, and to see new things as they emerged. Not that I set out to be an obituarist; events gave me no choice. My first map of Yugoslavia, like my own image of it, did not show internal borders. When I arrived, in 1987, it took a while to realize that Yugoslavia was less real than its component parts. Moving from Ljubljana to Zagreb to Sarajevo, I passed through three countries; at least three more lay beyond.

In earlier times this impression of difference would have been muted. In the 1930s I might have mourned the murdered King Aleksandar. In the 1940s Tito and his partisans would have won my heart and mind. Twenty years ago I might have lighted gladly on signs that nations had not vanished in the socialist federation. When I was travelling, nations were almost all there was. This spared me certain illusions; perhaps I indulged others, but I hope that wishful thinking is not among them. Yugoslav hearts have fed too much on fantasy; the task now is to help something better to come where Yugoslavia was.

I worked back from my preconceptions, unravelling them in a process of discovery. Each chapter, except one, describes a unit of the former state. Let the exception stand as a plea for wise treatment of regions in the Yugoslav space. If this plea reveals an illusion, so be it!

London, March 1992

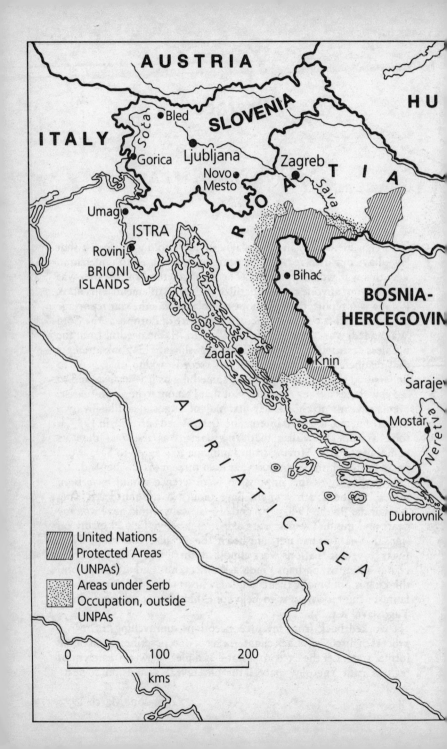

AUSTRIA

HU

SLOVENIA

ITALY

Soča

● Bled

Gorica

Ljubljana

Zagreb

Novo
Mesto

C
R
O
A
T
I
A

Sava

Umag

ISTRA

Rovinj

BRIONI
ISLANDS

● Bihać

BOSNIA-
HERCEGOVIN

Zadar

● Knin

Saraje

Mostar ●

Neretva

A
D
R
I
A
T
I
C

S
E
A

Dubrovnik

▨ United Nations
Protected Areas
(UNPAs)

▨ Areas under Serb
Occupation, outside
UNPAs

0   100   200

kms

What Was Yugoslavia?

Yugoslavia means land of the Yugoslavs – the South Slavs. In the beginning Yugoslavia was an idea. According to this idea, the Slav peoples who lived between the Adriatic and the Black Sea were bonded by kinship of race and language; therefore they should combine to realize their national essence in peace and harmony in their own state – Yugoslavia.

The idea contained a political project, because it could not be realized unless these peoples united against their Austrian, Hungarian and Ottoman (Turkish) oppressors. Yugoslavia became a rallying cry, for some. Most never trusted the idea even if they knew of it, or rallied to the cry even if they heard it.

Then Yugoslavia became a state, known now as the "first Yugoslavia" or royal Yugoslavia. First it was called the Kingdom of Serbs, Croats and Slovenes (1918–29); then it was called the Kingdom of Yugoslavia (1929–41). In 1941 this state was obliterated when Hitler invaded and dismembered it; the Germans kept a portion and gave the remainder to their allies.

There followed a double war: civil war among and within the peoples of ex-royal Yugoslavia, and war against the occupying fascist forces. During this conflict, the idea of a Yugoslav state – but a socialist federal state in which all nations would be free and equal – was kept alive by the partisan guerrillas, who fought the occupying forces, their quislings and collaborators, and other anti-communists. For the partisans were organized by the Communist Party of Yugoslavia, which was led by Josip Broz (1892–1980), known during and ever since the war as Tito.

When the war was won, Tito's Party founded the Federative People's Republic of Yugoslavia. This name was changed in 1963 to the Socialist Federal Republic of Yugoslavia. This was the "second Yugoslavia". According to its last (1974) constitution, the SFRY was a federation of six republics and two autonomous provinces. The head of state, after Tito's death, was a collective body, the federal presidency, comprising one member from each republic and province, plus the president of the League of Communists of Yugoslavia

(LCY) and the federal minister of defence. The presidency appointed the federal prime minister, whose government included equal representation of all republics, and at a lower level, the two provinces. The government was accountable to the federal assembly, a two-chamber body drawn equally from the republics and provinces, and responsible for federal legislation and the federal budget. Each republic and province possessed its own, similar structure of government, and a parallel LC structure.

At time of writing, the SFRY still exists, nominally. Unofficially the state has not functioned since the spring of 1990, when two republics blocked elections to a chamber of the federal assembly (parliament).

Or since 25 June 1991, when Croatia and Slovenia announced their independence from Yugoslavia.

Or since 27 June 1991, when the Yugoslav People's Army (JNA) attacked one of the republics.

As a term Yugoslavia was false: the Bulgarian, Croatian, Serbian and Slovenian languages are distinct, and anyway racial kinship proved too frail a bond against differences wrought by history and culture.

As an idea it was beautiful, inspirational, and delusive.

As a political project it was beautiful, inspirational, delusive – and sometimes expedient.

As a state it was unique and eventually impossible. Ripped from the grasp of dying empires and newer neighbours – including Bulgaria, the rival state of a South Slav people – the first Yugoslavia was a unitary, nation-state solution to a multinational question. Born in violence, it could only be maintained by force. As a federation, the second Yugoslavia seemed until the 1980s to have better prospects of enduring; in truth, the old multinational question remained unsolved beneath the mantle of Titoist federalism. This disintegrated half a century after Hitler smashed royal Yugoslavia.

Parts of ex-Yugoslavia may regroup and retain the name, but without two of its three founder nations, there can be no "third Yugoslavia".

Slovenian Spring

The Wall was the place to start, but how to find it?

"No problem," my friends in Slovenia had said, once they understood my mission. "It's small as Walls go, but you won't miss it. Get off the coach near the cemetery at Rožna Dolina and follow the road signs to the border."

The coach door sealed shut with a hiss, and I paused at the deserted bus-stop near the cemetery, letting my eyes adjust to the midday light, feeling the June heat on my skin. This, then, was the place: Gorica in Slovenian, Gorizia in Italian – in any language, the last divided town in Europe.

Ahead, on its green mound, rose the Franciscan monastery where the last of the Bourbons lie crypted in marble silence, disturbed only by birdsong and the occasional rustle of wreaths laid by French royalists. High above the monastery, the grey legend "OUR TITO" was inscribed hugely on the hillside. Leftwards, just beyond the monastery, lay Italy: the castle and avenues of Gorizia, then the monotonous vineyards of Friuli.

Dodging the traffic of Italian and Yugoslav family saloons, with windsurfing boards strapped on top and kids in the back, I crossed to the nearest pavement and padded toward the border, past scrappy vineyards under the lee of the monastery, through petrol fumes and summer dust. After a few hundred metres the road finished in a T-junction. Signs indicated the border in both directions. I noticed a tiny lane branching away from the road before me. A stone bridge carried the lane across the railway tracks that form the border-line at this point. It vanished into allotments between the railway and distant blocks of Italian flats. Barred to cars, bowered by trees in full leaf, this lane would be my secret route to the border; it might even lead to the Wall.

Instead it led to something like the opposite. Fifty metres past the bridge I became aware of a presence in the undergrowth. A soldier of the Yugoslav People's Army (JNA: *Jugoslavenska narodna armija*) stepped out and intercepted me. "You can't go here," he said, shooing me away with one hand as he swung his rifle behind his back.

"But isn't this the border?" I asked like a simpleton, gesturing at the empty lane.

He shook his head, smiling guardedly: "Back to the road, turn left, straight on, and cross at Rožna Dolina."

"Couldn't I pop across here instead?"

He shook his head again and pointed at the ruts and pebbles that separated his scuffed black JNA boots from my grimy trainers. "This is Yugoslavia," he explained sheepishly, "and that" – indicating an identical patch of lane, a few metres distant – "is Italy."

Nothing distinguished the two bits of lane: no sign, no barrier of any kind, let alone a wall rearing up to symbolize the junction of two states and two worlds, Eastern and Western, Balkan and European. All the same, if I walked on and ignored the amiable soldier's statutory warnings, he would have to shoot me. They did still shoot, in 1990, on the Italo–Yugoslav border, though less frequently here than further south around Trieste, and at smugglers, not political refugees. Everything and everyone, so they say, passes through this zone, from Albanian drug-runners to Filipinos without work permits.

There was nothing like a wall at Rožna Dolina either, and I pressed on to the next crossing-place, wondering if I had imagined the smudgy photograph printed a few weeks before in an Italian newspaper. Some six months after the breaching of the Berlin Wall, the Slovene mayor of Nova Gorica and the Italian mayor of Gorizia had made local headlines by calling for their towns to realize their vocation as "a laboratory for the common European house", and start the complicated process of integration.

When the Allies plotted the border in 1947, they dismissed the Yugoslavs' ardent protests and let the Italians keep Gorizia, except for the monastery, the grandiose railway station and some eastern suburbs. The Yugoslavs countered this injustice with revolutionary defiance: they would build their own Nova – new – Gorica just across the border, as concrete proof of socialism's superiority. Housing estates were arranged so that blocks of flats spelled the name of TITO, as a treat for angels and aeroplane pilots.

True to its conception, the town never outgrew the pallid angularity of a blueprint. My friend Ervin, who grew up in the never-completed second T of TITO, fled to Ljubljana as soon as he could and has stayed ever since, calls it the dullest of towns. The border was nothing interesting for him and his schoolmates; with their permits they could cross any time, and it was more fun to scamper in and out of Italy through the sewers. They used to play volleyball across ... the Wall! Here it was, in front of the Habsburg-butterscotch railway station. Standing knee-high, the

Wall is topped with robust green wire-mesh fencing that brings it up
to a couple of metres. The fencing is punctuated with dumpy posts
bearing the date "1947". I squatted to touch the coarse-grained
concrete, spored with lichen, unblemished by a single grafitto.

By now the Berlin Wall had been hawked like chips of seaside
rock, so successfully that preservation orders were slapped on the
last carious stumps. One of those chips sits on my desk, but because I
did not see it hewn from the wall with my own eyes, I can never be
sure that my cube of ice from the Cold War was not pinched from
a building site and sprayed with those authenticating daubs of paint.
No space for such doubt in Nova Gorica; the Wall here exists. Yet
what was it, what did this barrier mean? It seemed as devoid of wider
significance as the Berlin Wall was loaded with it. No books were
written about Gorica's Wall; no spies or movie stars vaulted it to
freedom or infamy.

In part, its obscurity was a matter of appearance. Flanked by car
parks, grassy verges and tranquil avenues, the Wall is more like a
school fence than a key strategic frontier. At the nearest crossing-
point the official folded away his newspaper and accepted a
cigarette. "The best thing would be to abolish the border here and let
everybody through," he remarked conversationally, leaning on the
jamb of his cubicle office. "I never check anyone's permit anyway."

Did the Wall's utter material modesty prove a triumph of
camouflaging by one or both of the states involved? Or did it reflect
the genuine ordinariness of the border? Since the 1960s both Italy
and Yugoslavia had wanted to minimize tensions along their
frontier. The claim that this is "the most open border in Europe"
became an official byword in Yugoslavia. An absurd claim, yet this
was the most demilitarized border between socialist Europe and the
West.

On the other hand, this reduction of tension would not have been
possible with any other of Europe's socialist states. Those countries
took leading roles in the Cold War between the Western, American-
led bloc and the Eastern, Soviet-led bloc. Their borders with
the West bristled with guns and animosity, both to enforce real
restrictions on movement of people and goods, and to demonstrate
most graphically their cast-iron political identity.

In this conflict of good against evil, there was no middle ground –
least of all in Europe, the heart and home of Cold War, where the
antagonism seemed sharpest and the rhetoric most clamorous, even
if the mortal price of that rhetoric was paid far away, by the
Vietnamese, Afghans, Angolans, Nicaraguans and other victims of
the superpowers and their proxies.

Yet Yugoslavia was not quite out of the middle. It became an anomaly within a world-system that, in principle if not in fact, refused to recognize anomalies. As a socialist state run by communists, it plainly belonged on one side of what Churchill called "this great world cleavage". In his epochal speech of March 1946, heralding the onset of Cold War, Churchill had no doubt on which side of the iron curtain Yugoslavia lay; Belgrade was included in his roster of "capitals of ancient states" within "the Soviet sphere". Ancient this state was not, but Yugoslavia unquestionably did lie within the Soviet sphere. The Yugoslavs were the most radical Bolsheviks outside the motherland – until 1948, when Stalin expelled the Yugoslav Communist Party from the Communist Information Bureau, the so-called Cominform, Stalin's club for co-ordinating his empire of satellites.

Yugoslavia ceased to be a member of the Soviet bloc without ceasing to be communist. For the next half-dozen years the Yugoslavs were immersed in a Cold War of their own, against the USSR and its bloc. Though the threat of invasion had ebbed by Stalin's death in 1953, the invective and the economic blockade lasted until Khrushchev sought peace in 1955. By this time the Yugoslav régime had charted its own course, parallel to the front line of East–West conflict. The Yugoslavs never belonged to the Warsaw Pact; they only became involved with COMECON, the Soviet bloc's economic organization, in 1964, and then with special status. As a socialist state Yugoslavia did not, of course, belong to Western alliances, yet it signed military pacts with Greece and Turkey, NATO's two Balkan members.

A chain of causality connects those far-off affairs, originating in the partisan war and revolution, with Gorica's present-day tranquillity. The ambiguity of the border was the ambiguity of Tito's Yugoslavia on the margin of the Cold War.

Any state with ambiguity as its cornerstone is bound to have a complex identity. Popularly in the West, since the 1960s, Yugoslavia meant sun-kissed Adriatic resorts, more interesting than Spanish costas though drab compared to French or Italian rivieras. For at the same time it meant communism, complete with red stars and busts of Lenin – but a friendlier communism, symbolized by Tito's stern or smiling face, redolent of paternal stability. More remotely, Yugoslavia meant the Balkans: swarming rivalries of unrememberable nations whose potential for violence and dissolution was somehow held in check by that face. It meant somewhere in the East but not quite of it – more advanced and liberal; somewhere categorically behind the West, where it could never belong because it was on the wrong side of the great chasm, if only because it couldn't be on the right side.

These paradoxes became clichés long ago. Nonetheless they describe the truth about postwar Yugoslavia. They explain why the place was more absent than present in the Western imagination, and why the West never grasped the rôle that socialism really played in Yugoslavia.

For their part, Yugoslavs knew very well they weren't East Europeans and were proud of the difference. East Europeans, too, knew that Yugoslavia was something else: freer and more affluent. The Yugoslavs reaped advantages from their ambiguity. Western governments paid them well for defying Moscow, while Khrushchev and his successors were content to let the Yugoslavs stand as proof of their tolerance. But when the Soviet empire collapsed in 1989, the Germans tore down the Berlin Wall and the Hungarians ripped up the barriers against Austria, the Yugoslavs had nothing to do. The world's sudden fascination with Europe's East–West frontiers did not disturb the convolvulus on Gorica's Wall; when a local Right-wing Italian politician took a sledgehammer to it, not even the regional press – always avid for political scandals – took much interest.

While a Westerner might suppose that the absence of obstacles to demolish in the name of freedom, democracy and European integration should have been felt by Yugoslavs as evidence of their head-start in the race, it confirmed instead their exclusion from the great transformations and the halo of hope that illumined them. Yugoslavia watched the changes sweep Eastern Europe with the disenchantment of an outcast, a once-favoured guest obliged to peer through the scullery windows at the jubilation within. And not one outcast alone but half a dozen, fist-fighting and shadow-boxing among the rubbish bins.

Like the East Europeans, most Yugoslavs were sick of one-party politics and of socialism. Unlike them, they had no outer walls to demolish; their demons lay all within. Their experience of socialism was complicated and diverse, not monolithic or merely oppressive. Their revolution had been genuine, neither forced on them by the Red Army, nor maintained by threat of invasion. On the contrary: in the aftermath of '48, that same threat united the Yugoslav peoples as never before or since. Their socialism could not be thrown off like a suit of someone else's clothes. In Yugoslavia, federalism and socialism were Siamese twins: organically fused. Their separation needed delicate surgery; otherwise the state itself might not survive. And not all Yugoslavs sought the end of socialism; the diehards included the armed forces and the leaders of Serbia, the largest republic. Surgery was not on these men's minds.

When two other republics finally departed the federation in June

1991, the result was Europe's first major war since 1945. The antagonists were not Italy and Yugoslavia, nor NATO and Yugoslavia, still less the Warsaw Pact and Yugoslavia. By a cruelly appropriate irony, the Warsaw Pact's dissolution was announced while Yugoslavs were shooting each other in front of Gorica's Wall.

*

The first republic to make the break was Slovenia, and its ten-day war erupted when the Slovenes declared independence on 25 June 1991. The immediate cause of fighting, however, was not the declaration, nor the high-spirited ceremony that night in Ljubljana. The decisive issue was control of international borders. When the Slovenes took over the border points with Italy and Austria, the JNA despatched columns of tanks from bases inside Slovenia to seize the border back. The Chiefs of Staff were acting unilaterally to keep the federation together by the only means they knew, but the federal government in Belgrade was compromised by their intervention; it had signalled to the JNA for help because it too desperately wanted those border posts. Customs revenue went directly to the federation; indeed, it made some 40 per cent of the federal budget, and Slovenia's borders were the most lucrative.

The motives for the war were federal-military and fiscal. Self-interest in socialist Yugoslavia was invariably dressed as something finer and higher, even when the need was less pressing than now, and the chiefs of staff gave their troops a grander rationale for violence against their own people. When the tanks rolled into Nova Gorica there was a shoot-out at Rožna Dolina; the JNA commander was killed and the bewildered teenaged conscripts were interned in a nearby school. "Why did you come here?" a reporter asked one of them. "To defend the borders," came the miserable reply.

"From whom?"

"We were told the Italians were attacking."

"Do you believe it?"

The humiliated boy lowered his eyes and shook his head.

Every shot fired in Slovenia drove another nail in the coffin of the Socialist Federal Republic. Even if the JNA troops had defeated the Slovenian Territorial Defence, the federation would still have lost, because the intervention proved it to be inoperative and inoperable. Western governments as well as public opinion appeared to accept for the first time that the federation was constantly in crisis because it *was* a crisis.

And the agent of this verification was historically the most self-effacing republic. Before June 1991 few foreigners could locate Slovenia on a map, where it resembles a chicken scampering under mother Hungary's wing. Fewer again could name a Slovene personage, past or present, or an event in Slovenian history.

In June 1991 the reason why most Slovenes wanted to leave Yugoslavia was so obvious that no one needed to ask. Before the JNA tanks converted Slovenes into freedom-fighters, however, the reason was simple and rather moderate; for breast-beating nationalism was restricted to a tiresome élite of writers and academics in Ljubljana.* Most Slovenes were fed up with Yugoslavia, above all for material reasons. Fed-upness was the common denominator, not anti-communism, for instance, as in neighbouring Croatia. (The League of Communists of Slovenia, renamed the Party of Democratic Renewal, polled more votes in the republic's first multiparty elections than any other party, though less than the Centre-Right coalition of six parties, called Demos.) As any Slovene would tell you, Slovenia had 10 per cent of the workforce yet generated 20 per cent of the gross national product of Yugoslavia. In fact, according to per capita income, the republic's federal contribution was not excessive; for Slovenia was the wealthiest republic. But here, as in Croatia, the reasonable suspicion that by the late 1980s the federation hampered development became tangled in a great many minds with the unwarrantable nationalist complaint that the federation had been ripping them off since 1945.

Underlying this complaint was a feeling that any contribution to the federation would be too much, partly because Slovenes wanted to be responsible for their own affairs, and partly because they thought the federation had become unfit to be subsidized. Nevertheless, until 1991 a looser kind of Yugoslavia – a confederation – would have been acceptable to most Slovenes.

The wherefore of independence is easily answered. As for *how* the Slovenes seceded, and with so few casualties, geography and ethnography go a long way to explaining. Wedged between Italy, Austria and Hungary, Slovenia shared internal borders with just one other Yugoslav republic – Croatia, with which it also shares the Catholic religion and an Austro-Hungarian legacy. The smallest republic after Montenegro, its territory was 8 per cent of Yugoslavia. Most significantly, its population is more nearly homogenous than

---

* I should say at the outset that the definition of nationalism I like best is Sir Isaiah Berlin's: "Nationalism is not consciousness of the reality of national character, nor pride in it. It is a belief in the unique mission of a nation, as being intrinsically superior to the goals or attributes of whatever is outside it." It is in this sense that I use the word and its cognates.

that of any other republic. More than 90 per cent of Slovenia's 1.9 million inhabitants are ethnic Slovenes, and 98 per cent of Slovenes in Yugoslavia live in their republic. (This concentration is rivalled only by the Macedonians, 95 per cent of whom live in Macedonia. The figures for Serbs and Croats are 60 per cent and 78 per cent respectively.)

Including the Slovenes over the border in Italy and Austria and the émigré communities in Australia and the Americas, the nation numbers two million souls. A small nation, with a small state. In Slovenia, the Ministry of Agriculture has one telephone line. The football commentator on national television works from Monday to Friday as a family doctor. It takes half an hour to look at all the pictures in the National Gallery. The total population is less than that of Manchester or Chicago.

Location, however, outweighs scale. "It's not how small a nation is," Ervin told me, raising a cautionary finger, "but whereabouts it happens to be small." Slovenia was small in the right place. It became fortunate in its neighbours; earlier this century Italy threatened to engulf the Slovenes altogether, while Austria and Hungary were both enemies too. Since 1945 all three have been a stabilizing influence. Internally, it was cushioned by Croatia from the brunt, first, of Ottoman imperialism and, since 1918, of Serbian centralism in Yugoslavia. By geographical good luck, Slovenes were englobed within the Habsburg Empire; oppressed, yes, second-class subjects, but not divided against one another by religious difference, at least not since the Counter-Reformation. Their identity, when they assembled one, was not adversarial or embattled, rather homely, withdrawn, depressive.

Under nineteenth-century Habsburg dominance the Slovenes gained some very limited experience of self-administration. In royal Yugoslavia they were for the first time titular subjects of a state; their representatives in Belgrade, outnumbered by Serbs and Croats, grew adept at playing both ends against the middle. After 1945, as a constituent nation of an increasingly devolved federation, the Slovenes were increasingly responsible for their own affairs, in effect an embryo national state.

With hindsight, the Slovenes used Yugoslavia to outgrow it, and they are the only certain beneficiaries of its ending. Each development in their history made the next one possible, and each was happening to them for the first time. In this too they were uniquely placed. Croats never forgot their sufferings in royal Yugoslavia, and the Serbs never let them forget how catastrophic Croatian statehood had been during the Second World War. Serbs themselves never forgot they were the lynchpin of Yugoslavia: the biggest nation, which made the greatest sacrifices to make Yugoslavia happen, and was forever entitled to the major say in running the place. Bosnia-Hercegovina and Macedonia were always junior partners, vulnerable to internal tensions and external pressure; mere survival and development absorbed most of their energy. Montenegrins tend to be either arrant Serbophiles or vibrant nationalists, reminding anyone who will lend an ear that Montenegro, no less than Serbia, was an independent kingdom before 1918.

Slovenia was scarred by no such memories. The Slovenes had never been within hailing distance of statehood, so they couldn't regret its loss. Nor had they been done down by other Yugoslavs. They were never involved in ethnic-territorial rivalry, which is the staple of Balkan political disputes. Croats and Serbs both insist that areas within the republic of Croatia really belong to them. Both nations look hungrily at Bosnia, which was the paramount motive for the original formation of Yugoslavia. Albanians and Serbs contest for Kosovo. These claims and counter-claims are transmitted down the generations like a congenital deformity.

In 1991 the guardians of united Yugoslavia let Slovenia go because it was not snared in the web of reciprocal grievances which, after the Titoist rhetoric of *bratstvo i jedinstvo* (brotherhood and unity) had peeled away and communism had retreated to its republican citadels, seemed all that held Yugoslavia together. For these reasons, and of course because it was the best-developed republic, Slovenia's standing toward the rest of the federation was uniquely arbitrary. By 1991 most Slovenes did not want independence from the SFRY any more sincerely than most Croats or many Serbs or Macedonians or Albanians wanted the same. Their frustration was no more democratic or selfish. Simply, their freedom of manoeuvre was enjoyed by no other nation or republic.

*

Gunfire and independence were still a year away when I left the Wall to take a bus northward, along the valley of the Soča river.

The other route from Nova Gorica into Slovenia follows a different, gentler valley: the course of the Vipava, curving toward its headwaters on a broadbacked mountain called Nanos. Over the saddle of land under Nanos runs the ancient route from the Adriatic to central Europe, trodden by Roman legionaries, railway engineers of the Austrian *Südbahn*, and partisan soldiers in the Second World War. As a watershed between the Mediterranean basin and the Danube, bearing its waters to the Black Sea, Nanos divides 'spheres of influence' millennia older than the Cold War. Slovenia is compact of these three worlds, Alpine, Adriatic and Pannonian: a triple bridge between Western Europe and the plains of Hungary.

The Alpine world begins a little way north of Nova Gorica. Before the Soča crosses the border to become the Isonzo, it bowls and hurtles through a landscape of pine-clad screes and cliffs ranged like giants' organ-pipes. The river is a startling turquoise hue and its valley is sublime, despite the occasional cement works and despite its past. At Kobarid – Caporetto – the Italian army suffered its worst rout of the First World War. Geology connived at carnage in this region: artillery shells burst the limestone into razor-like shrapnel. Though no traces of war are visible from the road, scars remain on the hillsides. Boys still dig up bones and helmets, and stumble upon caves littered with rusting guns.

Slovenia's heartland is not far away: a few miles east lie the lake of Bohinj and the peak of Triglav, prime symbols of Slovenedom. The Soča valley, though, is not yet quite Slovenia. Nor is it quite Italy. This is border country; even if the border is no longer contested and its history of conflict is all but healed, it will always have a hybrid identity. This should bring suspicion and instability, yet in this corner of Europe the border identity seems irrepressibly robust, like a mongrel dog. Perhaps the Balkans begin over the next range of hills.

I stayed overnight with a friend of Ervin, in a farmhouse with geranium windowboxes, on a hilltop high above the river. Juli the farmer welcomed me with homemade grappa blended with honey, and I listened to his stories as his wife watched television: *Cagney and Lacey* subtitled in Slovenian. Between the wars this area was part of the territory – amounting to one third of ethnic-Slovene land – which belonged to Italy. Mussolini's regime soon set about oppressing the Slavs: Juli was brought up with an Italian surname and forbidden to speak his language in public. Drafted into the Italian army in 1943, he promptly got himself captured and sat out the war in an American-run prisoner of war camp near Marseilles. He learned bits of English and French so he could chat with the GIs and chat up the French girls. Back home, which had become federal Yugoslavia, he settled into farming and marriage.

Now Juli is a citizen of independent Slovenia. I can picture his canny expression as he collected his new passport and fingered the new currency: first fascist Italy, then communist Yugoslavia, now democratic Slovenia ... Nothing short of another full-blown European war can touch this man; and he knows that his borderland has outlived European wars. This cool summer night he wore nothing above his baggy jeans but a string vest; in his sixties, his bronzed torso is creaseless like a doughnut. He lolled on a settle beside the wall as he talked, resting his broad balding head on a spade-like palm: a rustic Slovenian Buddha. Belgrade means less to him than Marseilles; Ljubljana, less than Udine across the border. He never leaves his hilltop except for business (at which, a rueful neighbour told me next day, he never misses a trick). He still knows four languages more or less, and his son will inherit his farm should he ever die, which I doubt.

From Juli's hill the road climbs and winds north, between the Soča and Italy. Odd to reflect that fifty years or more ago, this border divided fascism and democracy – however flawed Yugoslav democracy was in the late '30s, as Italy, Germany–Austria and Hungary hedged the young kingdom and exploited its weaknesses. As the decade wore on, and Yugoslavia kept skirting by hairs' breadths the horns of the Italo–German condominium, it looked more and more like a paper house shored up by fragile alliances. The Wilsonian vision of democratic states succeeding the Habsburg Empire, had curdled to a nightmare; only Czechoslovakia and Yugoslavia had resisted fascism, and their vulnerability seemed likely to be terminal.

So it seemed to British and French governments. From an anti-fascist perspective the Yugoslav shambles looked a little different. The glamour of its anti-imperial origins had been tarnished by all manner of outrages, including assassinations in parliament and a royal dictatorship. Even so, it was better than the alternatives. Among those who felt this was Eric Ambler, author of the best political thrillers of the prewar era. In *Cause for Alarm* (1938) the English hero and his Russian accomplice escape from Italy between Tarvisio and Kranjska Gora, a few miles north of Juli's hill. Fleeing the fascist police, they are grateful to be arrested by a Yugoslav frontier patrol, "suspicious but polite", and pleasantly informal.

Ambler put Yugoslavia in all his pre-war novels except the first, which invents Ixania, "a small Balkan state ruled by a Fascist-style oligarchy". (Fictional Balkan states were popular between the wars. As well as Ixania there were David Footman's Vuchinia in *Half-Way East* and Dashiell Hammett's Muravia in *This King Business*. If Yugoslavia could be written into existence by the great powers, after all, why should not novelists use their own creative licence?) Without offering any information about the place – none of the strenuous research that pads current-day thrillers – these books reflect Yugoslavia's peculiar status in the consciousness of 1930s Britain. It was more an atmosphere than a real place: a murky space of conspiracy and corruption, where every deceit was possible.

Ambler's characters are always on the move around Europe by train – you can smell the cinders on their jackets – and the railway tracks converge in Yugoslavia as if in a gigantic junction where the locomotives and rolling stock are blurred by a permanent fog. This ambience of Balkan bewilderment congeals to pea-soup density in *The Mask of Dimitrios* (1939). Most appealing among its gallery of crooks is the mysterious Peters, who praises Belgrade as "such a beautiful city. The views from the Terazija and the Kalemegdan! Magnificent!"

Belgrade turns out to have all the charm of a Chicago gangsters' convention. Yet (and here is Ambler's greatness) these books don't stop at conjuring an exotic image. They show real sensitivity to the dilemmas of border identity, particularly to the human cost of border changes. What pathos there is, for instance, in Josette's tough remark: "I was born in Serbia but I say that I am Hungarian because it sounds better." (From *Journey into Fear*, 1940.)

Uncommon Danger (1937) includes a character who speaks Slovenian – surely the only one in English fiction! Yet the effect of this detail is not to inform us that such a language exists. It slots into place as the kind of accomplishment that a fascist arch-villain like Stefan Saridza *would* have; it confirms his wickedness. "Slovenian" is interchangeable with "Bulgarian" or "Serbo-Croatian", for it signals nothing more specific than no-good, Balkan foreignness.

Danger is always an ingredient in this foreignness. Even in *Cause for Alarm* Yugoslavia is no simple haven. Early in the story, as his ingenuous English narrator reads a newspaper, Ambler makes him notice indifferently, as if remarking the cricket results, that "another Balkan state had gone Fascist". What's more, the "grotesque" and "inexpressibly ugly" General Vagas, a Nazi agent who rouges his cheeks and carries a deadly swordstick in his malacca cane, is a Yugoslav, and proud of it . . . because Yugoslavia was composite, and fascism was at home here too.

*

"The identity of Slovenia is more or less known to everyone," said the Adria Airways inflight magazine, pluckily, in spring 1991. Although Western awareness of Slovenia grew at the end of the 1980s and into the '90s, as it led its five partners in pursuit of political democracy and then in their even less certain quest for "sovereignty" (whatever exactly that meant), the *identity* of Slovenia remained unknown: not enigmatic, merely obscure – submerged within conceptions of Yugoslavia, as it had been for Eric Ambler's Englishmen in the '30s.

Other Yugoslav nations had more handy tags for foreigners: heroic Montenegrins, convivial Serbs, Austrophile (and "fascistic")

Croats, Muslim Bosnia and so forth. But Slovenia? The name floats in a weightless limbo, bearing no freight of associations, no patina of familiarity, yet no outlandish allure. Inside Yugoslavia too, Slovenes were a people apart. As we have seen, they stood at an angle to the rest of the federation.

It is no coincidence that the Slovenes arrived much later than the Croats and Serbs at a concept of nationality. Until the nineteenth century, the very meaning of the word "Slovene" was unsure; it might refer to any Slavs, or to those South Slavs who inhabited the region between Carinthia (Koroška in Slovenian) and Lake Balaton in the north, the Adriatic sea in the west, and the Croats to the south and east. The separateness of this community was given by its language, distinct from the variants of Croatian and Serbian, with written records dating from the eleventh century, and its own slender literature.

In the absence of any native political tradition, the self-appointed task of forging a national identity fell to the intellectual élite in the capital of Ljubljana. This was standard procedure among stateless peoples in nineteenth-century Europe, pursuing cultural homogeneity as the first stage of the journey to political self-determination. What differentiated the Slovenian project, almost from its commencement, especially from Serbian national awakening, was its stance towards its own folklore. Whereas the Serbs championed their heritage of popular epic poems as the linguistic treasury of Serbdom, the leaders of the Slovenian literary awakening decided that peasant traditions were insufficient for a modern national culture. They had no choice but to turn outwards and borrow from foreign cultures to suit their needs.

This decision was more than an incident in the development of the culture; it set a pattern that endures to the present – as will be seen. What's more, the sober pragmatism of the decision appears itself to be typically Slovenian. Rather than pretend to discover a medieval epic poem or two, the poets contented themselves with small-scale lyrics, and cultivated their melancholy Muse. The mood of their poetry is delicate, somewhat indisposed. Haunted by a Chekhovian sense of futility, of time passing unmeasured by external events, of life happening elsewhere, their verses venture nothing more exalted than a mute appeal to wind or stars. They are peopled by allegorical nature-women, fatal temptresses with the sunset flaring in their hair.

The aggregate Slovene poet of the nineteenth-century stands in the double shadow of the cathedral and the alms-house, reflecting on life's brevity, the failure of love, and the sad fact that the peasants don't read his works. His diffidence makes you want to shake him, yet he is familiar to a Westerner as the old bards of Serbia and

Montenegro, reciting feats of heroism against the Turk, cannot be. He speaks the language of selfhood, not drowning his individuality in the epic collective whole.

Greatest of these poets was France Prešeren, the avatar of Slovene consciousness. He tapped the same vein of fainting lyricism, yet achieved a unique flexibility of tone and range of style. His patriotic drinking song, "A Toast", chose itself in 1990 as the new anthem for democratic Slovenia. He also wrote a pseudo-epic poem for his people. Called *Baptism on the Savica*, it offers a myth of national origins, or rather of the origins of national identity. Its setting is Lake Bohinj, tucked among the Julian Alps only a score of kilometres from the majestic valley of the Soča.

The subject of Prešeren's pocket-sized epic is a real event: the forced conversion to Christianity of the pagan Slovene tribes in the eighth century. The characters are fictional.

The hero is Črtomir, last of the warlords to hold out against Valjhun, a German crusader. Črtomir is eventually driven into the narrow valley of Bohinj and besieged there for six months, before losing all his men in a last stand. He loves the maiden Bogomila, a votary of the goddess Živa, a Slavic Venus whose temple stands upon the island in Lake Bled, a few kilometres from Bohinj.

Finding himself the sole survivor of Valjhun's onslaught, Črtomir staves off thoughts of suicide by resolving to see if Bogomila is safe. He escapes down the lake, towards Bled, only to be met on the shore by Bogomila, who has come to find him, accompanied by a man who turns out to be an itinerant priest. She tells her warrior that the whole community at Bled was converted to Christianity by this priest. Now Bogomila sets to work on her lover: "Awake, O Črtomir, from your deep sleep, and bid farewell the errors of your youth." He meekly complies, through love for her and, it emerges, hoping his conversion will hasten their marriage. Of this delusion she rids him with truly virginal serenity. Christ is her consort now: "To God alone I have bequeathed my virtue," etcetera.

The priest steps in: Črtomir must cross the mountains to Aquileia, where the Patriarch will ordain him. Then he as well can wander the earth searching for pagans to convert. This instruction the warrior accepts without question: "You reason right, I cannot hope for joy, which always is and will to me be foreign." After a speedy baptism in the Savica – a mountain stream that flows into Bohinj from the Triglav massif – Črtomir departs. He and Bogomila never meet again.

It is fascinating to compare Prešeren's *magnum opus* with the Serbian epics about the battle of Kosovo, then recently published for the first time and probably present in the poet's mind as an archetype of national literature. Leaving aside the autobiographical dimension (Prešeren's own frustrated love affairs), the poem tells a story of self-denial and survival. Črtomir and Bogomila live in a world of forces that roll and shift around them, oblivious to their tiny will – like the Slovenes under the Habsburgs. If they persist in their inherited customs, they will be crushed, as Črtomir's troops are crushed by Valjhun. So they change, and their capacity for adaptation allows their survival, at least for an interval, until the next crisis breaks upon them.

Prešeren's lovers are glad to sacrifice mundane "joys" in order to serve spiritual truth. This is a thoroughly Romantic inflection, in keeping with Prešeren's aesthetic as well as his personal disappointments; yet it is in keeping too with the anti-epic modernity of the poem, whose characters are complex, divided against themselves, not one-dimensional heroes or villains like the Serbs in Kosovo songs. The only epic character is Valjhun, who experiences no inner conflict over the contradiction of slaughtering for the greater glory of God. And Valjhun is not directly seen or heard in the poem; his elemental presence would burst the seams of Prešeren's moral allegory.

Militarily, Valjhun is the winner. By the end of the story his victory has been utterly eclipsed, with the implication that he is a relic, while defeated Črtomir is the man of the future, ancestor of all the Slovene generations whose survival lay through flexibility and submission to *force majeure*. Črtomir escapes Valjhun by joining him, but that's not all: he upstages him by becoming a better Christian. For he knows the value of humility, he is able to throw away his sword and live by Christ's teaching. At a stroke the pagan warrior becomes more Catholic than the German crusader.

Črtomir's change seems impeccably high-minded or suspiciously nimble. It all depends on one's point of view. I remembered Prešeren's poem when an elderly Serb in Kragujevac chided me for commending Slovenia's slowly-slowly approach to independence. "No no," he said brusquely, "the Slovenes are simply a people without honour."

*

Bled, the site of Bogomila's pagan temple, lies a half-hour's drive from Bohinj. With its castled crag above the lake, and alps in the background, it was a favourite Habsburg resort, ideal for viewing mildly gothic scenery from the terrace of a luxury hotel. On fine summer days Austrian cars squeeze into the lakeside streets. Off-season too the place has a distinctly Austrian ambience, as so much of Slovenia does, from its emerald alpine meadows to the orchards and forests of Gorjanci.

The Slovene temperament is famously Austrian. This means: phlegmatic, orderly, hard-working, dull, piously Catholic, reticent, stingy. From Ian Fleming ("the apple trees and chalets were almost Austrian") to Claudio Magris ("Slovenia today is the most authentic Habsburg landscape"), visitors rarely fail to draw the parallel. Austria possesses a definite identity for Western visitors as Slovenia does not; so we reach for off-the-peg similes to help evoke the place. At the same time, the cliché does touch an intrinsic feature of Slovenia.

For the Slavs of the Alpine-Adriatic area, whose descendants only began to be specified as Slovenes at the end of the eighteenth century, conversion to Christianity meant Germanization. By the tenth century these tribes were under the feudal sway of German nobility who divided the territory into duchies and principalities. After 1274 "Slovenia" became part of the original Habsburg crownlands. Almost all "Slovenes" lived in the administrative regions of Carinthia, Carniola, Styria and Istria for the next six centuries, with a four-year interregnum of Napoleonic rule in 1809–13. So the Slovenes lived under German/Austrian domination for a millenium, from as early as 874 until 1918. The conditions for Austrianization could not have been more propitious.

By the time the French and American Revolutions, abetted by German philosophy, had grafted together the ideas of popular sovereignty and of ethnically-based national statehood, the Slovenes had no business to have survived at all as an entity. That they had, anonymously and unseen, is due to language and character, which Dimitrij Rupel, now foreign minister of Slovenia, defines as "authoritarian in 'internal communication' (as tyrannical fathers, husbands, bosses, teachers, and so on) and subservient in 'external communication'." (Remember Črtomir and Bogomila.) Back-handedly, survival was due too to their masters. If the Austrians hardly encouraged the local language – unlike the French during their brief tenure, who brought it into schools and law courts – at least they did not try to eradicate it. They gave the Slovenes representation at the Vienna assembly, and overall treated them much more liberally than the Hungarians dealt with the Croats.

Oddly, in view of the current post-communist renaissance of Catholicism, and a widespread identification of the Church with the nation's true interest, the worst danger to Slovenia's language, and hence to indigenous culture, came not from Viennese imperialism but from its own clergy, acting as the Vatican's fifth column during the Counter-Reformation. The Slovenian lands lay within the orbit of the Reformation, and the Protestant priests needed materials in the local tongue. In order to translate the testaments, a reformer called Primož Trubar had to separate the local vernacular from the neighbouring (Croatian) dialect. This wasn't proto-nationalism: his unlettered flock couldn't understand anything else. Trubar's *Catechism* and *Spelling Book* were the first printed books in Slovenian (1550). They gave the framework of a literary language.

When the Counter-Reformation arrived a century or so later, it wrought the Lord's vengeance. Impenitent Protestants were exiled and their possessions seized. Preachers' books were burned and their printing press destroyed. Legend has it that only two copies of the grammar survived. If so, those copies sufficed to carry the language through a century and a half of philistinism.

When they came, the first stirrings of Slovenian consciousness were not greeted with a chorus of welcome by the educated class. Not everyone agreed with Prešeren's and other liberals' belief that a modern literary idiom was the most urgent priority, so that Slovenes would not be obliged to use German for sophisticated communication. Church-oriented intellectuals argued that vigorous assertion of native language and culture was bound to create severe difficulties with Vienna. The Slovenian territory was a key strategic holding; it gave Vienna an outlet to the northern Adriatic, where Trieste was being developed as the empire's principal port.

But the Austrophiles overestimated the liberals' radicalism. Slovenes are never utopian; until as late as 1912, none called for separation from Austria. As long as the Austro-Hungarian Dual Monarchy existed, all three political parties in Ljubljana were reformist. Neither Yugoslavism nor its predecessor, Illyrianism, fired the Slovenes with much enthusiasm, chiefly because these ideas threatened to relegate their language to a Croatian-Serbian amalgam. Right up to the Second Balkan War, when Habsburg hostility to Serbia dismayed many Slovenes, clericals and liberals alike believed the nation's best future lay within Austria, the former for religious (anti-Orthodox) and the latter for cultural reasons. The small Socialist Party even favoured *expanding* the Dual Monarchy, as the optimal way to produce the correct preconditions for socialism. Joint autonomy with Croatia was the limit of their ambition, until the Duel Monarchy disintegrated and exposed the Slovenes to a victorious and expansionist Italy. At the end of 1918, when the Slovenes found themselves in the new kingdom, they were as surprised as anyone.

A stone's throw north of Bled, the border with Austria follows the crest of alps that mark the southern marches of Carinthia. The condition of the Slovenes in Carinthia has caused friction between Ljubljana and Austria on and off since 1920. In that year the dispute between the new Republic of Austria and the Kingdom of Serbs, Croats and Slovenes over rightful possession of Carinthia was settled by plebiscite. The majority vote for Austria could not have occurred without substantial support among Slovenes swayed by doubts about their economic prospects in the Yugoslav state.

The Carinthian minority has shrunk steadily from 80,000 to less than 18,000 – some 3 per cent of Carinthia's population. Slovenes aren't dying out; their spokespeople insist that they are still 10 per cent of the population. What has been happening since the plebiscite is the minority's steady assimilation.

No people would choose to live as a minority inside Austria; yet the pressures on Carinthian Slovenes to assimilate have been uniquely strong. Austria is the heir of Habsburg civilization, bulwark against Balkan chaos and defender of the faith. Slovene identity is not counterposed to that of the old imperial master. Quite the opposite; the Slovene nation hatched within Austria, which retains an aura of parental authority.

Slovene loyalty to Vienna was a byword in Habsburg times. The novelist Joseph Roth had fun with it in *The Radetzky March*, which opens at the battle of Solferino. There, a Slovene officer takes a bullet intended for the Emperor and lives for ever after on the glory of that moment.

The obverse of this loyalty was a distaste for the Balkans that is quite widely reciprocated in Yugoslavia's southern republics, where vox populi expresses either hostility, especially from Serbs and Montenegrins; resentment, as against the class swot; or baffled admiration, quite without envy. The sturdiest account I heard of a southern perspective came from Professor Djordji Marjanović, the founder of Macedonia's first opposition political party, the League for Democracy. "Slovenia is something exceptional," he said. "The 'Slovene Syndrome', we call it. It is an axiom of penology that you must not imprison anyone longer than ten years. Then people stop being citizens, they become another kind of human being, mentally so altered that they can't survive outside prison. So it is with nations. The Slovenes lived under German domination too long. If a people is to keep its pride, the maximum is 500 years, like the Macedonians. More than that is insupportable.

"In their thousand years of subjection to Austria, the Slovenes were 'the last hole in the flute', as we say. Suddenly, with Yugoslavia, they became the first hole. But it happened too late. They were a foreign body in royal Yugoslavia, before the war: Germanized to such an extent. They have the mentality of servants, and now they dream of returning to the breast that nurtured them. If they separate from Yugoslavia, they may well disappear within two generations, assimilated by the German nation. Look at Carinthia, where people just don't want to be second-class citizens, so they declare themselves Austrian in the census.

"Our [Yugoslav] hospitality is famous and stupid, at times quite perverse! But not the Slovenes. They aren't big thieves but little thieves, pickpockets – a bit here, a bit there. At least they did get something: by our standards, though not by yours, they are rich, and rich people always look after their money. I could give you many examples. The pattern was always the same, at every level: they knew how to take money, whereas we . . ." He rolled his eyes and smiled like a cherub. "We have a proverb: 'A poor man is poor because he squanders his chances.' This was our attitude. Yugoslavia can live without them. But if they do leave, I would insist on a clause in the contract, forbidding them to rejoin Yugoslavia – ever!"

Occasionally, though, Slovenes were up to mocking themselves. Ivan Cankar (1876–1918), a national figure second only to Prešeren, diagnosed the Syndrome very sharply, which did not prevent him displaying its symptoms himself. Once, famously, he called the Slovenes "a nation of servants", and sometimes despaired of rousing them to stop tugging their forelocks. He spared no local vanity in his descriptions of Slovene intellectual life, "enchanted within its own insignificance". Cankar's polemics can be as mordant as Swift, and the Austrian censor excised remarks like the following from his texts: "In olden times the minorities fared much worse than they do now. The majority used to nail them to the cross, burn them at the stake, stone them to death, quarter them, and even hang them by their necks. Now they only imprison or shoot them."

A Christly resignation crouches within this scathing satire, as a sort of concealed spiritual insurance: in case they can't throw off the oppressor, at least they will be morally superior – as Črtomir was superior to Valjhun. For Cankar's writing too yields to moods of swooning sadness and quietism. "Sing, O my soul, sing the song of sorrow . . ." At its best, this ambivalence serves Cankar's art fearlessly. In his sketches of the First World War, his knowledge that his hatred of the slaughter counts for nothing is tragically heightened by his nationality; how can a Slovene voice hope to be heard when all Europe is a pandemonium? He pictures his country as a colossal soldier's corpse, sprawled between the Adriatic and the Slavonian plain.

His best known work is a parable of the Slovene Syndrome. It tells of Jernej, a pious bailiff wrongfully sacked by his young master. He sets about obtaining justice. Not vengeance or victory: justice. The mayor angrily refuses to help; lawyers mock him; the cowardly priest won't risk upsetting the social order; the judge throws out his case. As in a fairy tale, Jernej's last hope is the emperor. In Vienna – which for him is remote like America – the police pick up the confused old vagrant and put him back on the train. Home again, he burns down his former master's farm.

No law existed to protect a bailiff from unfair dismissal, yet neither State nor Church would admit to Jernej that legal justice was not true justice. Cankar's tale is not, though, simply anti-Habsburg; Jernej's rotten master is no less Slovene than himself. Nor is it a fable of earthly corruption defeating virtue; for Jernej flatly insists that he doesn't want pity or charity; his forty years of service entitle him to rights – a word that hovers beyond Jernej's consciousness, out of his reach but within the reader's. The bailiff may be a bumpkin, but he will have his rights. When they are denied him all along the line, he doesn't knuckle under but takes the law into his hands.

Jernej's peculiar pride and doggedness came more than once to mind in 1990 and '91, when the Slovenes were manoeuvering towards sovereignty within Yugoslavia, or, if that proved unattainable, separation from it. Jernej's neighbours are stupefied when the old man burns the farm, just as the Yugoslav generals could not believe that Slovenia would fight the tanks in June '91.

Slovenia paid a Balkan price to escape from Yugoslavia; its independence was baptized with blood – the blood of the seventy-plus people killed in the ten-day war. The film director Dušan Makavejev was surely not the only Serb who, watching the Slovenes beat the federal army, thought: "Incredible! The Slovenes have turned into Serbs!" And I wonder if this purgative moment will come to be seen as the beginning of the end of the Slovene Syndrome. "This place was always screwed up," my friend Ivo – himself half Austrian – told me after the war. "Perhaps this victory was what we needed."

*

The goal of my foray into Carinthia was an artefact in the municipal museum in Klagenfurt. It stands on a low plinth in the first room: the stump of a stone column, perhaps a metre tall and almost as broad. Its Roman fluting has weathered into grey undulations. The details of the capital were obliterated long ago. No plaque disturbs the stump's anonymity by explaining its origins or presence here.

I checked no one was watching, hoisted myself onto its level surface and perched there. Footsteps were audible in an upstairs gallery; then silence. Nobody appeared, so I stayed put, legs dangling, musing on the democratic Slovenian backsides that had rubbed the pillar-top to smoothness, a millennium ago. Anywhere else in the Balkans – and not only there – this stump would probably be a national fetish: the object of tirades in parliament, the grail of an *ersatz* chivalric order, even the victim of cultural kidnapping. This is the sort of relic that nationalists dream of, the sort they once forged. For the stump is proof positive that the Slovenian tribes were united, back in the pre-national mists, by a ritual binding the lord to his peasantry.

In this case, not only does the stump attest to a popular ritual; the ritual itself was nothing bloodthirsty or regressive that might be tricky for postmodern democrats to accommodate. It was a unique precursor of contractual democratic procedure, with its own tiny, secure place in the history of political ideas.

The ritual was a vital stage in the investment of every duke of Carinthia until the Slovenes came under German domination in the ninth century, when the dukes became German too, though the ritual itself was unchanged. The site was *Gosposvetsko polje*, a meadow north of Klagenfurt. In his *Six Books of the Republic* (1576), the philosopher Jean Bodin gave the best-known description. "There is nothing to compare with this custom observed in Carinthia," he enthused, "where even today in the vicinity of the town of Saint Vitus [Sankt Veit in German, Šent Vid in Slovenian] one can see a stone or marble in a meadow. Surrounded by the people and leading a black cow with his right hand and a withered mare with his left, a peasant mounted this stone. This duty belonged to him by right of succession. He who was to be duke came forward accompanied by numerous nobles, all garbed in red, with banners carried in front of the duke. All were proper in dress except the duke who walked dressed as a poor shepherd with a shepherd's crook in his hand. The peasant sitting on the stone cried out in Slovenian: 'Who comes forward so boldly?' The people answered that this was the prince. Then the peasant asked again: 'Can he be a judge? Is he concerned with the well-being of the country? Was he born a free man? Does he serve the true religion?' They answered: 'He is and he will be.' Then the peasant slapped the duke gently. After promising the peasant that he would be exempt from public burdens, the duke mounted the stone, and brandishing the sword, he promised the people to be a righteous judge. He attended the mass still clad in the same attire. Then he donned the ducal vestments and returned to the stone, where homage and the oath of fealty were rendered him."

Though there was no mechanism for revoking the power thus granted, the notions of limited sovereignty and accountable rule plainly were present in the ritual, which Bodin interpreted as a clear instance of the transfer of sovereignty from people to ruler.

Bodin took his account from Aeneas Silvius Piccolomini, who worked in Carinthia before his election as Pope Pius II in 1458. Bodin's book was owned by Thomas Jefferson, who initialled the page describing the ritual. And Jefferson drafted the American Declaration of Independence. From Carinthia to Capitol Hill, the little ritual spins down its alpine stream, bobs up again in the European river, which sweeps it safely to the world-historic ocean. The Slovenes have a case for making much of their stump. Yet it stays amid the provincial bric-a-brac and stuffed wildlife in Klagenfurt, and no one in Slovenia seems to mind.

Is this the Slovene Syndrome again – a reflex of subservience, letting Austria obscure Slovenia's heritage? Or is their attitude merely tolerant, maturely disdainful of the kind of pageantry so in vogue in Croatia and Serbia? They were not always so coy or mature. During the First World War the Yugoslav Committee exploited the installation ritual for propaganda purposes, using it to contrast the South Slavs' early yearning for democracy with the belligerent feudalism of the Huns. A Slovene member of the Committee published a pamphlet in 1917 extolling the Slovenes' abiding belief "in the victory of democracy over autocracy, and with this faith in their hearts they are joyously awaiting the approaching day when the sun of liberty will shine over their cultural and geographical centre, 'white Ljubljana', blessing their happy union with their brothers, the Serbs and Croats."

Maybe this accounts for the Slovenes' silence about the ritual. They have long memories. By 1991 they were invoking the selfsame principle, democracy, as their rationale for sundering what had become a patently unhappy union.

*

My favourite building in white Ljubljana is *Nebotičnik*, standing fourteen storeys high on the main thoroughfare. An English traveller in the 1930s, when the building was new, was bemused by the Slovenes' pride in their "modern monstrosity". He didn't see the wit or adventure of building a scale model of a Manhattan skyscraper here. Nebotičnik looks as cosmopolitan today as then, when it towered above its surroundings; and the joke has improved with age. When I arrived from Carinthia, my nomadic photo-journalist colleague Crispin Hughes had been wandering around for a day already, hoping for images of Slovenia's drive to independence and finding the capital as lively as Chichester on a winter weekend. Then he saw Nebotičnik and cheered up. "Just looking at it makes me smile," he said, guiding me into the sombre foyer, where a white spiral staircase corkscrews through the core of the building to a rooftop café. The lift deposited us on the thirteenth floor, now leased to Ljubljana's first Chinese restaurant. Traffic hummed remotely, like a neighbour's washing machine. A single word is woven into the carpet on the stairs to the roof terrace: CLASS.

From the terrace Ljubljana lies all to hand; its comeliness and miniature scale become graphic. We saw icefields on the Kamniške Alps, baroque facades and spires in the old town centre, meadows and fir woods beyond the castle, factory chimneys drizzling smoke, the concrete geometry of a shopping centre and new apartment blocks. The fumes of low-grade petrol and brown coal don't reach this height, though the traffic doesn't ease until evening, when it dwindles as if by curfew. Recalling the travel-brochure cliché that in Slovenia you can swim in the Adriatic and ski on the same day, it was easy to imagine sea-salt and evergreen resin mingling in the breeze.

Ljubljana can seem the most livable of capitals. In winter, old ladies in fur coats cycle past Nebotičnik at stately pace, pursing their lips as the articulated buses overtake them with a groan. Braziers of roasting chestnuts glow on streetcorners, and the cafés have a welcoming fug. On summer mornings the riverside market buzzes, the colporteurs hawk magazines and books from trestles on the pavement, and café umbrellas flourish on the slabby embankments of the Ljubljanica river. The boom in private businesses at the end of the '80s brought delicatessens to all the main streets, glowing coppery emporia stuffed with cheeses and smoked meats. All in all, Ljubljana did not suffer from the ending of Yugoslavia; people weren't clamped in silence as in Zagreb, or falsely swaggering as in Belgrade; nor did you notice the bulge of pistols in belts, as in Bosnia.

On summer evenings the place to be is the old town, which defies the city's early-to-bed sobriety. The mustard baroque facades are overshadowed by black trees on the castle hill. Restaurant tables spill across the street, the cobbled lanes are filled with Fiats, BMWs, Zastavas and Volkswagens, and the bars stay open till the early hours (despite the Christian Democrat mayor's efforts to curtail their licences). The castle has been gutted and filled with a Hilton-style café, complete with ferns and fountains and a rustling grand piano. At such times Ljubljana seems an ideal miniature metropolis, borrowing a top-dressing of style – but not too sedulously – from the Italians, just over the western horizon, and owing its burgherish texture to Austria, an hour's drive to the north. The Balkans are a world away unless you notice the curly-haired Albanian and Macedonian waiters taking orders in five languages, or cross the river to the drab zone where Bosnian workers live.

On Sundays the entire city is deserted; since the JNA withdrew from Slovenia, conscripts no longer mooch along in pairs or threes, or drink away the tedium in the railway station's sordid bar. Then Slovenia shows itself as a tight, narrow-minded province watching its back and its purse, turning up its nose at the rest of Yugoslavia, or "the south". As used by Slovenes and Croats "south" and "southern" are terms of political, not physical geography; they include all areas outside Slovenia and northern Croatia – or, if a Croat is speaking, all of Croatia. I was once seen off from Ljubljana station by Tomaž Mastnak, a peace activist, democrat of the purest water, and a hammer of Slovene nationalism. "Where to now?" he asked.

"Belgrade, then Subotica."

"Well, I wish you a good stay in the south."

"But Subotica is north of Ljubljana."

"No-o," Tomaž hesitated, "are you sure? It's the south, I think."

Back at ground level Ljubljana's central European ambience becomes, if anything, more marked, especially around Prešeren Square, where the russet Franciscan church dwarfs the graceful Centromerkur department store, a white and green gem of art nouveau. There is more art nouveau in the shape of a once-shocking statue of France Prešeren. The clergy had always disliked Prešeren; when they saw the monument, with its bare-breasted Muse attending the poet (or seducing him, as solace for life's unfulfilment?) they swooped. The bishop of Ljubljana demanded the scandalous Muse's removal.

Luckily the mayor at that time (1905) was a free-thinking Liberal, not to be browbeaten. Ivan Hribar had been Ljubljana's first Slovene mayor since 1896, the year after an earthquake destroyed much of the town centre. He launched a competition for a master plan of reconstruction. Over the next decades two young entrants, Jože Plečnik and Maks Fabiani, were responsible for much of the city's distinctive look. Of the two architects, Plečnik built far more in Ljubljana. Without Hribar, who definitely ranks as a Slovene hero, Plečnik would not have been given the chance to evolve his vision of the capital. And without Plečnik, Ljubljana would look altogether different.

The junction of Plečnik's Ljubljana and Habsburg Ljubljana is most graphic when you turn from Centromerkur towards the Ljubljanica river, channelled between high embankments, spanned by the Triple Bridge and bordered on its far side by the arcades of the market place. Embankments, bridge and arcades are all Plečnik's work. They display to the full his grandiosity, which is likeable exactly because of its pocket-sized scale.

What the ensemble doesn't show so well is Plečnik's quirkiness, his taste for collage and quotation. For this you must walk downriver, to the pharaonic sluice at Pregrada, or upriver, to the functionless columns on Shoemakers' Bridge, or north, to the bizarre city cemetery at Žale with its double-decked forest of columns.

The difference is not one of contrast but of modulation. A Slovene patriot, Plečnik was immersed in Austrian culture, and not in its provincial forms; he had studied with Otto Wagner, no less, while Wagner was replanning Vienna. Perhaps this accounts for Plečnik's confidence when the chance to redesign Ljubljana fell into his hands. His work drew on Italian and Austrian baroque, on classicism and Italian mannerism (the mature Michelangelo) as well as Viennese Secession, all mingled with the originality of genius or mangled with the gusto of inspired amateurism. Each view has its advocates; Plečnik remains controversial. What's certain is that when the foundation of royal Yugoslavia created the opportunity for a national architecture, he was the man for the moment.

The Slovenian revival of the 1980s rediscovered Plečnik too. Proudly national in loyalty and outlook, always popular with the Church, he has been fêted with international exhibitions and lavish monographs. Maks Fabiani, by contrast, is almost forgotten here. His work in Ljubljana, Gorizia, Trieste and Vienna proved the vitality of Habsburg traditions, as if flowing electrically down the tracks of the *Südbahn* after the death of the empire. His training and early style were similar to those of Plečnik. Fabiani's internationalism, though, was of a different cast, not a matter of garnering motifs for a national project but of working within functional modernist canons. He spent his old age restoring the hilltop village of Štanjel in western Slovenia. No one who dreamed of a canal to join the Adriatic and the Danube can be said to lack vision; yet Fabiani was never tempted by monumentality, unlike Plečnik, whose sports stadium in Bežigrad – the home of Olimpja, the city football team – reminded me of the much bigger arena used for the 1936 Berlin Olympiad, even before Ervin told me that this was the venue for the Slovenian quisling government's celebration of Hitler's birthday in 1943, when choirs sang an ode to the Führer. On an autumn afternoon, when leaves scuttle along the terraces and a dank wind stirs the goal nets, it is easy to suppose that celebration was the stadium's apotheosis, and it has been running to seed ever since.

*

As Plečnik's star rose, others' fell, and none harder or farther than that of Edvard Kardelj, whose very name has been hurried out of view. Kardelj Street no longer exists, and the university is no more the "E. Kardelj University of Ljubljana". His bronze statue on the western edge of Revolution Square may not stand much longer, and libraries will never hold the other monument planned after his death in 1979: the *Complete Works*, in sixty-nine volumes. The publisher cancelled the project after volume one, "though I was surprised how good the sales were," he says. "Four hundred copies isn't nothing, after all." But four hundred! Twenty years ago every school and government office in the land would have shelved its Collected Kardelj in pride of place, somewhere under the regulation portrait of Josip Broz Tito.

Whatever happens to his name, Kardelj's complex legacy will live in the bloodstream of independent Slovenia for some time to come – and not only Slovenia's. Kardelj was the senior Slovene in Tito's Yugoslavia, and his influence on Yugoslav socialism was second only to that of the Old Man himself, whom he served with absolute loyalty through four decades. His final act of deference was to fall ill and die a few months before his ailing chief, whom he would probably have succeeded.

Kardelj's name went, while Marx Park and Kidrič Street stayed, because he is something of an embarrassment in post-communist Slovenia. He personifies the depth of Slovenia's complicity in socialist Yugoslavia, its responsibility for the political system which the new government prides itself on dismantling. This complicity had become quite difficult to descry by the late '80s, when Slovenia was so at odds with the rest of Yugoslavia. But complicity there was, or rather full involvement from 1941 through to the '80s. In the first flush of revolution, and then in their resistance to Stalin, Slovene communists were as fanatical as any. Yugoslavia's worst series of show trials took place in Ljubljana, where political opposition was obliterated as it was everywhere else. That period too, well symbolised in the hideous statue behind Revolution Square of Boris Kidrič, the other Slovene in Tito's postwar politburo, is part of Slovenian history, no less than the liberalization in the '80s.

Kardelj was in the thick of all political battles, internal and external. As foreign minister during the crucial period after 1948, he laid the foundations of the non-aligned foreign policy. As the architect of the so-called "system of self-management socialism" and the prime mover of the devolutionary 1974 constitution, he was socialist Yugoslavia's ideologist-in-chief, the surveyor of Yugoslavia's own road to socialism.

He looked like a surveyor, too, nondescript beside Tito's glamour. However much the Marshal appeared to stand alone at the helm, it was Kardelj who charted the course, and Tito knew it. "Kardelj was so quiet that you hardly noticed him at first," he said. "But decisions were made, aims were achieved, and then you realized it was he who had made the proposal, persuaded others to accept it, and put it into effect. No setback dismayed him ... an honest man and a true revolutionary." Plenty of Yugoslavs, surveying the post-communist political and economic chaos of their country, must wish Kardelj had been a bit dismayed by the setbacks that afflicted his labyrinthine schemes.

By the end of the war Kardelj, Aleksandar Ranković and Milovan Djilas were established as Tito's trio of advisers. Djilas was disgraced in 1954, Ranković in 1966, and a host of other leading communists in the late '60s and early '70s; but Kardelj never – in his lifetime. Though his heyday already seems a lifetime away, measured by every political standard Kardelj's career was outrageously successful, almost without parallel. To describe him like this is to use terms that Kardelj himself would never recognize. Careerism and ambition were for bourgeois leaders, and Kardelj was a revolutionary whose beacon was the red star of Yugoslavia.

When Ervin played me his cassettes of Kardelj speaking, I was caught unawares by his halting, pedantic speech and wondered for a sentimental moment if his species of public figure will be seen in Europe again: the pre-televisual, styleless kind of ranking communist politician maligned in the West as wicked, as if all of them were embryonic dictators. If it was possible for this dubious genus to spawn a giant, it was Kardelj. He understood many things, especially about nationalism and small nations. Decades before the transformations of 1989, he knew that Stalinist "internationalism" – a weasel-word for Soviet domination of Eastern bloc countries – would create by inevitable dialectic "the opposite effect: the strengthening of nationalism from a nation's resistance to oppression." He knew too that "among the peoples and republics of Yugoslavia there are not only different but also certain objectively contradictory interests." As a Slovene who had grown up in Serb-dominated royal Yugoslavia, he realized that Yugoslavism was "a form of great-state bureaucratic centralism", and therefore small nations would inevitably suffer in a centralized Yugoslavia. This conviction runs like a thread through Kardelj's endless reforms of Yugoslav socialism and federalism.

Abstracted from context, he shrinks at once. Listening to his speeches, I tried to picture the man at an American political primary, dowdily besuited, blinking behind bottle-bottom spectacles at the tickertape and cheerleaders. It has been said that to the end of his life, Kardelj, who had no charisma and was never under the electoral pressure to acquire any, looked like the schoolmaster that he was in the 1930s, in Yugoslavia and Moscow, where he taught at the Lenin

School. He sounds every bit the teacher on these recordings; but he also sounds like a schoolboy who knows the dragons under the bed will devour him unless he repeats the tongue-twisting spell without a slip. The puckered concentration is audible as he extracts words from the unwieldy lexicon of Yugoslav political vocabulary.

Kardelj more than anyone else was responsible for this vocabulary. Like some perverse lexicographer, he obscured the original sense of words and invented barbarous new terms. In mature Kardeljese, a business became an "organization of associated labour"; a manager, an "individual business organ"; a worker, an "associated socialist producer". Local tax was "self-contribution". And Edo Kardelj produced this jargon by the yard, as repetitious and prescriptive as board-room minutes.

Language-mangling came as the last chapter in Kardelj's life. Forty years before, he published a children's book called *Our Marvellous World: a Journey through Time*. In this Marxist allegory, a Mr Omnipotent guides a little boy called Stefan through history on an aeroplane, showing him how human life has always been driven by economic forces, and convincing him that the class of producers are now coming into their own: a classless society is finally at hand. Stefan is overjoyed.

Socialists love ideology: the smell of printer's ink, the monkish study of sacred works, the sabre-rattle of polemic – all to prove that ideas control reality, and the right ideas create the best of worlds. Marxists love ideology with a special passion; when they win power, they enthrone ideologists, firstly to lay down the correct plans about everything, and then, when power implements the plans and they don't work, to deny they didn't work or to justify the failure and make it beautiful. Ideology begins as high priest at the court of power, declines to the rank of handmaiden, and finishes as the despised apologist.

When Stalin expelled the Yugoslav communists from the Soviet bloc, they were left with a gaping hole in their ideology. By fits and starts, they devised a creed of their own, called self-management socialism, or just self-management – the socialism could be taken as read. From about 1950 until Yugoslavia split apart, self-management was the official Yugoslav system; in 1991 the federal armed forces fought for the principle of self-management.

While self-management could be dressed up by Kardelj and others as a respectable concept in its own right, it was first and always functional, invented to bestow ideological legitimacy and consistency on political measures. Whether or not Yugoslavia was a totalitarian state in the full sense, self-management was a totalizing ideology, no less than the Stalinist system. Self-management was everywhere and everything, filling every crack and corner. It made every couple a threesome and eavesdropped every conversation. It wrote all the editorials in all the newspapers, it embraced every sinner and kissed every baby. The world could be interpreted through self-management as through gender, astrology, or the profit motive. Its utter inclusiveness is well caught in my favourite passage of Kardelj, from a 1964 report typically titled *The Socio-economic Tasks of Economic Development in the Forthcoming Period.* "Our activities," Kardelj exhorted, must be directed "toward building an integral system of socio-economic relations, in self-management frameworks, along the whole chain of labour and creativity – from man's labour in his basic production unit, through his work collective, to combined enterprises and business associations and the entire social economy; at the same time" – he continues, taking a breath but not risking a full-stop – "all productive labour must be integrated with every other social activity having a share in social labour, up to and including science and culture." In brief, everything must be integrated with everything and everyone with everyone. Kardelj wanted the system of society to resemble the structure of his prose: each separate item linked to every other, "along the whole chain".

After 1950, when Kardelj and Djilas stumbled upon the idea as much by luck as judgement, self-management was presented as the ultimate theory and practice of democratic socialism. It was the fruition of seed cast on the stony ground of war and irrigated there with heroes' blood; for the mechanisms of self-management had grown, so it was claimed, from the People's Liberation Committees which organized the partisan battalions in the Second World War.

In terms of political organization, self-management transformed the Communist Party of Yugoslavia from what Kardelj called "a classical political party", meaning the usual Leninist organization that substituted for the state in other communist countries, and monopolized every aspect of power. In the self-management system, the League of Communists (as the Party was called after 1952, to signify its new rôle) was in theory the workers' helpmeet and guide in their march towards total empowerment. Unlike other CPs, the League did not usurp the coercive functions of a state. Rather it was, in theory, a transcendent arbiter, upholding both sides in any dispute as impartially as Solomon: it was an arena, where conflicting interests could be harmonized for the sake of the single overarching interest – the development of socialism.

Alongside the League were other mass "socio-political" organizations: the Socialist Alliance of Working People, the Union of Socialist

Youth, the War Veterans' Association, the trade unions. Every adult Yugoslav was a member of at least one of these.

In terms of the federation, self-management meant the principle of devolution. Powers and competences were devolved from the federal centre to the six republics and the two autonomous regions, each of which gained its own League of Communists and mass organizations, its own constitution, assembly (parliament), civilian defence, and budget.

In terms of democracy – and Yugoslavia claimed to have the only democratic socialist system anywhere – self-management meant the installation of a multiple hierarchy of assemblies, from the community to the republic and then the federation. Not every adult Yugoslav participated in these assemblies, but a huge number did; by 1986, when the Yugoslav system was at its most baroque, 649,525 delegates were elected to "self-managing organizations and communities and socio-political organizations". The delegate system, which Kardelj pictured as the "backbone" of self-management democracy, was supposed to be more democratic than bourgeois parliamentary democracy because it went beyond accountability by empowering "the broad working masses" directly. When professional politics had been wholly supplanted by the delegate system, society would be directly responsible for its own affairs.

In the workplace, self-management meant the hierarchy of workers' councils established to let every associated socialist producer have his or her say in running the enterprise and "directly controlling surplus value and capital accumulation". By 1986 more than 613,000 individuals participated in the "organs of worker self-management".

In economic terms, self-management meant workers' councils and an end to centralized planning. In terms of property, self-management meant the creation of a new category of ownership. Soviet-type socialism had merely exchanged private property for party-state property. The Yugoslavs therefore invented "social property", defined by Kardelj as "simultaneously the collective, class property of all workers and a form of individual ownership by everyone who works".

In foreign policy, self-management meant non-alignment: independence between the two blocs of Cold War antagonists, and later, formation of the Non-Aligned Movement.

Militarily, self-management meant the network of civilian defence militias, and Committees of General People's Defence and Social Self-Protection in every workplace, school and community. These committees drew upon the Leagues of Communists and trade unions, officials from the state administration, and army and police commanders.

Educationally, the study of self-management was compulsory in all sociology, law, and philosophy degree courses.

The Yugoslavs claimed that self-management was not a static dogma but an evolving principle. And they were half-right, for self-management was pragmatic in its origins as well as its later history, and adaptable as East European socialism could never be.

Stalin was its parent. By denying Yugoslav communism the sustenance and legitimacy of the Soviet model, he left the Yugoslavs no option but to carpenter an ideology of their own. This did not have to be tackled immediately; the first priority for Tito and his Party was sheer survival. As fighting revolutionaries who had just won a guerrilla war, strategies of survival were second nature to them: internal discipline (i.e. police-state terror), diplomacy and military prowess. Ideology could wait until it was clear enough that Stalin and his allies would not invade. Even then Tito was reluctant to challenge the USSR on ideological grounds. "They know all the right quotations," he bluntly told Djilas and Kardelj, who persisted, explaining that workers' self-management "would be the beginning of democracy, something that socialism had not yet achieved", and what was more, "could be plainly seen by the world . . . as a radical departure from Stalinism". At this Tito "paced up and down, as though completely wrapped in his own thoughts. Suddenly he stopped and exclaimed: 'Factories belonging to the workers – something that has never yet been achieved!' . . .". A few months later, Tito explained the Workers' Self-Management Bill to the National Assembly. The ball was rolling.

As the threat of invasion receded, there were other incentives for the Yugoslavs to change their ideas. The break with Moscow and the Cominform's economic blockade made it easier to accept that their pre-'48 policies had not proved very successful. The economic effects of Stalinist centralization and collectivization were disastrous. The political effects were not much better. Further, the new régime still faced a host of internal enemies: Albanian rebels in Kosovo, Slovene bourgeois, Croat Catholics, royalist Serbs. When war ended in 1945 some 40,000 anti-communist irregulars and bandits were still hiding out; the last of them were not mopped up until the mid '50s. Violence could be used against these enemies, and it was – the full range, from arbitrary interrogation to mass slaughter.

Yet Tito and his top echelon were not natural tyrants. They were too conscious that tyranny breeds hatred and is a poor substitute for rule by consent. By the summer of 1945 Tito already realized that bloodletting had become counter-productive. Since 1918 the tumultuous multinational reality of Yugoslavia had broken a constitutional monarchy, a royal dictatorship, and a fascist occupation; it might break communism too, unless the Party legitimated its rule and broadened it base.

As we saw, Kardelj the Slovene knew that differences of interest among Yugoslavia's peoples and republics were "objectively contradictory". The fulfilment of one people's or republic's wish was incompatible with another's (such as territorial rivalry between Serbs and Croats). Self-management was invented to cope with these contradictions; not to dissolve them – Kardelj knew that was impossible – but to muzzle them so they could cohabit. This could only be managed by straddling the contradictions with a further, colossal contradiction: the supreme power of the LCY, and the goal of building socialism.

Acceptance of these realities spurred the reappraisal of Soviet doctrine. Still, the reappraisal would not have happened if the Yugoslav communists had not believed implicitly in themselves and their cause. The USSR and its satellites insisted that Yugoslav arrogance and nationalist "deviation" had left the socialist fraternity no alternative but expulsion. If the Yugoslavs were not guilty, as they insisted they weren't, then the other side must be responsible for the schism.

Deference to the Soviet motherland was instilled in the Yugoslav leadership's brains, which is another reason why they marked time for two years after the split. When they did look closely at Soviet socialism, they found, to their amazement and relief, that Stalinism constituted the true deviation. Under Stalin, communism had become bureaucratic and dictatorial. Capitalist relations of production had not been supplanted: the working class was still alienated and exploited, because it still had no control over surplus value. The identity of the exploiter had merely been replaced; the workers were now exploited not by private capital but by the very organization that supposedly embodied their interests – the Communist Party of the Soviet Union. Under Stalin, the CPSU had assumed the apparatus and structural power of a state. At the same time – unlike a Western democratic state – it monopolized political and economic life. Capitalism had become state capitalism.

Deprived of "socialist internationalism", the Yugoslav Communists sought new legitimacy in their own achievement. They looked back at their own finest hour when they won the war by winning support from people of all nations, faiths and classes. This magnitude of support reappeared in 1948, joined by anti-communists and other former enemies – not, as the Party knew, because of any fondness for socialism but from patriotism and a blank refusal to be pushed around. The Party's best justification of its monopoly of power, and its best hope of uniting the nations behind its power, lay in perpetuating its original tradition. To be durable, the new ideology must be fashioned from native materials. Who, after all, should understand the tenacity of national loyalties better than Yugoslavs, whether communist or no?

Kardelj and others returned to Marx's own writings – the fountainhead – and found evidence to vindicate the lesson of their own experience: that maximum direct participation was essential for democratic socialism. (Essential too, politically, for a monopoly party to govern effectively.) Political structures must be permeable and open; otherwise bureaucratization ensues, as surely as tar gathers in a smoker's lungs. The CPY could not afford the Stalinist luxury of bureaucratization or its twin, disaffection.

The key text was *The Civil War in France*. Nobody knows quite what Marx meant by "the abolition of the state", but the historical model in his mind was very likely that of the Paris Communards of 1871, whose aborted plans he described at enthusiastic length:

> The Communal *régime* once established in Paris and the secondary centres, the old centralized Government would in the provinces, too, have to give way to the self-government of the producers . . . the Commune was to be the political form of even the smallest country hamlet . . . The rural communes of every district were to administer their common affairs by an assembly of delegates in the central town, and these district assemblies were again to send deputies to the National Delegation in Paris . . . The few but important functions which still would remain for a central government were not to be suppressed . . . but . . . discharged by Communal, and therefore strictly responsible agents. The unity of the nation was not to be broken, but, on the contrary . . . to become a reality by the destruction of the State power which claimed to be the embodiment of that unity independent of, and superior to, the nation itself, from which it was but a parasitic excresence.

Kardelj would have read this with recognition as well as relief. Like the Communards, the Yugoslav communists had forged their revolution in bloody conflict. Like them, their vision of communism was fiercely pure. Like them, they had known the euphoria of total participation, when every warrior was a political activist and every activist bore arms; when guerrilla campaigning bound each to all in pure comradeship, with no mediating structures to get in the way and dilute their revolutionary energies. The partisans' forest hide-outs had been their Athenian assembly: the site of direct democracy.

Unlike the Communards, the Yugoslav communists had the fortune of ruling a society long accustomed to self-management, albeit of a different, pre-modern kind. Behind the direct democracy of the partisans lay the centuries-old peasant experience in Serbia,

Montenegro, and much of Bosnia and Croatia, of living in *zadrugas*: "self-managing" households of extended families which owned, produced and consumed communally. Peasants were 75 per cent of the population in 1945; by evoking ingrained co-operative traditions, self-management presented socialism to this majority in a palatable form.

For all the similarities, the Yugoslavs were determined not to join the Communards on the list of history's losers. They would save their revolution by radicalizing it: by instituting what other communists promised – "the self-government of the producers".

And yet . . . the Socialist Federal Republic of Yugoslavia did not become the first true instance of a workers' state. No matter how often Kardelj reiterated that self-management socialism was well on the way, it never arrived. A twist of the spanner here, a new gasket there, and the machine would definitely work, he promised; it could not *fail* to work.

It didn't work. The economy lurched from bad to worse, and only Western credits, and the remittances of a million guestworkers in the West, baled it out. There were more and more strikes, and strikers were tricked and bullied by management, as under capitalism. The republican Leagues of Communists squabbled and schemed like Tammany Hall careerists. The tally of political prisoners kept growing.

Anybody can tell you why self-management never reached the promised land. Diehards say the system wasn't communist enough, reformists that it was never reformed enough, liberals that it was never liberal, democrats that it wasn't democratic. Plenty call Tito a dictator; others lament his leniency. Cynics blame human fallibility. Workers say their participation was rigged; managers, that the system maximised inefficiency. Wise humanists, who abound in Yugoslavia though they never make the front page, know that totalizing systems never deliver.

The key to self-management's failure is rather simple. The system was devised to serve two purposes, which turned out to lead in opposite directions. On the one hand, it was a system of maximum participation, federation, devolution: a pluralistic system. On the other hand, it was intended to let the Communists keep their monopoly of power.

Ideologically, self-management was moderate and inclusive; but it had its limits. The liberty granted by self-management could not be used to question the League of Communists' "leading role" as "the organized vanguard consciousness of the working class and the working people generally". Like their Soviet counterparts they had no choice but to curtail free expression, because their only justification for keeping a monopoly of power was that they had a monopoly of truth.

In theory, the delegate system ensured fair and equal representation of all citizens in the hierarchy of self-management councils and committees, at the workplace and in higher political structures. Yet not so; there was an agency at work, filtering out the wrong people and privileging the right ones, defining the terms of the agenda. This was the League of Communists. Nowhere did the constitution say that LC approval was essential for an aspiring schoolteacher, journalist, or manager. Yet everyone knew the value of a "red card".

This reserve of power, incarnated in the majestic person of Josip Broz Tito, was the hidden god in the self-management system. Kardelj, though, theorizes as if there were no hidden god, referring to the LCY as one among other "subjective forces of socialism", along with "social-political and social organizations, as well as science, scientific-specialized institutions, professional services, and also our responsible state organs" etcetera. But these organs and institutions were ultimately politically controlled; self-management entailed no division of powers. Although the League was devolved to the republics, a devolved monopoly is a monopoly all the same. Socialist Yugoslavia's power-élite retained its power, guaranteeing self-management's failure in its own terms. For socialism's promised land could not be reached without throwing open all political and social institutions to democratic mandate. This is what the students in Ljubljana meant in 1968 when they demonstrated for "real" self-management.

In 1968 it was still possible to hope that Yugoslav socialism might be reformed. The late '60s was a period of genuine liberalization, and this liberalization can be credited to the *success* of self-management. Freed to advance along the road to socialism at their own pace and in their own national patterns, the republican leaderships were making real social and economic progress. To keep making progress they needed more devolution, and this clashed with the second purpose of the system. Smelling danger, Tito and his old guard purged the reformists, then revamped the system by stealing the reformists' economic ideas while condemning their political liberalism – all in the name of socialism and anti-nationalism. The system was still ingenious, still moving, and still widely seen as legitimate. But the more complex self-management became, the further it ramified through society, the more glaring was the contradiction between its double purposes.

The League of Communists was locked in a self-defeating strategy; it became ever more obvious that its unaccountable power was the subject of self-management. The manifest subjects – the working class and all working people, etcetera – were ever-more sceptical spectators. Inadvertently the monument in Revolution Square reveals these subject/object relations. It shows Kardelj leading a band of associated socialist producers into the radiant future. Yet only Kardelj's features are defined; the workers are indistinguishable. This is the proletariat as a symbol of itself: the ghostly ideal proletariat of self-management.

Did the hideous jargon of self-management conceal an awful truth: that Yugoslav socialism was not really different from Soviet socialism? Plenty of people in ex-Yugoslavia told me so, but what they mean, I think, is that it was no better. Less dictatorial, it was more confusing, mainly because of its trick of involving everyone, and conjuring itself out of sight. "It was the most perfect system among the one-party states," writes Slavenka Drakulić, "set up to internalize guilt, blame, failure, or fear, to teach you how you yourself should censor your thoughts and deeds and, at the same time, to make you feel you had more freedom than anyone in Eastern Europe."

Drakulić's bitterness has surely warped her vision; and this too is part of self-management's dismal legacy. For Yugoslavs did have more freedom. Quite how much varied from republic to republic and from year to year. Back in the '50s, the communists wanted to devolve without altering their control. Instead, as shall be seen throughout this book, the different Leagues of Communists came to take their bearings from their republics – not least because self-management made it hard to isolate themselves from popular feeling in their constituencies. Rather than communizing the republics on Yugoslav lines, the communists were republicanized on national lines. This took some time to happen. After the '74 constitution there was nowhere for the self-management system to go except into complete devolution – a confederation of sovereign republics – which was unacceptable, as always, to communists. As long as Tito was alive the tension could be held in balance, because he was obeyed by one and all. When he died, Yugoslav unitarism died as a federal project. When it reappeared a few years later, it was as a nationalist project, sponsored by the biggest republic.

However, Drakulić does put her finger on a crucial source of self-management's insidious appeal. People lacked arguments against the system. Maximum participation in politics by the maximum number was the explicit goal; and there were no Leftist arguments against that, only liberal ones – which were taboo. From the point of view of power, anyone who opposed the system was still supporting it, as long as he or she kept participating. Whatever opposition the communists could neither stamp out nor cajole, they could usually pre-empt. It is difficult to confront power that keeps dispersing itself, difficult to attack the monopoly of a system which has already denounced and, apparently, renounced its own monopoly. Likewise, as if mimicking another theological sleight of mind, Kardelj knew it was wiser to tell people that self-management was their right than to instruct them about their responsibility. Hence the 1974 constitution referred to citizens' "inalienable right" to self-management.

No wonder the most obvious aftermath of self-management is utter confusion. The system of total direct empowerment disintegrated, leaving people politically inarticulate, unable to analyse power or to define priorities. When false communities of self-management melted away, people fled to their nations and churches, the only real communities that had not been swallowed by socialism.

*

The cutting edge of democratic change in Slovenia was citizens' groups, known as new social movements, and concerned with peace and ecology, feminist and gay issues, and new age spirituality. The term *movement* refers not to size – no more than a few hundred people were active in these groups, except on big occasions. What it describes is their spontaneity, raising social issues outside the capacious frame of official organization.

But first, breaking the ground, came the punks. In the early 1980s an extraordinary range of Slovenes got involved in the punk scene. The present head of sociology at Ljubljana university had a band called Papa Kinjal; his lead singer, now completing her doctorate at the philosophy faculty, remembers they were thrown off the stage at a punk festival in Trieste in '82, midway through their first number – a rare accolade! Peter Lovšin, lead singer with the Bastards, is a sports journalist at the daily newspaper *Delo*, as well as editor of *Privat*, Slovenia's first hard-core porno magazine. Boris, an editor at the radical news magazine *Mladina*, started the Bitches in his home town of Idrija, halfway to Nova Gorica. Punk arrived there before Ljubljana, he says, because it is that much nearer to Italy. After their gigs in the castle dungeons, the Idrija punks sometimes clashed with their arch-enemies, the rockers. Motorbike chains crunched on leather jackets in the midnight streets. Ervin organized punk concerts in cellars. He keeps fond memories of all-night jams at the K4 and FV clubs, sweat coursing down the walls and an unearthly din blaring as the Stray Dogs and the Pulp did their thing.

Punk was a homegrown product for domestic consumption. The last band, Nyet, broke up in 1985. To a Westerner, the blanket influence of Skychannel and MTV – both popular with Ljubljana's rocking class – appears a decisive reason why no phenomenon as intensely local as Slovenian punk is likely to recur. Yet the movement's unrepeatability has less to do with the media and the music industry than with the scope of political change. Punk was the creature of a unique moment, and history has turned its parents to dust and shadow.

Whereas dowdy Ljubljana gave nothing to Yugoslav rock in the 1970s, when bands from Belgrade and Sarajevo made all the running, in the '80s Slovenia was the champion republic of subculture. The reasons for this bizarre pre-eminence illuminate too the larger enquiry: how did the Slovenes democratize themselves at the end of the '80s without strife?

First, a negative condition. Punk and the other new social movements would not have taken off if Slovenia had not been permeated by all manner of Western influences. If British, American and German punk rock was the model, the ears that picked up these new sounds had been following Western rock music since the Beatles, watching Hollywood films and television, reading British spy thrillers, studying French structuralism, wearing Italian clothes (budget permitting). The punk generation of teenagers and students knew the styles of European and Anglo-American mass culture from inside and out. Because of Slovenia's location, and because it was the most prosperous of the republics, young Slovenes could afford habits of consumption beyond the reach of other Yugoslavs. On the other hand, they were not subjects of this culture – how many foreign films or rock bands or genre novels mentioned Yugoslavia, let alone Slovenia?

Yet unlike their Western counterparts, especially in Britain, young Slovenes bore no burden of anxiety about cultural Americanization. They were cosmopolitan enough to have the confidence to be parochial. Free to accept Western mass-culture as a repertory of styles, they pounced on the do-it-yourself forms of punk and applied them to their own context as Slovenes in a decaying authoritarian state. At the same time, as we saw, they were spared the fixation with national grievances and resentments that do such damage in Croatia, Serbia, and Kosovo.

Above all, they picked on the punk theme of alienation, which carries different resonances in Ljubljana than in New Jersey or Hamburg. Punk alienation meant spleenish boredom, anarchic narcissism or designer nihilism, and in socialist Yugoslavia these poses did more than upset parents and teachers. Self-management was supposed to have eradicated the social spaces where alienation breeds. Total participation was the refrain of Yugoslav socialism. In practice, by the '80s – after Tito's death – the authorities were ready to settle for apathy. But aggressive apathy? That was too much! Punks were berated by the press and harassed by the police. Because this was Yugoslavia, not Eastern Europe, they weren't locked up or forced underground, unlike the "Lennonists" in Prague or the surreal "Orange Alternative" in Poland. And genuine social outrage at the punks, among the war veterans for instance, was not strong enough to close down the punk scene. The sweaty cellars stayed open. Records were cut.

The punks had support too, in the media, the university, and even the administration. It amounted to a pro-punk movement, parallel to the real punks and allowing them space to be active. These pro-punks weren't numerous, but the fact of their existence in a one-party system says much about Yugoslav socialism. These same individuals later backed the new social movements. In particular the Youth League of Slovenia, formerly an efficient nursery for budding apparatchiks, became a hotbed of subversion; its officers organized peace demonstrations, subsidized the ecologists, and defended the gays. *Mladina*, the Youth League's dull official organ, became the liveliest news magazine in Yugoslavia. By the late '80s the movements' spokespeople could discuss their demands with ministers. Even Ljubljana's police chief indicated a certain sympathy for the punks and peaceniks.

Like their punk forerunners, the new social movements had no equivalent in Eastern Europe. They belonged to the political opposition, certainly, yet had as much in common with "alternative society" in the West as with the dissident enclaves of Prague or Warsaw. ("'Dissident' was a dirty word here," Ervin told me, "because dissidents want power and we didn't. We just wanted to bring the system down." *He* didn't want power; other self-styled dissidents are now sitting pretty in the Slovenian cabinet.) They had a freedom of action that East German or Czech dissidents could only dream of. Because power was relatively enlightened in Slovenia, not vindictive, dialogue was possible between power and the social movements, which worked by intelligent agitation, pinpointing sympathisers in the administration, being serious while refusing to be "socially responsible". They staged peaceful demonstrations, held public meetings, publicized secret information, circulated petitions, and lobbied the appropriate offices.

While the activists of the new social movements challenged this system, a constellation of philosophers and sociologists in Ljubljana – Tomaž Mastnak, Slavoj Žižek, Silva Meznarić and others, who were activists themselves as well – developed a critique of Yugoslav socialism. Life under self-management was totally politicized, and the best way to attack the system was to attack the form of this politicization, rather than to dispute its ideological content. This attack should start by clarifying power – what it was, where it lay, who had it and who didn't – because the hallmark of the self-management system was, as Žižek put it, "total non-transparency". The system had erased the boundary between state or public life and private life. The latter was the sphere of civil society and no state that denied the autonomy of civil society was democratic. Citizens have the right not to be politicized – the right to be punks.

This liberal theory harmonized with the social movements' work, because their common concern was democracy, not nation. Hence the peace movement's campaign against militarization was a campaign for democracy. The peaceniks wanted people not to be inculcated from kindergarten age with enemy images and soldierly values. The theorists wanted people not to have to participate in defence committees and militias, which extended political control over citizens by meshing them in the structures of state defence, under the guise of empowering them.

By their writings and actions, the democratic movements accustomed the Slovene communists to the notion of political pluralism. They proved that there might be life after the end of the one-party system; that society – not the official fiction of a seamless self-managing society, but actually-existing society – was fit to cope with multiparty politics. The communists were able to adapt, and their reward was reaped at the ballot box. In retrospect, the face of change belongs not to a punk or peacenik but to Milan Kučan, leader of the League of Communists and now president of the republic. His dutiful, rumpled features and sober speeches seemed a pledge of sanity amid turbulence. People who were nervous about leaving Yugoslavia trusted a man who warned, as late as 2 June 1991, that "the shortest way to independence is through long negotiations, even if at this moment they appear futile". In his own words, Kučan evolved "from an apparatchik into a politician". A humble claim, it may sound, but true politicians – workaday artists of the possible – are a precious commodity in Yugoslavia.

Running as a party, the social movements polled under 2 per cent of the votes in the 1990 elections, confirming that they had lost the initiative to an older generation of anti-communist academics and Catholic nationalists who had kept their distance from the unruly movements when they needed support, and in some cases even attacked them.

One band from the heyday of punk became Slovenia's prime cultural export since the polka-dot tie. Not just the best-known Yugoslav rock group, Laibach was the only band from socialist Europe to win Western renown. Established darlings of art-house culture, they perform from Warsaw to New York. In Britain in the late '80s, their records outsold all other foreign independent-label albums.

Laibach (the German name for Ljubljana) is phenomenal by any standards. It is made to last, and could have originated nowhere but Ljubljana. In retrospect, its career has followed an arrow-straight course. The band's style was immediately notorious. With their sledgehammer percussion, hunting horns, ranting lyrics, and khaki uniforms, they looked and sounded like fascists. They turned audience-assault into a facet of their art. When a rock band calling itself Laibach kitted itself in peaked caps, jackets and jodhpurs, and barked songs about "strong men of the nation" and so forth (often in German), it was evoking the Second World War, when the city was occupied by the Nazis for a year and a half. Open discussion of this period was taboo because it would have begged the question of fascist collaboration in wartime Slovenia.

By bringing militarism and totalitarianism to centre-stage, the band's style broached further, equally taboo questions about the unaccountable power of the régime and the rôle of the armed forces in that régime. Laibach flouted these taboos in a way that was blatant and ambiguous, iron-fisted and enigmatic. Their militarism was thoroughly aesthetic: a matter of attitude and pastiche, not of commitment. The band did not "believe" the political symbolism of their own style; they performed as if they were, so to speak, just following orders. "For us," says Žižek, "their fundamental cry was 'We want more alienation.' "

When the band made its first, electrifying appearance on television in 1982 most viewers were shocked and many were outraged. The War Veterans' Association condemned the band as fascists. It is unlikely that the band's critics grasped the complexity of its message. Even if they appreciated its subtlety, this could only have enraged them further; for the message challenged authority at its weak point. The band used totalitarian motifs with no irony or humour – though one could never be sure they weren't absolutely ironic, sending everything up, including themselves. To its critics, Laibach was not even honest about its fascism!

Laibach joined a collective enterprise called *Neue Slowenische Kunst*, or New Slovenian Art. Its other components are IRWIN (visual artists), New Collectivism (posters, graphics and books), Red Pilot (theatre), New Builders (architecture), and Retrovision (film and video). Together under the NSK banner or separately, they communicate with the public by issuing inscrutable bulletins. Politicians or journalists studying these statements found little to enlighten them.

For instance: "NSK is based on the principle of a conscious abandonment of personal taste, judgements, convictions, voluntary depersonalization, the willing adoption of ideology". Or this, from Laibach: "Politics is the highest form of popular culture and we, who create the contemporary European pop culture, consider ourselves politicians." As with their performances, the band's statements evade commitment.

Like Laibach, the other organs of NSK are studiedly avant-garde, and specialize in exploiting Slovenia's ambiguous heritage of totalitarianism. Their products are cool, gestural, anti-naturalistic; they want your attention, not your emotions. Laibach are media manipulators rather than musicians. IRWIN's paintings are more interesting to discuss than to look at, like Red Pilot's productions for the stage. Far from trying to be personalities, NSK artists subsume themselves in a collective identity, with no more individuality than the marionettes of a puppet theatre.

Laibach's political difficulties ended in 1986, when the Youth League began to support it. The band looked farther afield, and its first appearance in New York was only a matter of time. Retrovision filmed the audience. "Art-fags from Europe!" spat one man, hurrying away. Another spectator was more thoughtful. "I think it was neo-fascist but I'm not sure. I had this incredible subconscious urge to *march*, this feeling I was being made part of a nation that's not mine." "Is that bad?" asked Retrovision happily. "Oh no," said the man, "I just want to know if it's serious or not."

While Laibach and the rest of NSK are masters of paradox, at least one irony seems to escape their control. Behind the avant-garde brilliance, NSK owes its success to the traditional Slovene virtue of hard graft, husbanding narrow talent as doggedly as any farmer tilling his patch of mountainside.

A farmer's toil is never done. NSK have announced their "next step": "rewriting *Das Kapital* to make it relevant again for the future".

*

The spirit of mid-to-late '80s Ljubljana endures in *Mladina*, though on diminishing returns.

When this weekly magazine bought itself out of the state publishing enterprise in 1990, it became the first independent news publication in Slovenia. Nothing else changed about the magazine; its premises in a ponderous Habsburg block near the railway station are still threadbare and smokefilled. Most of the staff are in their late twenties; I am currently the London correspondent.

Independence has been *Mladina*'s watchword since the punk wave washed the magazine out of conformism. Led by a generation of journalists who had graduated from the student radio station, *Mladina* began to behave like a free press. It invented investigative journalism in Yugoslavia, ignoring republican boundaries. It supported the new social movements before they were fashionable.

By 1987 everyone was discussing *Mladina*. The Slovenian Assembly, five minutes' walk away, watched it like hawks, quite often condemned it, and occasionally banned it – which was good for publicity. The Chiefs of Staff in Belgrade were outraged by its campaigns against arms sales to Third World dictatorships, and against conscript labour used to build generals' seaside villas. In London, the *Guardian* opined that *Mladina*'s "journalistic standards would put most western magazines to shame".

The magazine's apotheosis came in spring 1988, when its editor and two contributors were court-martialled for possession of "military secrets". It was an open secret that the JNA had been spoiling for a fight with *Mladina* and other dangerous elements in Slovenia.

The journalists denied the charges. They were known as critics of the military, and clearly they were being set up. Yet the rumoured contents of the secrets were all too plausible; they related to the role to be played by the JNA's Ljubljana garrison in a hypothetical military clamp-down in Slovenia.

The prosecution of the journalists gave a great fillip to nationalist and democratic sentiment. For the first time, the entire spectrum of Slovenian society united behind the reformists. Even the republican presidency and the LCS expressed reservations about the trial. A Committee for the Defence of Human Rights was formed the day after the four were arrested. (The fourth was a warrant officer who had supposedly leaked the secrets.) In a matter of weeks half a million signatures were collected – a quarter of Slovenia's population. The street in front of the court was filled with crowds who strewed flowers and played music. A rally in the centre of Ljubljana drew the biggest crowds in the city's history.

This tremendous mobilization was spurred by indignation at militarist arrogance *per se*, but also at its imposition from outside. The prosecution was rightly seen as directed from Belgrade. Almost as much as the arrests, what galled the Slovenes was the use of Serbo-Croatian in the courtmartial. This flouted the constitutional right of everyone to be tried in their mother tongue; it was stark proof that this was an *anti-Slovene* trial. The feminists, punks and war veterans joined ranks behind the accused. The JNA had succeeded beautifully in widening the pro-democracy constituency in Slovenia.

Mladina's circulation soared to 80,000. It could do no wrong, and its halo endured as long as Franci Zavrl, the boisterous editor, remained behind bars. (Nominally, at least. Serving his sentence in an open prison with a friendly governor, he spent his days editing the magazine in his office and his nights in prison. When he arrived after lights-out, he had to escape *in* over the perimeter wall. On his release in early 1990 Zavrl threw a party where leading apparatchiks rubbed pinstriped shoulders with teenagers in ripped T-shirts and green Mohican coiffures. Only in Slovenia . . .)

All good things must end. By the elections in April *Mladina*'s circulation had sunk by half. Other magazines stole its winning formula of investigation, wide-ranging cultural coverage, and offensive satire. It could no longer trump its rivals by "going further", because any magazine could now go anywhere. For the first time *Mladina* felt the pinch of competition. Its sensations became strained; a fake photomontage of the assassination of Serbia's President Milošević, for instance. It decided to cultivate professionalism: if it couldn't be notorious, it would be the best. Reporters were despatched to Ulster, Lebanon and other Balkanish hotspots. It introduced a double-page parliamentary column. Worthy innovations, but the pursuit of excellence proved dull for journalists who had helped bring down a political system and enjoyed themselves hugely in the process.

A year after the elections *Mladina*'s anti-clerical, anti-nationalist stance was increasingly unpopular; people had less money to buy magazines; and there were signs of political burn-out among the population at large. Ervin shook his head. "In the good old days before democracy there were two poles in this society: civil society, or the democratic public, and on the other side, those imaginary Bolshevik hardliners. It was so simple! Now we attack the government – which makes worse mistakes than the communists did – but unlike the communists, it doesn't actually *mind*." I was tempted to preach about repressive tolerance and the infinite cunning of capital. Instead I said that *Mladina* still outdoes anything I can buy in London. This cheered him up. The British press, he tartly reminded me, is hardly an inspiration to anyone.

Ervin will keep cropping up in this book. He needs an introduction. A decade older than most of *Mladina*'s staff, he is (though he'd deny it) the magazine's star reporter, interviewer, columnist. He has never been on the payroll; a born freelance, he means to stay that way, at least until *Mladina* gets serious.

Ervin is an obtrusive presence. Very tall and bulky with it, hirsute and shambling, he is a physical event in himself. More like a wall than a fly on the wall, he registers every word and gesture in a room, even when his own stories are flowing. He reads philosophy like novels, coins epigrams in three languages, contradicts himself at every turn. He compensates for caffeine and tobacco gluttony by "not really drinking", except wine, bourbon and single malt. He can abstain but not be moderate. Quite the contrary: Slovene moderation is a favourite target for attack, and reasonableness is but one English 'virtue' that disgusts him, at least when I'm around. In fact there's no pleasing the man; he criticizes Slovenia with relish until any foreigner joins in. Half Italian himself, he has no compassion for the Slovenes and their mealy Austrophile airs, their don't-stare-in-public primness. Most unusually, he has a romantic fondness for the south. "Of course the Serbs are a disgrace these days," he nods sagely. "Don't forget, though, they were the best people in this country: no one else could touch them." Until the war in Croatia, nothing made him merrier than displays of Balkan honour or sheer bloody-mindedness, jamming the jaws of Western rationality, dumbfounding the righteous Slovenes.

He once vowed to emigrate if Slovenia became independent. "But where can I go?" he asked when I reminded him. "In Serbia or Montenegro they would send me to fight the Croats. In Croatia, well, I don't want to live there anyway. Bosnia is all screwed up, and Macedonia is too far away . . ." Myself, I can't imagine him anywhere else.

Ervin isn't the only know-all at *Mladina*. When Ivo isn't writing or editing the magazine, he translates German philosophy into Slovenian, or reads comic books. When Marcel isn't writing or editing, he reads pulp fiction or watches movies, or both simultaneously.

One day I visited the office and found no one there but Marcel. I had just finished *Cause for Alarm*, so I enthused about Eric Ambler's sense of Yugoslavia as a middle zone of deception and instability. "Yet Ambler's postwar books," I said, "skirt Yugoslavia. Though he sympathised with the Left, it's as if he lost interest once fascism was beaten. Which is odd, for there was plenty of ambiguity and shadow about Yugoslavia after 1948. Ambler was typical, too; I can't think of any genre fiction inspired by socialist Yugoslavia."

"It's true about Ambler," Marcel nodded, stubbing out a Marlboro and swinging his chair round. "And when he does include postwar Yugoslavia in a plot, he writes around it rather than about it, as if the place is too equivocal to be trusted at the centre of the story. Likewise Ken Follett and Helen MacInnes. Graham Greene tried to write a Cold War screenplay, a spy story with Yugoslavia as the villain, but it didn't work. The film was called *The Stranger's Hand* and it sank without trace, Greene said, because the split with Stalin had turned Tito into 'a kind of white-headed boy of the West'. The real reason is less interesting: it's a dog of a film."

He rocked back in the chair and folded his arms. "Now Bond," he said, "James Bond. He's one of us."

"Pardon?"

"One of us. On our side."

"There aren't any Bond books about Yugoslavia," I said confidently, "or any Yugoslavs in the stories. Only *From Russia, With Love,* and then . . ."

"Just for a chapter or two, I know. But Yugoslavia is often present, though never prominent; that's part of the point — Yugoslavia *shouldn't* be prominent in those Bond plots about good and evil, heroes and villains. It figures in the appropriate way, framing the stories like the empty margin of a page."

"For instance?"

"Beginning at the beginning: early in *Casino Royale,* the first Bond book, a medical officer at the Yugoslav Embassy in London is killed by SMERSH. Fleming gives the date: 7 August 1948 — a few weeks after Stalin threw Tito out of the Cominform. The assassin is Russian, of course. The book wasn't published till 1953, but Fleming didn't forget these things. He knew Yugoslavia's status.

"Then, Bond's first date with the beautiful double-agent, Vesper Lynd. He cites the *četnik* leader Mihailović's last speech at his trial in '46. You know, the famous sentence: 'the gale of the world carried away me and my work'. At the end of the book Vesper quotes the line back at Bond in her suicide note. Unbelievable!"

"Unbelievable," I agreed. "But how does this put Bond on your side?"

"Because it constructs Yugoslavia not as a land of commie bad guys but as a complex place with a history. The Embassy officer and Mihailović: two victims, you see? Fleming — or Bond, whichever you like — sympathised with us. He *knew* us. You needn't take my word for it; my theory is underpinned by Bond's own weird thoughts near the end of *Casino Royale.* Recuperating in hospital, he suddenly becomes a theologian of Cold War. 'In order to tell the difference between good and evil,' he says, 'we have manufactured two images representing the extremes and we call them God and the Devil. I've been thinking about these things, and wondering whose side I ought to be on.' An absolutely Yugoslav reflection! Bond feels that he's a man in the middle, caught between these extremes, as Tito's Yugoslavia stood between God and the Devil — the Free World and the Soviet bloc. No wonder Bond knows the Mihailović quotation: it would stick in the mind of anyone caught in the great game of East–West conflict, yet who can't convince himself that his own side is what it claims to be.

"Not convinced? Then think of those two killers in *Casino Royale* who murder innocent people with a Molotov cocktail – they are Bulgarians. Almost Yugoslav, you see – the same neck of the Balkan backwoods. But *not* Yugoslav. The pattern is repeated in *For Your Eyes Only* when Bond sits in a Paris café, reflecting how Paris has pawned its heart 'to the tourists', the 'Russians and Roumanians and Bulgars, pawned to the scum of the world who had gradually taken the town over'. Or later in the book, remember the Albanian opium-smugglers? Again, not Yugoslav! In Bond's mind Yugoslavs aren't part of the Eastern riffraff.

"Don't forget that Eastern Europe barely figures in the Bond books – less than Yugoslavia, and never positively. There's the passage in *Diamonds Are Forever*, when Bond compares a roomful of American gangsters with other villains he's encountered. 'Bond remembered cold, dedicated, chess-playing Russians; brilliant, neurotic Germans; silent, deadly, anonymous men from Central Europe'. Of course the central Europeans are 'anonymous'; what else would they be? When Fleming wrote the book in '55 or '56 central Europe was one huge Soviet backyard, stretching from Budapest to the Baltic. Horrible. And not like us.

"Mihailović figures again, by the way – in *Thunderball*, mentioned as the archetype of resistance leaders. And a few pages later, in the famous SPECTRE boardroom scene in Blofeld's Paris head-quarters, Fleming tells us there are 'three tough Yugoslav operatives who had resigned from Marshal Tito's Secret Police'."

Spying my chance, I pounced. "So what? There are fifteen other villains around Blofeld's table too."

"Seventeen, actually. Three mafiosi from Sicily, three Corsican villains, three ex-Gestapo officers, three Turks, and three Soviet agents. From Eastern Europe, though, there are only one Pole and one East German, making up the full SPECTRE complement of twenty. Fleming gives Yugoslavia numerical parity with the USSR; the other socialist states have just one apiece, because they're only satellites. That's another point to us! And isn't there even a touch of delicacy about the word 'resigned'? Not 'purged' or 'defected'. As if the Yugoslav secret police was a rather civilized operation, don't you think, like the British civil service?"

The phone at Marcel's elbow rang. He took the receiver off the hook, lit another Marlboro, and resumed.

"The only other Yugoslav in Bond is the improbably-named Bertil, a SPECTRE agent with 'bad teeth', we're told, who has a tiny but crucial off-stage part in *On Her Majesty's Secret Service*. Blofeld has him killed for making a pass at one of the English girls at his eyrie in the Swiss Alps. A bad guy maybe, but a victim too. More than anything else, his execution shows up Blofeld's bestiality. In terms of plot, we might see his death as a Yugoslav sacrifice to the West, because it helps Bond to see through Blofeld's disguise. And his name may be silly, but at least he *has* a name, unlike those 'anonymous men from Central Europe', or that Bulgarian plastic explosives expert in the same book, the one who used to work for the KGB. Fleming and Bond didn't like Bulgarians, but ah!, who does?

"Anyway, the key text – you're right," he added kindly, "is *From Russia, With Love*. The Yugoslav part comes when Bond and the gorgeous Tatiana are . . ."

"On the Orient Express. But there are no Yugoslav characters, are there?" I said hopefully.

"True," Marcel conceded. "And that's neither here nor there. The whole scene is crammed with perceptions about Yugoslavia. First, it's the route through Bulgaria that is called 'the northern route through the Iron Curtain'. Fleming knew *we* hadn't been behind the Iron Curtain since 1948.

"Second, it's when the train is racing through southern Yugoslavia that Fleming writes that romantic sentence about James and Tatiana: 'The flame that suddenly lit between them – between the two secret agents, thrown together from enemy camps a whole world apart, each involved in his own plot against the country of the other.' A *profoundly* Yugoslav sentence; it is a thought that could have occurred nowhere else. It follows then, when Bond muses on the Cold War context of his present escapade, that Fleming gives him the clinching insight: '*And Yugoslavia? Whose side was Tito on? Probably both.*'

"I see you're convinced. Anyway, I've reached my last shred of evidence. While Bond waits for Tatiana in Istanbul railway station (homage to Ambler?), he reads off the destinations on their train: 'Istanbul–Thessaloniki–Beograd–Venezia' and so on. 'One of the most romantic signs in the world,' he thinks. Now, Bond is 007: the double-O prefix signifies his licence to kill. And 'Beograd' is Belgrade with an O. Yet once he is on the train, inside Yugoslavia, the text only mentions 'Belgrade'. There's no O in Belgrade. And indeed Bond *doesn't* kill anyone inside Yugoslavia in this book or any other. Or any Yugoslav for that matter. As if Yugoslavia disarms Bond, revokes his licence to kill, because Cold War rules didn't apply here."*

---

* Reality has caught up with Marcel's semiology. At the end of 1991 a private training school for bodyguards opened in Belgrade. Its proprietor, Zoran Marković, "who comes from a police background" and hopes "to create a superior type of bodyguard", tells his students that " 'the last thing in the world they want to do is to kill someone.' " The name of his establishment? – The 007 School. (From *Politika the International Weekly*, 7 December 1991.)

Marcel looked at his watch; a stack of videos was calling him home. As he hurried toward the door, my memory sparked into life for the first time that morning.

"Wait, you've forgotten Bond's cigarettes."

He turned and frowned. "Sixty a day, specially prepared by Morlands of Grosvenor Street. What about them?"

I tutted. "The tobacco, Marcel, the tobacco. It's Macedonian, 'fragrant but powerful' . . ."

*

Boris the ex-punk editor had arrived halfway through Marcel's performance. Now he looked up from his Applemac screen. "See how much you learn when you're with us!" he teased. "Now, perhaps you can do something for us too. It's high time you wrote an article. Why don't you go to Kočevski Rog on Sunday and cover the ceremony."

Kočevski Rog is a remote region in south Slovenia, the last great forest in the country. Through the spring and summer of 1990 its name had been on many lips, for Kočevski Rog was the terminal destination for many thousands of Slovenes (and Croats and Serbs) transported as prisoners from Allied refugee camps in Carinthia, at the end of the Second World War. There, cloaked by the forest's silence, which had sheltered the Slovenian partisans during the war, the prisoners were slaughtered as quislings, as enemies of the people and the revolution.

They were buried in a cave. The cave was sealed with explosives. Until spring 1990 access to the forest was forbidden to all, on the pretext that it contained a top-secret military base. The massacres were a taboo subject until the late 1980s, when references to those events of summer '45 began to be made by historians and oppositionists. In fact the killing was always an open secret among locals, who knew what they had heard and seen, and knew too to keep their mouths shut. A British journalist, Anne Dacie, travelling in northern Slovenia in 1946 recorded hearing that "8000 *domobranci* men and women had been . . . shot [or] pushed over a precipice" somewhere, in "a valley where entry is forbidden". This was well-founded rumour: the estimated total of domobranci victims has not changed, though exact figures will never be known, because records have not survived, if they were ever kept. British sources indicate that a further 12,000 Croats, 5,500 Serbs and 400 Montenegrins were repatriated from Carinthia; presumably the total of victims here and at other sites in the Republic is in the order of 25,000.

The civil war that raged throughout Yugoslavia within and

parallel to the anti-Axis war took different form in different regions. Partly because the Slovenian theatre was remote from the main conflict, in Croatia and Bosnia, and partly because of bad memories of royal Yugoslavia, the partisans here tended to view their struggle as national rather than all-Yugoslav, until they were knocked into line. Meanwhile, in Slovenia as elsewhere, the CP commissars manoeuvred to bring other anti-fascist resistance groups under their control. When this was consolidated via the Slovene Liberation Front – an anti-fascist coalition run by the Communist Party – the partisans began liquidating their opponents inside the resistance.

After the Axis invasion of Yugoslavia, which carved up Slovenia between Italy, Germany and Hungary, the Italians interned the officers of the Royal Yugoslav Army, then released and armed them to form the White Guard, which became the Home Guard (*domobranci*). These collaborationist forces served the Slovenian quisling government under the Italian and Nazi occupations. As such, they and the partisans were deadly enemies throughout the war, competing for both present and future survival.

Through the late winter and early spring of 1945, as German defeat loomed closer and the partisans closed upon Ljubljana from the east and south, the quislings headed north. Their only chance of survival was to reach the Allies in Austria or Italy before their compatriots caught up with them. Refugees poured over the border to surrender in droves, not only Slovenes but Croat *ustaše* and *domobranci*, Serbs from the forces of General Nedić in Belgrade, Montenegrin *četniks*, several thousand Cossacks with their White Russian commanders, Polish Ruthenes from a Waffen SS division, Vojvodina Germans from the 'Prinz Eugen' SS Volunteer Mountain Division. . . .

Fascist flotsam from all around central Europe and the Balkans was beached in Carinthia. Partisans marauded in the hills around the refugee camps, while in Belgrade the new government pressed Yugoslavia's claims to the Austrian province. Witnesses have described the utter chaos of the scene – a microcosm of Europe at the war's end, when entire populations were in flight. These refugees' situation was horribly clear. They knew the kind of justice they could expect from the partisans, whose definition of collaboration yawned as blackly as any pit in a forest. Any farmer who had succoured a Home Guard fighter at gun-point might be denounced as a collaborator; likewise any peasant overheard by the wrong ears criticizing the partisans. Back in 1941, officers of the Royal Yugoslav Army who refused to join quisling forces had faced deportation to German labour camps. Throughout Yugoslavia the war left no room for neutrality. Alongside genuine quislings were a good many innocents, swept along in the whirlwind.

The new régime was not interested in differences among the motley crowds on the wrong side of the fence. Once the massacre was done, the régime needed to cancel the legacy of wartime hatreds. This it did by burying them. In the 1980s, as communist power waned and national consciousness waxed, the massacre in Kočevski Rog was adopted as a cause by several politicians and academics. This abcess in national history, they argued, must be lanced. Mrs Spomenka Hribar was expelled from the League of Communists of Slovenia for breaking the taboo. Her campaign for a Ceremony of Reconciliation became one of the Demos coalition's election promises in 1990. The Ceremony was scheduled for 11 a.m. on Sunday 8 July.

Boris did not have to ask twice. After I agreed to write a report, he expressed scepticism about the whole business. "They call it 'reconciliation', but for whom? *I'm* not being reconciled to anyone. In fact I'm not involved at all. This is typical Demos: inventing emotive rituals to homogenize the nation, when only a fraction of the nation is really involved."

I went, watched, listened and wrote:

"On the press coach to Kočevje I met a man from Litija, hitching a ride to the Ceremony. 'There are always winner and losers, in every situation,' he said, seeking to explain the event to a foreigner. 'How the winners behave toward the losers – *that* depends upon culture.'

"The first thing to say about the Ceremony of Reconciliation is that its culture was civilized. The atmosphere was intent and gentle. The matter of historical winners and losers was negotiated with tact by the speakers and by the 20,000 Slovenes who had made their way to the forest.

"Everyone disembarked near a row of little wood and canvas kiosks, selling video cassettes of this same place, as well as souvenir knick-knacks, books and pamphlets about the atrocities, lapel badges, funerary candles, and postcards of the large carved crucifix erected beside the newly-laid path into the forest.

"Beyond the crucifix this path divided. One fork led up the hillside to a high clearing. An altar stood under a canopy upon a raised platform of scaffolding and boards. The air, loud with insects, was tangy with resin. The other fork wound up between rocks into dark shadow, to the mass grave. Here the crowd thickened and moved slowly. Old people picked their way over the rough ground, some muttering the Hail Mary, a few bearing crutches. I walked beside an old crone whose legs were swathed in bandages. She carried a stick in one hand, and tears gleamed in the creases of her cheeks. Protruding from the earth above the pit was a large mossy boulder, illuminated with funerary candles; their red plastic cases glowed in the green penumbra. Other candles were placed in the pit itself, and white carnations were scattered on its sides of shelving rock. The sobbing became audible as people reached the lip of the pit. A few yards away from the path, the forest's stillness was untainted. A bird sang nearby.

"When the service began the hillside above the altar was packed with people. All generations were present, from grandmothers to infants on their fathers' shoulders. The average age was at least fifty. To judge by the singing, the expressions on faces and the queue for communion, the service meant most to the older ones: women in shawls and high-laced shoes, clutching rosary beads and lace-edged handkerchiefs, and men perspiring in felt hats and best black Sunday suits.

"The Ceremony commemorated the dead through Catholic ritual, and articulated the reconciliation in terms of faith and forgiveness. Archbishop Šuštar [the Primate of Slovenia] made two last-minute changes in his homily. Listing groups for whom prayers should be offered, he qualified 'partisans' to 'Slovene partisans'. Then, imagining what the dead might say now to the living, he inserted 'Yugoslavia' after 'fatherland' as also needing help for a better future.

"At an occasion which conjures a national community, any exclusions gain extra significance. Šuštar was surely right to add the name of the federation. The same name was prominent by its absence from President Kučan's speech, which was altogether less confident and political than the Archbishop's. This was the Church's day, and Kučan's manner acknowledged that he was second fiddle. His was a good speech, drawing the necessary distinctions, speaking of history rather than faith, and even slipping in an apposite quotation from Marx.

"As people drifted away, I asked ten men and women, all aged sixty or more, why they came. Six believed their fathers or brothers were killed there. Others had been imprisoned in Germany or Novo Mesto. They had travelled from all over the country, and one from Canada. All were glad of this day, when they could bury their relations at last. 'Now I can die in peace,' as one old man said.

"The air was thick with untold stories, suppressed experience. An ancient man in loden green told me about his prison in Novo Mesto: 'Sixty-eight prisoners to a cell for a fortnight, with nothing to eat but a cup of rotten beans. I haven't only come to see – this is a pilgrimage for me.' His voice rose excitedly, and others crowded round to hear. A soft-voiced woman from Kočevje told what the domobranci did to a man in her village, how the partisans treated people who were forced to help Germans or Italians, how she heard the gunfire in the forest . . .

"If there was any urge to recriminate at Kočevski Rog, I did not notice it; only grief and satisfaction at a long-overdue task now achieved.

"Of course, the event has a present political meaning too, and Slovenes who do not want the coming 'time of peace' (to quote Kučan's closing phrase) to be supervised too closely by the Church, may see potential cause for concern in the cordial handshake of Church and State in the forest."

Ervin's reaction to my article was succint. "Sentimental claptrap. That woman's tears may be real, but the Church's manoeuvres for influence are real too in Slovenia today, and rather more important, if you don't mind."

He had been revolted by the media competition for stories of the latest *cache* of bones to be unearthed; every week produced evidence of further horrors. And he rejected the rehabilitation of domobranci. "I'd have shot them too," he declared. "They were backing the fascists, and I don't like fascism."

"But they weren't all collaborators," I protested.

"No doubt, but that doesn't excuse the domobranci, nor does it mean the partisans were evil to eradicate their enemies. 'Revolutionary justice' is what winners do to losers, and in that situation, either the fascists won or the communists, and the fascists didn't, thank God."

He and Boris were in a minority, as they wanted to be. Public response to the Ceremony was positive. Hailing the event as an example of the Slovenes' own sort of greatness, Mrs Hribar proudly said that "communism and anti-communism have been relegated to the past."

*

I took my article to the office and handed it to Boris with relief. Too much mud sticking to my shoe-soles, too many bones under my shoes. July was blazing, and Ljubljana was draining daily westward, to the sea. "No one's here now except people who wish they weren't," said my friend Miha, who was delivering his own weekly column. "We're going to Umag this afternoon. Come along!" I said I would follow the next day; I had one more appointment in Slovenia.

Bogenšperk castle stands on a high ridge due east of Ljubljana, commanding a wide view towards the valley of the Sava. Its walls are freshly whitewashed; its squat turrets are roofed with mottled ruddy-brown tiles. An apron of grass between the car park and the castle gate is neatly mown. A mob of chattering jays chase each other around the apple orchard below the western wall.

The scene is idyllic, as so much of Slovenia is, but in no way grand. Bogenšperk looks much like other little castles that dot these hills, if better preserved than most. Yet this is the most important castle in the country; on a cultural map of Slovenia, this ridge-top would be the midpoint. For Bogenšperk was once the home of Baron Valvasor, and Valvasor, as the enthusiast selling T-shirts in the castle courtyard told me, was "a great Slovene, maybe the greatest!" It was an apt tribute; Slovenia did not exist as an idea in Valvasor's lifetime, let alone as a territory. By affiliation, however, he was absolutely Slovene – the first citizen of Slovenia.

Janez Vajkard Valvasor was born in 1641 in Ljubljana, then the capital of the Habsburg province of Carniola, which covered roughly the same territory as the present republic. After joining campaigns against the Turks in Slavonia he went travelling in Scandinavia, Paris, Spain and Tunis, returning home in 1672. He bought Bogenšperk, where he lived for the next twenty years, leaving only to battle the Turks once more, in Styria in 1683.

While his fellow barons slid after their soldiering into the hunting, drinking, belly-broadening round of provincial baronetcy, Valvasor was insatiably curious and bookish. He was also a sort of visionary. His portrait shows an amiable, bumpy face with wisps of moustache and watchful eyes, flanked by armour on one side and a library on the other: renaissance man, *il sloveno universale*!

Unlike Montenegro or Serbia, Slovenia is not a land of heroes. Its culture does not venerate heroism; its partisan brigades in World War Two were named after poets, not warriors. Valvasor's appearance was suitably unimposing, diffident, but he was the genuine heroic article. He had discovered in his travels that no one abroad knew anything of his beloved land. Ensconced at Bogenšperk, he conceived a tremendous plan to present Carniola to the world in words and images. He brought printers, draughtsmen and coppersmiths from as far away as Holland. He assembled a library of several thousand volumes, and set to work. Treatises on heraldry and mathematics, illustrated editions of classical Roman poetry, inventories of the castles of Carniola, streamed from Bogenšperk's presses.

Meanwhile he never stopped researching for his own *magnum opus*. His study occupies the topmost room in the northwest tower, behind a recessed door; he cloistered himself here, away from guests and his team of assistants. The work was published in Nuremburg in 1689 under the title *Die Ehre des Hertzogthums Crain* (The Glory of the Duchy of Carniola). Running to fifteen volumes – 3,532 pages with 528 original copperplates – this work is about everything. It catalogues valleys and mountains, towns and boroughs; charts rivers and underground lakes; investigates dialects and flora; records customs, crafts, superstitions and monastic orders; summarizes the history and the legal system. Its maps and diagrams were state-of-the-art. Its inductive methods of research were unheard of, hereabouts. Its humorous, moralizing narrative remains highly readable. It has been a superlative resource for every generation of writers and scholars. And its author bankrupted himself by publishing it. Already ailing, he sold Bogenšperk and his other properties in 1692, including his library. He died a few months later.

His book seems a model of Slovenia in its variety and obscurity, and in the sheer fact of its existence: for it is the single bloom in the cultural desert of the Counter-Reformation.

Valvasor suffered the fate of greatness in a small nation; inside Slovenia, every schoolkid knows about his book; outside, no one has heard his name. "I lived outside Slovenia for thirty-seven years," said Archbishop Šuštar recently, "and I have seen that it is not known at all." He was speaking in the spring of 1991, weeks before his country's name was blazoned on front pages across the world. Where Valvasor failed, the Chiefs of Staff of the JNA succeeded.

After touring Bogenšperk I sat a while in the courtyard, sipping coffee. The chatty T-shirt vendor was demonstrating to a visiting couple how he impressed Valvasor's coat of arms on his shirts, and telling stories about the castle: how the partisans were stopped from burning it in 1943, how marriages are solemnized in Valvasor's library. The man of the couple was craning forward to hear; lean, with a tanned, high-boned face under a mane of white hair, he was perhaps seventy, a decade or more older than his companion. His lips and dark eyes were smiling as he listened; once or twice he responded in an exotic mixture of Slovenian and Russian. His companion glanced around the courtyard. When she noticed the makeshift bar, she whispered to the man and led the way to the table next to mine.

The couple had a special reason to be here; Philip owned a castle that was pictured in Valvasor's great book. The castle lay an hour's drive south-west, near Novo Mesto; they were on their way there now. Would I be interested. . . ?

Novo Mesto is a market town perched on the river Krka – an oily, torpid stream these days, thanks in part to the car factory which keeps the town affluent. To the south–east rise the hills of Bela Krajina and Gorjanci: first line of defence against the Ottomans for four centuries. The hill are studded with castles, some converted into hotels, others restored and open to visitors. Others again are uninhabited ruins. One of these is Philip's.

The partisans reached Hmelnik in high summer of 1942. Legend has it that among them was a cabinet maker who had made the family's silver chest; he led the fighters past the customary linden tree beside the drawbridge, under the portcullis and straight to the treasure. Two partisans went to bury the chest in the woods nearby. Neither men nor chest were seen again. Whether the story is true, the partisans did destroy the castle with dynamite and flame: the end of baronial exploitation, with a vengeance. The castle blazed for five days and nights. An effort has been made recently to restore the walls. The weedy courtyard is littered with planks and masonry and scaffolding. The surviving rooms are blackened with grafitti and smoke. In Valvasor's copperplate of 1679, the building and estate are spruce as a Surrey stockbroker's mansion.

A melancholy sight it seems to me. Philip grew up here in the '20s and '30s before he was swept into the war, most of which he spent in Soviet prison camps (where he learned his Russian). He remembers being woken in his bed by the gardener's singing as he walked up from the village at dawn. Now he and Christa live in Germany, and even if he weren't the last of the von Wambolts he knows no future generations would have grown up in castles. The fact doesn't distress him in the least. "Am I sad when I come here? A little maybe, underneath I'm more concerned with the present. The trouble with the old aristocracy is that they think they're still an élite."

The old aristocracy was not Slovene but Habsburg; castles and estates were owned by Austrians, Hungarians, even Italians. Philip's grandfather bought Hmelnik from a Triestine family; later he opened a school for the village boys, while his wife started sewing lessons for the girls. There is talk of returning the castle to its last owners, and Philip is negotiating with lawyers in Novo Mesto, pursuing a cloudy idea to use the site as a foundation for young people, something progressive and international.

Below the wall stands the chapel, roofless and overgrown, unreachable through brambles and acacias. Philip spied a lone rose blooming in his mother's garden beyond the chapel, but we couldn't reach that either, though we tried, pricked by thorns and prickling with sweat, stumbling over charred beams.

Nothing melancholy, though, about the view from the empty windows across the curling Temenica valley, dappled with cloud shadows, toward the mantle of Kočevski Rog, forest of bears and dreadful secrets. Philip remembers pointing down at the tiny figures harvesting in the fields and begging his father for some farmers to play with. Despite the vast backdrop of the forest, this is a pocket landscape, proportioned for childhood and a child's eye. Wilderness and plump cultivation, fir trees and vineyards, evergreen darkness and golden light mingle in the valley. Orchards and vineyards cover the southward slopes; near the village, strips of maize and kitchen vegetables gather round the terracotta tiles and crimson spire of its whitewashed church.

Leaving by a back lane, we stopped in a four-house hamlet where Philip's family rode to Mass every Sunday. A woman shyly invited us to take our ease under her chestnut tree. She brought wine and biscuits, and coaxed her two blond children to come and sit near us on the grass. When she discovered Philip's identity, the woman's eyes widened. "Oyoyoy!" she murmured, standing to clasp his hand in hers. "A pity," she said, "your family doesn't still live at Hmelnik. Then my daughter" – who wants to train in hotel management at Novo Mesto – "could come and work for you." The daughter smiled discreetly and said nothing.

Istran Summer

When Ljubljana empties in August each year, Miha comes to Istra for a holiday in his grandmother's bungalow by the sea, and this summer I came too.

The bungalow is a solid stone structure with its own lawn sloping beneath umbrella pines down to the fissured limestone pavement that stands in for beaches, all down the eastern Adriatic. The pines are beautiful. Their trunks are ruddy as the Istran soil, and the grass under them is matted with needles. In the midday lull, tawny squirrels with feathery tails skip, freeze, skip across the grass, and once a hoopoe stalked back and forth for half an hour, the first I ever saw.

Our nearest town was Umag, where the Hotel Adriatic advertised its casino with handbills in the shops: "Roulette, Black Jack, and Sloth Machines". But no mechanical help was needed: the Istran summer evaporates your energy all by itself. Politics disturbed no one's daydreams on the coast, and the only national question on anybody's mind was one that unites rather than divides: what Albert Camus once called "the nationalism of the sun".

A wave is a rare event on this coast. After picking a path between sea-urchins that sway in the water's lens, you roll on to your back, tread water, turn somersaults, watch the windsurfers sliding by. A rare crawler ploughs a furrow across the bay. Beyond the pine-topped promontories Umag's giant concrete factory is weirdly profiled against the sky: installed by fascist Italy, taken over by Yugoslav communists, and due for closure any day now.

Posters in Umag and other towns try to whip up interest in 'Topless Boxing' competitions. The tourists are more interested in the fruit market, or hushing their kids, or glancing at the trinkets hawked on the quay. Macedonian waiters flash their teeth, posing for snaps with pasty Dutch girls. The Byzantine basilica in Poreč smells of salt; its mother-of-pearl mosaics scintillate in the shallow sunbeams of early morning. Potatoes in the market are crusted with warm red earth, and the plums have a soft bloom. Sea and sky merge milkily, before the sun burnishes a horizon into view.

Istra is a place for holidays of placid routine, and nowhere more than in the workers' camps along the coast. One of these is tucked away in the woods near Miha's bungalow. Dozens of minuscule pastel-coloured cabins with tiny concrete verandas. No privacy and no entertainment, no noise above a murmur from a whitewashed bar-restaurant at the hub of the camp. We found the campers on the nearest bit of shoreline, stretched on their towels, eating fruit, and working their way through the daily paper.

This is 'syndicalist tourism' and it meets a need for affordable holidays. Workers came from all over the federation, and Istran camps were the most popular. Miha says they cover their costs, but how many more summers will they last? They have nothing to do with commercial tourism, and besides, the new government in Croatia won't want these mementoes of socialist Yugoslavia.

After a few days Miha and I were joined by Crispin the photographer, in transit to Dubrovnik. He walked straight from the car, through the bungalow and into the water, shedding camera bags and sweat-starched clothes as he went. Over supper he elaborated a brainwave that inspired him as he splashed about. He fancies that swimming tours of Istra and Dalmatia just might catch on. The basic package could be attractively cheap: a bathing costume, flippers, a waterproof rucksack for a change of clothes, an optional lightweight tent, and there you would be, as free as the dolphins that sometimes sport in these waters. Free to meander from Umag to Montenegro, tracing a white wake of pencil-thin arabesques upon the map's duck-egg blue, emerging in the south well exercised, and rimed all over with a thousand tiny saline scales.

When fighting erupted the following summer, first in Slovenia, then in Croatia, it put paid even to such daydreams, as it did to regular tourism. Although Istra saw no fighting, its coast emptied. Holidaymakers fled to Italy by ferry from Pula and Poreč. Once the fighting in Slovenia had ceased, Miha drove down the deserted highway from Ljubljana to check his little property was intact. Umag was a ghost town. "*Istria infelicissima e abbandonata!*" exclaimed a Triestine scholar in 1819. In 1991 Istra was once again most wretched – and abandoned, until its hotels filled with refugees from Dalmatia.

Istra is the stalactite that hangs into the upper Adriatic: a limestone peninsula some seventy kilometres long, shelving westward to the sea, cleft by green valleys, its hilltops dotted with ash-grey and terracotta villages.

Geography has demarcated the territory with, by Yugoslav standards, unique clarity. Nobody passes through Istra; one goes *into* it, as into Calabria or the Mull of Kintyre. It has always been a region in the fullest sense, with its own history, dialects and folklore. Like nowhere else in the federation except Vojvodina, it generated an identity beyond ethnic and national difference.

Its most successful governors have always respected its people's wish for self-administration. The conquering Romans endowed its coastal towns with constitutions that lasted into the middle ages, through occupations by Goths, Avars, and Byzantines. It was the feudal rule of the Patriarchs of Aquileia, at the northern tip of the Adriatic, that drove these towns into the Venetian Republic during the thirteenth century. Though the eastern interior still belonged to Austria, most of Istra stayed Venetian for 500 years, until Napoleon frowned at the mouldy Republic and it collapsed.

Under Venice, the four cities of Istra were self-governing – Capodistria, Cittanova, Parenzo and Pola, now Koper, Novigrad, Poreč and Pula. The smaller towns were "free communities", entitled to administer their own affairs. After brief interludes within the Illyrian Provinces of the French Empire, and as an appendix to Bonaparte's Kingdom of Italy, Istra became Austrian in 1814, then Austro-Hungarian in 1867. It sent its own deputies to the parliament in Vienna, and became a fashionable resort after the *Südbahn* connected Fiume (now Rijeka) and Vienna.

Among the bookshelves in Miha's bungalow I found a pocket-sized, scarlet cloth-bound guide printed in Bohemia in 1913: the nick of time for the last season on the Austrian riviera. The *Handbook of Dalmatia, Abbazia, Lussin Etc., including The Albanian Coast* has a brief chapter about Istra; the section about Abbazia (Opatija), then "among the most fashionable sea-side places of the world", includes a list of physicians: Dr J. Cohn, Dr P. Corpocich, Dr A. Craciunescu, Dr G. Fodor, Dr X. Gorski, Dr J. Knöpfelmacher, Dr K. Szegö . . .

With Jewish, Romanian, Hungarian, German and Croatian names, the list epitomizes the late Habsburg world. As the *Handbook* reminded its readers: "**Passports** are convenient, but not absolutely necessary for travellers in Austria-Hungary. . ." A passport-free zone from Dubrovnik to Krakow! Now documents are needed to pass from Umag to Portorož, a twenty minute drive.

After the Dual Monarchy became the largest casualty of the First World War, almost the whole of Istra was awarded to Italy. After the Second World War the Allied Council of Ministers awarded the peninsula to Yugoslavia, though without the coveted strategic port of Trieste at its northern apex. This was the only significant change to the country's pre-war borders. Italian *Istria* had become Yugoslav *Istra*. Almost all of it lay within the republic of Croatia, though the northern coast and a wedge of hinterland were deemed Slovenian. As with all internal Yugoslav borders, this one was invisible, until 1991, when Slovenia erected border-posts along backroads to mark the limits of its new sovereignty. As yet the border is still more symbolic than real; officials wave through nine cars in ten. But one's heart sinks at the omen of borderlines gouging into Istra yet again. Although it witnessed atrocities under Italian and Yugoslav rule, this stalactite never bred hatred among its people, whose regional loyalty now irks the republican governments.

In Croatia's 1990 election a majority of Istrans – not just the Italian community – voted communist, on the principle of better-the-devil-you-know. President Franjo Tudjman was so offended by the unpopularity of his radical nationalist HDZ party (*Hrvatska demokratska zajednica*, the Croatian Democratic Community), which swept to victory in the election, that within weeks of taking office his ministers were discussing how to repopulate Istra with Croats from Romania; who would, of course, express their gratitude in future polls. Small wonder that even anti-communist Istrans viewed the arrival of democracy with mixed emotions.

If Miha's bungalow had been built a hundred and fifty years ago, its owners might have seen the boat that carried Sir Gardner Wilkinson past this coast, on his way south from Trieste to Pola. Though he did not pause here, Sir Gardner duly noted the view of "Omago, sitting on the water's edge; and the inland Buia beyond, with its church crowning the hill on which it stands". There is no further mention of Umag or Buje in his redoubtable *Dalmatia and Montenegro; with a Journey to Mostar, and Remarks on the Slavonic Nations, &c. &c.* Nor any mention at all of the territory between the shore and the hilltop. It is simply elided by that semi-colon.

This was sensible. Wilkinson was curious to meet the prince-bishop of Montenegro; he had a lot of travelling ahead of him and no reason to pause here. And indeed he *didn't* miss anything by not stopping – nothing except the ordinary life of Istra.

What gulfs of difference that semi-colon reveals, deeper than the waters between his boat and the shore. For Sir Gardner disposed of nothing less than the power of freely-chosen movement. This incalculable privilege conferred another: the power to observe without obligation, without any awareness of himself as an actor in the scene. Sir Gardner was a doughty explorer, knighted for his contribution to Egyptology. Our sense of the malign influence that well-intentioned outsiders can have upon indigenous cultures did not exist for him because it has been generated by changes – including mass tourism – which were not perceptible in the 1840s.

By a twist of modernization, the increasing fraction of humankind which inherits Sir Gardner's power of movement is ever less able to grasp the meaning of deracination. By the same paradox, those who experience that deracination at first-hand are worst placed to communicate its meaning. We know anything of life inside the semi-colon only because that way of life was shattered after the Second World War. When the partisans annexed the Italian territories in Dalmatia and Istra, with their half-million inhabitants, most of the Italians plus a number of Croats and Slovenes fled to Italy. This drove the new régime to even harsher measures against the Italian minority, amounting at times to terrorism. Village priests were hounded and even murdered. Sixty-three of the ninety-two Italian schools were closed. Toponyms were Slavized. What fascist Italy did to Slavs before the war, socialist Yugoslavia now did to Italians.

That post-war exodus was the last big thing to happen to Istra, and its effects are inscribed on the landscape. Historically, it conformed all too neatly to the tradition of forcible immigration and depopula-tion that President Tudjman has threatened to revive. When it had defeated its Hungarian and German rivals for Istra, which lay devastated by war and plague, Venice welcomed Slav, Greek and Albanian refugees from the Ottoman Turks. In this century Italy and Yugoslavia both imported their own nationals to shore up claims to ownership.

The exodus dragged to the mid '50s, affecting the whole peninsula. Eventually it numbered at least 300,000 people. Among the refugees was the Tomizza family from the village of Materada, midway between Buje and Umag, in the heart of Sir Gardner Wilkinson's semi-colon. Young Fulvio Tomizza was twenty when he joined the flight to Trieste. He found work there as a journalist and published his first book a few years later. Called simply *Materada*, that first novel is set in 1954, perhaps the nadir of the area's postwar history. The London Memorandum had just sealed Yugoslav possession of Istra and Italian possession of Trieste, prompting a final rush across the border. Tomizza's miniature epic shows the exodus at fever pitch, destroying the community by bringing out the worst. Prudent farmers grow sly and suspicious, marriages buckle, children despise parents, brother fights brother. The settling of old scores is on everyone's mind.

Materada is devouring itself at such a rate that people are relieved to get away, "and the ones who stayed were almost apologetic for not having left already". Not that the place had been a paradise before; its tragedy is that events far beyond the villagers' control now exploit their weaknesses, hammering into the hairline fractures of dormant tension, injecting hatred into minor feuds. In the narrator's imagination an air of apocalypse hangs over Materada. The very land is emptying, "as if abandoned to perpetual night".

The plot turns on exactly this question of the land and who possesses it. Francesco Kozlović, the narrator, farms his uncle's land, to which he is bound by wordless peasant loyalty. The two little local towns are the axis of his universe. "Buje was the capital of the world for us," and, "for me," he confesses, "Umago is the most beautiful place on earth."

The ailing uncle has made a will leaving half his land to his son, who lives in Trieste, and the other, richer half to Francesco and his brother Berto. But they all know that this second half is marked down for expropriation by the communists when the old man dies.

Francesco doesn't want to emigrate. He has worked this land, made it fruitful; it belongs to him and his sons after him by elemental, indisputable right. He takes his case to the officials; they sympathize but won't intervene because, though Francesco helped the partisans in the war, he still won't join the Party. Then they change their mind and offer him a way to get the property, but only by laying false charges against his uncle, who is legally unassailable. The evils of traditional injustice and "revolutionary justice" mirror each other. Francesco is revolted, and accepts he and his family have no choice but to follow his neighbours into exile.

Crispin went his way, then Miha's friend Mojca arrived from Ljubljana. The three of us drove through Materada and Buje to Motovun, one of the hoary hilltop towns in the interior.

The road spiralled from the river valley towards the town walls. Except for a few old people on the balcony of a pensioners' home, who peered at us a moment and resumed a solemn debate about which owned the most teeth, we had the place to ourselves. Miha noted a children's playground, new since his last visit. "The place must be picking up."

The walls – "of venerable age", as the 1913 *Handbook* safely observes – are presented as the town's prime tourist attraction. They completely encircle the place, making a citadel of the centre, and they were needed, too, seven centuries ago, when Motovun had a spell of independence as the Republic of Montona, before submitting to Venice as protection against more rapacious predators. In return Venice demanded wood from the local forests to build her navies, stone from the quarries, and a legion of reserve soldiers, 4,000 from all Istra.

Relics of Venice are all around. The Lion of Saint Mark is embossed on the gatehouse, and the cathedral's main treasure is a silver-gilt altar that belonged five centuries ago to the commander

Bartolommeo Colleoni, he of Verrocchio's tremendous equestrian statue in Venice. The cathedral was locked, so we paid a few dinars to make a circuit of the walls instead. Miha was right: Motovun was reviving; the shells of old buildings were being cleared and repaired. On the terrace outside an unexpectedly smart hotel, the first diners were eating *tartufi* – truffles, a speciality – washed down with *teran*, a sharp Adriatic wine.

An empty café in a cellar under the walls was pumping disco beat into the evening air, which absorbed it utterly. We sat in a Venetian loggia overlooking the valley of the Mirna and absorbed the view, all purple and grey in the grainy dusk-light. Only the shreeing of swifts as they swept in arcs high above, where insects floated on warm currents, disturbed the peace. The valley bottom was squared into large cereal fields. Except for patches of vineyard on the lower flanks of the valley, the rest of the landscape was more or less unfarmed. The tops had presumably always been wild – left to sheep and goats, during the centuries when Istra exported wool. Otherwise, signs of lapsed cultivation were everywhere: overgrown orchards of fruit and olive trees, empty farmhouses, crumbling terraces, fields and hedgerows gone rankly to seed. Istra stretched away like a secret garden, intimate, still, rich with potential.

The stillness seems a fact of nature, but it is not so. The desolation was produced by humans, and it proves the absence of those thousands that fled in the '40s and '50s. From Roman times Istra was assiduously farmed, and travellers were always impressed by its fecundity. According to legend Saint Jerome was born near Koper, though he preferred the ecstatic hardship of an anchorite's life in Palestine. Probably Istra never suited ascetics. "A country so bountifully favoured by nature," enthused one Victorian Englishman, "would at all times have enjoyed the prosperity which seems now to be its portion, had it not been the bone of contention between neighbouring powers, who ended by making a desert of it."

In his memoirs, the Triestine Giani Stuparich (1891–1961) celebrated Istran abundance. "The cultivated land reached as far as the eye could see, and Istria kept arriving in our house with its gifts. Father had many friends there, in all parts. Besides the prawns and figs from Cherso [present-day Cres], there were sea-bream from Cittanova [Novigrad] and oysters from Quieto [the estuary of the Mirna river]; demijohns of oil arrived from Umago and casks of wine from Parenzo, and slender bottles of a delicious rosé wine from Dignano [Vodnjan]; there were kid-goat, hare, and sheep's milk cheese from the interior, and peaches and grapes from Capodistria and Isola [Izola]."

The sad serenity of the landscape is in the people too. A Slovene journalist who investigated the post-war exodus wrote recently that "Very few regions in Yugoslavia endured after the Second World War such a dramatic change of populations, of cultures, of customs, and also of economic activity." While this is true, and some of the exiles in Italy remain unreconciled, inside Istra there is a shared sense of loss and a distaste for nationalisms, and a shared resignation too, born of the certainty that whatever happens, Istra is peripheral. A resignation that creeps into a province when it can't keep its youth.

In Motovun and Buje and Grožnjan, the minority language became audible at twilight. Old women chatted in Italian as they hobbled home with bags of shopping or sat in their doorways. A shopkeeper leaning on his counter – at forty the youngest Italian in Grožnjan – nodded back, without turning, at the waxy portrait of Tito on the wall and murmured, as non-Slavs did throughout Yugoslavia, that the minorities were safer when *he* was around . . .

Even without ethnic strife, Istra's depopulation might have happened anyway. Throughout the Mediterranean basin the pull of urban industries has emptied the land of peasants. Thirty years ago, before its empty farmhouses became the second homes of Chiantishire, Tuscany looked much as Istra looks today. Not that this observation consoles Miha, shaking his head at the landscape: "It's such a pity. Don't you see Istra should be the Yugoslav California? Our Silicon Valley? It has everything going for it, but nothing changes."

*

Marine life has been scraped from the bed of the upper Adriatic, and these days the fishing fleets are sparse. Among the boats that leave Rovinj each summer dawn, one belongs to Ligio Zanini. He rises at four and is soon nosing his skiff out of the harbour towards the balmy islands that fringe this part of the coast.

He learned to fish as a boy in the 1930s, long before he trained to be a schoolteacher, and when fishing was the town's main business, not tourism. A kilo of choice fish earns more than the weekly value of his wretched pension. Not that money is the sole reason for his expeditions. "It lets me be free," he says, showing white teeth in a wide smile and spreading his arms in a favourite gesture, generous and explanatory. "And gives me space to think."

For years his boat has been visited by a herring gull, which perches on the stern. Man and gull are on such good terms that the man wrote a book called *Favalando cul cucal Filéipo*, which, translated from dialect, means "Conversations with Philip the Seagull". The dialect is Rovignese, evolved from the vulgar Latin that endured here when the Roman colony named Arupinum or Ruginium after the russet, bauxite-rich earth, had become a Byzantine and then a Venetian fishing town.

Zanini is the last poet who will write spontaneously in Rovignese. The audience is small: no more than 500 of Rovinj's 9,000 people know the dialect; perhaps two or three thousand others around the world understand it. Volumes of his poetry are printed by small presses in Friuli and Croatia. His masterpiece, *Martin Muma*, an autobiographical narrative composed in secret over many years, was published in Rijeka in 1990, shortly after Croatia's first open elections.

"This is the story of an Istrian . . ." *Martin Muma* begins, placing its infant author in the world of 1927, when Rovinj was still Rovigno. To the west, Winston Churchill, "then Chancellor of the Exchequer in Baldwin's cabinet", was in Rome, expressing his warm regard for Mussolini. Eastwards, Majakovski, the poet laureate of Bolshevism, was lauding a decade of Soviet rule.

These thunderclouds on either horizon roll closer through Martin's idyllic boyhood, and force him in his early teens to make enough existential decisions to fill a long lifetime. His Istra was milled like a handful of wheat between fascism and communism. The outbreak of war in 1939 found him in Pola, studying at the teachers' college, where he became active in the *Gioventù Antifascista*, the youth wing of the Italian Communist Party. "Ah, what a communist I was!" he beamed, as we sat drinking warm beer in his narrow pink house on the harbour front. Papers and books were heaped on a bare wooden table, and the windows were wide open to the sunset. Reflected light danced on the ceiling. Outside, the summer crowds rustled by. Zanini raised his bottle in a mock-salute to his naïvety. "We Italian comrades were fighting for a socialist Italy on one side and a socialist Yugoslavia on the other, and eventually for a world socialist union. Then it wouldn't matter where they put the borders around Istria." He paused to cut up a cigarette and pushed one quarter of it into a holder. "We were like almond blossom in January, killed by the first frost!"

Zanini and his comrades were surrounded by more enemies than they knew. Italian partisans in Istra were fighting not only the fascist troops of Germany, Italy and Croatia, and local anti-communist militias. They were undermined by their Yugoslav comrades, who did not want the Italian communists to be too successful or popular, as that might hinder post-war annexation of Italian territories. Subversion was easy because of the Yugoslav population's distrust after two decades of persecution. Eventually the local Italian communists submitted to the Communist Party of Yugoslavia, which eliminated doubtful Italian resistance leaders and betrayed others to the Nazis, even some who freely accepted Yugoslav command.

Although Zanini was disenchanted by Tito's régime, he toed the line. Taking Yugoslav citizenship, he transferred to the CPY along with other Italian comrades. "Lots of the Italians in Rovigno were communists, and stayed," he told me. "In Parenzo they were all bourgeois, so they left." The other students at the college called him a Titoist because he criticized the Italians who abandoned Istra, and refused to join their patriotic protests against Yugoslavia.

He held firm until 1948, when the expulsion from the Cominform blasted his internationalist dreams. An emissary arrived from Zagreb to test the loyalty of the Pula communists. As the Italians confessed one after another that they could not go against Mother Russia, young Ligio, the white hope of the cell, sitting in pride of place, could see the emissary score a line with his pen through each name.

His own turn came. "I cannot agree with the comrades who have already spoken," he began, to the delight of the pen-wielder. "But neither can I agree with the comrade from Zagreb." The whole dispute, he went on, boils down to a shepherds' quarrel: the big shepherd in Moscow with the moustache wanted to fleece his own sheep *and* to grab the lambs that belong to our shepherd in Belgrade. The Party had become nothing more than a trap for fools, an instrument of power wielded by scoundrels. For his part, Zanini wanted no more of it; he slapped his Party card on the table. "From now on I simply want to be a free citizen."

As he rose to go, the emissary crossed out his name with two lines. A few weeks later he was arrested, sentenced to eighteen months' imprisonment, and despatched to Goli Otok, Naked Island, a parched limestone reef south of Rijeka. Known nowadays as the Yugoslav gulag, Goli Otok was the camp where thousands of real and alleged *ibeovci* (Cominformists) were kept for 'corrective punishment', far from public view.

In prison Zanini learned the techniques of survival, and to quarter his cigarettes. He also seems to have discovered, with relief, a vital margin of liberty, which he refused to compromise by collaborating in his own "re-education" or pledging support for Tito, "that Stalinist against Stalin". Zanini settled his accounts with communism, paid for his delusions, and after three years achieved release on his own terms. He managed to pick up the pieces of his life, and made a career as a teacher; this was Yugoslavia, after all, not the Soviet Union or Eastern Europe, and the worst post-'48 paranoia was spent.

The prison term took away a slice of his life, but he emerged shriven of complicity with the power-system. Describing this to me, and in *Martin Muma*, Zanini is marvellously light-spirited, though his poetry can be bitter, haunted by phantasmagoria from his past. Never again was he tempted by political activism, though he gave his blessing to "his children" in the independent pressure group called Gruppo 88, which opposed nationalism as well as the communist régime; for Zanini detests Italian and Slav chauvinists alike. As for the Slovenes, "their nationalists are worse than the Serbs, by the way, and maybe than the Croats," Zanini warned, because he suspected me of letting them off too lightly. "Don't forget why so few Italians are left in the Slovenian part of Istra. The Slovenes are more cunning. Serbs will give you their heart — the Slovenes, never."

His regional identity rockets him to a cosmic viewpoint, bypassing nations entirely. "The illusion that anyone possesses territory is so damaging. What matters is to walk lightly on this earth. Bickering about whose culture is better than whose: what nonsense! Culture is universal, and we have to be eclectic. Like republican Rome, not imperial Rome. Pluralism!" He reached for a well-thumbed copy of William James's *A Pluralistic Universe* and flourished it under my nose. "Like this! Culture belongs to everyone. From slave songs came spirituals and the blues, which are played now in the same theatres where Verdi is performed. Think of it! Even those wretched and despairing people brought their little flower to the house of culture . . ."

The points of light in a person's eyes don't always change with the years; Zanini's skin is minutely creased by sun and seawind, yet his gaze is positively boyish. His hopeful smile, his prickly truculence (which I'm told about though do not glimpse), might be called boyish too. By recovering his independence he reconnected with an adolescence cut short by war and tyranny, and dialect keeps that link alive in his poetry. As we strolled past his boat moored in the old harbour, past kiosks selling a rainbow-range of German and Italian magazines, Zanini, with a red handkerchief round his head ("like a Pioneer!"), a threadbare cotton shirt and faded tennis shorts, looked like *homo istrianus*.

One of his young admirers from Gruppo 88, now a member of parliament in Ljubljana, describes Zanini as a living archive of Istran experience: "When *he* dies, that'll all be gone."

"To be a free citizen": where had that notion sprung from? Young communists aren't supposed to speak the language of citizenship, after all. Then I realized the answer lay all around. The entire littoral between Trieste and Kotor was under the sway of Venice for centuries, then under Napoleonic France, and its Latinate republican traditions were not extinguished by Austrian rule.

When Zanini made his stand in 1948, he was appealing to a right that cannot exist under communism: the right of the individual to withdraw, unmolested, into private life. Like any other individual right, this can be guaranteed only where the separation of government powers is ensured. The Illyrian Provinces of the French Empire were no more democratic than anywhere else in Europe in 1810, but they were not absolutist. Bonaparte sought to promulgate the *Code Napoléon* as rapidly as possible, and the Code did declare the equality of citizens, the inviolability of private property, the end of hereditary nobility, and the emancipation of civil institutions from ecclesiastical control.

It is tempting to interpret an elementary separation of powers in the assemblage of Venetian-Gothic and Renaissance buildings in the main square of Koper, where the municipal governor's crenellated palace and the urbane loggia face each other on either flank of the cathedral. In Koper and the other coastal towns, a web of narrow streets winds inward from the seafront to squares where the winged Lion of St Mark is carved upon a belfry modelled more or less exactly on San Marco in Venice: a hexagonal cone atop a high, square tower.

These are the insignia of what Italians call Istro-Venetian civilization, and it is rare to find a vista between Koper and Trogir that lacks evidence of its long tenure. The white stone walls of old Rovinj shimmer with light reflected from water that is never far away, and echo to its lap against the piers and outer walls. This intermingling of elements is utterly Venetian, and has long fascinated Istrans. Giani Stuparich never forgot the "land and sea, fields which mix their green with the blue of the sea, inlets of azure water penetrating the green land: *this* is Istra." The triad of sea, land, stone: blue, green, white – and such white! Istran stone "seems compact of salt's bright yet shaggy crystals. Air eats into it, the brightness remains." Venice built itself with this stone, "essence of the sea", and plundered Istra's forests. In return, it invested in Istra's own culture. Franciscan, Dominican and Benedictine monasteries were established. Venetian nobles employed Istran scholars to educate their sons. Links were fostered with Tuscany, too; Petrarch cultivated Istran humanists, and Dante himself may have visited. The Renaissance brought painters and sculptors and their patrons across the Adriatic; as witness the palaces and altarpieces from Koper to Dubrovnik. These connnections survived to a later age; the violinist Giuseppe Tartini (1692–1770) was born in Piran. Though he lived and worked in Padova, musicology honours him for a distinctly Istran accomplishment. Tartini it was who discovered the "difference tone" – a third note that is heard when two notes are played steadily and intensely. In modern times the beauty of the Istro-Venetian achievement has been exploited to bolster minority demands that Istra really *belongs* to Italy. (Victims of the crippling delusion Zanini mentioned; Italians can be as Balkan as anyone else.) During and after the First World War the Italians manoeuvred to ensure territorial gain. The Yugoslavs contended for possession, but when America and the European powers washed their hands of the Adriatic Question, Italy got its way, despite the fact that the Slav population of inland Istra, away from the Italianized coastal strip, was estimated at 90 per cent of the total. (Not by Italians, of course. There is even today no consensus on the Italian and Slav proportions of Istra's population before and after both World Wars.) What Italy failed to win at the negotiating table, it soon secured by buccaneering, when the poet d'Annunzio seized the port of Rijeka in 1919.

Yugoslavia was compelled to guarantee the rights of the Italian minority in Dalmatia. No reciprocal obligation was laid upon the Italians, who set about stripping basic cultural rights from the Slavs and the Slovenes in the large triangle of territory north of Trieste that Italy also gained at Versailles. When the fascist government came to power in 1922, oppression of Slavs became a matter of legal and political principle. It was a criminal offence to speak or sing publicly in Slovenian or Croatian. A schoolmaster could spit into the mouth of a boy heard using his native tongue; surnames were Italianized; Italians were encouraged to immigrate and so dilute the Slav majority. Any publication casting doubt on the Italian origins of culture in the region was banned.

A middle-aged Slovene described to me his humiliation at school in Postumia (Postojna), when an Italian schoolmaster ridiculed him before his giggling classmates for being "a dirty Slav". "And I was clean, *clean*, my mother scrubbed us every day, but it was summer and I was brown." The boy's helpless hurt was vivid in the man, half a century later.

And all in the crusading name of patriotism and superior civilization; fascist posters rallied citizens to "the holy battle for Italy". Nowhere was Italian fascism more virulent than in Trieste and the Adriatic territories, because nowhere was Italian chauvinism better rooted than here, where Italians and Slavs had always lived side by side, though never as equals. The Slavs were peasants and manual workers, or at best, clerks in the Habsburg bureaucracy, while the Italians were professional middle class.

Yugoslav victory in the Second World War turned the tables. The Italians fled and began to organize themselves in Trieste. Relations between the *esuli* (exiles) and the rump that stayed behind have been bitter. The exiles were doubly aggrieved: they felt ignored by Rome – sacrificed to diplomacy with Belgrade – and betrayed by the Italians who remained. Most of the latter, meanwhile, despised their own official representatives as mouthpieces of the Yugoslav régime.

Even today, Italians are liable to cite Dante as proof that Istra, mystically, *is* Italian. When this line was offered to me by one of the leaders of the exiles in Trieste, I objected that an outsider, scanning the map, might suppose Istra belongs with its Yugoslav hinterland. "No no," came the testy answer, "it's a natural part of the Italian peninsula. Ljubljana and Zagreb are over the Alps."

While such dogmatism isn't now typical of Istran émigré politics, the Slovenes and Croats seem to have recovered better from their maltreatment than have the Istran Italians, doubtless because the Slavs 'won' the last showdown. Trieste, after all, was never a Slav city, so the Slovenes could not lose it. The *istriani*, by contrast, still feel they were expelled and robbed.

Fascist oppression doesn't feature much in Italian evocations of life before the exodus, which conjure Istra as an Adriatic land of lost content. Marisa Madieri, who fled with her family from Fiume to Trieste in the summer of 1949, and whose book *Watergreen* is calmly free of resentment, sees her home town from a ferry on the Quarnero, in the 1980s: "If I shut my eyes, I can see our old house near the Baross docks, and granny Quarantotto's house near Piazza Dante. I don't, though, know where to place granny Madieri's house. I would never be able to find it now . . . Atlantis remains lost at the bottom of the sea, covered with shells and seaweed, shining like stained-glass fruit."

If this tender tone is due partly to memories made selective by time and hurt, it was also produced by the fact that Italians were able to live on the Istran coast almost without meeting Slavs, who tend to figure in these writings as local colour, servicing the Italians as nannies, boatmen, shopkeepers. The grandsons and granddaughters of those shadowy figures are rarely moved by Italian elegies. Aren't the middle-aged authors all too often, the Slav Istrans argue, the same people who deserted Istra in their youth?

Dealing as they usually do with infant experience, these memoirs don't avow any political designs; yet they are not neutral. In the late 1950s, when the Istran issue looked so tragic to Italians, Giani Stuparich wrote his account of growing up before the First World War. "At that time we didn't make any distinction between Trieste and Istra, for us it was the same land. Only later did we learn at school that the history of Istra had at certain times in the past been different from that of Trieste. But in essence we boys were right to feel that Trieste was Istra and Istra was Trieste: one geographical, natural reality, a unit, a single region."

Thus far, thus good. But should this single region be part of a single state? And if so, which one?

The young Stuparich had belonged to a political movement that sought the redemption of Trento, Trieste, Istra and Dalmatia for Italy; so his reply to my questions, which is evident anyway in his yearning prose, is easy to guess. Ligio Zanini's answer would be that Istra belongs to those who love it unpossessively; but his platonic anarchism would cut no ice in the bumptious parliaments of Slovenia and Croatia.

Trieste's inclusion in Italy is no longer challenged; nor was Dalmatia's in Yugoslavia. Serbia and Montenegro want some of the Croatian coast, as does the federal navy. It is extremely unlikely that they will succeed in keeping the portions they occupied and laid waste in 1991. Either way, Italy is not a contender. For its part, Slovenia's Italian minority guarantees the existing borders, and in 1990 the exiles started talking with their co-nationals who stayed in Istra.

Paving the way for this rapprochement was the appearance in 1987, three years before the elections in Slovenia and Croatia, of Gruppo 88, a group of young journalists and others campaigning for the Italian minority and the rights of all Istran citizens. This grew into a broader-based movement for self-administration, called the Istran Democratic Convention (*Dieta democratica istriana, Istarski demokratski forum*). With several thousand signatories from all three national groups, this is a prototype for a regional assembly, a forum where Istra's future can be debated.

The Convention upholds an idea whose time has either come and gone, or not yet arrived. Certainly the obstacles to Istran self-government are formidable. Ljubljana's government is Austrophile and ignores proposals from the Italian minority. Zagreb, meanwhile, mutters about Italian infiltration of Istra. Both states are too primitively centralist not to suspect any such project as the Convention, and after the events of 1991, Croatian and Slovenian governments for a long time to come will tighten rather than devolve their powers.

*

The bungalow was emptying. Miha was due back in his office, Mojca was needed at the university. I went south, catching coaches down the coast to Pula and the islands of Brioni.

Like military towns everywhere, Pula has a fusty, hole-in-corner atmosphere, a pungent aura of neglect. Near the coach station stands a broken, bone-dry fountain, erected in the '50s to commemorate the socialist feat of completing Istra's water system. First-storey balconies on the peeling housefronts wear their iron railings like wreaths. On the ground floor, faint television murmurs and dinner-time odours linger around the half-closed shutters. Bored ratings sprawl in café chairs. Weeds grow between the cobbles.

The Austrian *Handbook* could take for granted that the harbour would be "crowded with imposing men-of-war, looking like huge colosses threatening even in their immobility." Pula was Austria's prime naval base and it became Yugoslavia's. As a garrison town on the western edge of the country, it was a fitting venue for Tito's speech of 11 November 1956. Tito had an appointment to address the Army Club here, and he used it to present the official Yugoslav position on the Hungarian revolution, which had been crushed by Soviet force a few days before.

His task was a ticklish one. Khrushchev had taken pains, the previous year, to restore relations with Belgrade. This was a plume in Tito's cap. The Soviet chiefs swallowed pride by coming to him, and the joint declaration followed the Yugoslav agenda by stressing sovereignty and equality. Tito's return visit to Moscow a year later brought further triumph. Interest in Yugoslavia's experiment in socialism flourished among the Soviet satellites, though not without sniping from conservatives throughout the bloc. Meanwhile the country's links to the West did not suffer.

Then came October '56. Khrushchev had consulted Tito through-out the year over the turbulence in Hungary and Poland. He was keen to keep the Marshal onside, as the communist with the most presitge worldwide, thereby showing his restless satellites that an innovator could stay amicable with the USSR, and also giving him a purchase to rein Tito in. That September they spent two "holidays" together. Yet Tito still did not grasp the other man's intentions and limitations. What with the Belgrade Declaration, followed in February '56 by Khrushchev's momentous secret speech denounc-ing Stalin, the Yugoslavs believed their Soviet counterparts truly accepted the legitimacy of separate roads to socialism. Tito had been warning Khrushchev that the Stalinist leadership in Hungary spelled trouble, yet certain aspects of the revolution must have gratified him; the attack on Stalinism and the demand for autonomy from the USSR showed the Hungarians treading in Yugoslav tracks. Then, as Stevan Pavlowitch observes, Tito's "attitude towards Hungary changed as soon as the new government in Budapest announced a return to the system of multi-party democracy." When Khrushchev and Malenkov visited Brioni secretly on 2 November, presenting their plan to invade, Tito acquiesced.

Publicly, though, it would hardly do for the Yugoslavs to support the invasion. His Pula speech was an artful performance. Tito conceded there had been "counter-revolution" in Hungary, instigated by "reactionary elements" who "intervened in the uprising and exploited it for their own purposes". Even so, Soviet intervention had been "a great mistake" and had dealt "socialism a terrible blow". Yet "if it leads to the preservation of socialism in Hungary, i.e. the further building of socialism in that country and peace in the world, then one day it will appear as something positive, on condition that the Soviet troops withdraw the moment the situation in Hungary is settled and peaceful." He pledged support for Kádár, the new leader.

The day never dawned when the invasion of Hungary appeared "as something positive", but Tito's equivocations served their purpose of uncoupling him from Soviet aggression without offending the Kremlin too gravely. The West, meanwhile, was too immersed in the Suez crisis and outraged by the USSR to spare much attention for Yugoslavia, which anyway had won approval by granting sanctuary to Hungarian Prime Minister Imre Nagy in its embassy.

Western communists were traumatized by the invasion; in Britain the Party lost one third of its membership. A number of the resigners discovered an interest in self-managment socialism; which, as Tito's manoeuvres had shown that his rapprochement with the Soviet Union outweighed the fate of Nagy and his reforms, may be thought ironic – typical, too, of Tito's phenomenal talent for having his cake and eating it.

Trips to the archipelago of Brioni leave from Fažana, a fishing village north of Pula. Waiting for the next departure, I sat in the shade of an umbrella pine, facing the islands across a cerulean channel, and rummaged through my bundle of guidebooks.

The 1913 *Handbook* was novelettish. "Only a few years ago, these islands were very unhealthy, feverstricken, deserted places." Thanks, however, to one Herr Kupelwieser, an entrepreneur from Merano who bought the islands in 1893, Brioni was transformed into "a first-class winter resort, answering to all exigences of modern times." My Yugoslav guide, published in the '60s when mass tourism along the Adriatic was ballooning, mentions everything about Brioni except the most salient fact, which glowers behind these sentences like a nightclub bouncer: "There are hotels on the eastern side of Veliki Brion. The islands are not open to tourists." This, though, is contradicted by Charles Cuddon's sterling *Companion Guide*, which said the islands *were* visitable but not how to reach them. The 1989 *Blue Guide* went further but disdained to grasp the nettle.

Veliki Brion "was the summer residence of President Tito". True, but there was more to the Old Man's relationship with Brioni than that . . .

The salient fact – always public knowledge anyway – is that Brioni was Tito's personal archipelago, his Chartwell, Camp David and Kremlin, rolled into one. From 1949 until his death in 1980 it was a summer residence where he withdrew with family and friends, pottered with his hobbies of photography and metalwork, and cultivated his garden. Yet it was also the showcase where he received presidents, princesses, and film stars, as well as a bunker where he could convene Party meetings and orchestrate secret operations with no risk of publicity.

In 1983 Brioni was proclaimed a National Park and Memorial Area. Veliki Brion, biggest of the fourteen islands, was opened to visitors, who flock here through the summer months and can now stay in the hotels once reserved for nomenklatura. The tourism is packaged, and trippers who hope to nose around Tito's house, stroll in fragrant woods of holm-oak, or swim in the pellucid sea, are bound for frustration. Still, the tour is enjoyable, made more interesting by the organizers' uncertainty whether they are paying homage to Tito and his works or offering a seaside excursion for all the family. The result is a weird combination of the two: a commercial Tito theme-park that defers to the Old Man constantly but less than half-heartedly. Brioni assumes Tito's greatness without trying to demonstrate it, or even caring about it.

Ashore, we were ushered into a motorized train which trundled off towards the safari park at the island's northern tip. We passed the foundations of a first-century *villa rustica*; Brioni was a resort for rich Romans from Pietas Iulia (Pula). There are Byzantine and Illyrian remains too, but no evidence of Venice's long tenure; the story seems to be one of malaria and neglect down the centuries until Herr Kupelweiser came to the rescue. He built hotels and roads, landscaped the park, planted trees, laid out a golf course, racecourse and tennis courts. The First World War ended Brioni's glittering success as a high-society playground, and when Tito arrived after the Second War, he found only fishing families and a little school that taught in the Italian language. He closed the school, and used army and prison labour to build new villas.

The Serbo-Croatian carriages of our train were full of families and couples; the Italian and German carriages had a few dozen trippers. Besides me, the English-language wagon could only muster a hefty Swedish couple. The publicity promised expert guidance, and our language graduate from Zagreb, neat in drip-dry blouse and navy skirt, looked the part. But she soon lost heart or interest, falling quiet for long minutes. The wagon was stifling; we perspired in silence as the train looped around the inlets and headlands. The Italian-language guide never paused for breath; we could hear her babbling like a steeplechase-commentator. Were we too few to warrant the effort? Or too dull? Feeling sorry for our girl and somehow responsible for her apathy, I plied her with questions. No, you can't visit Tito's house, that's on a small island in the Memorial Area, for special guests only. Yes, three villas are still kept for élite politicians.

Then the Swedish man spoke up. What became of the fishing village? Did Tito throw the people off? The guide gazed blankly back. "Come on now, how was it?" he persisted, winking ripely and nudging his wife. The wife giggled obligingly, which gave our girl a moment to recover her poise. "Before the war the islands were private property," she explained blandly, "and after the war they were nationalized." The Swede knew all about these euphemisms, and he guffawed. "So that's how he did it, eh!"

Yugoslav visitors to Brioni are told the truth: that the islanders were moved to Fažana at the end of the '60s. Our guide did not enthuse about Tito or defend him with a joke; neither admiration nor irony was detectable. There was no sign that respect for the Old Man made her reluctant to criticize, or that fear held her in check (for criticism of Tito was still outlawed). Nothing as personal as fear. It was as if an enormous, leaden cliché had rattled down like a portcullis of pure habit as soon as the sailor's question was out of his mouth. Hence her reflex obedience to the fading dogma, her lip-service to a cult that persists somewhere far away; to an idol hewn from rock and exfoliating into facelessness upon a distant peak, an idol whose priests have absconded yet who in the presence of heathens cannot quite be ignored, although too decrepit to require any but token devotion, even at a five-star shrine like Brioni.

Whatever detail is provided about Tito's activity on Brioni has been not so much laundered as bleached. Nothing about the Central Committee sessions convened here to stamp them with Tito's personal authority. Nothing about the "very strange scene" which occurred in the harbour on the evening of 2 November 1956, when Khrushchev and Malenkov arrived, both seasick in the "howling gale", for a secret all-night summit about Hungary with Tito, Kardelj, Ranković and Mičunović (whose celebrated diary I am quoting). Khrushchev insisted the Yugoslavs should "understand us properly"; should accept, in other words, that "counter-revolution" in Budapest was impermissible.

Nor is there any reference to the purges effected here over the years, none more important than that of 1 July 1966, when

Aleksandar Ranković, federal vice-president and chief of the security services for twenty years, was forced to resign.

If all this, which has long been public knowledge, is omitted, of course the really disgraceful stuff never gets a look-in. It must be said that Brioni's subtropical beauty, and the indolent heat of a summer afternoon, do ease the bleachers' task. At the end of the tour, sitting gingerly on the hot stones of the pier, paddling my feet in the sea as we waited for the return boat to Fažana, I contemplated Tito's cruise-liner yacht moored across the harbour. Try as I might, I couldn't focus my mind on the skulduggery that the yacht witnessed one afternoon in 1973 or '74 when – if the scabrous memoirs of the Romanian ex-spymaster Ion Paçepa can be trusted – Tito entertained Nicolae Ceauşescu. He wanted to cajole the Giant of the Carpathians into helping him entrap a troublesome Yugoslav dissident by luring him to Bucharest. The Incarnation of the Highest Aspirations of the Romanian People was chary of bad publicity. Tito, flattering and puissant, prevailed.

By the early '70s Brioni had become thoroughly surreal, hosting an inner-party purge one day, Ceauşescu the next, and Sophia Loren at the weekend. All the other residents had now been removed; Brioni was Tito's domain, and its versatile hospitality reflected the unique chameleon character of its owner's status, both nationally and internationally, which waxed ever greater and more legendary as the years passed and he approached Methuselan realms of old age, it seemed without losing a jot of health or vigour. Of course this status was cultivated by Tito himself, with his superb intuition for his own image-management. For instance, in the early '70s he backed two prestige film productions about the partisan war, *The Battle of the Neretva* and *Sutjeska*, both tedious and boasting star-studded casts.

Tito was impersonated in *Sutjeska* by handsome, rakish Richard Burton. Filming was fraught with difficulties, and during a break Burton and Elizabeth Taylor were invited to Brioni. Taking the chance to study his rôle-model, the actor was disturbed by unexpected ambiguities in the atmosphere. According to Burton's diary, the Old Man and Madame Broz regaled their guests with "long stories which they don't allow the interpreters to interrupt". Burton noted "the remarkable luxury unmatched by anything else I've seen and can well believe Princess Marg[are]t who says the whole business makes Buck House [Buckingham Palace] look pretty middle-class." Yet he also noticed "the nervousness with which the servants serve us all" on board the yacht. "Am still worried by the atmosphere of dread which surrounds Tito", runs a later entry in his diary. "Cannot understand it. Neither can the rest of us."

His unease was heightened by some surprising news. It seems Tito told him that he had always refused to shoot captured enemies. Burton was impressed, and not surprisingly was later "a little put out" when he heard that people in Dubrovnik "had been shot in the Yugoslavian 'purge' in 1948". He determined to find out if the orders to shoot had come "from the top. If so I shall be a disappointed man". Whether Burton settled the question his biographer doesn't say, but his reaction speaks volumes about Western wishful thinking.

Had our guide been told not to disturb our illusions, or was she being spontaneously coy? I couldn't bring myself to ask, but she brightened up when our convoy reached the tiny safari park. Now she could fall back on a neutral ground of data and statistics. The two elephants rubbing their flanks on a wooden stall had been presented by Indira Gandhi. The pair of camels were a gift from Muammar Qaddhafi. Zebra, antelopes and other beasts had been donated by some of "the ninety state leaders from fifty-eight countries and over 100 presidents" who had visited the islands. Altogether Tito had hosted "over 1,400 political meetings on Brioni, including 250 foreign delegations, and he set off from here on over fifty peace missions". By now I was scribbling to keep up.

Last stop on the tour is the 'Tito on Brioni' photographic exhibition, introduced with the caption: "On these islands the Yugoslav socialist system was created and the foundations of non-aligned movement were laid." The islands' credentials as a holy site could not be clearer, but again the ambivalence looms through: there is no information about the System or Movement, not even a chronology or list of achievements. Either the organizers are assuming that the whole world already knows, or they are loath to profane these institutions by describing them. Or – a third alternative – they were embarrassed by these institutions and decided the best way of discharging their duty was to keep mum.

Among the scores of photos, there is not a glimpse to be had of Ceauşescu, or for that matter of Burton and Taylor. Qaddhafi is here, strutting in a long cape past a parade of guards on the quayside. And of course the famous photograph of Tito with Nehru and Nasser here in 1956 – the first meeting of non-aligned leaders.

We drifted through the roomsful of images of politicians, mostly leaders of non-aligned nations, unremembered by white Westerners. After a quarter of an hour one head of state resembled another, and I went downstairs where stuffed Brioni wildlife poses behind glass amid papier maché scenery. My thoughts retraced our convoy's route to the safari park. I knew from the *Handbook* that imported fauna were nothing new: "Hagenbeck [?] had a farm built on one of these idyllic spots, where he is elevating ostriches; there is also a game-reserve." Yet the present safari park is something different. The animals were gifts from member states to the father of the Non-Aligned Movement. We had driven bang through Yugoslavia's foreign policy.

*

It is still an open question whether the Indian elephants and Libyan camels will not outlive the cause of their transportation to the Adriatic.

The Non-Aligned Movement (NAM), launched on Brioni when Tito hosted Nasser of Egypt and Nehru of India, still exists. With a membership of ninety-eight states and two liberation movements, it includes two-thirds of the total membership of the United Nations.

In reality the NAM has been posthumous for a long while. Its best achievement was always its own creation and survival, and the collapse of superpower antagonism has removed the reason for persisting, just as it removed vital props that held Yugoslavia itself together.

Can the Movement disband, happy that its proclaimed goal – to overcome the Cold War – has been attained? Sadly, no. The 'new world order' proposed by Western policy-makers is something very different from that envisioned by NAM in its early days. The end of Cold War reveals to Third World states new kinds of powerlessness, not least by dissolving their ideological leverage against superpowers and their rich allies.

Whether as Movement or policy, non-alignment has never been easy to discuss from a First or Second World standpoint, due to a genuine problem of communication, and to sheer political hostility. This is hardly surprising, given that from its inception non-alignment set itself against the division of Europe and the world into rival camps. As an organization of Third World states – except for Yugoslavia and Cyprus – with an egalitarian, neutralist, pacifist programme, the NAM would never have impressed the Western ministers and mandarins, even if its original even-handed denunciation of both blocs had not been corrupted by a pro-Soviet slant that became really disabling in the 1970s.

Yugoslavia adopted non-alignment as its foreign policy in the mid '50s, and it remained ever after as a pillar of its socialist edifice. What people tell you now is that the only load ever borne by this pillar was the burden of Titoist vanity, pretending to exert a global influence far beyond Yugoslav means or needs. As the Father of the Non-Aligned Movement, Tito indulged his offspring; yet he served the Movement tirelessly. Or was the Movement serving him? As Yugoslavia was the

Movement's bridge and pivot, the Marshal had an excellent pretext for globetrotting and constant top-level summits.

With self-management and social property, non-alignment was the third ingredient of Yugoslav socialism, and the régime never squandered an opportunity to trumpet its virtues and its benefits for the rest of the world. Its survival into the present seems to many younger Yugoslavs worse than anachronistic. When I asked Desanka, a thirty-year-old Serb from Croatia, what non-alignment means to her, she shrugged: "Tito's foreign policy. Relations with Third World countries. Helping other peoples, but not really . . ."

To the disenchanted generations born since the '50s, non-alignment was ideological posturing hyped as a substantial principle. In hindsight Yugoslavia's rôle – an anomaly within an anomaly –was more of a liability than a privilege. Perhaps it is difficult to do justice nowadays to non-alignment. It relates to a dead world that oppresses the living, faced with the death-duties that are psychological as well as economic. Even Yugoslavs who defend non-alignment and its Movement are hard put to deny that, even when NAM was a live rather than a dead letter, it was always a letter: a symbol of something that never arrived, to wit a global coalition of progressive, anti-imperialist states against the nuclear-armed might of the blocs.

Five conditions attached to membership of NAM. A country should have an independent foreign policy based on peaceful co-existence and non-alignment with either bloc. It should support national liberation movements. It must not belong to any multilateral military alliances, or bilateral or regional defence pacts, related to great power conflicts. Last, it must not accept foreign military bases, in the context of great power conflicts. In practice, only members of the North Atlantic Treaty Organization (NATO) and the Warsaw Pact were excluded.

'Active co-existence' or 'active neutrality' were the Movement's watchwords, and the agency through which the Movement operated was the United Nations. Without the General Assembly as its arena and the Charter as its great backdrop, the Non-Aligned Movement could never have happened.

In the small print beneath the banner headlines of non-alignment, membership had different meanings for different states, and for no state were these meanings more complex than for Yugoslavia. For a year after their expulsion from the Cominform, the Yugoslavs minimized the significance of the break. When in June '49 the USSR dropped support for their claim to Carinthia, they could no longer avoid concluding that the Eastern bloc was closed to them.

Tito and his men rose to the occasion. At the United Nations in New York, Edvard Kardelj, now minister of foreign affairs, denounced the "countless frontier incidents and troop movements amounting to military demonstrations" against Yugoslavia by Cominform states. Yugoslavia was rewarded with election to the Security Council as a non-permanent member for 1950–51.

This reception promised the possibility that the UN might serve Yugoslavia as a forum for an alternative bloc, with a constituency just then arriving on the scene: the new nations of the Third World. By the late '60s more than half the UN member states had become independent since 1945. In the magically egalitarian chamber of the General Assembly, Upper Volta possessed the same voting power as the USA and the USSR. The Yugoslavs were not slow to realize that the new states rarely wanted to plunge into a superpower's sphere of influence, and that their collective voting power might swing behind a state that led the way in neither-East-nor-West politics. The Assembly's decisions were not binding, of course; but you had to start somewhere.

As time passed, the Yugoslavs became reassured that the West would not stand by if the Soviet Union invaded. In 1952 the General Assembly vote on Yugoslav complaints about the Soviets' threatening posture backed Belgrade overwhelmingly. The Yugoslavs started to turn their exclusion from both blocs to their advantage.

At the Security Council the Yugoslavs had worked with Egypt and India, as well as new states run by the radical governments of the euphoric post-colonial era. The Asian Socialist Conference of 1953 confirmed a widespread desire among Asian leaders for an independent socialism. The five principles of peaceful coexistence formulated by Nehru in 1954, then the ten principles enunciated at Bandung in 1955 and the New Delhi Conference the same year, demonstrated Asian solidarity against colonialism.

Like many Third World states, the Yugoslavs had made their own revolution and were immensely proud of the fact. Like many of them too, they were poor, strategically vulnerable, riven by tribal suspicion and fear. The Yugoslavs didn't try to preach. Incredibly for a European leader, Tito wasn't patronizing. Nasser's reaction after his first meeting with Tito was revealing: "He had no pretensions. He did not try to impress me that he was a more important person than I was, or a better soldier, or knew more than I did about anything. We got along well together." And he backed his words with action; in the '50s Yugoslavia sold arms to Burma and Egypt when the two blocs refused.

Internal pressures also pointed to non-alignment as a safety valve. The sprawling diversity of the Movement, which included every kind of régime from parliamentary democracy to theocratic despotism, answered to Yugoslavia's own diversity. The Yugoslav Party had its own Right and Left, and after the trauma of '48, the leadership had to frame a foreign policy that would appeal to as wide a spectrum as possible. Non-alignment had the virtue of not distressing those fractions that favoured closer ties with either East or West. The simple nobility of its aims would win the rank and file. Its North-South emphasis was valuable in a country which enclosed Alpine tidiness and Levantine poverty. Further, it was grandiose enough to satisfy revolutionaries who had won two anti-imperialist struggles of their own, against fascism and then Stalinism. The Eastern and Western blocs may have been out of bounds to them; but were the blocs not oversubscribed? In the mid-twentieth century, how many small states could claim to be framing an original foreign policy – one that would influence a hundred states? When Tito said in 1967 that "our country is playing a rôle as if it had a hundred million rather than twenty million", the old revolutionaries' breasts surely swelled with pride.

The Yugoslav leaders were psychologically geared for non-alignment. As partisans negotiating with the Western Allies and the Soviet Union, Tito and his men had had to convince the sceptical Anglo-Americans that they were not Moscow's puppets, while not allowing the Soviets to accuse them of weakening their socialism. Tito's extreme agility in walking this plank came in useful when Yugoslavia needed UNRRA aid after the war, and was essential after 1948, when the plank narrowed to the width of a tightrope.

The Movement's limitations were laid bare at its founding summit, at Belgrade in September 1961. The convocation of representatives from twenty-eight states was a coup for the Yugoslavs, marred only by the fact that the week's high-point was not the agenda of discussions about disarmament, self-determination, and global inequality. What reverberated round the hall and out into the waiting world was Tito's silence in his opening speech about the resumption one day before of Soviet nuclear testing.

Khrushchev had warned Tito: "then we'll see who is relevant". For once, Tito miscalculated. Henry Kissinger used to refer smugly to "the alignment of the non-aligned"; the pity of it is, he was right. And it got worse. When Cuba gained chairmanship of the Movement in the '70s, any pretence at even-handedness went out of the window. The invasion of Afghanistan in 1979 was the first occupation of a non-aligned state by a superpower; Cuba blocked calls for an emergency meeting and led the handful of pro-Soviet votes in the UN against a resolution condemning Soviet aggression. The next summit communiqué chastised the United States twenty-three times and the USSR not once, although more than 100,000 Soviet troops were occupying a NAM state. (The Movement proved equally helpless to arbitrate in the wars between Libya and Chad or Iran and Iraq, all member states. It is a condition of the NAM's existence that it enforces nothing, that it has no sanction.)

Tito's omission caused glee in both blocs because it confirmed their supremacy. Despite the display of summitry, the NAM was and would continue to be trapped by its own powerlessness. As a coalition of political and economic weaklings, its only chance to exert international pressure lay in solidarity. But these states could not afford solidarity, for technology, loans, food and expertise were to be had from the blocs.

This contradiction was abetted by another. Solidarity required the maximum number of members, but the wider the membership, the less efficient the Movement. The quest for numbers was as successful as the Movement was ineffectual; its 1983 Summit was the largest convention of heads of state and government ever held.

Given the impossibility of the NAM backing its sonorities with action, members used the Movement to pursue their own interests, especially when shifts in superpower relations minimized the Movement's room for manoeuvre. Tito's own first diplomatic interest was, as we have seen, to keep his relations with the Soviet Union in good repair. What he never forgot, however, is that the NAM should flirt with the Soviet Union, not be seduced. When the Movement's internal balance shifted under pressure from Cuba's blatant pro-Sovietism, the octogenarian Tito called for a return to "first principles" and the "democratization" of the Movement.

Those first principles, however, had nothing to do with democratization as such; and this is the other side of non-alignment and its futility.

The term 'movement' connotes spontaneous, open-ended, grassroots radicalism. Yet the NAM wasn't a movement in this sense at all. No more spontaneous than NATO or the European Council of Ministers, it bore the same relation to democracy as Tito's Brioni did to mass tourism. Genuine political movements are water to the stone of state, and states are bound to be antagonistic to the anarchism, volatility and autonomy of movements – especially if these shared the declared aims of the NAM. When Tito called for democratization, you can be sure he did not mean throwing the conference open to any impartial agitator for disarmament and redistribution of resources. For neither he nor other NAM leaders wanted to risk awkward questions about resource distribution, rights, and militarism in their own states.

It was militarism that divulged most glaringly the Movement's democratic deficit. It gained much credit and momentum from its demands for nuclear disarmament, and active neutralism was a genuinely radical notion, compatible in theory both with grass-roots pacifism and the NAM's statist kind. Its excellent premise was that disarmament would not happen by waiting for the superpowers to come to their senses, so neutralism must be enacted as, in Tito's words, "a dynamic process in the course of which an easing of tensions, a gradual elimination of blocs, should be achieved". Despised by Western states, the NAM in turn disdained the mass peace movements which were its only potential partners in the West. For it demanded a new world order in the most reactionary way. Non-alignment meant heads of state, mostly unelected and more or less anti-democratic, sweeping to conferences in limousines with armed outriders. It meant costly ceremonial in the midst of deprivation. Dictators shaking hands for the cameras. State media broadcasting vapid communiqués. Careers and expense-accounts for bureaucrats. Arms sales by one NAM state to another. Elephants and camels to Brioni.

*

From Pula I caught a coach to Opatija and Rijeka. Eastern Istra falls in ramparts to the wrinkled waters of the Kvarner gulf. The coastline is breached by one tremendous valley, where the river Raša once marked the boundary between Italy and medieval Croatia.

Hereabouts is mining country, or was until recently, and it bears the scars. The coach eased round the hairpin bends down to the mining plant broiling in the valley bottom. Nobody at the bus stop or anywhere in sight; the buildings look deserted; a huge roadside grafitto says *Prizemljenje u pakao*: Forced Landing in Hell. Until a few years ago miners' pay was among the worst in Yugoslavia – lower than factory cleaners' – and the Istran mineworkers' traditional defiance was broken in 1987, when they staged the longest strike in Yugoslavia's postwar history, and lost. The immediate motive for the two-month stoppage was a pay cut imposed as an austerity measure, but the miners were protesting too at their abysmal living conditions, and demanding an investigation into spectacular misuse of company funds – the miners' own funds, according to self-management law. Neither grievance was seriously considered by the authorities; opposed at every level of the system, threatened with dismissal, the strikers were forced back to the coalface.

Grinding gears, the coach hauled itself from Raša up into

Podlabin, which means Under Labin and is a fitting name for this fringe of raw cubic buildings around a wooded hill on which, almost concealed by its trees, squats the walled town of Labin. It looks like the fortress that it was; Venice called Albona *la Fedelissima*, the most faithful, recognizing its resistance to marauding Uskok pirates.

From the coach stop Labin's main gate is only a quarter-hour's walk away. The road opens into a small flagged square, with a Venetian loggia on one side. Labin's hub, it is an elegantly proportioned civic space. Rackety buses shudder in and out; old men in berets, retired Bosnian miners presumably, repose in the shadow of the war memorial to the partisans. Labin is as pretty as Podlabin is nondescript, but the hill is so riddled with mine shafts that the town, sinking under its own weight, is being evacuated.

Coal has been mined here for two hundred years by Italians, Croats and Bosnians, and by 1921 the miners had sixty years of militancy behind them. As soon as this part of Istra was ceded to Italy in 1920, fascist *squadristi* began harassing the miners' leaders. When they started on the union secretary, one Giovanni Pipan, the miners took to arms, mustered their own Red Guards, and seized control of the mines.

The Republic of Albona held out a few weeks, until the Italian army suppressed it in April. Dozens of miners were arrested and tried. Though they won their case in court, Albona's radical days were numbered. The revolutionary wave that swept Italy after the First World War had subsided without ever quite breaking. Mussolini rode the reaction, and was welcomed to power by parliamentary vote in 1922. Among the many miners who emigrated from Albona in the early '20s was Pipan, who crossed the Atlantic, became involved with the bakers' union in New York, and was assassinated there for his activities.

I learned about Pipan in Labin's museum, housed in a baroque palazzo on a winding cobbled street above the square. Among the Roman remains in the entrance hall stands a fragment inscribed with the legend RES PUBLICA ALBONESSIUM, and I was musing on this proof of republicanism down the millennia when I found myself inside a coal mine. Labin is so proud of its heritage that it installed a miniature mine inside the museum. A wooden ramp slopes steeply down to a level complete with railway lines and wagons. You have to bend double to weave between the wooden pit props, past the conveyor belt, to the coalface. Only the walls and roof are unauthentic, and at one point a rent in the canvas gives a glimpse of sky. No one else was in the museum. The level stretched ahead, round corner after corner. Weren't there too many corners? I wondered for a moment if I had missed the exit. The whole effect is convincingly claustrophobic, made more peculiar by a powerful reek of drains. Soon this will be the last coal mine in Istra.

A modest exhibition upstairs displays flyblown photostats of documents. As I skimmed an Italian police report, a name caught my eye. A week before the Republic was defeated, a dozen *squadristi* tried to beat up a "well-known agitator" called Anton Ciliga, but were routed by a hundred "armed Slavs" who chased the Italians into a barracks.

Nothing more is said about the well-known agitator; when the museum was founded in 1960, Ciliga's incredible career was too scandalous to mention.

Born nearby in 1898, Anton Ciliga joined the Socialist Party of Croatia as a student in 1918. He "evolved towards Bolshevism" – in his own scientific-Left phrase – and was soon "taking an active part in the Communist movements of Yugoslavia, Soviet Hungary, Czechoslovakia and Italy". He was despatched in 1926 to Moscow to represent the Communist Party of Yugoslavia, and to study at the Comintern school, the one where Kardelj taught in the '30s.

Disillusionment with Soviet Russia began almost at once. Over the next two years, as Stalin outflanked Trotsky in the struggle for supreme power, the young Istran became convinced that the Trotskyite argument was correct: the Soviet leadership was betraying the masses who had made the revolution. After Trotsky's expulsion from the USSR, a witch-hunt started for his supporters. Ciliga was arrested and sentenced. The CPY, toeing the Comintern line, duly expelled its emissary and abandoned him to his fate. Paradoxically, his Italian passport saved his life – that, plus a streak of native cussedness. After firing off a series of protests to Moscow he was released, after more than five years in prisons and labour camps.

In captivity he pondered "the enigma of the Russian revolution": to wit, "how has it come about that all that constitutes the October Revolution has been entirely abolished, while its outward forms have been retained; that the exploitation of workers and peasants has been brought back to life without reviving private capitalists and landowners; that a revolution, begun in order to abolish the exploitation of man by man, has ended by installing a new type of exploitation?"

Ciliga's account was published in the West as *The Russian Enigma* in 1940, before Hitler's invasion of the USSR turned Stalin into an ally. A year later the author was thrown into the concentration camp at Jasenovac, run by the *ustaše* (Croat fascists). This time it was the Communist Party of Croatia that had betrayed him. Again he lived to tell the tale, and 1951 saw the appearance of a new book, this one attacking the Yugoslav Communists for double-crossing their own revolution.

Ciliga had given up trying "to separate the positive acquisitions" of Bolshevism from "its more threatening phenomena". The '70s found him in Rome, editing *On the Threshold of a New Dawn*, an émigré magazine. Now he has survived the Party that twice deserted him, and witnessed some sort of a bloodshot dawn.

The Russian Enigma reveals nothing of Ciliga's pre-Soviet exploits, but a memory of his homeland does once peep through. Watching the arctic sunset in Yeniseisk, eastern Siberia, shortly before his release, "I look on the river, tranquil, powerful, wide as a sea . . . and I remember another sea, my own, my Adriatic." From the ramparts of Labin – or better, from the road beyond Plomin – his Adriatic is magical to see, azure beneath a summer haze, its scrubby whaleback islands trailing southwards out of view.

Labin is Istra at its most redoubtable. The last Yugoslav census, in spring 1991, offered twenty-five categories of national identification, plus 'Yugoslav' and 'Regional'. Despite the worsening crisis and the Croatian government's efforts to infect Istra with its own virulent nationalism, the townspeople registered the highest proportion of 'regionals' anywhere in the federation: 36 per cent. Will Zagreb take the hint, or grit its teeth at this provocation? When an English journalist visited the Labin coalfield in 1946, with destruction all around, a "wizened Italian miner" told her that "here they were all in the building of a new house for Europe, a house which *everyone* shared!" Probably the old man died of pneumoconiosis and his mine closed with no provision for its workforce. Still the Istrans keep building their house for Europe, and still the surrounding powers haven't learned not to meddle.

Bridges of Bosnia

Jebeš zemlju koja Bosnu nema! runs a pithy saying, full of fond exasperation. "Fuck the country that hasn't got a Bosnia!"

The coarseness is fitting; refinement is not among Bosnia-Hercegovina's qualities. Here a traveller from the north meets the Balkans – "the south". Streets are dustier, buildings are more dilapidated, shops are plainer, cars are older, people are more hospitable (and poorer) than in the regions I had left. Coffee is Turkish and food has Turkish names. Minarets pierce the skyline. The towns are at once bustling and becalmed. Human contact becomes warmer and more direct; politics, on the other hand, becomes oblique. Bosnian space-time is more dilated than our northern kind; men who spend years as guestworkers in Germany, having their days sliced and parcelled in factories, revert effortlessly to a more languorous Bosnian tempo. Goats and cattle graze the city verges. Things don't function – hence the exasperation. (I know a Croat woman who swears never to return to Bosnia because of the lavatories.) As for the rough fondness, it emerges patronisingly in the many jokes about Bosnian stupidity – jokes that Bosnians crack too; unlike other Yugoslavs, they laugh at themselves.

Beyond the humour, this affection stems from a sense or intuition among more open-minded people that Bosnia was the heart of Yugoslavia, both literally – the geographical centre of the federation lay a few kilometres from Sarajevo, capital of BiH as the republic is known – and metaphorically. BiH is impossible to subdivide along ethnic lines. Moreover, it is a mixed republic by statute as well as in fact. The population is 41 per cent Muslim, 31 per cent Serb, and 18 per cent Croat; all three of these peoples are the constitutional subjects of BiH – none of them is a minority. The communists were clear about this from the start, stating in 1943 that the future Bosnia-Hercegovina would be "neither Serbian nor Croatian nor Muslim but rather Serbian and Croatian and Muslim". This was a noble formula, and, insofar as Yugoslavia was ever a multinational state rather than a state comprising many nations, BiH was its truest fragment, the place where the old

Yugoslav idea of kindred peoples in harmony stood its best chance to be realized.

Conversely, if the peoples of this republic – where 27 per cent of marriages are mixed – could not live together in peace, Yugoslavia was past redemption. When war came in 1991, everyone knew that Bosnia-Hercegovina was a powderkeg, and feared the worst. Yet, despite frequent alarms, the conflict kept not spreading across the border from Croatia. If this proved that Bosnian harmony was much more than a slogan, and that its leaders were expert firemen, dousing sparks of conflict before these flared out of control, it also confirmed the republic's helplessness. As Croats, Serbs, Montenegrins and the Yugoslav people's army killed each other over the border, BiH could only watch and wait for its fate to be decided.

Of course, this helplessness merely followed from the facts; and Macedonia, which likewise had no wish to join the fighting, was in the same position. Yet BiH's impotence was uniquely poignant and illustrative; it demonstrated the peculiarity and eventual failure of Yugoslavia's federal system. Perhaps, too, its welcome tranquillity in 1991 had a graveyard quality: ratifying, so to speak, the disappearance from the human gallery of that elusive ideal hybrid, the Yugoslav.

Officially the SFRY never intended to create Yugoslavs. As a "socialist federation of free and equal peoples", peoples not individuals were the subjects of its liberty and egalitarianism. The Serb-dominated Kingdom of Yugoslavia was portrayed by the communists as a prison-house of nations, which it had indeed been for Muslims and non-Slavs – also, to be sure, in the eyes of Macedonian and Croat separatists. Instead of the *narodno jedinstvo* (national unity) of royal Yugoslavia, the communist watchword was *bratstvo i jedinstvo* (brotherhood and unity). Yugoslavism was in disgrace: a mask for "Serb bourgeois hegemonism", etcetera. Unofficially, communists and other optimists hoped that *jedinstvo* would grow as *bratstvo* became a normal way of life and class differences were triumphantly demolished by socialism.

Thus the first post-war constitution, modelled on Soviet lines, defined the six republics as "sovereign". In reality they were no more sovereign than in the USSR itself. A bargain was implicit. In return for ceding political power to the Party and its organs, the republics were granted an array of political institutions and cultural rights – folklore, languages, academies, and so forth. Within the forms of folklore, however, political blood never ceased to pulse. When self-management reforms began in 1950, national grievances soon bubbled out. As a counter, the Yugoslav idea was revived, tentatively, not as a substitute for national cultures but as a common aspiration, a form of socialist patriotism. The revival could only be half-hearted, because Yugoslavism was seen by too many people as inherently coercive, and the leadership knew that its legitimacy lay in its approach to the national question and its success in developing the country, not in championing a new kind of assimilation, let alone in waging class struggle. In the '60s, as the republics began to wrest economic and then political functions from the federal centre, Yugoslavism faded away and was scarcely heard of again.

The non-viability of Yugoslavism except for foreign consumption was not a problem in itself for the leadership, but it symbolized an essential political dilemma: how to free the nations without inflaming nationalisms, or losing communist control of political and economic life? It was, in the end, a dilemma without a solution. Concretely, the wellbeing of one nation offended another. When the Serbs in Croatia felt secure, the Croats felt aggrieved; when the Albanians of Kosovo ceased to be second-class people in their native land, the Serbs felt insulted and threatened.

Complicating matters still further, in the latter case the Serbs had a certain constitutional warrant for their grievance, because some peoples in the federation were created more equal than others. That first constitution of 1946 recognized five nations: Serbs, Croats, Slovenes, Macedonians and Montenegrins. Other Yugoslavs, from the Hungarians of Vojvodina to the Vlachs of Macedonia, belonged to minorities. In the '60s the minorities were redesignated "nationalities", to signify that their status was not different in kind from that of the nations. Real progress was made in developing their cultural rights, as later chapters will show; no other socialist or Balkan state could compare with Yugoslavia in this respect. Still the difference remained; indeed, multicultural concessions confirmed that nations were the political subjects in federal Yugoslavia. Only nations had their own republics, and only Yugoslavs were nations.

Officially the republics were not national territories – hence embryo nation-states – but federal units where the nations and nationalities lived. A Serb in Slovenia had the same rights and status as a Slovene; likewise a Montenegrin in Macedonia. Subsequent constitutions revoked the sovereignty of the republics. The 1963 constitution transferred sovereignty to the peoples of the republics. This more unitarist formulation actually heralded the decisive republicanization of Yugoslavia. The last constitution (1974) enshrined the result of this process, defining the SRFY as "a federal state having the form of a state community of voluntarily united nations and their Socialist Republics". Sovereignty now lay in the "sovereign rights" that the "nations and nationalities shall exercise

in the Socialist Republics, and in the Socialist Autonomous Provinces
. . . [and] in the SFRY when in their common interests".

How remote this was from the communists' initial hope that,
given time and correct policies, the bonds tying nations to their
historic territories would fray, releasing the peoples to float and
mingle as socialist Yugoslav patriots. For by 1974 no one could
doubt that the republics were indeed national; and how could it have
been otherwise, when they bore the historic names and existed
within, very largely, their historic borders? And when, moreover,
that same 1974 constitution was the climax of a decentralizing
process in Yugoslav federalism?

Plainly it was contradictory to empower the republics while
keeping the nations tightly in check; yet what else could be expected
of an anti-nationalist system that created new political nations – first
the Macedonians and Montenegrins, and finally, in 1964, the
Muslims? Socialist federalism created these contradictions, yet
communist power furnished means to contain their effects, as long as
that power was itself undivided.

Ultimately Tito was the sole guarantee that this circle could be
squared. More than a system, Yugoslav federalism was a technique
that depended in the last analysis on Tito's authority and native wit.
It functioned by balancing the biggest nations, sometimes using the
nationalities, ensuring a parity of grievances as well as of rights.
Serbia, the dominant nation in royal Yugoslavia, was weakened by
turning pre-war "South Serbia" into the republic of Macedonia, by
making Montenegro a nation in its own right, and by creating two
further federal units within Serbia: the "autonomous provinces" of
Vojvodina and Kosovo. The Serbs of Croatia and Bosnia, meanwhile, were over-represented in their republican élites, as a kind of
compensation that also curbed Croatian ambitions. Persecution of
Catholic clerics in Zagreb was matched by persecution of Orthodox
clerics in Belgrade. After breaking the reform movement in Croatia
in 1971, Tito moved to purge the Serbian reformists.

The import of these manoeuvres was not much considered abroad,
largely because abroad did not want to know. European nationalism
seemed to belong to history, and everyone particularly wanted
Yugoslavia to endure. Wishful thinking quite swamps analysis in
this, for instance, from the 1974 edition of *Encyclopaedia
Britannica*: "Although there are likely to be difficult years ahead,
politically and economically, the Yugoslav system is so deeply
rooted, and the survival of a strong, independent, nonaligned
Yugoslavia is so vital to the maintenance of European stability, that
the country will undoubtedly survive the shock of Tito's departure."

Western strategists wanted Yugoslavia to be strong; ordinary

Westerners assumed it was. No one did more to encourage this assumption than Tito himself, of course, which is why he is authoritatively credited, by Djilas among others, with a naïve faith in Yugoslavism. My own hunch is that the old illusionist was far too astute to believe his own spells, and I feel vindicated by Phyllis Auty's experience when she interviewed him in 1968. The exchange did not find its way into her biography of Tito, and I am grateful for permission to quote her recollection of it here:

> I asked Tito if he thought Yugoslavism had come into existence during the postwar period. He laughed, and replied: "Yugoslavism? It does not exist, but maybe one day in the future it will come." Jože Smole [a federal minister], who was also present, drew in his breath with horror at such frankness.

*

In historical and cultural terms, the decision to elevate the Muslims as the SFRY's sixth nation was no less than justice. In terms of federal politics, it was a Titoist balancing act *par excellence*, in a Habsburg tradition. By promoting the Muslims, Bosnia-Hercegovina was effectively promoted too; although BiH did not formally become a national entity, it now had a nation of its own, like the other five republics. And promotion brought a measure of protection, from the Croat and Serb revanchists in whose eyes Bosnia-Hercegovina was an artificial entity perpetuated by the communists to deny their own respective claims.

The 41 per cent of BiH's population that is Muslim comprises more than 80 per cent of all Muslims in ex-Yugoslavia. Yet the proposition that they identify with this republic more closely than the other national communities does not hinge on statistics – nor on the obvious truth that they have nowhere else to call their own. Today's Muslims are descendants of the Slavs who converted to Islam during the four centuries when Bosnia and Hercegovina were Ottoman possessions. A Bosnian entity predates the Turkish conquest; there was a medieval kingdom of Bosnia, which captured Hum (Hercegovina) from the Serbian empire. The reason why many Christian Slavs 'turned Turk' – embraced Islam – has much to do with the popularity here in the century or so preceding the Ottoman invasion of Bogomilism, a heretical dualist sect. Both Western and Eastern Churches persecuted the Bogomils so remorselessly that thousands took sanctuary in the faith of their invaders. In a phrase of the epic poets, Bosnia became "the lock, the lock and the golden key" of Suleiman's immense empire.

Those shadowy beleaguered Bogomils, of whom almost no trace

survives, were the ancestors of today's Bosnian Muslims, caught between the frying pan and the fire.*

It is more than a happy accident that the most grimly memorable wisecrack of the war in 1991 was made by Bosnia-Hercegovina's President Alija Izetbegović, a Muslim. Having to choose between Presidents Tudjman of Croatia and Milošević of Serbia, he remarked, is like having to decide between leukaemia and a brain tumour.

To anyone reared, as I was in the '60s and '70s, on the Gladstonian tale of Turkey as the sick man of Europe, it could seem ironic that the Bosnian Muslims became, within a life's span of Turkey's final expulsion from Yugoslav lands, the guardians of civilization against Christian warmongers. Not that religion played more than a small supporting rôle in war propaganda in 1991; yet it should be remembered that, although Ottoman depredation is proverbial, the worst atrocities recorded in Bosnia were wrought by Catholic ustaše against Serbs and by Serb četniks against Muslims during the Second World War, when the Muslims suffered worse losses than any other national group in Yugoslavia.

Nor were the Muslims a party to the single most portentous act of violence in Bosnia. My first destination, when I arrived in Sarajevo shortly before the November 1990 republican elections, was the street corner by the river where Gavrilo Princip fired the shot that killed the Habsburg heir, Archduke Franz Ferdinand.

In 1914 the tectonic plates of imperial interests converged and overlapped in Bosnia and Hercegovina, the two Ottoman provinces that had been under Habsburg administration since 1878. In 1908, Austria-Hungary sealed its possession of the provinces by formally annexing them, to stop the Kingdom of Serbia gaining from the collapse, then plainly impending, of Ottoman Turkey. The annexed Serbs were doubly bitter against the Habsburgs. Key figures in Vienna, though not the ancient emperor himself, yearned to destroy Serbia. Behind Serbia stood Russia; behind Austria-Hungary, Germany. When Franz Ferdinand spurned wisdom by visiting the capital of Vienna's newest provinces on 28 June – so adding insult to Serbian injury† – those continental plates were pinned by a bolt no

---

* "In Bosnia the Bogomil religion had its longest and most successful innings. But its whole history and the bathos of its end shows that . . . [i]t had been carried on there by the forces of nationalism, as a national alternative to Orthodoxy with its Byzantino-Serb influence and the Catholicism of Hungary and Dalmatia." (Runciman.)

† 28 June is *Vidovdan*, St Vitus' Day, observed by Serbs as a day of national mourning for the battle of Kosovo, 28 June 1389, when the Serbian army was defeated by the Ottomans.

stronger than a man's life: the life of a stout red-faced man who strutted like a marionette as he left the town hall to drive along the embankment where Princip waited to shear the bolt.

Two footprints are set into the concrete paving at the spot where the assassin stood. An autumn drizzle turned everything grey, and I wondered if the sky had been clear on that summer day, and if a satellite photograph would have registered a commotion rippling from the epicentre, the first shudders as the old order ruptured.

Looking up from those waterlogged footprints, I noticed a very elderly gentleman observing beadily from the embankment, the only other person in sight. He wore a mackintosh over a woollen waistcoat and watchchain; a felt hat sheltered his whiskery face. Approaching suddenly, he pointed at the footprints, shook his head, indicated a spot directly across the empty road, and nodded intently, jutting his chin out. His mime achieved, he pattered away with a startling burst of speed – too quickly to see if he was grinning a Bosnian grin.

Whatever the Austrians said and others chose to believe, Princip was a Serb idealist, not a tool of Belgrade, where the government had no wish just then to furnish the enemy with its longed-for pretext to invade.

This is not to deny that Serbia viewed Bosnia-Hercegovina (43 per cent Orthodox in 1910) as Serbian land crying out for redemption. Language was taken as the basic criterion of Serb identity, and according to the supreme authority on these matters, the purest vernacular was spoken in Bosnia and Hercegovina. Croat extremists too looked hungrily upon the Habsburg province, claiming – indisputably, for what it's worth – that much of north-western Bosnia belonged to the medieval Croatian kingdom. By these competing claims, Bosnia caused the Yugoslav nations to be yoked together in 1918.

In royal Yugoslavia, where the Muslims of BiH were classified as nationally uncommitted, Serb and Croat leaders reiterated the claims, and until 1943 the communists were unsure whether BiH should be assimilated to the Croatian or Serbian republic in their projected federation, or stand by itself.

When BiH's free elections were held at the end of 1990, its integrity was again an issue, not challenged in so many words by Croatian and Serbian parties but looming implicitly in their aggressive stances. The Serbian leader threatened to boycott the elections, as being "against Serbian interests". Then he set up a national council to run Serbian affairs – an act of defiance that proved how impotent the republican authorities were, now that communist power had vanished like water into sand.

National and ethnic distribution in Yugoslavia

The Croatian party in BiH was an offshoot of the radical nationalist HDZ which had already come to power in Croatia. One of its spokesmen told the BBC that "the idea of a Bosnian nationality in our time is unacceptable"; and its leader in BiH had been sacked, allegedly for enthusing too warmly about the republic's inalienable sovereignty. I called to see their vice-president, a grey-faced man in a dog-collar. "Our programme," Father Baković explained, looking me dourly in the eye, "is for the rule of law, political pluralism, marketization, and Western democracy. For Yugoslav confederation, with Bosnia-Hercegovina as a sovereign member. And for the rights of the Croats in Bosnia-Hercegovina."

A familiar shopping list, except for the last point. What did this entail?

"Bosnia is an old Croat land, it was *never* an old Serb land. Two sides of Bosnia face Croatia," he said urgently, "whereas only one side faces Serbia. We want to join the European Community, and fight communism and Serbian hegemony."

Swiftly he had found his theme, and further questions merely egged him on. The Serbs boast how democratic they are, but look at their treatment of Kosovo. The Serbs want to absorb Macedonians, Jews, Vlachs, Roma; Belgrade sucks money from everywhere in Yugoslavia. The constituency boundaries deliberately disadvantage the Croats (did he know that the Serbian party made the identical complaint?). Resenting Father Baković quite as much as he resented the Serbs, I made an excuse and left him, still fuming and woebegone.

sDA (the Democratic Action Party), the Muslims' national party, had a discipline problem too. Its leadership had split, and if the press could be believed, one faction was riddled with fundamentalists baying support for Saddam Hussein, while the other was élitist and paranoid.

The leader of the smaller faction looked spruce in a tailored blazer and tie, like the successful businessman he is. Adel Zulfikarpašić was the only politician in Yugoslavia who drove a Rolls Royce. He had recently returned to Bosnia after a lucrative career in Switzerland to help launch sDA, which proclaimed the unity of the Muslim nation in Yugoslavia, staging huge rallies and signing up 700,000 members within three months. (So it claimed; party membership figures had to be treated as ideal truths.) Then he fell out with the other founders of the party, who expelled him and two others. These three formed MBO (the Bosnian Muslim Organization) less than two months before the election.

Zulfikarpašić tried to sound confident. "We have the Bosnian intelligentsia in our hands," he said. "We will make a liberal European party with an open democratic structure. We're getting thousands of letters and telegrams of support. Half the local councils say they are with us. We can count on 60 per cent of Muslims."

How could he be sure? It was obvious why Muslims would vote for the sDA: it championed their national interest. But a Muslim party that stressed liberal democracy rather than identity: what did *that* mean in 1990?

He grew heated. "It's ridiculous to claim that so many people should have just one party. True, we Muslims are frustrated, a little repressed, and the reaction is to be united, but this is absolutely not logical. I would *like* us to unite and fight for Muslim emancipation, but the party of unity has to be a democratic, European party." His eyes dilated behind his spectacles, and he seemed panicky, out of his depth. Perhaps those decades in Zürich had unfitted him for politicking. Even his Rolls Royce seemed a dubious asset in a bankrupt republic where 70 per cent of the electorate had elementary education or none at all.

On, then, to the rival leader, Alija Izetbegović, now the president of the republic. "Our concern is with all three million Muslims in Yugoslavia," he explained. A compact figure radiating assurance and wily caution, he was twice jailed in the '70s for agitating the Muslim cause. "Perhaps you from Europe cannot understand this, because for you Muslims are defined by their faith, whereas here they are in the first place a national group.

"By their oppression the communists created this longing among people to express their religious or national identity. Perhaps in four or five years we shall have passed through the minefield to the horizon of civil society! For now, unfortunately, our party *must* be sectional. The parties that try to represent everyone are small and weak. There is real risk of civil war here; our main aim as a party is to keep Bosnia-Hercegovina together. We're entering a very uncertain period and until now Muslims have had no political leaders. We need a *big* party, then we need political power."

Both parties held public meetings the next day at noon. SDA rallied in the football stadium, while MBO forgathered in a theatre. SDA supporters arrived early from the provinces; gangs of teenage boys sauntered through the city centre, waving green banners and chanting "*Ess-day-ar! Ess-day-ar!*" to the tune of "Here we go!" By noon some 20,000 people half-filled the stadium. Every banner, symbol and speech reiterated Muslim solidarity. A jerky figure on the podium tried to get the crowd to sing the SDA anthem, but couldn't elicit an echo from the terraces, where men in tasselled fezes and blue-grey shiny suits squatted beside women (outnumbered five to one) in loose pantaloons, smoking, chatting in undertones, squinting at their neighbours, buying peanuts and Coke, patiently waiting for the leaders, who finally arrived in a motorcade through the stadium gates.

I dashed to the theatre. Not a fez in sight. These were urban Muslims, a few hundred, sitting with legs crossed and lips pursed, listening to speeches about democracy and the dangers of clericalism. Mr Zulfikarpašić presided in an atmosphere of waspish tedium.

The supranational parties were better organized and equipped, and much nicer to visit. Plump secretaries supplied coffee and fruit juice while professional gents smoothly explained how democratic their party was and how retrograde the nationalists were.

These parties included some hybrids that had no chance of surviving the ballot box. The DSS (Democratic Socialist League) was cobbled together by prudent Bosnian communists who realized that their own gruesome record put them beyond salvage. It was a letterhead party except in the capital, where it was based, brazenly, in the League of Communists' own headquarters. There, in his spacious office, Mr Ibrahim Spahić churched his fingertips and discoursed. "Bosnia-Hercegovina isn't an excuse for Yugoslavia," he murmured, "it is the reality of Yugoslavia. It has its own internal resistance. There can't be a simple analysis of Bosnia; as soon as you try, it all slips away. Yugoslavia cannot be divided. I don't think any Yugoslavs truly want to separate. Eclecticism is the destiny of the Balkans; that's what I believe in. Sarajevo is cosmopolitan, there's a mentality of bridge-building here, produced by all these centuries of living together, and we want to take this as the basis for building a new identity."

"Are you still a member of the League of Communists?" I asked indelicately, after an hour of these pleasing bromides.

"I have been since 1979, though I never belonged to the apparatus. I had enormous problems with it." He knew that I knew his *curriculum vitae* punctured this claim; so why did he say it? Perhaps because it refused not to be said. All at once he looked coy: "Are you *irritated* that I'm still a member?" This ranking politician wanted some kind of exoneration from an unknown freelancer armed with a notebook and a tenpenny ballpoint. It was an odd moment, and quite as true a symptom of the end of communism as anything else.

The League of Reform Forces was the only party that contested elections across Yugoslavia. It was the baby of Ante Marković, the federal prime minister whose draconian economic reforms made him popular in 1989 and '90 with the World Bank and Western governments. The Reform Forces was founded in July 1990, and contested the elections in BiH, Macedonia, Serbia and Montenegro. Its chief in BiH was the rector of Sarajevo University. "We are the only option between the communists and the national parties," he told me, "so our supporters wouldn't vote for anyone else. The nationalists are against us more than the communists, because they feel we're the threat. If we aren't a strong factor in a coalition government, we'll be a strong opposition. And don't forget that many people who won't vote for us now *will* support the Reform Forces in the federal elections."

Another hybrid was the DS (Democratic League), spawned from the wreckage of Bosnia's Socialist Alliance, the umbrella organization for trade union, youth, student, women's and war veterans' associations, all under the political "guidance" of the League of Communists. As the Socialist Alliances ceased to function in 1989 and 1990, they split and evolved in ways that reflected the sort of pluralism evolving – or not – in different republics. In Slovenia and Bosnia, components of the Socialist Alliance found new life as political parties, competing more or less genuinely with their former colleagues in the League. In Serbia and Montenegro, by contrast, the Alliances combined with the Leagues in powerful and well financed party-state blocs. (Only in these two republics did communists win in 1990.)

The DS derived from the Youth League, and the youth vote was its target. Its office was staffed by student volunteers moving coloured pegs around constituency wallcharts. Rock videos played on the MTV monitor in the corner, above shelves full of Lenin's collected works. Nobody buttonholed me with complaints. On the contrary, Kasim, the energetic campaign manager, filled my hands with pens, notebooks, lapel badges and condoms decorated with the party logo. Normal electioneering trinkets weren't normal at all in Bosnia; those condoms lay in my palm like flamboyant omens of defeat.

Away then to a meeting some twenty kilometres from the capital. But for the lorries pounding through to the coast, Pazarić would be any backwoods village. Beyond the houses fringing the road, blackness veiled the open hillside under a cold three-quarter moon. A girl tugged her goat home from its forage on a building site. A policeman sauntered toward the meeting hall, where cars and newcomers had caught his eye. In the ante-room half a dozen chess matches were in progress, beside a rack of trophies. The obligatory portrait of Tito showed him concentrating on a chequered board. At other tables, dominoes and cards were slapped down. Spectators rested stubbly chins on the backs of their reversed chairs. Men in berets, and one or two in Albanian skull-caps, smoked and talked with amicable, emphatic gestures. No women in sight, except a waitress with a tin tray. After being looked up and down, we were ignored.

The meeting started with thirty people in the hall; a few more drifted in. Nazif Gljiva, a celebrity folk-singer and the party's candidate for president of the republic, barked a forty-second speech. Young Rasim Kadić, party president, stood at the microphone like a trooper at ease and rattled through his speech, staring blankly over the audience's heads. (Was this typical martial style another partisan legacy? A huge, sombre portrait of Tito surveyed the audience from the wall beside the stage . . .) He explained the DS's background and its multinational programme, and attacked communist corruption. At question-time a voice from the back asked why Rasim criticized the communists when they were good to him as the Youth League's last president. Visibly defensive, Rasim fired back that he had never accepted a car or apartment. The meeting closed with a song from Nazif that should have been rousing but wasn't.

At the *post mortem* in a nearby restaurant, the singer told his team that Bosnia has two thousand villages like Pazarić, full of uneducated people who don't know what politics is, what they can do, what's right and what's wrong. Only the nationalist parties and the communists exist for these people. No one disputed this; Gljiva knows Bosnia from the roots.

Kasim whispered that Nazif would like to be interviewed, so I called questions across the clatter of cutlery. "I'm forty-one," boomed Nazif, "born in a potato field, the ninth of ten children. My father had to rustle horses with the gypsies to get money, and I stole food when I was a boy. They jailed me the first time for stealing two chickens. I never spent a *day* in school: *prison* was my education. Now I'm a rich man, my songs sell millions of copies. Look, I wear a Rolex watch and a diamond ring." His small, burly frame was encased in a well-tailored suit. Though his square-jawed face rarely smiled, his nonstop patter and childlike egotism radiated benignity.

"Don't take the watch off, Nazif," someone jested as he passed the Rolex round for inspection. "It might disappear!"

"No-o-o, I'm the only thief in this room, and the watch is mine. Why should I be president of Bosnia? Because I know what's right and what's wrong, and there's the beginning and end of it. There should be ten parties for every nation: having just one is fascism. Everything I do is by instinct, I have excellent antennae for what the Bosnian people think, and I *love* them. When *I'm* president *they* will be president . . ."

The gloom had evaporated. The restaurateur dug out a video of Halid Bešlić crooning Nazif's songs. The waiters served creamy venison *burek*, bowls of *klepke* with sour cream and garlic, and ever more Johnnie Walker. The three-man house band beamed like courtiers behind Nazif's chair and struck up a medley of his tunes. The table cried for Nazif, who fished out a thousand-dinar note for the band and obliged in an ululating tenor, hand on breast: "Tell my mother I will go to war for you, my Bosnia . . ." His largesse enveloped activists, journalists, waiters and musicians. They all sang along, and we all loved him.

"There are a dozen Gljivas in every Bosnian village," a Croat friend said when I told her about my evening, "and you'll never know them. Crazy, crazy. Only in Bosnia."

Last stop on my pre-election tour was the League of Communists. The Central Committee building was a white rectangular block with no entrance visible from the road, and nobody coming or going. No one moving inside, either; only white corridors punctuated by rubber plants and closed doors.

Zlatko Lagumdžija gave me the Communist view. Dr Lagumdžija studied systems analysis at UCLA, teaches at the university, runs his own business, and sits on the presidency of the BiH League of Communists. "Parties here divide into three: parties of politically prehistoric nationalist madness; early capitalist parties, ranting about the free market; and reformed parties of the Left. Our first goal is for the second and third groups to win a majority over the first and help it disappear. It will be disastrous if the national parties come to power even if they don't foment civil war. Their leaders would be fine farmers or supermarket managers, but not leaders of the republic, *please*. They remind me of the joke about Mujo and Suljo [the stock featherbrains of Bosnian humour, both Muslim]. Mujo says: 'Cyrillic, that's the alphabet for us, that's our history, our roots.' Suljo disagrees: 'Latin is the alphabet of Europe, the future.' They start fighting, and a passing policeman drags them apart. At the police station an officer takes down their statements, which they have to sign. Both mark a cross!"

It was too late. Come polling day, Mujo and Suljo ignored the revamped League. Communism in BiH had produced tough operators who ran the republic like an Ottoman *pashalik*. For a long time, indeed, their Titoist recipe of forced-march industrialization plus "brotherhood and unity" had much to contribute. The régime only foundered after a series of spectacular scandals in the mid-to-late '80s.

Whatever its record, though, by November 1990 the domino effect guaranteed electoral oblivion for the League, and for the other, untainted supranational parties too. The Slovenian and Croatian elections had already brought secessionist governments to power. The Croatian and Serbian parties in BiH had exclusively national programmes: the social content in their manifestoes was padding. The Muslims had no option but to homogenize. Mr Izetbegović predicted that MBO would take one or two per cent of the Muslim vote from SDA. This is what happened, and I was thankful; the "period of uncertainty" facing BiH was even graver than pessimists were guessing. He gave an impression of understanding very well the liberal values that his rival Zulfikarpašić had nailed to his mast; unlike the other man, though, he knew that Bosnia's Muslims might be swallowed up unless they united.

The national parties had nothing to offer in terms of economic revival; the supranational parties were right about that, but who cared about economics when bodily security was at stake? Such matters, anyway, had always been controlled from afar, and if bad turned to worse the family would not let one starve.

In this sense the reformed Communists and the Reform Forces and even the Democratic League (excepting the bizarre Mr Gljiva) were true legatees of the system they wanted to replace. Their rational, all too rational conceptions were just as unreal as the jargon of self-management socialism; they knew what was best for Bosnia-Hercegovina, like the old Communist leaders, but could not give it what it wanted. The difference was that the new supranationalists were competing for power, the state was not their monopoly, and their call for brotherhood and unity plus free market economics was not underwritten by the armed forces. The army, indeed, kept mum throughout the campaign, watching developments from the barracks above Sarajevo.

What the supranationalists couldn't know is that the crisis and war in 1991 would rob them of the chance to fight another day. "We want to reform the system *through* the system," said suave Dr Lagumdžija; yet the only reformable content of the system was its kernel of power, which could be nationalized by the communists (as in Serbia and Montenegro) or transferred intact to anti-communists (as in Slovenia and Croatia) or split between the two (as in Macedonia and BiH). With this kernel removed, the system was dross.

Nothing proved this so well as the fate of Ante Marković and his Reform Forces party. In his own words, Marković stood for "an undivided Yugoslavia with a market economy, political pluralism, democratic rights and freedoms for all citizens." This was music to Western ears and to Yugoslavia's own cosmopolitan élite, though not to the primitive republican governments, especially in Serbia, which rightly foresaw their control over their economies being undermined by the Marković reform programme. Concretely, his authority as federal prime minister derived from the federal assembly, which was an early casualty of the breakdown of inter-republican relations. The assembly was unable to agree a procedure for elections. Without a functioning democratic parliament drawn from all republics, Marković could be ignored by republican governments. Nor could he pass any legislation, let alone enforce it. He was powerless to stop republics from defaulting on, and plundering the federal budget, for which he was responsible. He couldn't be replaced and legally he couldn't resign, because no competent body existed to elect a successor or accept his resignation.

The champion of all-Yugoslav democratization had no democratic mandate. In theory he might have remained in office for life. In fact "the last Yugoslav", as the press dubbed him, resigned in December 1991, on the grounds that the armed forces had appropriated 80 per cent of the federal budget for 1992, and he was powerless to prevent it.

He had stayed at his post through the autumn of war, chauffeured around Belgrade and guarded by a detail of US Marines lent by the American ambassador. For Marković was in fear for his life, expecting to be ambushed by Serbian guerrillas. It was an ignominious end. He and his programme are destined to survive in footnotes – the last of the Yugoslav might-have-beens.

The Cassandras warned that if national parties won in BiH, what future could the republic have? And if BiH, the Yugoslav microcosm, had no future, what chance did the federation have?

This prophecy shivered the spines of foreign correspondents (mine, too) but was wrong on two counts. Nothing that happened here was decisive for Yugoslavia. Events marched to a tune composed in Belgrade and Zagreb; if those governments are determined to foment war in Bosnia-Hercegovina, nothing can stop them. Secondly, the harmony of BiH depends not upon amalgamating its nations but – as Tito realized so well – upon balancing them. The Bosnian Serbs and Croats borrow extra strength from their own national republics, but the Bosnian Muslims outnumber them and their leaders were nimble enough to improvise alliances as necessary. The warning should, then, be reversed: if supranational parties had won the elections, Bosnia-Hercegovina would have had no chance of remaining impartial as war raged beyond two of its three borders.

This three-way balance of strength and fear was socially destructive and humanly exhausting. In Sarajevo the effects of the ending of Yugoslavia were etched on people's expressions. Forcing them into one-dimensional identities appeared physically uncomfortable, like putting gravel in their shoes or ripping a wall off their apartment block. Forty-eight nationalities live in this city. The mingling of nations and faiths has become second nature where the Catholic and Orthodox cathedrals, the mosque and the synagogue lie within a 400-metre square. Half a century of secularization has surely drained much of the militancy from these symbols of faith. The synagogue is now a Jewish museum, the old stone *hammam* (baths) is a casino, and the Orthodox congregation I saw was grey-haired. Shari'a courts were closed after 1945, and the veil was banned. Still, it isn't hard to tell the Muslim women apart, at least those from out of town, by their headscarves and beige raincoats, and the way they avoid eye-contact.

The loveliness of Sarajevo's setting amid steep green hills offsets the high-rise brutalism of the suburbs. In the city centre, it frames every vista like a poem. The *baščaršija* (bazaar) is still the heart of the city, if not its pulse or wallet. Along its cobbled alleys boys hawked flick-knives and plastic lighters off trestle tables. Shops sold leather-ware, jewellery, copper pots and wooden pattens, the first I ever saw outside a museum. Chimney smoke wreathed the minarets and the *medresa* (Koranic school). For real latter-day craftsmanship, though, the ordinary car-owners are hard to beat. At any moment, half the bonnets in Sarajevo have men bent beneath them like surgeons, clutching tins of red paint and rolls of sticking-plaster. Beneath the clatter of two-stroke engines, a deeper backbeat drones: generators for cement-mixers and pneumatic drills. Every way I turned, men were knocking walls down or plastering them up. The air was mizzly with brick dust and exhaust fumes.

Miskina is the artery, a pedestrian street lined with smarter shops and cafés. Stalls sprout soon after dawn, vending perfumes, shower lotions, one-size spectacles, yellow plastic razors, rings with huge stones dyed every colour of the spectrum. Hairspray, carrier bags, Marlboros by the two hundred, white ankle socks, telephones, tights, shirts, non-stick pans, Swiss chocolate. A cache of new leather belts pulled a little crowd. Rain conjured umbrellas, furled like early daffodils.

Come nightfall, the *korzo* begins: a procession of amorous entangled couples and teenage groups arm-in-arm, dressed to the nines or slumming in satiny track-suits. Impossible not to be cheered by watching them, and, later, by meeting Mrs Sultanović (*that's* a Bosnian name) at her Solaris Non-Stop Video and Photo Store. She runs this leisurely business from home, which is a Jewish merchant's house, vulnerably wooden from its rooftiles to the fret-work on its ground-floor balustrade, and still intact after a hundred years, standing fast against the blaze of history.

*

I moved south toward Mostar and the heights of Hercegovina. An hour out of Sarajevo, rounding a bend near Jablanica, a collapsed railway bridge came into view. Half of it spans the Neretva river; the other half jack-knifes up the side of the river's deep gorge.

The bridge was blown fifty years ago, in the battle of the Neretva, one of the most dramatic engagements of the National Liberation War, as the years between 1941–45 were officially known in Yugoslavia. The wreckage has been kept as a relic, for the battle of the Neretva was honoured as "the battle for the wounded". The partisans refused to leave their 4,000 wounded behind as they forced a way across the river, at huge cost, fleeing the German assault against their base in northern Bosnia, to the relative safety of Montenegro. The blown bridge became a giant staircase for Tito's guerrillas.

My 1980 Yugoslav guidebook says this "famous battle" was waged between "the occupation forces and the Yugoslav Liberation Army". In truth, the partisans' escape route to the south-east was blocked not by German or Italian troops but by other Yugoslavs who, acting in concert with the Axis, fought their countrymen tooth and nail. These so-called četniks were, in their own eyes, less of an "occupying force" here than the partisans, for they were mostly Montenegrins, fighting on the frontier of their homeland, whereas the partisans came from all over Yugoslavia.

This slippery reference to "occupation forces" was quite standard. As the founding event and symbol of socialist Yugoslavia, the legacy of the National Liberation War had to be protected as the star-spangled banner is protected in the United States, but much more fiercely because its enemies were legion.

The war was won by the partisans, organized and led by the Communist Party. This victory was one and the same as revolution against the state of royal Yugoslavia, represented by the king and his government in London, where they escaped soon after Hitler's invasion in April 1941. The partisans fought in the name of all Yugoslavs for the sake of all Yugoslavia; their enemies were the occupying fascist forces from Germany, Italy, Hungary and Bulgaria, and the numerous quislings and collaborators who supported these forces. Within the anti-Axis war, therefore, was a series of incredibly savage local wars. Come 1945, the enemy leaders were caught (whenever possible) and prosecuted in show trials. Lesser collaborators were hounded, disgraced, murdered, expelled from the country. Then a veil was drawn; officially, socialism was healing Yugoslavia of those bourgeois nationalist diseases that underlay collaborationism, so further examination of those terrible years when some 6 per cent of all Yugoslavs died, mostly at other Yugoslavs' hands, was unnecessary. In reality the régime knew that its constitutional myth would not survive free examination; for, far from settling the difference between winners and losers, victory had added another cause for bitterness.

Though they might not say so now, for a long time most people wanted to keep the veil drawn; nothing, they thought, was to be gained by digging into wartime scars. But the euphemisms and suppressions had their price, as became horribly clear in 1991, when the great multinational event shivered into national shards, razor sharp and poison-tipped.

Communities traumatized by wartime atrocities had no chance to grieve, blame, expiate, comprehend what had happened. Only the "victims of fascism" were commemorated, indeed fetishized as martyrs for socialist victory; monuments were raised in their memory; streets and factories were named after them. This cult harboured its own distortion. Many of the partisans had indeed died for a principle, an idea of a new, better Yugoslavia striving for birth from the ashes of the old kingdom. Others were whirled along like leaves in a hurricane, killed protecting their nearest and dearest. Meanwhile the shades of all the others – those who chose fascism and those who merely found themselves on the wrong side for reasons they may not have understood – languished in the upper air like lost souls, unforgotten, mourned in private, bequeathing an inflammable mix of guilt and unappeased resentment to their families and villages. More unfinished business, festering in official oblivion and passed like an heirloom from one generation to the next.

Yet it would be falsely fatalistic to conclude that what was repressed has returned to wreak vengeance. In 1990 and 1991 the repressed was invoked; whatever crimes those lost souls had or hadn't committed on earth, they now became victims of new exploitation by political and intellectual élites in Serbia and Croatia, the two largest Yugoslav nations and the most mutually hostile during the war. (As we saw, the Slovenes made, characteristically, a separate peace with the ritual in Kočevski Rog in July 1990.) The wartime epithets, četnik and ustaša, were now heard on everybody's lips, from presidents to peasants; Croats were now "fascist ustaše" and Serbs were likewise "Great-Serbian chauvinist četniks", not because the terms were literally true (in more than a few ageing individual cases), nor because the galloping crisis in the early '90s resembled the disintegration of Yugoslavia in the early '40s. These labels were revived as abuse and incitement, to antagonize the other nation and to rouse one's own to wrath. Almost overnight, in an atmosphere of hysterical revelation unchecked by scholarship or humanitarianism, censorship became publicity. As the army bombarded towns in eastern Croatia, Belgrade television relayed the exhumation of Serbian remains from caves in Bosnia-Hercegovina, where the ustaše or partisans had dumped them. The camera lingered greedily on grief-drawn faces as plastic sacks of nameless bones were passed from hand to hand; the soundtrack was a requiem mass. In Croatia, meanwhile, President Tudjman led a demagogic effort to downplay the ustaša role in wartime slaughter.

The real story of the partisans, četniks and ustaše has little to do with the recent trading of insults and hatred.

It begins in March 1941, when the Yugoslav government signed protocols acceding to a Tripartite Pact with Germany and Italy. Yugoslavia at that time was hemmed on three sides by Axis or Axis-aligned powers: Italy, Greater Germany, Hungary, Romania, Bulgaria and Albania. Only Greece to the south, attacked by Italy in October 1940, was fighting the Axis. Prince Pavle (regent for the underage Petar II Karadjordjević) yielded to German pressure and signed the Pact as a despairing strategem to save his state, knowing that the Slovenes and Croats favoured a concession that would lift the threat of invasion, and hoping that the Serbs would tolerate it. They didn't. Encouraged by British secret agents (Britain had its own strategic reasons for wanting to tie the Axis down in the Balkans), Belgrade rose against the Pact: demonstrators brandished the famous slogans, '*Bolje rat nego pakt!*' (Better war than the pact) and '*Bolje grob nego rob!*' (Better the grave than slavery), and a near-bloodless military coup wrested power from Pavle and his government.

Churchill declared the Yugoslavs had found their soul; Hitler prepared to annihilate the rebels "with merciless brutality". He struck on 6 April; a week later the Nazis marched into Belgrade. An armistice amounting to unconditional surrender was signed on 17 April. The young king and his new government had fled. Italian and Hungarian forces had joined in the invasion; now – with the Bulgarians – they assisted the dismemberment.

This wholesale obliteration of the state was not a single event. Germany wanted to crush the Serbs, because of Hitler's own obsession with them and because they were rightly seen as the key opponent among the Yugoslavs. So the Germans did not try to dominate the whole country; so long as they could pillage Yugoslav resources and keep the main transport routes free, they were largely content to control the cities and leave much of the remainder to allies and quislings, and to the guerrilla resistance bands hiding in the hills and forests, provided these kept out of the way.

This policy spared vital German divisions for the war in northern Africa and, soon, against the Soviet Union; it also had the advantage of bleeding potential anti-Nazi activity by reviving old expansionist dreams and inter-ethnic hatreds. The Germans' principal ally was Italy, which, until it capitulated in 1943, dominated the western third of Yugoslavia; thus it acquired southern Slovenia and most of Dalmatia. Bulgaria annexed Macedonia, Hungary took a large slice of the territory 'stolen' from it after World War One, and Kosovo-Metohija became part of a Great Albania under Italian aegis.

Of the two collaborationist régimes, one was Serbian, a proxy to help the Germans keep order in Serbia. The other was Croatian, and

How Yugoslavia was carved up, 1941–1945

in ideology and practice it was altogether more horrific. Consideration of the so-called Independent State of Croatia (NDH: *Nezavisna Država Hrvatska*), run by Ante Pavelić and his ustaša movement, and disposing of some 250,000 men, will be kept for a later chapter; suffice here to say the NDH included Bosnia, Hercegovina and Srem – from Kotor to Zagreb and almost to Belgrade. While gratifying its leadership's thirst for territory, this posed a problem: how could the NDH be the Croats' national state if almost half the inhabitants of this huge area were not Croats but Orthodox Serbs, Muslims, Jews and so forth? The fascists who wanted to run the NDH found a suitable solution: convert a third of the Serbian population to Catholicism, kill a third, and expel the rest. Ustaše assassins turned the land into a slaughterhouse; statistics are still bitterly contested, but perhaps

350,000 Serbs died at ustaše hands, as well as thousands of Jews, gypsies, and anti-fascist Croats. Two to three hundred thousand more Serbs were converted. Thousands were expelled eastwards, into the rump Serbia.

This genocide was terminally debilitating to the NDH. Under pressure from their German and Italian overlords, the ustaše curbed their blood-lust, but too late to stop the Serb-inhabited regions of the NDH becoming rich recruiting grounds for the two main guerrilla forces, namely the partisans and the četniks.

When the state died in April '41, most of the Yugoslav army units surrendered. Their Serb officers were taken away to prison camps in Germany. Others took to the hills; a group led by Colonel Draža Mihailović aimed to become a nucleus of resistance to the invaders, mustering guerrillas in the name of the old Yugoslav state. Calling themselves the "četnik detachments of the Yugoslav army", they made their way to the mountains of west central Serbia, where other officers joined them, as well as politicians from Belgrade. Mihailović set about bringing other četnik bands under his command.

In September a weak radio signal from Mihailović was picked up in Malta. This first indication of anti-Nazi resistance inside Fortress Europe was gratefully seized by the Allies and especially by the exiled government in London, which made the colonel its Minister of War and Deputy Commander-in-Chief of the Yugoslav Army in the Fatherland, and promoted him to the rank of General.

By early '42 Mihailović had already clashed with the other concerted anti-fascist resistance: the partisans, organized by the Communist Party of Yugoslavia, led by its general secretary Josip Broz, soon and forever after known by his *nom de guerre* of Tito. The CPY was the only political party with an all-Yugoslav programme, and the only one that hadn't disintegrated. Outlawed in 1921 and led from abroad for most of the interwar period, its members were at home underground. Tempered by persecution, and by the Spanish Civil War – where some 1,200 Yugoslavs saw action, of whom a quarter returned to fight as partisans – the CPY was inured to war conditions. It was fitted too by virtue of the ruthless internal discipline that Tito imposed after he took charge in 1937.

Their first hitch was more ideological than practical; in spring 1941 Hitler and the Soviet Union were allies, so how could the CPY fight Germany? After the end of May, however, when Broz learned that Germany planned to invade the USSR, they prepared to act. On 22 June the invasion began. On 1 July the Comintern signalled new commands: "The hour has struck when communists must launch an open fight against the invaders. Without wasting a moment, organize partisan detachments and start a partisan war behind the enemy's lines".

Another potential difficulty loomed. Broz had made it clear that the coming struggle would be for social as well as national liberation. Yet Moscow demanded a common front against the fascists; the CPY should subordinate any political ambitions of its own to the imperative of collaboration with other resistance forces. To begin with, in Serbia and ustaša-terrorized regions of NDH, joint action with the četniks worked well enough. But the basis of co-operation was too fragile to last. Only Moscow's injunction prevented the partisans from treating the četniks as their enemy, and only uncertainty about their own strength stopped the četniks from reciprocating in kind.

Not only were the two movements bound to despise and distrust each other; their strategies of resistance were increasingly incompatible. After the first autumn of occupation, when the Germans retaliated savagely against Serbian civilians for guerrilla actions and sabotage launched from "liberated" areas, the četnik idea was to hunker down and outlast the occupation. When the Germans were retreating, they would rise up, finish off any Wehrmacht stragglers, take revenge on domestic enemies, and assume power.

It was a coherent, pragmatic response to a dire predicament. The quota for reprisals had been set: 100 Serbian hostages would die for every German killed, and fifty for each German wounded. No one knew how long the war would last; everyone knew the četniks lacked resources to threaten the occupying forces. Already the towns of Šumadija, Serbia's heartland, had been decimated by reprisals. The četniks refused to risk more of the same.

Why not, given that the stakes were anyway so high? Because –and here one approaches the core of the strife between četniks and partisans – Mihailović was running a Serbian operation with a pan-Serbian or Great Serbian ideology. The četniks were almost exclusively Serbs and Montenegrins, not because they didn't seek the liberation of other Yugoslav territory, but because they were drawn from the Serb-dominated ranks of the pre-war officer corps, and sought the restitution of a Serb-dominated monarchic state. For the non-Serbian population, the četniks' sole positive attribute was that they weren't Axis fascists; for some, indeed, such as the Albanians of Kosovo, or many Macedonians, they were more dangerous than the occupying forces.

The "national question" had not been interred along with the state; on the contrary, inflamed and aggravated on every side, it was about all that remained of Yugoslavia. From the perspective of the minority nations, Mihailović had nothing new to offer. His ideal postwar

Yugoslavia would have been the same unitary settlement as before, except tighter, more closely supervised by the army, to forestall the sort of crisis that had allowed the Croats to win autonomy in 1939.*

The partisans, by contrast, were committed to a revolution that would inaugurate "liberty, equality, and brotherhood for all the nations of Yugoslavia. In this consists the essence of the national liberation struggle." So said Tito in 1942; and, however tinny the partisan cry of brotherhood and unity was to sound in later decades, whatever the failure of socialist Yugoslavia to deliver "national equality, social justice and individual liberty", and for all the needful debunking of partisan myths, it has yet to be proved that the partisans were any kind of chauvinists.

They were committed to total war against the fascists and collaborators, with no quarter given or asked. Nothing else would help the Soviet motherland in her plight. To warriors with revolution as their ultimate goal, *tabula rasa* looked less terrible. Of course this was a callous strategy; but it also took the initiative, and answered the extremity of the times as Mihailović's waiting game did not.

So the četnik–partisan partnership was short-lived. It seems the royalists attacked first, in October 1941, trying to nip the rival movement in the bud. In any case Moscow's word, now as in the future, was not enough to bind the CPY, and Tito's forces gave as good as they got.

Soon afterwards the Serbian uprising was quelled by the Germans. The partisans were chased out of Serbia, while Mihailović's men reverted to their waiting game. Over the next two years, as both the resistance and civil wars shifted back to battlegrounds in the NDH, partisans and četniks attacked each other from end to end of Pavelić's puppet state and in Montenegro, taking few prisoners.

It was a war without fronts, or with a thousand fronts shifting every day. The historian Vladimir Dedijer spent most of the war with the partisan command, keeping a famous diary throughout; his entry for 3 November 1942 records how the "general situation" looked on that particular evening:

> The enemy is waging a sharp offensive in the south. Prozor has been occupied. The Italians are in it; the četnik-bandits have returned to Hercegovina. The Fifth and Tenth Brigades did not go to Hercegovina because they received no orders. Now they have penetrated in the direction of Glamoč. The Dalmatians fought bravely at Aržano, but

---

* The *Sporazum* (agreement) of August 1939 created a Croatian administrative unit within the Kingdom of Yugoslavia. Croat extremists were unimpressed, and Serb extremists were outraged. The map on p. 266 marks the extent of the Croatian unit.

the ustaše managed a surprise breakthrough over Cincar and occupied Livno from the rear. They destroyed one of our supply units; we lost about thirty soldiers. Now the front is between Livno and Glamoč. From Jajce and Mrkonjić the Germans, with the četniks and ustaše, are waging an offensive in the direction of Mlinište and have committed a mass of atrocities. They even burned down some villages in which there were četniks, including the village of Dragniće. Mrkonjić has changed hands three times . . .

The četniks' priorities made them more interested in defeating the communist-led resistance than in harrying the occupiers. To this end they negotiated all manner of arrangements, first with the Italians and later even with the Germans and ustaše, combining with them against the local partisans. The četniks received arms and salaries – or at a minimum, peace and quiet – to hunt the partisans down.

It didn't work. Apart from their political shortcomings, the četniks were less a unified force than a league of warlords, some of whom did not even seek the restoration of Yugoslavia, as Mihailović did; whereas the partisans were usually fiercely disciplined, with an efficient command structure. They disposed of some very able commanders, and, as they well knew, their stance on the national question gave them a head-start over any other anti-Axis force. The longer the occupation lasted the more people, left with nothing to lose, gravitated towards the partisans as the most effective resistance fighters and, increasingly, as the destined victors who would soon control the country.

Those two years, as Tito's government-in-waiting played cat and mouse up and down the wooded ravines of Bosnia and the stark moonscapes of Hercegovina and Montenegro, settled the outcome of the war. As early as March 1943, when the Axis, intending to smash the partisans once and for all, drove them out of their Bosnian base at Bihać down towards the Neretva, where they broke through četnik lines, the writing was on the wall. In the months after that "battle for the wounded", the partisans confirmed their military superiority. That November, at the supremely confident second session of AVNOJ (Anti-fascist Council for the National Liberation of Yugoslavia) back in Bosnia at Jajce, they laid the foundations of a socialist federation. A few days later, at the Tehran Summit, Roosevelt, Stalin and Churchill recognized the partisans as an Allied army, and didn't mention the četniks. The watershed was crossed; the partisans could almost freewheel to victory.

Abandoned by the Allies in 1944, Mihailović battled on, first in tandem with the Serbian quisling régime, finally almost alone. He evaded capture until March 1946; the outcome of his show-trial in Belgrade was a foregone conclusion. The demise of Yugoslav communism has seen Draža Mihailović's star rise again. Today his portrait is brandished at Serbian demonstrations; Draža lapel badges are sold in Belgrade; the label četnik was accepted proudly by Serb irregulars fighting across Croatia in 1991. He has entered the pantheon of Serbian heroes, in part for opportunist motives (as a famous victim of communism), partly because the trajectory of his life, mingling courage, chauvinism and blindness, and culminating in hideous defeat borne with such pyrrhic dignity that his executioners looked jumped-up and sordid, was indeed archetypally Serbian.

Concurrently with the restoration of Mihailović's prestige among Serbs, repeated efforts have been made in Britain and America to revise the accepted version of Britain's wartime rôle in Yugoslavia by arguing that there was no military or wholesome political reason for the Allies to drop Draža and the četniks as the official anti-Axis resistance. They were only dropped, the argument runs, because of skulduggery and gullibility among the individuals who influenced the switch.*

The skulduggery was perpetrated by British Leftists who exploited their positions of authority to show Tito and his bandits in a favourable light, while the gullibility was evinced by other, right-thinking Brits who allowed the partisans and their backers to hoodwink them.

The fact that the revisionists' case withers under scrutiny doesn't lessen its fascination – the fascination of the entire episode – by a jot. For their allegations are no more extraordinary than the unadorned facts of the case.

Britain was in direct if shaky contact with the Yugoslav resistance from the first, by radio and a series of envoys. When it became known that Mihailović did not have a monopoly of resistance, Britain's priority was to encourage what Anthony Eden, the secretary of state for war, termed "a united front of all patriots in Yugoslavia". Through 1942 and into 1943, the Allies (which, in respect of Yugoslavia, meant the British) looked solely to the četniks, despite Mihailović's quiescence and indications that his commanders preferred to hammer the enemy within – using the Italians –than to fight the Axis. Meanwhile reports kept being filed, and German signals decoded, which suggested that more effective

---

* While I wrote this chapter the revision was rehearsed again, in the pages of the *Guardian*: "The British role that left Yugoslavia in the lurch" by Jessica Douglas-Home, 9 November 1991. And as I checked the proofs, a documentary programme peddling the same line was broadcast on BBC television ("Tito – Churchill's Man?", BBC2, 26 February 1992).

resistance was being put up by these mysterious "partisans" in regions where Mihailović's writ did not run.

In May 1943, after long consideration, the order was given to approach resistance groups outside Mihailović's home territory of Serbia. Liaison officers parachuted to the partisans were impressed by what they saw. Their reports persuaded Britain to strengthen relations, at first under the familiar illusion that both forces could be persuaded to work together. Milovan Djilas bluntly recalled that "the British wanted us to tie down as many German and satellite divisions as possible, which suited us, on condition that we be given aid and recognition as the only Yugoslav force." Such recognition came, implicitly, at Tehran, and explicitly at the subsequent British conclave at Cairo. Henceforth supplies were dropped exclusively to the partisans.

What especially absorbs the revisionists is the run-up to that first official mission to the partisans. Liaison with the Balkans was mediated by the Cairo headquarters of the Special Operations Executive, and SOE Cairo in 1942–43 was a set-up to warm the heart of any right-wing conspiracy theorist.

Lieutenant (later Major) James Klugmann was employed in the Yugoslav Section there, and Klugmann was a lifelong open communist, from his conversion at Cambridge in 1931 to his death in 1977. Indeed, he was for decades the pet intellectual of the British Communist Party. In the crucial months preceding the May mission, Klugmann was working under Major Basil Davidson, who after the war became widely known as a Leftist writer on African history and politics. Davidson's other assistant in Cairo was Captain F. W. D. Deakin, an Oxford don (SOE also stood for Scholars & Other Eccentrics) who happened to have been Churchill's literary assistant before the war. The fourth suspect, from the revisionist point of view, was Brigadier C. M. Keble, chief of staff to Lord Glenconner, who ran SOE Cairo.

Late in 1942 Keble had become vexed by London's refusal to alter its exclusive support for Mihailović, despite such *sotto voce* admissions as this, from Lord Glenconner: "As we know, any activities in Yugoslavia should really be attributed to the Partisans." With Davidson's help and, no doubt, Klugmann's encouragement, Keble resolved to do his utmost to change British policy. Fortune favoured him: thanks to Deakin, he had direct access to the Prime Minister when he passed through Cairo early in 1943. Via the young don, Keble put his report into Churchill's hands. Churchill had been aware of the controversy about Mihailović simmering in the Foreign Office and SOE London for months, and he would have been reading top-secret Ultra signals intercepted from the Germans. He was persuaded by Keble's argument for maintaining support of Mihailović in Serbia, while seeking contact with "other resisting elements" elsewhere. Thanks to the PM's personal intervention, the Foreign Office's and SOE London's abiding reservations, not to mention the attitude of the king and his government in exile, were sidestepped.

Later in 1943, convinced that relations must be developed with the partisans, Churchill intervened again by despatching Fitzroy Maclean as a "daring Ambassador-leader to these hardy and hunted guerrillas". Maclean's special status as Churchill's emissary gave his first report, written after a few weeks with the partisans, a unique significance. It was overwhelmingly favourable to Tito's forces. The rest is history – or, the revisionists argue, conspiracy.

Whatever one's opinion of the switch, anybody might be startled by the coalition of talented and diverse people who achieved it. From Klugmann the commie to Maclean the Conservative member of parliament, the soldiers and diplomats who set their shoulders to Tito's wheel were a rum assortment.* It is true that the anti-communists among them, including Churchill himself, were eager to underestimate the partisans' ideological loyalties. Yet Maclean had no illusions on this score; and his observations that Mihailović had "no prospect of uniting the country", and that failure to help Tito would rather drive him into Soviet arms than weaken his prospects of final victory or his commitment to communism, were well founded and farsighted.

What this unique cross-bench support proves is less a Leftist, anti-royalist or anti-Serbian conspiracy, than, first, the Homeric appeal of the partisan movement and of Tito personally; and second, the sheer effort that was required to haul an inert policy into line with Yugoslav realities and Allied interests in the Balkans. For – contrary to the revisionists' casual assumption, and to old soldiers and seadogs such as Rear-Admiral Sir Morgan Morgan-Giles, DSO, OBE, GM, DL, who recently issued the magnificent boast that "British involvement ... undoubtedly determined the whole post-war history of Yugoslavia" – Britain neither forged the partisans nor guaranteed their victory, let alone the nature of the post-war régime. If any outsider may be credited with some such powers, it was Hitler.

When I contacted Sir Fitzroy Maclean and Basil Davidson with a view to asking about their parts in the Yugoslav war, Sir Fitzroy

---

* "The officers of one of the Maclean missions in Croatia, Major Randolph Churchill, Captain the Earl of Birkenhead, and Captain Evelyn Waugh, were recruited in the bar of White's Club by Randolph Churchill, who stood as a Conservative candidate in the 1945 general election." (McConville.)

agreed to meet, then fobbed me off ("I'm afraid I'm rather putting the clamps down on anything about Yugoslavia for the time being. The situation's all too complicated"). Likewise chary of revisionist inquisitions, Basil Davidson refused to be interviewed, but he did answer correspondence. His last letter ended: "What I hope is that the grandeur of the partisan resistance, in human terms, in moral terms, will remain a central part of your vision of those tormented years: its heroism, but also its success, no matter how obscured it has become in the minds of youngish people today. We British had our part in that, and not easily and not painlessly; and this is something of which one can be proud, even if pride of that nature is no longer fashionable."

Amen to that. Yet – a last point – fashion is not quite the issue. The values of the partisan war were experiential, not transmissible; yet not just the passage of time has made the war as remote from younger Yugoslavs as Anderson Shelters and Woolton Pie from their British contemporaries. That epic and tragic struggle was milked for every drop of legitimacy it could confer upon the Yugoslav system. Hence the Western revisionists' zeal to expose the partisans finds an echo within the country in a widespread cynicism about all things communist.

Perhaps the present war will prove a turning point in the partisans' reputation. There were "ustaše" and "četniks" in 1991, and the federal army has disgraced its origins by imitating, under cover of anti-fascist rhetoric, the Germans and Italians of fifty years ago, by stoking local conflicts and arming bandits to slaughter villagers. But there were no "partisans" – none. The best partisan legacy was unexploitable in this dirty sectarian war. When the killing has stopped and the fog has cleared, that legacy will still be present in the collective memory – not merely in the Museums of the Liberation gathering dust throughout the ex-federation – to shame today's obsessed and manipulated aggressors.

*

British involvement in wartime Yugoslavia has a pendant in the little-known story of the *omladinska pruga*, the youth railway. In 1947 volunteers came to build a rail line from Šamac to Sarajevo.

Anyone was welcome, but of course young communists were keenest to spend their summer toiling in darkest Bosnia, when the Federative People's Republic of Yugoslavia had been dubbed "Satellite Number One" in the Western press. Some 200,000 people worked on the railway, including some 450 British.

I looked up four of the Brits to ask them about the *omladinska pruga*. Their memories trail cloudlets of glory, from an era when they, their leftist hopes for Europe, and socialist Yugoslavia were in their first ardent and ascetic flush. Peter Worsley, now a Professor Emeritus of sociology, went to Yugoslavia from an international youth festival in Prague. "That was thrilling, young people from Korea to Canada and everywhere in between. We were invited to a work camp in Slovakia, then on to Bosnia. The Yugoslavs showed us what to do and left us to it. At the international camp we worked hard but not unduly. We used to hear how serious the British were. I don't remember any political meetings at our camp, and when I went down the tracks, there were the Brits discussing dialectical materialism!

"At the end of the war, you see, and before the Cominform split, Yugoslavia was *the* country we could support unreservedly, without condition, for their resistance movement was untainted by nationalism or reaction."

The historians Edward and Dorothy Thompson had volunteered too; the first of Edward Thompson's many books was a slim collective volume that he edited about the experience. Dorothy Thompson agrees with Worsley that Yugoslavia's appeal was that it was authentically communist. "One didn't have the feeling of being in a satellite at all, whereas in Bulgaria [at a similar camp in 1948] it was clearly a banana republic tacked on to the Soviet Union."

Edward mentioned "our own revolution" in the British Brigade. I smiled: "You didn't mention *that* in your book." "Of course not," he said drily. Dorothy elaborated: "We had these brigade commanders who didn't do any work. They swanned around the place, and there was a feeling we only needed a working commissariat, not a bureaucracy. Edward and I didn't instigate this, but somehow we became involved. He ended up as brigade commandant and I as secretary and cook."

As the founder of the Merlin Press, Martin Eve is Edward Thompson's publisher to this day. In 1947 he was the British Brigade's choirmaster. "We didn't go because it was 'Yugoslavia'," he said. "We went because it was the *most communist place* we could go. I still consider the best of my political education happened in those six or eight weeks. It had to do with discovering collective rather than individual goals. Now the phrase is hedged around with doubts, but then 'building socialism' meant something very simple. And that's what we were doing.

"I went to Bulgaria the following year, and it was markedly less enthusiastic at a deeper level. That pointed up the spontaneity and genuineness of the Yugoslav experience. It was quite difficult to adjust when we came back to Britain. My first memory is of queuing for a bus and feeling the difference: no one spoke to anyone else, let alone greeted strangers or helped each other. Today London still has bomb sites from the Second World War; in 1947 there was an immense amount that needed doing. Filled with enthusiasm for this kind of thing, some of us approached the Ministry of Labour, not as communists of course – under the British-Yugoslav Association auspices. With a little bit of help from government, we said, we could organize a workcamp. The response was totally negative. In the end they said the only task where we could contribute volunteer labour was in processing football pool coupons. It didn't seem the same as building a railway in Bosnia!"

*

My last Bosnian destination lay to the east, in the valley of the Drina, primordial among Balkan boundaries. When Theodosius the Great divided the Roman Empire in 395 AD, the Drina was the junction of its Eastern and Western halves. Later the river's middle course separated Bosnia and Serbia; which it still does.

Much of this course cleaves through gorges, and the little town of Višegrad lies on a rare terrace of level ground where a tributary joins the Drina. Višegrad stands midway on the direct route between Belgrade and Dubrovnik. It was among the first Bosnian towns to fall to the Turks, and in the sixteenth century the enlightened Grand Vizier, Mehmed Pasha Sokolović – himself a Bosnian Christian by birth – ordered the construction of a bridge to span the river at this important juncture, where troops and trade passed constantly. After four centuries the bridge still bears all the traffic on this route; my coach trundled across it and left me in the little square, near where the caravanserai that could accommodate 10,000 camels, mules and horses once stood.

I knew about Višegrad and Mehmed Pasha from the magnificent novel by Ivo Andrić (1892–1975). *The Bridge on the Drina* chronicles the building of the bridge and the events that occurred on and around it, through the ages, until the First World War. The scene never shifts from this remote corner of Bosnia, but the subject is immense: the retreat of Turkish power "like some fantastic ocean tide", and the irruption of modernity. The story is told as if Andrić had stood in this square beside the bridge for those hundreds of years, overhearing conversations, jotting down legends, observing the gyrations of history and human dreams. Nothing escapes his eye and empathy; the attitude of a gypsy executioner impaling his victim is recounted as intimately as the agony of a girl forced into an unwanted marriage.

Andrić's name is Croat and he called himself a Serbian writer; yet he was a Bosnian artist, for the characters who call forth an extra measure of compassion from this impassive creator are the stoical Muslims who fight against Ottoman decadence on one side and infidel backwardness on the other: the vizier who "could never think of Bosnia without a sense of gloom"; the keeper of the caravanserai who "had long become reconciled to the idea that our destiny on this earth lies in the struggle against decay, death and dissolution, and that man must persevere in this struggle, even if it were completely in vain." Andrić much respects this lucid resignation, perhaps because in his own youth he had experienced its opposite: revolutionary idealism. As a member of the Young Bosnia movement, he had been imprisoned by the Austrians in the First World War.

Near the end of *The Bridge on the Drina* a Yugoslav nationalist and a Muslim discuss the future. The date is 1913, and Bosnia is buzzing with rebellious energy. Toma and Fehim meet on the bridge, and Toma does most of the talking. "You will see," he says passionately, "you will see. We shall create a state which will make the most precious contribution to the progress of humanity, in which every effort will be blessed, every sacrifice holy, every thought original and expressed in our own words, and every deed marked with the stamp of our name. We are destined to realize all that the generations before us have aspired to: a state, born in freedom and founded on justice, like a part of God's thought realized here on earth." These yearning generalizations are alien to Fehim, who cannot express why he knows his friend is wrong, so keeps silent. Andrić keeps silent too, condensing his wisdom into an image; as they walk back to town, "one or other of the pair" tosses his cigarette stub over the parapet, and it falls "like a shooting star in a great curve from the bridge into the Drina".

Freed from the responsibilities of fiction, the older Andrić was not optimistic for Yugoslavia. "Our people's lives pass," he wrote, "bitter and empty, among malicious, vengeful thoughts and periodic revolts. To anything else they are insensitive and inaccessible. One sometimes wonders whether the spirit of the majority of the Balkan peoples has not been for ever poisoned and that perhaps they will never again be able to do anything other than suffer violence, or inflict it."

After strolling across the bridge I found a smoky, listless tavern, ordered a coffee and hoped someone would start a conversation. The berets and a lone fez showed that I had picked the Muslim local (Višegrad is two-thirds Muslim). A Turkish word, *sevdah*, evokes the peculiar suspended torpor in Bosnian cafés, especially Muslim cafés in the provinces. *Sevdah* is a condition of the Bosnian soul, a ruminative pessimism brought on by heartbreak or simply by too much staring through grimy windows at cars and cattle passing randomly into and out of vision. At the tail-end of a day measured in cigarettes, coffee grounds, and desultory chat, this randomness can seem devasting, proof of fate's calm ill-will toward all human aspiration.

I sipped coffee and tried to write letters, but *sevdah* or maybe plain tiredness sapped the muscles in my hand. Two characters at another table invited me to join them. One returned to contemplating the wall; the other wanted to talk politics. With a great show of secrecy he pulled out an SDA membership badge and flashed it.

"Why do you support SDA?" I asked.

He drew back in surprise. "Because they're much better than MBO," he said. "SDA is the only party. I still don't know what their programme is, it's true. Somehow they don't say!" He shrugged and rolled his eyes complacently.

His friend revived, and fixed me with a bleary gaze. "Bosnia is my *mother*," he growled slowly. "The Slovenes have *their* mother, the Croats have their Croatia. I have Bosnia and I *love* her so much. There is no other Bosnia in all the world, from Japan to South America, and here is where I want to be, here with my Serb and Croat brothers." The other man winked at me and stage-whispered, "Pay no attention, he's a communist!" The other was too far down to be roused; peering at the ashy, stained tablecloth between his elbows, he murmured, "Life." Pause. "Life."

The waiter stood us a final round of *rakia* and pulled up a chair. When he learned I was a foreigner, he gravely presented me with his cigarette lighter. So I gave him my last pack of cigarettes, because he was fresh out. Now I was out too, so he insisted I have one of mine, and I did the honours with his lighter. Bosnian protocol.

We walked back to the river through empty streets. Night air revived the philosopher. "Pluralism is coming, look" – pointing at election posters on the walls – "and we must keep it when we get it. Tell me, why do French and English and Americans dislike all Muslims?" I didn't try to answer, and he didn't press. "You go to your church and worship Christ, I go to the mosque and worship Allah. There is only one god in the universe. Everyone lives beneath one sun and lives but one life." We had come in sight of the bridge, and suddenly he was worried that its perfection had eluded me. "Built by Sinan in 1571," he said, gesturing at the shadowy arches, "the Turkish Michelangelo, *better* than Michelangelo." Did I know about the great flood of 1896, for instance? He lead us into the hotel above the riverbank; a photo on the lobby wall showed the bridge wholly engulfed by a colossal sleek torrent. The water vanished, the stones remain.

*

They tried so hard. When war came, the Bosnians really tried to keep the fighting out of their republic. At time of writing (early March) they had not failed, despite six months' predictions of impending slaughter. It is nice to think that Bosnian habits of tolerance had weathered the storm. Perhaps they did; yet the non-arrival of war was calculated. The Muslims wanted an independent BiH, and did *not* want to be part of Croatia or, more to the point, of rump Yugoslavia. The Croats preferred a sovereign BiH, but if the Serbs started carving the republic into ethnic portions, or tried to keep it all for their rump federation, they would not stand idly back. The Serbs – or rather, their political leaders, who sang Belgrade's tune – wanted as much as they could get.

In truth, a carve-up would have suited neither side. In a quarter of the constituencies of BiH, no nation has a majority. If Croatia were to walk off with the regions where Croats are a majority, it would leave most Croats behind. As for the Serbs, fully half live outside majority-Serb constituencies.

The result was a stand-off, with the Serb spokesmen threatening a bloodbath whenever the (Muslim) leaders of the republic tried to edge a little closer to independence. These threats were mainly intended for the ears of the European Community; for the Serbs' bottom line was that BiH should not be recognized in its existing borders and with its existing form of government (which guarantees a controlling hand for the Muslims).

The United Nations special envoy, Cyrus Vance, made peace in BiH his first priority. If this was easier to preserve than Vance may have expected, it was in large part because, as autumn dragged into winter, the federal army pulled back from Croatia and then, in February, from Macedonia, Bosnia-Hercegovina was stuffed with soldiers and weapons that had nowhere else to go. The JNA high command promised the government in Sarajevo not to force a political solution; in return, the government treated the army with understanding.

This entente brought a kind of stability. When Serbs boycotted the republic's referendum on independence at the end of February, and then set up roadblocks in Sarajevo in protest at the near-unanimous vote for independence among Muslims and Croats, the army helped defuse the tension. With the UN peacekeeping force of 14,000 about to arrive at its headquarters in Sarajevo, President Izetbegović –

whose maxim throughout had been "If there must be war, better tomorrow than today" – was entitled to a little optimism. "I believe civil war is no longer a threat," he said. "That danger belongs to the past." As for the future, that was at last becoming more clear. International pressure for a solution to the deadlock grew irresistible; in March, the European Community and the United States made plain their intention to recognize BiH as an independent state. The Serb leaders bowed to the inevitable, and dropped their maximal demand to "stay in Yugoslavia". Instead they agreed on 18 March that the republic "would be a state, composed of three consitituent units, based on national principles". This proposal appealed too to Croat radicals. "Cantonization" became the diplomatic buzz-word. It seems so improbable that a Swiss model of anything could be grafted onto Bosnia-Hercegovina; but stranger things have happened here.

The Dark Side of Europe

First stop on the northern route into the province of Kosovo is a ravaged industrial town called Mitrovica, where nitrite deposits carpet the earth like thick frost. Then the landscape flattens into a dusty plain, ringed by a rim of mountains. My bus swept along the arrow-straight road, past men in white felt skullcaps and battered suits, squatting on the verge or tending black buffalo; past the JNA base where tanks are serried in full view like showroom cars. Then down the hill to Prishtinë, capital of Kosovo.

The town appears all at once, filling a hollow in the plain. Rust-red and green towerblocks crowd the view, pushing through a sprawl of concrete and breezeblock, scored by roads and waste ground. When the ethnologist Edith Durham first caught sight of Prishtinë in 1908, she noted the same colours: "red roofs, green trees, and white minarets". Trees and minarets there still are, but less abundantly. In other respects Kosovo and its options have changed little – so little that it stands as the epitome of insoluble problems and answerless questions in south-east Europe.

Drawing her conclusions after that journey, Edith Durham wrote: "The claims of Greek, Bulgar, and Serb in the Balkan peninsula are well known; so are the desires of Austria, Russia, and Italy. But it has been the fashion always to ignore the rights and claims of the oldest inhabitant of the land, the Albanian, and every plan for the reformation or reconstruction of the Near East that has done so has failed." Three years after these words were published the Albanians gained their own state; but Durham's warning still stands. Of the 40 per cent of Albanians who live outside their national state, the vast majority lives in Yugoslavia. At least 70 per cent of this majority are Kosovars – Albanians of Kosovo. They now number some 1.7 million, and when the federation allowed their rights and claims to be rescinded by force in 1989, it set a fateful precedent. A pattern was cast of achieving national goals by unilateral and, when necessary, violent action. The first victim, after the Kosovars, was the federation itself.

The Kosovars took no part in the war of 1991, nor were they

allowed a voice at the peace negotiations organized by the European Community. Whatever form the post-Yugoslav settlement takes in the southern republics, it looks dead set to ignore the Kosovars' wishes; if it does, it will fail.

Kosovo is a small territory, some hundred kilometres square, boxed by the state of Albania to the west, and by Macedonia, Montenegro and Serbia. Or rather, by the rest of Serbia; for Kosovo lies within Serbian borders. This territory (Kosovo in Serbian, Kosova in Albanian) is known to Serbs as the "cradle of Serbdom", and almost all insist it must be integral to any Serbian state, governed by and for Serbs. Kosovars, on the other hand, see the place as home, and they – now 90 per cent of the population – want to live here unmolested, managing their own affairs like any other Yugoslav people.

The problem, apart from Serb extremism, was that the Kosovars were not quite a Yugoslav people. Only Yugoslavs were constitutional nations in the SFRY, so the Kosovars were barred from having their own republic. Before 1968 there was not much demand for a republic. When this demand swelled to a chorus in the '80s, it coincided with the arrival of an aggressive revanchist leadership in Serbia. Indeed the republican movement in Kosovo helped to spark the revival of Serb chauvinism, which the leadership spurred on and exploited – by harassing the Kosovars.

Kosovo's part in the ending of Yugoslavia was complex, but the crisis turns on a simple enough contradiction. One party to the conflict holds that Kosovo patently is not and should not be part of Serbia; the other denies that Kosovo can be anything else.

The effects of the crisis are simple too, dreadfully so. Since Serbia cancelled Kosovo's autonomy, more than eighty Albanians have been killed. Some 75,000 – from surgeons and magistrates to manual labourers – have been sacked from work, sometimes for refusing to sign loyalty pledges or to accept Belgrade's writ, sometimes with no pretext. Albanian-language television, radio and daily press have been shut down. Schools are closed, because teachers refused to implement the "uniform teaching plan and programme of Serbia", which would privilege Serbian language and history above their own and their pupils'. Albanian students are banned from most faculties of the university.

In effect the Kosovars are under occupation, humiliated and terrorised. Wedding guests are stopped by the police and told to hand over their jewellery. Taxi-drivers are waved down and ordered to pay a wad of notes on the spot, or lose their licence. A priest is arrested on public order charges and jailed when police find cassettes of Albanian music (from Tirana) in his possession. Anyone who is not an "honest Albanian" (loyal to Belgrade) lives in fear of dismissal from work, a knock on the door at night, and worse. And the oppressor wants no dialogue with the oppressed; only minimal co-operation, as from livestock or a captive tribe.

*

There are no street signs in Prishtinë, so I gave up trying to find my friends' address on foot and took a taxi. "Are your friends Albanian?" asked the driver, keeping his eyes straight ahead. I nodded. "So you're a journalist," he said neutrally.

We stopped in front of a curving row of apartment blocks. Ragamuffin gypsy boys were selling bananas off a wet cardboard box on the pavement. A horse-drawn wagon passed by, a man in a doctor's white tunic clutching the reins. An elderly BMW rumbled along in the other direction; a rap song blared from its windows: "Get off my back or I'll hit back and you don't want that . . ." A hunched old woman in headscarf and pantaloons led her cow to graze on the litter-strewn verge. In the background a metal rubbish container was in flames. A gang of little boys raced by, yelling "Kill Albanians! Kill Albanians!" at Kosovar girls, who ignored them and concentrated on stepping gingerly through the mud – mud was everywhere. Further away, two armed policemen slouched outside the radio and television centre, now closed. The flower border outside the Grand Hotel was bare and fenced with barbed wire. (Inside the hotel, I later learned, 307 Albanian staff had been sacked and replaced with 107 Serbs and Montenegrins.) After dusk the streets would be almost empty except for packs of feral dogs that roam and scavenge, and silent but for rare bursts of gunfire.

Xhemail was at home. I left my bag with him, and went to keep an appointment with a local Serb journalist. Perhaps she could explain why Kosovo had come to this.

Vesna was afflicted with a snuffly cold; it gave her a suffering, reproachful expression that suited her well. "Believe me, they had everything. No nationality in the world had what they had. Then they wanted even more, in 1981: to secede and join Albania. That was their big mistake," she said bitterly. "Serbia will never let them take Kosovo, because this *is* Serbia."

This "everything" was Kosovo's rights as a member of the federation. The 1946 constitution created an Autonomous Region of Kosovo-Metohija (Kosmet) within the republic of Serbia. One motive was to mete "freedom and equality" to the Kosovars; the other was to clip the wings of Serbia, far the biggest and most populous republic. Not until the '60s, however, did nominal autonomy become substantial; then, in the space of a few years, Kosovo gained far-reaching rights. It was upgraded to the rank of province, like Vojvodina in the north of Serbia. While their "limited sovereignty" left both provinces subordinate to Serbia *de jure*, in practice they were self-governing. To some extent Kosovo even influenced foreign policy: cultural links with Albania were permitted for the first time. The provinces had a share in federal government, and were protected by an all-important clause preventing any alteration to their autonomy unless this were approved by the province itself. In this Vesna was right: the Kosovars were granted extraordinary rights, as a minority that was widely seen by other Yugoslavs – especially by Serbs – as innately separatist, waiting only for a chance to annex Kosovo to the state of Albania. What she didn't add was that Kosovo is an extraordinary case, and not only because the minority is 90 per cent.

The "big mistake" in 1981 was a wave of demonstrations in Prishtinë, led by students. Among mundane demands for better accommodation, they chanted "Kosovo Republic!" and waved placards with slogans supporting Enver Hoxha, the dictator of Albania: "Long Live Marxism-Leninism! Down with Revisionism!", and "Unification of All Albanian Lands!" A state of emergency was declared, paramilitary police arrived with tanks and machine guns. A dozen demonstrators were killed. Belgrade denounced the protesters as counter-revolutionaries and separatists. Mass arrests followed, then purges from the provincial League of Communists. Over the next eight years 584,373 Kosovars – half the adult population – were arrested, interrogated, interned or repri-manded. Seven thousand of these were jailed, hundreds more dismissed from school, university and work.

We were sitting in a Serb café near Vesna's office, a seedy place empty this wet afternoon except for a clutch of red-eyed men getting soused on *rakia*. "Serbs are something special," Vesna was saying. "Nobody likes us. We are like the Jews – truly. And Kosovo is our Jerusalem. You know what the mystery is? Our religion. Orthodoxy has made us masochistic. Read Dostoyevsky, you will understand."

"What about the mass sackings? What do you think of that policy?"

"*No one* was sacked, believe me," she pleaded confidently. "They refused to work, on their leaders' orders. They are primitive people, their way of life is 500 years out of date, and they are manipulated by their leaders, especially by Rugova. A high birthrate is their tactic to dominate here. Ah, you don't know how it was before. Anarchy, it was political anarchy."

"And now?"

"Now . . . it's not good, I know. I think there will be war. Everyone has guns; my colleagues all carry pistols. But it's better for Serbs than it was."

I splashed back to Xhemail's flat through the mud, no wiser as to how Kosovo could be "better" if the police had become highwaymen and war was imminent. I have never been in a more dispiriting and claustrophobic place. The Albanians know they are under siege. The Serbs and Montenegrins appear blindly, vindictively glad that the Albanians have been put in their place. Only a few seem aware that Kosovo's future looks worse than ever, or to care that the current policy cannot be sustained, if only because it is insanely unproductive. More than a fifth of bankrupt Serbia's 1991 budget was absorbed in policing the once autonomous province and subsidizing the importation of Serb and Montenegrin workers, who demand hefty hardship allowances.

Vesna is not an extremist by the standards of Serb political and public opinion. In the late '80s a collective hysteria about Kosovo gripped Serbia and Montenegro. It was an official hysteria, disseminated by politicians, intelligentsia, and media. The Kosovars were accused of every imaginable crime. Almost every printed or spoken mention of Albanians was prefaced with the epithets "separatist terrorist". Mass rallies of Serbs and Montenegrins, transported with grief and yearning for Christly vengeance, demanded a day of judgement. Scholars did their bit by extolling the medieval Serbian empire that allegedly (not actually) met its end here at the battle of Kosovo in 1389, and praising the glorious Serbian monuments that still stand here. The clergy called for Orthodox churches and nuns to be saved from the Muslims. Poets denounced Albanian backwardness and depravity. The bones of Prince Lazar, who led the Serbian army to defeat at the legendary battle, were borne around Serbia as holy relics.

Facts were scarce amid the delirium, but were hardly the point. Truth was a necessary casualty of this mobilization, and its medium was myth. When one Djordje Martinović claimed in 1985 that two Kosovars had raped him with a broken bottle, he became a national martyr, an archetype of Serb suffering and Albanian (Muslim, Ottoman . . .) evil. A poet likened him to the Serb rebels impaled by the Turks of old. In due course the courts and medical examiners agreed the man was unbalanced and his wounds were self-inflicted; but who cared?

A Croat journalist investigated the many allegations that Serb and Montenegrin women were being raped in Kosovo. Records showed no disproportion among Albanian and Slav criminality in the province, and a lower than average number of rapes. Researchers in

Belgrade bore the journalist out; but by the time their dull book of statistics was published in 1990, who cared?

If the official figures proved that hundreds of thousands of refugees had *not* crept over the border from Albania, and hundreds of thousands of Serbs and Montenegrins had *not* been scared into fleeing the province, who cared? There was no separatist movement of any substance, but who cared? The Kosovars' weary insistence that separatism was not the issue, only confirmed their perfidy.

Identical hate-filled, panic-mongering rhetoric was used about Kosovars by gutter journalists and prestigious professionals alike. The Serbian Association of University Teachers and Researchers penned an open letter "to the world public". Titled "The Truth About Genocide in Kosovo and Metohija", the authors concluded that

> Albanian terrorist beasts rampage today in Kosovo and Metohija, attacking and destroying everything that is Serbian. They break into Serbian homes and terrorize the few unfortunate souls still remaining there ... We are compelled to address you at this time since the Albanian terrorists are today attacking the Serb and Montenegrin population in Kosovo and Metohija with all kinds of modern weapons, and with the aid of infiltrated trained terrorists from Albania and other countries, so that blood is even shed, while Serb women and children are evacuated, abandoning their homes to the devastating rage of Albanian terrorists.

They adduced no evidence.

Another document was the petition addressed in 1986 to the federal and Serbian assemblies by 200 leading intellectuals. Claiming that 200,000 people had been forced out of Kosovo since 1966, and that 700 settlements had been "ethnically 'purged' ", the petitioners explained that the "expulsion of the Serb people from Kosovo and Metohija has already been going on for three centuries. Only the protectors of the tyrants have changed: the Ottoman Empire, the Habsburg Monarchy, Fascist Italy and Nazi Germany have been replaced by the Albanian state and the ruling institutions of Kosovo" where "Stalinized chauvinism" has been instituted, fusing "tribal hatred and genocide masked by Marxism". Then the petition gets specific: "Old women and nuns are raped, frail children beaten up, stables built with gravestones, churches and historic holy places desecrated and shamed, economic sabotage tolerated, people forced to sell their property for nothing." Nor does this criminality lack a covert strategic aim: "The first goal is an ethnically pure Kosovo, to be followed by further conquest of Serbian, Macedonian and Montenegrin territories." No attempt is made to warrant the monstrous accusations.

These texts are worth sampling for several reasons. One might say that they, and countless others like them, spelled the end of federalism. Their method prevents any response but total assent or total antagonism. They abolish the criteria by which truth can be known. They create, by reaction, the symptoms which they claim to diagnose. They foreshadow the propaganda that was unleashed by the same institutions in 1991, which accused the Slovenes of shooting their prisoners in the neck, and demonized the Croats as ustaše fascists. Indeed, "propaganda" seems not quite the right term for something that rises so naturally from the cesspool of "unfinished business" that for certain nations at certain times comprises the sweetest proof of identity. Yet propaganda it was; its goal was to create an unstoppable popular momentum for abolishing Kosovo's autonomy. And it succeeded.

Apart from confirming the ghastly standards of Yugoslav journalism, and revealing the paranoid aspect of Serb culture, these successes are witness to something else: the paucity of free, unofficial communication among the peoples of Yugoslavia. My impression is that only a small minority of Yugoslavs had or wanted to have more than superficial knowledge of any nation but their own. Neighbours who nodded and smiled on the stairs never crossed each others' thresholds, never gained each others' trust by exchanging favours or gossip. And why should they? Federalism meant non-interference, after all; but the freedom to stick with one's own kin turned out also to be the freedom to let one's image of other peoples remain blurred by the accumulated dross of prejudice and distrust. This was not a failure of Yugoslavism but of pluralism, of integration. Albanians were always outsiders in Yugoslavia, and Serb polemics were able to amalgamate living Albanian persons into the figure of one terrorist separatist rapist because their audience had no touchstone of experience by which to assess the frenzied indictments served up for months and years on end.

"So what did Vesna have to say?" asked Xhemail, half-trying to keep a sardonic twist out of his voice. Among Albanians the use of the first name does not signify acquaintance; Xhemail does not know Vesna, nor she him, and probably they will never meet. Feeling like a messenger from another world, I summarized her opinions. Xhemail glowered and jumped up from his chair. "And do you believe her?"

"You know I don't but—"

"What you must see", he interrupted, "is that for Vesna and god knows how many more of them, 'political anarchy' is when Albanians are equal with Serbs and Montenegrins. And that's that."

Was this the essence of Serbian rage against Kosovo's autonomy? The more I discovered, the more I agreed with Xhemail that banal chauvinism ("they are a primitive people") underlay the Serbian clamour for order and justice.

The origins of this chauvinism predate 1918 by a millennium and more. The Balkan peninsula was not empty when the Slav tribes invaded in the sixth century; as the great Albanian writer Ismaïl Kadaré recently observed: 'The medieval Balkan epic of the Albanians and the South Slavs is a bloody tale . . . this migration was accompanied by bloodshed, massacres, and atrocities of every kind.'

The Albanians survived, and are autochthonous where they live today. The earliest Ottoman records prove that Albanians inhabited Kosovo in the early 1400s, within a lifespan of the battle of Kosovo, where Catholic Albanians fought and lost alongside the Serbs. In later centuries, as the Serbs drifted northward, the Turks encouraged Albanians to move into Kosovo in greater numbers.

Ottoman administration quartered the Albanian lands. Most Albanians adopted Islam to escape taxation; like the Bosnian heretics, they had no reason not to convert. Albanians had no church or memory of statehood as sources of loyalty. A sizeable minority remained Catholic; a few were Orthodox. Regardless of faith, all social life was regulated by the _kanuni_, the adamantine laws of clan society; and everyone spoke Albanian, a language unto itself.

Bismarck said there was "no such thing as Albanian nationality", and he was right according to the definition of nationality then current; the Albanians were a people without state, government, or sovereignty. National consciousness, however, was on the way, and it waxed as Turkish power waned. When the great powers assigned Albanian areas to Montenegro in 1878 a resistance movement began in western Kosovo. The League of Prizren called for Albanians to unite in the cause of autonomy within the Ottoman Empire. The project failed, but Albanianism had arrived to stay. When the Turks lost the Balkan War of 1912, it suited the great powers to sponsor an Albanian state as a block to Montenegrin and Serb expansionism; the Serbs' ambition for a coastline was thwarted, and they disputed the border well into the '20s.

The Albanians were dissatisfied too, for the new state included less than half the Albanians. The remainder lived in Serbia, Montenegro and Greece, which all wanted Albanian territory but not Albanians. When Serbian troops occupied Kosovo in 1912, to liberate it from the Albanians who had just liberated it from the Turks, much blood was shed. After the First World War Kosovo was allotted to Yugoslavia rather than to Albania. The Kosovars again revolted and were again crushed.

Between the world wars Yugoslav Albanians were treated as a nuisance. The Serb-dominated government denied the existence of "national minorities in our southern regions", while conducting secret diplomacy with Turkey to achieve a final solution by deporting all Albanians to Anatolia. Albanian lands became the wild west of the triune kingdom, offering rich pickings for smart Slavs. Some 65,000 Serb colonists settled in Kosovo alone; more than 200,000 Albanians were removed from the kingdom. When they invaded in 1941, the Axis powers knew the value of anti-Serbism among Albanians; by annexing most of them to a Great Albanian puppet state, with their own cultural rights, the Italians ensured that resistance was exceedingly weak. Besides, partisan actions were organized by local Serbs and Montenegrins, the perennial enemies, in the name of a state that Albanians loathed, and of an ideology that meant nothing to them. In April 1941 the Communist Party organization in Kosovo numbered only twenty Albanians among its 270 members; a pro-fascist movement called *Balli kombëtar* (National Front) was much more popular.

In November 1941 an Albanian Communist Party was launched at the initiative of the CPY, which hoped to win the support of Yugoslav Albanians by offering the example of their kin over the border waving the red flag as they fought the fascists. But nothing persuaded the Albanians to trust the Yugoslavs. Early in 1945 thousands of Kosovars rebelled, provoked by rough treatment of collaborators and the innocent, and partly by the dashing of their hopes of incorporation into Albania. Kosovo was declared a war zone. Some Kosovar partisans, until then loyal soldiers of Tito, refused to assist the pacification, which was violent and prolonged.

Relations with the rest of the federation could not have started on a worse footing. The hollow autonomy of Kosovo-Metohija did not compensate Albanians for being divided four ways – between Kosmet, southern Serbia, Montenegro and Macedonia – and being denied national status.

Through the next two decades matters did not improve; in the mid 1950s the security services declared a state of emergency in Kosmet. Predictably, rebellious Kosovars came to idealize Albania, ruled by the Stalin-worshipping dictator Enver Hoxha; so their nationalism took the weird form of anti-revisionist (i.e. anti-Titoist) Stalinism.

The man responsible for police tyranny in Kosmet was Interior Minister Ranković, a Serb. (He is still a diabolical figure to Kosovars; people who weren't born when Ranković fell from power in 1966 told me about the mansion near Peć where he exercised *droit de seigneur* with Albanian brides.) Policy changed after 1966 and accelerated after 1968 when protesters in Prishtinë demanded a

Kosovo Republic – "KR". The province got its own administration, legislature, militia, police and supreme court – everything short of republican status. Albanians were given their quota of jobs. Prishtinë got a university, Albanian became an equal language in schools and media, and the Albanian flag, stamped with the Yugoslav star, was legalized. The Institute of Albanology, shut down in the 1950s, was reopened.

No effort is needed to imagine the resentment stirred among Serbs and Montenegrins, who had monopolized power and privileges in Kosovo. Certainly injustices were committed: one hears of honest Serb managers supplanted by incompetent Kosovars. Doubtless, too, some Kosovars in villages took the chance to settle old scores. A list of Serbian grievances in Kosovo was suppressed in 1977 – partly at the behest of the provincial leadership, which turned a blind eye to cases of Albanian chauvinism. But the local bureaucrats did the bidding of the federal powers, which, so long as Tito was alive, forbade any questioning of Kosovo's status.

In other words, real autonomy was imposed communistically – undemocratically, insensitively, and corruptly. Orders arrived from on high, for implementation by apparatchiks. But the intention to let the Kosovars become political subjects in Kosovo was valid and positive. Unfortunately, Socialist Yugoslavia set about the job the only way it knew.

Kosovo was always the poorest, most backward part of Yugoslavia. Centuries of Ottoman rule and twenty years of Serbianization left it, in 1945, without so much as a kilometre of asphalted road. Modernization had to start from scratch, and while the pattern and terms of investment prevented Kosovo from accumulating capital and developing its own professional class, still, the province advanced in giant strides. The post-Ranković reforms then matched the material gains with political and cultural rights.

And here's the rub. Any dialectician could have foreseen that the concessions of "limited sovereignty" must sharpen the hunger for more. By creating the space and tools for an Albanian intelligentsia, the federation gave a hostage to fortune; for the new intellectuals might not dance to the federal tune. In 1981, when the demonstrations happened, Prishtinë university had 26,000 students: more than one in ten of the town population. These students graduated with no prospect of work in their field; for Kosovo still squatted at the top or bottom of statistical tables. The most densely populated region, it had the highest demographic growth in all Europe, the highest rate of unemployment in Yugoslavia, the lowest average wages, and the highest ratio both of students and of illiterates.

Adding to the ferment, the educated class of Kosovars was

"nationalized" in the 1980s no less rapidly than the same people in other republics. Resurgent Serbia lifted its shaggy head, looked south, and beheld an increasingly articulate and confident community. The villages might still be dirt poor and backward, but in Prishtinë the reforms had produced, for the first time in history, a generation of people like my friends Xhemail, a journalist and aspiring philosopher; Mufa, rock musician extraordinaire; Jusuf, a medical student; Arta, poet and interpreter. But everyone knew that political progress was precarious and revocable as long as Kosovo was a province; hence the demand for KR.

In Serb nationalists' eyes, the spectacle of Kosovo outgrowing its rôle as province was outrageous. The Albanians were getting too big for their boots and must be cut down. Traditionally, they were manual workers, itinerant handymen, greengrocers, miners. When anti-Kosovar agitprop called for equality as well as order to be restored to the "anarchic" province the outspoken historian Rexhep Qosja commented: "The final aim is a kind of equality the Albanians have known only too well: equality with the woodcutters, coalmen and peasants who were beaten by gendarmes whether they said 'Good morning, sir' or whether they didn't."

Vowing to end the "genocide" and restore the errant province to the bosom of Serbia, the Serbian régime under Slobodan Milošević began by passing racist laws. Restrictions were placed on land-sales to Albanians and on the movement of people in Kosovo. The legal code was altered to treat certain common crimes as anti-state activity if the victim's nationality differed from the perpetrator's.

Constitutional amendments were drafted to neuter the two provinces' autonomy. Before these could be promulgated the provinces had to give their approval, and this required doctoring their leaderships. By the autumn of 1988 Milošević was ready to move. In October the League of Communist chiefs in Vojvodina were ousted. On 17 November the committee of the LC of Kosovo met to discuss (that is, to accept) the resignations, tendered under Serbian pressure, of its president and her predecessor, Azem Vllasi, who now sat on the federal executive committee of the League of Communists.

Every soul in the province knew what was at stake, and there was open resistance for the first time since 1981. On the morning of the 17th, 3,000 miners set off from Trepča, a centre of worker militancy, to walk the forty kilometres to Prishtinë. They camped outside the headquarters, along with students and children who had joined the march. Other demonstrations were held across Kosovo, to no avail: the committee buckled. The federal League did its bit by sacking

Vllasi and reiterating support for the constitutional changes. Now just the approval of the Kosovo assembly was needed.

Again the miners intervened. On 20 February 1989, 1,300 of them announced a hunger strike until their demands were met: "no retreat from the principles of the 1974 constitution"; resignation of the new placemen on the committee; democratic debate of any constitutional change to Kosovo's status; and an end to "the discriminatory policies of Slobodan Milošević".

The hunger strike was front-page news throughout the federation; support for the miners and their cause was voiced in Slovenia and Croatia. But again the republics signed on Serbia's dotted line; on 26 February the federal assembly approved the proposed amendments, as well as "special measures" for the province.

"Special measures" meant tanks patrolling the streets of Prishtinë and helicopters drumming overhead as the assembly considered the amendments. Before the vote each member was interrogated by the state security police. In the voting, 175 supported the amendments, ten were against, two abstained. In effect, the assembly had consigned itself to oblivion. Protests began across Kosovo: mostly teenagers of both sexes – the stone-throwing Kosovo intifada, treated to tear gas, water cannon and bullets. (Among their slogans: "Better the grave than slavery", the Serbian anti-fascist cry from 1941.) Six days later twenty-four Kosovars were dead (official statistic) or 100 (Reuters) or 140 (Ljubljana Radio). On 28 March the Serbian assembly ratified the amendments, with the support of its Albanian delegates.

Why did the other republics accept Serbia's flagrant bullying and violations of statutes? Montenegro's leadership needed no persuading; it had been cleaned out in the same fashion as the provinces'. Macedonia complied because it too favoured tough treatment of Albanians. The leadership of Bosnia-Hercegovina was weakened by scandal and corruption. Slovenia and Croatia, on the other hand, were gulled; the kickback for abetting Serbia's assault would, they hoped, be Serbian tolerance of controversial steps that they wanted to take in their own republics.

In the event their cynicism was repaid in kind. The Milošević régime's appetite for centralization was unsated; far from viewing more kindly the western republics' calls to reorganize the state on a looser confederal basis, Serbia and its ally Montenegro refused point blank. And their refusal now carried more weight in the federal apparatus, where Serbia retained the provinces' quota of representation, using the extra muscle to push its own interests.

The republics had persuaded themselves that Serbia would calm down once its heart's desire was granted. Albanians were the third largest nation in Yugoslavia, after Serbs and Croats, but they had no allies; no republic supported them, and nobody liked them. They were expendable.

What nobody grasped at the time is that federal Yugoslavia could not outlive Kosovo's autonomy for long. Perhaps it is fitting that a non-Slav people was so fateful for this misnomer of a state, yet the most helpless victims of this demise – discounting perhaps the Croatian dead – are this same people, the Kosovars. They alone stood four-square in the path of Serbian ambitions, and only they could have been sacrificed with so little compunction by republics which were in no other sense Serbia's allies.

*

As Serbia squared up for its constitutional mugging of Kosovo and the other republics cheered or watched, the Albanians' reaction was astonishing.

Their former apparatchiks fast became superfluous. Belgrade needed a handful of "honest Albanians" to decorate the League of Communists and to fill seats in the federal assembly and federal presidency. The remainder was discarded or tactfully withdrew.

I encountered one of the cast-offs, quite by chance. My friend Besim and I were sitting in a café when a well dressed, jowly man at another table caught our eye and approached. This was Besim's uncle, who had, I knew, resigned his membership of Kosovo's presidency in November 1989 – months after the end of autonomy.

"Wouldn't you like to know *why* I resigned?" he asked shyly, when Besim introduced us. "I could no longer accept the policy of Belgrade towards Kosovo. Then I came to see that the real problem lay with communism itself, and I resigned from the League of Communists too. I saw, later than other people perhaps, for I was a fanatical communist, that they [sic] had made three principal mistakes. By taking private property from individuals, they took away their motivation to work. Self-management made a cleaner equal to a doctor, so it meant bad management. Lastly, non-alignment meant cultivating profitless relations with African and Asian countries. Far from Europeanizing those countries, we Africanized and Asianized Yugoslavia."

A clean sweep! "But", I asked, "did Yugoslav communism change so much within one year that a 'fanatic' could resign from the presidency and the League?"

"Yes it changed," he said, "it lost all its power." I still don't know whether he misunderstood my question or understood it better than I did myself.

"What do you think of what I've said?" he asked, looking me in the eye at last. What ran through my head as I produced, shamelessly, the requisite murmur of grateful surprise, was something Ervin in Slovenia had told me about the miners at Trepča. When they planned their famous hunger-strike of February 1989, Ervin visited the miners and saw them shaking their heads and muttering: "We'll be screwed by the Albanians, it's the Albanians who'll do us in, we know it . . ."

All that Besim's uncle and his kind could do for Kosovo in its extremity was to get out of the way. The work of rallying people and articulating resistance fell to new organizations, principally the Democratic League of Kosovo, which called for open dialogue and peaceful solutions. By the end of 1990 the DLK claimed 700,000 members and its leader, the tousle-headed, dishevelled Ibrahim Rugova, was a hero to the Albanians, a wolf in sheep's clothing to Serbs, and a household name everywhere.

I visited Dr Rugova at his headquarters in the Writer's Union, a humble shack behind the football stadium. He is a literary critic by profession, trained at the Sorbonne in Paris, and the public image of the DLK is very much identified with his manner, which is low-voiced and undogmatic. "Serbia is determined to pretend Albanians are separatist," he said hoarsely, lighting the first in a chain of Dunhills. "It isn't true. The DLK is accepted around the world as democratic, not separatist. We want Kosovo to be part of a Yugoslav federation, and participate in European integration."

Thanks in large part to Rugova, Kosovo has won many tokens of international support. He has toured Western capitals, and is particularly persuasive at the European Parliament. Yet this backing is rhetorical; if the Euro-MPs and the parliaments of Austria and Belgium condemn human rights abuses in Kosovo, so what? The Council of Europe's commission to Yugoslavia in October 1990 acknowledged that Kosovo was an internal Serbian matter when it reported "problems with minorities" in "some parts" of the federation, as there are in "nearly every European state". President Milošević blithely offers Northern Ireland as a parallel; Dr Rugova points out that even the Basques in Spain have more rights than his people.

A third comparison, even more dismal, occurs to me: Tibet. While China cites ancient history to justify "reuniting" Tibet with "the great family of the motherland" (by invading it, colonizing it and laying waste its culture), Britain, for instance, readily recognizes Tibet's "autonomy" and speaks in weasely terms of China's "special responsibility". Like the Dalai Lama, Dr Rugova lacks everything but good intentions, the love of his people, goodwill where this doesn't make a difference, and implacable enemies where he needs goodwill. Like him again, he has a long-term strategy that twins non-violent resistance at home with campaigning abroad on a platform of human rights.

This is pragmatic, since as long as Serbia denies there is a deadlock in Kosovo, the DLK's and other groups' efforts to break the deadlock will count for nothing. Yet there is nothing inevitable about their non-violence. No less than the Serbs and Montenegrins, Albanians have a tradition of armed revolt. Thousands of Albanians in royal Yugoslavia joined guerrilla bands to attack law courts and trains, terrorize officials, and rustle the colonists' cattle on a grand scale. Today, too, there are extremists waiting for the signal to start an uprising.

Dr Rugova explained their non-violence in terms of patience rather than pacifism. "Our political secret is to combine traditional and current thinking. Fighting was always the last resort for Albanians. Now, too, we have learned that non-violence is the modern European preference."

With nothing to lose, and no interlocutors among Serbian political parties, the Kosovars' minimum demand escalated. On 7 September 1990 a meeting of all independent groups – old dissidents and ex-apparatchiks, democrats and traditionalists – gathered to constitute the Republic of Kosovo. Like desperate illusionists, the Kosovars began to act as if their republic really existed. They boycotted the Serbian election, which returned Milošević and his Serbian Socialist Party to power with a mandate for their policy of restoring the pre-1941 status quo, when Kosovo had been a district of Serbia, and was no more autonomous than the Bantustans of South Africa. Milošević began planning the recolonization of Kosovo-Metohija (as the Serbian media now called the province).

Puzzled, I asked Xhemail why they had not taken the chance to send their best people to make a racket in the Belgrade parliament; after all, Kosovo has more than 20 per cent of Serbia's population; even forcing the government to silence its legal representatives would be useful. He insisted they had no alternative: "We are open to all solutions except one: to be under Serbia. For this is Kosovo, not Serbia. This new Serbian constitution says that everyone in Serbia is equal as a citizen. Well," he rolled his eyes, "I'm not equal *because* I'm Albanian. We ignore their new constitution, their election, everything – there is no way to accept the Serbian rules of the game."

It has taken the iron discipline of Albanian tradition to sustain a strategy of non-violence; the patriarchs of the chief families in Kosovo decreed that no Serb or Montenegrin would be touched, and none has been.

This discipline is visible everywhere in the deference of young to old, female to male. Xhemail is twenty-five; he lives with his parents, as all young people do, and gives his wages, paltry as they are, to his father. His mother asks permission to visit her family, out of town. Hospitality is sacred, and guests are lavished with the best a household can offer. There is nothing cold about this propriety, no implied superiority. To me it was wonderful and oppressive; it cocoons an outsider with the warm human contact of an immense extended family that seems to connect every Kosovan hamlet like an organism. Inside this family no one is off limits, no one neglected, and the enemy of each is the enemy of all.

Until this century Albanians had never – except for a handful of high-fliers in the Ottoman hierarchy – lived in a state they accepted as their own. Their ethos evolved as self-preservation against a hostile world, and it gears them for endurance. One of Ismaïl Kadaré's best novels chronicles the life of a city in wartime. The city is Gjirokastër in the Second World War but it stands as an emblem of all Albanian lands through history. "At dusk the city, which through the centuries had appeared on maps as a possession of Romans, Normans, Byzantines, Turks, Greeks and Italians, now watched darkness fall as part of the German empire. Utterly exhausted, dazed by the battle, it showed no sign of life." Tender life does pulse within the carapace of "ancient stones", folded safely away, awaiting better times.

In Kosovo today, no one can predict better times. Wearing his philosopher's hat, Xhemail observed, one evening as we watched a venomous news report on television about separatist terrorists, that "verbal violence in the Balkans *entails* physical violence". Mufa the rock musician chipped in: "Playing with fire – that's politics in the Balkans. From outside it looks too crazy, but the fire is real, and so is the dynamite stacked all around."

How many years will it be until verbal solutions entail real solutions? Obsessed with what has happened to them, Xhemail and his friends cast around for a *deus ex machina*. Could Kosovo be a United Nations protectorate, like Namibia? Might the European Community take a decisive stand for Kosovars' rights? It was painful to answer such questions honestly, and sometimes I equivocated, ashamed that Europe ignored these shipwrecked missionaries of the "modern European preference" for non-violence and dialogue, and somewhat haunted by Ervin's breezy cynicism: "This Gandhian trip of theirs is picturesque but it won't do. A few thousand dead might have secured their autonomy. Now they'll have to shoot their way out of Serbia or learn to put up with it."

Meanwhile the crisis suffocated the community, forcing it to batten down. Cultural life more or less ceased, pluralism withered in the bud, Prishtinë became a cauldron. Under such pressure, I wondered, will Kosovar traditions round on the new, democratic ideas that arrived here in the last twenty years, and devour them? In Kadaré's novel, two unmarried teenagers caught kissing in an air-raid shelter, during a bombardment, are hounded to their deaths by scandalized elders . . .

One remarkable achievement in overcoming bad tradition suggests I may be too pessimistic. As late as the mid-1980s, blood feuds in Kosovo threatened the lives of as many as 17,000 people. The number of feuds is much smaller – one feud can implicate all the adult males in a family. Since 1990 a concerted effort has been made by enlightened students and Albanologists to stop blood vengeance. At great open-air ceremonies, several hundred feuding families forgave each other and vowed not to perpetuate the cycle of revenge. The reconciliations continue, despite official displeasure; for the authorities see them as proof of dangerous homogenization.

Arta the poet took me to see the poorest quarter of Prishtinë. "Come to Vranjevc," runs a line in one of her songs, "the dark side of Europe." Vranjevc looks like a *favela*. Youths from this warren of shacks and unpaved lanes have nothing to lose by confronting the bullets and tear gas; since the demonstrations of 1989 it has gained a second name – *kodra e trimave*, hill of the brave.

This quarter is treated as a no-go area by Serbs and Montenegrins. I heard no Serbo-Croatian and saw no uniforms here, though it was difficult to see anything in the late afternoon murk. We picked our way along the fences, through puddles and mud. The first man we met, making his way home, invited us for a coffee. Behind the fence, a neat path of paving stones set in the mud led to a tiny two-room dwelling. A slight, gaunt-faced man in his forties, Hashim has lived here twenty years; he and his wife have nine children. We took off our shoes and were shown into the guest room. The walls of whitewashed hardboard glistened with damp. The spartan furnishings were arranged with care: two low settees separated by a low table with a patterned cloth. A handbag, decorated with a scrap of lace, hung from a nail near a poster of Shkurte Fejza, Kosovars' favourite folk singer, cross-dressed as a legendary warrior.

Hashim had been sacked from his labouring job after twenty-eight years. He was one of 5,000 laid off without explanation. His neighbour, who joined us, had been dismissed two months before from his job as a hospital porter, along with 350 others, from doctors to cleaners, all Albanian. The state pension is 700 dinars per month: not enough to keep Hashim's family in bread. So how did they eat?

He shrugged: one way or another, and neighbours help when they can. Fuel is a bigger problem: last year his neighbour gave Hashim a lift into south Serbia, where he foraged enough wood to last the winter. This year, though . . . He shrugged again.

His wife (she wasn't introduced by name) brought a tray of coffee and apples. Hashim had accepted our cigarettes and now offered his own. The sun had set, and the room seemed suddenly colder and damper in the light of its single bulb: I inhaled hot smoke gratefully, wondering how they survived. "Are all your neighbours as patient as you?" I asked crassly. Yes, said both men, of course they are. Without patience we'd be destitute or dead. Our hopes lie with Rugova – who knows where we'd be without him? As for the future, well, if things don't get better, they'll get worse.

Arta whispered in my ear: "You see, patience is a sign they're *still alive*." As we rose to go, Hashim rebuked us for not touching the apples – we should take them to eat as we walked . . . The children had arranged our shoes on the doormat; they crowded silently round to help us and watch, eyes like saucers in the dusk, as we left.

*

Stripped of propaganda and paranoia, what remains of Serbian claims that Kosovo belongs to less than 10 per cent of its population, and that 90 per cent must live here on sufferance?

"Historical right," said Mufa the musician. "That's not their main argument, it's their only one." Because medieval Kosovo had belonged to Serbia, and again from 1912 to 1918, Serbia is eternally entitled to possess the territory. This mystical notion of right goes unchallenged by Serbia's own democrats and intellectuals.

It was impossible to feel the weight of this right in Prishtinë, so I went to Gračanica to see the church. Everyone agrees that Gračanica is sublime, a glittering gem in the treasury of Serbian medieval architecture. I inspected the intricate patterning of the tawny bricks and stones, and the tiny dome riding its cross of cupolas. I admired the dense geometrical harmony of the whole. Inside, I could appreciate the famous frescoes of King Milutin (who built the church around 1320), his queen Simonida, the family tree of the Serbian dynasty. Orthodox churches cherish mystery, and Gračanica has mystery enough to spare; it dwells in the antique gloom, and in the candle-light playing on the frescoes and around the massive pillars, bigger than the spaces between them. Yet the mystery was tainted. Only that week the television news had shown četniks – armed Serb irregulars – taking an oath of loyalty in the churchyard.

I tried Prizren, a market town near the Albanian border. In the

Serbian empire Prizren was Carigrad, their Constantinople. "Where is Prizren, the glorious city?" asks the old song. "Where are the imperial palaces? Where is Dušan's golden age which wonders wrought? Kosovo, Kosovo has swallowed all." It is a lovely town; history that was torn out of Prishtinë is intact here. Yet it is Turkish beauty and Albanian history that strike the visitor. The perfectly proportioned bridge over the Bistrica stream, Sinan Pasha's mosque, mortared with goat hair and eggwhite, adorned with frescoes of fruit and flowers like a Palladian villa – these are Turkish. The museum of the League of Prizren is a shrine of Albanian nationhood. Imperial palaces there are none.

Orthodox shrines abound in Kosovo, and anyone can understand Serbian sorrow that the territory around them is no longer populated by Serbs. Yet these monuments are symbols of Serbs' "historical right" to Kosovo; the basis of that right is even more mystical. It is a battle fought – and lost – here six centuries ago.

It was time to visit the battlefield. I retraced my route to Prishtinë, then hitched a ride to Gazimestan, north of the town. This is it: the "field of blackbirds", site of Prince Lazar's defeat in 1389. A dirt track curves from the road into empty moorland, where a grey stone tower stands on a rising. A café, fenced with barbed wire, is the only other building.

Other than the wind, only crows broke the silence, clattering and screaming against a crimson sunset. The rim of far mountains darkened. Nature was giving me the works.

No eye-witness accounts of the momentous battle have survived, and the earliest reports indicate much uncertainty about the outcome. Some claimed glorious victory for the Christian army, led by Serbs and comprising Croats, Hungarians, Vlachs and Albanians. What confused the chroniclers on both sides is that both leaders had died on the field, Lazar conventionally and Sultan Murad against the run of play. Adding to the confusion, both sides appeared to retreat after the battle.

In truth the Ottomans had won, but Serbia did not finally succumb for a further seventy years. Lazar had ruled a declining empire – the golden age was long past by 1389 – and the field of blackbirds was one in a series of defeats.

Over the centuries this truth was woven into a tapestry of myth, and in the process transformed into something rich and strange. It began with the sermons and hagiographies written to commemorate Lazar. Casting the story of his defeat in a messianic mould, the monastic writers made a cult of the prince as a martyr who sacrificed himself for Serbia's sake. Far from belittling Serbia's defeat at Kosovo, as one might expect, the emerging mythic version made the defeat responsible for all the subsequent sufferings of its people. "Kosovo, Kosovo has swallowed all." This defeat was a measureless cataclysm, shattering the empire, dividing the people and leading them into captivity.

The monastic texts become the substance of popular ballads. Handed down to each generation, these epic poems were the cultural patrimony of Serbdom. They inculcated a reverence for the defeat, and for the heroes of Kosovo: holy Lazar; Miloš Obilić, who infiltrates the Ottoman camp and kills Murad; Vuk Branković, the traitor who abandons the Serbs for the Turks; the Kosovo Girl, who tends the dying warriors with wine and water; the Mother of the Jugovići, whose nine sons are all killed. These figures became archetypes of Serbian virtue and villainy.

At the heart of the messianic myth is Lazar's choice. On the eve of battle, says the epic, the Mother of God offered Lazar the choice of a heavenly or an earthly empire. If he wants the latter, he should drive the Turks away. If the former, he should prepare himself and his "seven and seventy thousand soldiers" for destruction. Lazar weighed the options:

> "Kind God, what shall I do, how shall I do it?
> What is the empire of my choice?
> Is it the empire of heaven?
> Is it the empire of earth?
> And if I shall choose the empire,
> and choose the empire of the earth,
> the empire of earth is brief,
> heaven is lasting and everlasting."
> And the Emperor chose the empire of heaven
> above the empire of the earth.

To a non-believer, of course, this looks like a cheat, for it merges the contradictory satisfactions of being the winner and the loser; the most humiliated, the most suffering, and also the best. To a believer, the totality of loss bore the promise of restoration – provided that the Serbs did not forsake their faith. The loss can be redeemed, but only if it is never forgotten. If it is mourned wholeheartedly enough, unceasingly, and if Serbs never comfort themselves by falsely lessening the tragedy of Kosovo, then the seed of that distant defeat will bloom into something more wonderful than victory.

When the new intelligentsia of independent Serbia discovered, in the nineteenth century, that the Kosovo myth had persisted among ordinary folk during centuries of oppression, it made a latter-day, secular cult of those archetypal heroes and their defeat. Plays were written about Obilić. Vidovdan, or St Vitus's Day, the day of the battle became a national anniversary. Philosophers pondered "the

Kosovo idea", "the Kosovo commitment", "Obilićean thought", "the Vidovdan duty". Newspapers admonished politicians for betraying "the Kosovo ethos".

The myth served the ideology of Serbian unitarism. Bosnia should be joined to Serbia not for mere expansionist reasons, but as a sacred duty to avenge and reverse the injustice of Kosovo. Because Kosovo was the ultimate good cause for Serbs, no sacrifice was too great for it. When the Serbian army marched south, in the Balkan War of 1912, illiterate soldiers knelt and kissed the soil of Kosovo, and were surprised to be ordered on; Kosovo was regained, what need to go further?

The myth has the true Christian disdain for middle ground; when aroused, it drives its believers to incredible feats; in slacker periods, it encourages chauvinism and boastful whingeing. It turns anyone who disagrees or doubts into an enemy and an inferior being. By definition, no evil can be done in its name (perish the blasphemous notion!), and its roots are secure among the people; thus the myth can be abused by populist leaders for their own ends.

As a pre-modern myth of identity, it can be bent to totalitarian ends. A hundred years ago, the Kosovo idea gave a metaphysical lining to the Yugoslav idea. "For more than five centuries Kosovo was the banner of our national pride, the sum and substance of our national unity", wrote the Yugoslav Committee in 1916. (The Croat sculptor Meštrović planned a gargantuan temple for Gazimestan, bigger than St Peter's in Rome.) But this did not last; it is a Serbian myth, and when Serbian interest clashed with other Yugoslavs' interests, it was pressed into the service of a bad, imprisoning cause, and the faithful Serbs did not even realize what had happened.

It is no accident that the kingpins of Serb culture today are obsessed with Kosovo. The aesthetic consequences are tacky – papier-mâché medievalism – and the political consequences are disastrous. Far from helping the nation to understand its identity, these intellectuals chorus the ancient lamentations, encouraging their congregation's hopeless clamour for an earthly as well as the heavenly kingdom.

When Matija Bećković, president of the Serbian Union of Writers, averred that Kosovo would be Serbian even if not one Serb lived here, was he serving Obilićean thought? When Dobrica Ćosić, the supreme ideologist of Serb nationalism, declared that "Albanians decompose the ethnic and social structure of Yugoslavia", was he advancing the Kosovo ethos? Do the thugs of *Božur*, a Serb-Montenegrin organization, obey the Vidovdan duty when they terrorize Kosovar peasants? Was Milošević true to the Kosovo commitment on the six hundredth anniversary of the battle, when he assured half a million Serbs on this spot, some of them sporting fake medieval armour, others dressed as the Kosovo Girl, that "the Serbs throughout their history never conquered or exploited anybody else"?

The answers are all yes. If Serbia is to start living in the present, it must lay its beloved myth to well-earned rest in the graveyard of folklore, and return Kosovo to its people, all the people who live there.

Montenegro: 'Favoured Above Millions'

Autumn dusk fell as we hauled over the hills north of Peć and tipped into Montenegro, chasing our headlamp blaze all the way to Titograd.

It was the last coach of the day, and almost empty by the time we stopped at a roadside restaurant near the Morača gorge. One passenger crossed the silent road and rinsed his face in a stream tinkling down from steep meadows. A scarved Muslim woman lifted her solemn child from the coach and followed her husband into the building. I walked around the coach, exhaling the last stale air of Prishtinë from my lungs, looking up at the immense blueblack silhouettes that blocked out the stars on either side of the valley.

In Kosovo I had grown used to an atmosphere of murmuring intrigue and cowed alertness in public places. Here, men looked up from their beer to see new arrivals, but not to trap and judge their reactions. I relaxed. Another republic, another country.

Titograd, capital of the republic, was quiet as a village. Impatient to reach the mountains, I hitched a ride to Cetinje and left the lights of the plain behind.

I awoke in a crater of green, surrounded by grey mountains. This was Cetinje, capital of old Montenegro, Tennyson's "rock-throne of freedom". My first goal was the highest of these peaks: Lovčen, already flushed with morning sun – a golden reef shouldering the clouds.

Again I was lucky, and soon hitched a lift into the wilderness of the Njeguši range. The road climbed like a staircase. Only a rare stone cottage with a vegetable patch showed a human presence.

Lovčen is visible from far and wide, but the point about it, the reason why it stands as the emblem, the very hub of Montenegro, is not its scale (1,749 metres) but its supreme place in Montenegrin identity. For Lovčen is the mausoleum of Montenegro's paragon, Rade Petrović (1813–51), the *Vladika* (Prince-Bishop) Petar II Petrović-Njegoš, known universally as Njegoš.

This mountain haunted Njegoš's imagination, and he asked to be

buried in a simple chapel on the summit. The chapel was eroded by
the storms that buffet the peak, and it had to be restored in 1879.
When Montenegro capitulated to the Austrians in the First World
War, one of the victors' first acts was to exhume the Vladika and
carry him back down to Cetinje. The job was clumsily done; for
years to come sharp-eyed pilgrims found stray bones beside the
path. In 1925 the remains were carried back up the mountain for
interment in a new chapel. Aleksandar Karadjordjević, King of the
Serbs, Croats and Slovenes, officiated. Since Aleksandar's grandfather was King Nikola Petrović of Montenegro, his presence was a
matter of family piety as well as homage. But it was more than this;
a parable of power was enacted when the living Karadjordjević – a
Serb – buried the greatest of the Petrovići. The new Yugoslav
kingdom could not accommodate two dynasties; grandfather
Nikola had died in exile in 1921, and his descendants were
banished from their native rocks.

Visitors can drive almost to the summit, then climb the last
hundred metres through a stone gallery. The first school party of the
day was still negotiating the hairpin bends far below as I emerged
onto the crest.

It is the airiest of burial-sites. The sky wheels overhead, wind
rustles in your ears, clouds drift and merge at your feet. The African
immensity of the view streams away in every direction. Titograd is a
smudge to the east; to the north-west, the bay of Kotor is etched into
the coast like blue satin. The hazy ranges to the south are Albania.
Italy was somewhere over the western horizon.

From Lovčen one can survey almost all of Old Montenegro – the
fabled Montenegro that Njegoš ruled, that Tennyson and Pushkin
sang, that Gladstone eulogized as a lone beacon of freedom, where
Christian warriors defied the Ottoman Empire. It was a realm that
belongs to legend, not to real history; even standing here, I could
hardly believe that old Montenegro was more than a figment of
Turk-hating politicians or pan-Slavic poets.

Yet its reality is a matter of record. Until 1878, it was the only land
of free Slavs outside Russia. It measured some thirty by sixty
kilometres, and in Njegoš's day, numbered fifty or a hundred
thousand souls. Njegoš ruled as bishop, judge, legislator, governor,
and commander-in-chief. He was a crack shot, and once led an
assault on Podgorica (renamed Titograd in 1946). He was the
greatest poet yet seen in these lands, and his *Gorski vijenac* (The
Mountain Wreath) is the greatest work of Yugoslav literature. He
stood over two metres tall, and was extraordinarily handsome.

He had fascinated me since I read his last will and testament, in
which the conventional Orthodox thanks to God are transmuted

into a hymn, serene and half pagan – a valediction to the world as imagined, surely, from memories of Lovčen:

> Thanks be to Thee, O Lord, for having deigned to bring me to the shore of this Thy world, for having been pleased to nourish me in the rays of this, Thy wondrous sun. Thanks be to Thee, O Lord, for having favoured me above millions on earth in soul and body. Ever since my childhood, as often as Thine unattainable majesty has moved me to hymns of divine rapture and awe before Thy great beauty, so often have I beheld in horror and bewailed man's wretched lot. Thy word has created all from nothing. To Thy law are all things subject. Man is mortal and must die.
>
> With hope I come before Thy sacred altar whose radiant glory I glimpsed even from the shore which my mortal steps have measured. I go calmly at Thy call, either to abide in eternal sleep in Thy bosom or to glorify Thee forever in deathless choirs.

A genial host, Njegoš received a string of inquisitive visitors. Their memoirs vouch for the sensational strangeness of the Vladika and his minuscule principality. What these foreigners underestimated – and Montenegrins themselves usually kept quiet about – was the rôle of ordinary politics in keeping that independence. From the start, Montenegro's leaders had to play off the surrounding powers to preserve their autonomy.

By the end of the fifteenth century Montenegro had been incorporated into Ottoman territories, but the Turks' grip was never secure; although large-scale attacks continued into the nineteenth century, they settled for a policy of minimal management. The degree of interference depended on the Montenegrins' own compliance and diplomacy, and partly on the whim of the vizier of Skadar. In 1718 a treaty between the Habsburgs and the Turks granted *de facto* independence to the defiant mountaineers, who were more lightly taxed than the empire's other Christian subjects. In 1838 the Turks recognized for the first time "the independent territory of Montenegro". The attacks continued, but recognition on paper was recognition nonetheless, and besides, there was always something papery about Montenegrin independence, even when it was most bloodily defended. Although negotiating skills have no place in the legend of old Montenegro, the tribesmen were astute politicians; they reached a *modus vivendi* with the Ottomans, averting attacks and exploiting divisions.

Several Turkish expeditions reached Cetinje. Montenegro could have been quelled. The coast was held by Venice, then by France, then Austria, while Turkish control began on the plain north of Lake Skadar. It suited both powers to let Montenegro preserve its insolent, ineffectual sovereignty. The border raids were tiresome for the

Turks, but the enclave of Slav freedom could be used as a counter in diplomacy with the Russians.

Still, diplomacy or no, both before and after Njegoš it was a land of incredible extremes; too small to be true, and larger than life. The first printing press in the Balkans was operating near Cetinje by 1493, within two years of Caxton's death. On the other hand, into the twentieth century Turk-killing was still a rite of passage for young men, as well as a favourite pastime.

Everything about Montenegrins was extreme: their poverty and courage, their self-mythologizing, their fanaticism. (The story goes that in the Russo–Turkish War of 1878, only one Montenegrin was taken prisoner by the Turks, against 6,000 killed.) Even in physical terms they are phenomenal, for Montenegrins are the tallest Europeans. Whether or not they have the best eyesight of any people in the world, as they boast, one sees very few bespectacled Montenegrins.

Their longevity is attested. A Napoleonic colonel told of his encounter with a family of seven living generations, aged 117, 100, eighty-two, sixty, forty-three, twenty-one, and two years. One pictures the dumbstruck Frenchman with his braid and epaulettes, briskly reconnoitering a Montenegrin village and finding himself all at once in a tableau from the Old Testament.

Njegoš bestrides this astonishing country, and where should he be buried except on the highest peak, guarding his people, lodged as in an ark above the blasted landscape that writers compare to a petrified sea, a lunar desert?

Yet the form of this ark gives pause for second thoughts about old Montenegro. The Vladika's bones lie in a grandiose mausoleum, designed by Meštrović and completed at vast expense in 1974. And a tasteless edifice it is. Two giant free-standing caryatids in the courtyard and a carved eagle inside the building have a pasteboard solemnity, like props from an Indiana Jones movie. The figure of Njegoš looks too old and plain.

Would any art seem coarse in this sublime setting, or was Meštrović simply past his best? This bloated statuary might be proof of failing senses, or inept assistants, but one wonders if the very commission was somehow blighted with kitsch. Is something amiss with the cult of Njegoš and the heroic self-image of Montenegro? When news started coming through in the autumn of 1991 about Montenegrin paramilitaries marauding into Hercegovina and rampaging up the coast, my doubts about the mausoleum gathered into a pair of troubling questions. What was the connection between the self-image of Montenegro revealed on Lovćen, and this murder and mayhem? And how was it that a people famed for honour and independence were now the most servile nation in Europe, lick-spittles to Serbia in a shameful war?

Answers to these questions begin on Lovčen. To be sure, Njegoš's mountain is the mystical seal of Montenegrin nationhood; the Austrians understood this very well when they stole the relics away in 1916. Montenegrins have only to lift their eyes to Lovčen to know where they always belonged and will belong. An outsider assumes that therefore the Montenegrins know who they are. Yet it is not so; the issue of their own identity divides them more deeply than any other people in the Balkans.

*

The Montenegrins' dilemma sprouts from a bifurcated root. There are two competing theories of ethnogenesis, neither of them verifiable and both freighted with ideology.

The better-known theory dates Montenegro's real foundation from the battle of Kosovo. It holds that, in the decades after 1389, an élite of survivors of the Ottoman onslaught fled to the tiny Serbian principality of Zeta, between the Lovčen range and the Zeta valley. Here they settled in their twenty-four tribes, scratching a subsistence and plundering the Turks.

For those – always a popular majority inside the country – who believe that Montenegrins are a branch of Serbs and that Montenegrin history is a phase within Serbian history, or an adjunct to it, this theory is sheer common sense. According to them, Montenegro's historical mission was to preserve the essence of Serbdom through the centuries when Serbia proper was occupied. To quote one of Milovan Djilas's fictional characters: "I am not a Montenegrin because I am a Serb, but a Serb because I am a Montenegrin. We Montenegrins are the salt of the Serbs. All the strength of the Serbs is not here, but their soul is." On this view the Montenegrin nationality evolved in the past couple of centuries. Recast in Marxist terms, this was the basis for the CPY's recognition of Montenegrin nationhood in 1945.

The other theory maintains that Montenegrins are a unique hybrid of Slav and Illyrian or Albanian descent. The Serbian principality of Zeta existed, but before Zeta was Duklja, originally the Roman colony of Doclea, and a Catholic domain until the Serbian empire absorbed it. Roman rubble can still be seen in the meadows near Titograd where the Zeta river flows into the Morača, but nobody knows much about Doclea, or Duklja either – which makes it easier for proponents of this second theory to submit Duklja as the Avalon of Montenegro. Extremists in this camp even deny that Montenegrins are Slavs at all.

These theories are each plausible and implausible in complementary ways. The first is scientifically outlandish; these mountains and valleys were not empty when the Serbs arrived; whatever the influx after 1389, the new arrivals were bound to have mixed with the incumbents. What's more, ethnologists say that the structure of Montenegrin zadrugas was very similar to those of the Albanian tribes to the south; likewise the tribal laws. Intermarriage too could occur.

In short, the pro-Serbian theory is strained at best, and at worst chauvinist. On the other hand, there is no question that Serbism was the breath in the Montenegrin body – at least until an independent Serbia was born in 1878. The Kosovo cult was stronger here than anywhere; the Church taught the tribesmen that revenge for Kosovo was the highest of duties. Slaying Turks was not only a profitable pleasure and a source of status; it was righteous vengeance against the killers of Prince Lazar.

The pro-Dukljan theory, by contrast, is sensible about origins (except in the extremist version), but slippery in other respects. Sociologically speaking, there was a Montenegrin culture; the independent tribal way of life was specific to this area. But its values were Serbian. Here as in Prizren, "Kosovo, Kosovo had swallowed all . . ."

*

Cetinje is a town with a superiority complex and its head in the clouds. Proudest of all the proud Montenegrins, its 12,000 people rather look down on outsiders, meaning people from Titograd or Nikšić, let alone the rest of Yugoslavia. "They think they're all royalty, the best, the ones who can quote *The Mountain Wreath*," said my friend Rada, from Titograd. "Cetinje is beautiful, of course, but," she added slyly, "it's also the only town in Yugoslavia without a river or a railway."

Even the *korzo* at dusk leaves the main street more than half empty, and the rest of the day passes in a placid routine of old ladies with shopping bags, cars pottering slowly along the avenues, a scattering of kids on bikes, moustachioed men in the cafés on the main square, tracking passers-by with their eyes as they talk. Kosovo and its griefs are remote – like Northern Ireland from Canterbury.

There is some industry, in the notoriously profitless form of a refrigerator factory. What visitors see, though, is what they come for; the cluster of Petrović palaces, the monastery, and the nineteenth-century embassies, built by the great powers when Prince Nikola gained a coastline, and with it strategic value, in 1878. These mementoes of lost grandeur decay in overgrown gardens.

Until the gains of the 1870s, Cetinje was Montenegro's only town. Even so, it wasn't an urban environment. When Njegoš died it had 120 inhabitants, half of whom were guardsmen in the militia. There were a dozen stone buildings besides the monastery, and a rough-hewn palace. The tower behind the monastery bristled with Turkish heads, and the chieftains' senate house doubled as a byre for the horned cattle.

The palace is the *Biljarda*, built by Njegoš and named after the billiard table he imported from England. I visited his gloomy rooms, hoping to glean traces of the living man. His ornate autograph passport is here, with his pen, a few sheets of *The Mountain Wreath*, and a case of his books: Voltaire, Molière, Schiller, Pailliet's *Manual of Civil, Commercial and Criminal Law*, twenty-four volumes of the French *Dictionary of Conversation*, well thumbed; a selection from Dante; Montesquieu's *Spirit of the Laws*; a treatise on intestinal worms.

Not much else survives. For tangible humanity, the Prince's Palace, a hundred metres away, is the place. Nikola built it early in his long reign (1860–1916), and his wiliness and vainglory are everywhere on display, as if he had left a week ago. The living quarters are lavishly furnished with the 'gifts' that he was pleased to accept from the ambassadors. Downstairs are battle standards shredded by Turkish bullets and green banners captured from the Turks, near cases of medals and coins minted for the pocket kingdom. (Nikola made himself a king in 1910.)

By the end of the century Montenegro was lampooned as a Balkan Ruritania, yet Nikola himself stands on the near side of modernity. The pistol in his belt was decorative. He wore national costume because foreigners were tickled to see it, and his own people trusted it; his portrait in the Palace shows a politician, and judging by his lucrative ploys with the great powers, he was a good one.

Njegoš, though, belonged to immemorial, benighted Montenegro – as he knew too well. "One may expect anything from such a people", he wrote about his tribesmen. "Woe unto him who is their ruler. This is the saddest fate in the world." And to his friend Vuk Karadžić, the Serbian folklorist and language-reformer, he lamented: "at times the hard and bloody struggle overwhelms me, and I curse the hour when this spark rose up from the ashes of Dušan's greatness and into these mountains of ours."

If a date can be put to the founding of Cetinje, it is 1484, when Ivan Crnojević established the Orthodox monastery. His line soon perished, and authority came to be vested in the Orthodox metro-politan (bishop), elected from the monks at the monastery. Yet the metropolitan's power was limited; he could advise the chieftains, not compel or punish them. If he persistently flouted tribal wisdom, he might even be deposed.

The metropolitanate became the hereditary privilege of the Petrović clan. With Metropolitan Petar I, whose long rule began in 1782 and ended with his death in 1830, the effort to organize the Montenegrins started in earnest. After defeating and killing the vizier of Skadar, in 1796, Petar tried to establish a legal code and a law-court. Petar had won the chieftains' respect; they accepted his innovations, then ignored them. Tribal law remained the strongest sanction, and it was left to Petar's nephew Njegoš to push the modernization forward.

Adding princely power to religious authority, Njegoš became the Vladika. Unlike Petar, who regarded Montenegro as a separate entity, Njegoš was an ardent Serbophile, and made his eyrie into the centre of free Serbdom. Vuk Karadžić, who wrote the first good book about Montenegro, was his confidant. His boyhood tutor was Sima Milutinović, author of famous plays about Miloš Obilić and the Kosovo Girl. Matija Ban, Serbian revolutionary and the first man to use the word Yugoslavia in print, was a secret visitor.

Njegoš's Serbism was couched in the mystery of the Kosovo myth and inflected with Orthodox pan-Slavism. In this visionary sense he was a Yugoslav *avant la lettre*. Yet he was practically minded too. He did his best to foment uprisings against the Turks in Bosnia, Kosovo and Macedonia in 1848. These schemes came to nothing, but with his measures to regulate his wild Montegrins, he laid the foundations for the state which came to formal existence in 1878.

Njegoš's struggle was so hard because the Turks had such an advantage of power, but also because his tribes' independence had never been curbed. Although he was their bishop and commander, he, like his predecessors, had to move cautiously.

The tribes had evolved a structure of self-administration beneath a spiritual leader. Tribes were composed of clans, and the clans, of zadrugas. Every adult male participated in his tribal council and in the assembly in Cetinje. Important decisions were taken on the basis of free discussion. Social status was not conferred by the metro-politan. It was gauged by the condition of one's *obraz* (literally, cheek), which depended on clan or tribal approval. Censure blackened obraz just as recognition of achievement whitened it. For women, obraz was tarnished by sexual transgression. For men, it was inseparable from *junaštvo*, the quality of being a good warrior.

In the teeth of opposition, Njegoš gave Montenegro the appur-tenances of a secular state. He instituted a militia and a senate of chieftains, who came to fear and even hate him when his reforms sapped their power. As soon as he could, he abandoned the cassock for national dress. He, who declared himself "the enemy of inhuman anarchy and disorder", defined Montenegro's borders, founded schools and started taxation. This last step was bitterly resisted: tax was something for *raya* (Christian subjects in Ottoman land), not free Montenegrins. Sometimes he had to bribe the chieftains to pay up.

A Russian officer told the story of a band of Montenegrins being ferried aboard a Russian navy vessel during the campaign against Napoleon. They were astonished to learn that they couldn't disembark without permission. "If you like to do a thing," they said, "what right has another to forbid you?" These were the men whom the Vladika wanted to forge into citizens.

The feuding had to stop, as had the freebooting heroics. Tribal law – *lex talionis*, "an eye for an eye" – had to yield to a civil code. Njegoš knew as well as anyone that the tribesmen's independence was the source of Montenegro's glory; and he shared their invincible pride. (When he visited Rome, terminally sick, he baulked at kissing the chains of Saint Peter. "A Montenegrin," he said simply, "does not kiss chains.") Yet the necessity was overriding. Montenegro's highest duty was to remain Orthodox and Turk-free, and the tribes were weakened by inveterate feuding.

Montenegro could not be reformed without destroying traditional Montenegrin virtues. This is why Serbism was, for Njegoš, a tragic vocation as well as a vision. He saw himself as its instrument, acting a rôle that had been ordained by the defeat at Kosovo. Somehow Montenegro – "the bloody Serbian rock", as he called it – had to endure at the crossroads of this contradiction: Serbism and the Turks.

Njegoš was a poet, and he conceived this plight in poetic terms. Its essence, as he saw it, was the clash between inner principle and external force. What dignified the conflict with tragic horror was the fact that some of his people betrayed the principle and changed sides. For the Turks were mostly not Turkish at all, but ethnic Albanians and Montenegrin-Serb "renegades" who had converted to Islam or at least paid it lip-service.

The renegades imperilled the Montenegrin mission, and were an obstacle to any Vladika trying to unify the tribes. This was why Turkish rule was an evil with which no truce was possible. With some of their number constantly going over to Islam, the Montenegrins were split one against another, within tribes and clans. "Brother beats brother, brother cuts down brother," keened Njegoš, "the ruins of our empire have curdled our blood."

From where Njegoš reigned in embattled isolation, the main

barrier between the South Slavs and liberty was their refusal to seize the opportunity. Letting themselves be divided, they connived at their impotence. When Habsburg Serbs and Croats fought the Hungarians in 1848, Njegoš almost despaired. For the Serbs of Vojvodina to be freed, Hungary had indeed to be beaten; but this war was fought at the behest of the Habsburgs. Didn't the Slavs realize they were exchanging one captivity for another? "O wretched Slavs," he wrote in a blaze of frustration, "what would Europe do without such slaves? Were it not for them, Mein Herr would have to take off his gloves and effendim benim put aside his pipe, and they would be compelled to become blood brothers, had not their good fortune given them the Slavs. Yes, our race is owned like cattle by other nations, and whoever has the largest herd is the richest. Whoever has the slightest doubt that the Slavs were born to be slaves, let him look upon their actions today. Can there by anything more loathsome in the world than their blindness? I am always amazed, and can never get over my astonishment, that shameful slavery can be so precious to some men. They are like dogs, for a dog tugs to gain his freedom, but once he gains it, he runs back to his leash to be tethered."*

The theme of internecine strife gave the poet the subject for *The Mountain Wreath*, the epic poem that recounts the massacre of "renegades" by the warriors under Metropolitan Danilo Petrović, in 1702.

As a matter of record, the renegades may have been expelled, not killed. As a matter of national myth, the tribes amputated their unsound limb in order to be whole. In Njegoš's hands the massacre becomes a sacrificial sin, committed for freedom's sake but at the price of fratricide. Evil is perpetrated so that evil shan't prevail. Montenegro becomes an entire moral universe, governed by laws that limit the choices open to men and heighten them so that each option is terrible in its own way. Njegoš's Montenegrins are free as Antigone was free: to live ignobly or lose her life for higher values.

---

* An archeology of Serbian/Montenegrin political rhetoric might do worse than start with this magnificent denunciation. It is a short way from Njegoš's eloquence and passion to the swaggering demagogy that masks real objectives under self-pity or muscle-flexing aggression. President Milošević of Serbia updated this demagogy for the age of soundbites with his famous promise to the Serbs of Kosovo that "Nobody will beat you again," his cry of "All Serbs in one state!", and his declaration that "Serbia will be united or it will not exist." When Branko Kostić, the Montenegrin member of the federal presidency, told a news conference during the ten-day war in Slovenia that he would rather eat roots than bow to foreign pressure, he was tapping the same vein of nationalist unreason and paranoia.

When Gladstone and others extolled Montenegro as a latter-day Sparta and likened its warriors to the heroes of Thermopylae, they were, whether consciously or not, evoking an image that Njegoš had already invented. For he compared his land to ancient Greece, and his Danilo faces a predicament borrowed straight from the world of classical tragedy. Danilo has not only to obey a higher law than kinship, he has to betray kinship. His situation is that of Shakespeare's Coriolanus, or of Lucius Junius Brutus, the consul who ordered his own sons' execution for conspiring against Rome, and of whom Plutarch wrote that "either the greatness of his virtue raised him above the impressions of sorrow, or the extravagance of his misery took away all sense of it; but neither seemed common, or the result of humanity, but either divine or brutish."

Montenegrin and Serbian culture is so imbued with the ethos of *The Mountain Wreath*, one easily forgets that it is literature, not history. Actually the choices confronting Montenegrins were not equally terrible. Montenegrins could defy the Turks, or submit. Pragmatically, the second course had more to offer: a quiet life, certain material privileges. This is why Njegoš's poem depicts any weakening of commitment to Orthodoxy, the legacy of Kosovo, the unity of the tribes – in a word, to the nation – as the blackest of crimes. For Njegoš, both as Vladika and as poet, was rallying his people to the banner of Serbism.   This is not to deny the reality of Montenegrin valour, but to point out that the ethos of old Montenegro was not a neutral or natural product of circumstances. It was a case of national ideology *in extremis*. The contempt for compromise and rationality, the mystique of self-sacrifice, the capacity for endless cruelty – these were not native to the rocks of Montenegro but imported along with Orthodoxy and the cult of Kosovo. Njegoš's poetic genius gathered the elements of drama that lay to hand and condensed them into a national epic. He did not invent the elements, as other sources prove. The Russian naval officer mentioned above, who witnessed the Montenegrins' fanatical patriotism in action, recalled: "When the country is in danger, they forget all personal feelings of private advantage and enmity; they obey the orders of their chief, and, like gallant republicans, they consider it a happiness, and a grace of God, to die in battle. It is in such a case that they appear as real warriors: *but, beyond the limits of their country, they are savage barbarians, who destroy every thing with fire and sword.*" This touches the quick of old Montenegro, where the divine was a hair's breadth from the brutish, heroism was treachery's blood-brother, and whoever was recognised as chief commanded life and death.

In those times the country practically always was in danger, so this insane fealty could hardly be abused. But, as the recent history of Kosovo has proved, national myths outlive their function. In 1991 the anti-Turk reflex was still strong enough to turn Croats into Turks and Montenegrins into savage barbarians.

*

So far, so clear. Their ethnogenesis did not worry the Montenegrins. Complications did not begin until the 1900s. The transcendent idea of Serbdom was one thing; the reality of Serbian state power was another. In this respect, Montenegrin disenchantment has resembled that of Croats who yearned for Yugoslavia more selflessly than anyone until Yugoslavia happened, and then became its bitter enemies.

Nikola offered in the 1860s to abdicate in favour of the Serbian dynasty, if their prince proved capable of uniting the Serbs in a single state. This turned out to be a final gesture of Petrović self-effacement before the greater good of Serbian resurrection, for in 1878, with the birth of an independent Serbia and recognition of Montenegrin statehood, relations between Cetinje and Belgrade became competitive, as did those between the three ruling dynasties – the Petrovići in Montenegro, the Obrenovići and the Karadjordjevići in Serbia.

Montenegro had lost its mission; it could no longer be the supreme guardian and prophet of Serbism. Meanwhile, Montenegro's sheer success in gaining new territory presented a challenge. While enriching the country, this expansion corrupted its purity by bringing the mixed populations of towns, as well as Muslims and Albanians, within the principality. In the Balkan Wars, Nikola conquered yet more land, in Metohija and Sandžak and on the shore of Lake Skadar. Montenegro in 1913 was four times the size it had been in 1860 – bigger than it is today.

Nikola promoted his country by exploiting the great powers' competitive interest in Montenegro, while allying his family with as many royal houses as possible. He married two daughters to Romanov grand princes, another to a Battenberg, and a fourth to the King of Italy. Most significantly, he paired his eldest daughter with Petar Karadjordjević. At that time (1883) the Serbian throne belonged to the Obrenovići, so Princess Zorka was marrying an heir without prospects. What the alliance offered Nikola was a chance to grasp back the captaincy of the 'true' pan-Serbian project; for Milan Obrenović was tainted by Austrian sponsorship, whereas Petar was the grandson of Karadjordje himself, the founder of independent Serbia.

When Aleksandar Obrenović and his Queen were butchered in a

coup and Petar was enthroned, the tables were turned on Nikola. The Petrovići became a branch of the Serbian royal family. By now (1903) Montenegro was acquiring social tensions. Montenegrin students in Belgrade despised the antics of the Cetinje court. Nikola's acumen looked like despotic cunning, and his steps to constitutionalize his rule were less than convincing. Serbia represented the progressive as well as the economically sensible option for increasing numbers of his subjects.

Matters came to a head when the Balkan Wars (1912–13) gave the two states a common border. In the eyes of Nikola's opponents, Montenegrin independence had become positively unpatriotic. The old king allowed free elections, which the pro-Serbian party won. Negotiations for military, diplomatic and financial union with Serbia were interrupted by Austria-Hungary's attack on Serbia in July 1914. Nikola rallied to the cause, and appointed the head of the Serbian military mission as the chief of his supreme staff. The six-man staff included four more Serbs; the Montenegrin army indirectly took its orders from the Belgrade government.

When Serbia was beaten in 1915, the subversion of Montenegrin sovereignty became a matter of urgency. Otherwise, after the war, Montenegro and its dynasty would profit from Serbia's loss. Nikola was inveigled into pressing for peace at the end of 1915, and left Montenegro in January 1916 – for ever, as it turned out.* Believing that its king had abandoned it, the army capitulated, though still undefeated. The Austrians occupied Montenegro, and refused to negotiate with such of Nikola's ministers as remained. The king's deluded flight had discredited him; he tried to exert authority from his refuge in France, but had no chance against the combination of Austrian force and Serbian diplomacy. Serbia's government and king were intent on the postwar incorporation of Montenegro into Serbia, and Nikola had no leverage to back his suggested compromises.

At the end of 1918, with the war won, Serbian troops entered Montenegro to demobilize the remnants of the army, preempt Italian schemes to reinstate Nikola, and supervise preparations for a vote on Montenegro's future. Elections for a Great National Assembly of the Serb People in Montenegro (note how the title prejudges the issue) were held in November. The unionists were dubbed the "whites"

---

* The Serbophile understanding of this crucial episode is very different; it casts Nikola and his kin as an *ancien régime* of decadents, who fled "to save only their titles – without idea or conscience; just to save their heads – nameless and faceless – as though there had never been anything – neither battles nor poetry." (Djilas, *Njegoš*.)

and their opponents the "greens", after the colours of their lists of candidates.

Polling was arranged in conditions that ensured a white victory (which doesn't mean the whites might not have won fair and square). On 26 November the Great Assembly voted to unify the two states under the Karadjordević monarchy. A few days later the union merged with the ex-Habsburg lands as royal Yugoslavia.

An armed uprising followed in old Montenegro. Its chance of success was reduced even further by disagreement among the greens; some demanded independence, others favoured federation within Yugoslavia or equal partnership with Serbia; some were diehard monarchists, others were republican patriots. Where they agreed was that this union was brutal annexation: no less than Serbia, Montenegro had been a sovereign state, not a region within Austria-Hungary, and it had been treated worse than a colony. They were burned by the flame they had guarded so long.

Henceforth everything in Montenegro came in two colours, not the scarlet and black of national costume but the green of Montenegrin autonomism and the white of pan-Serbism. Villages, clans, and even families were split. Inevitably Cetinje was the centre of greenery, yet the queen's own brother was white, while a local fraction of the Communist Party was green.

Socialist federalism seemed to engulf this demarcation by absorbing Montenegro's two tones into a larger palette. Then federalism died and history came out of its cupboard, rattling its bones and stalking across Montenegro's mountains in green and white-striped seven-league boots. Cetinje became again the core of resistance to Belgrade. I visited a couple of ardent Liberals who live two minutes' walk from Nikola's palace. (In the December 1990 elections in Montenegro, the Liberal Party had a green programme of Montenegrin sovereignty in a confederated Yugoslavia.) Sitting in their apartment, which is painted in red and black down to the doorknobs and tablemats, they described their hopes of gaining an autocephalous Montenegrin Orthodox Church, and the return of the Petrović dynasty.

And the greens are still divided among themselves. When I asked other Liberals about the Church and the monarchy, they frowned like grown-ups being pestered to join children's games. "Pay no attention," said Slavko Perović, head of the Liberals in Cetinje. "All that's irrelevant. We are a party of social democrats, not romantic traditionalists."

The British embassy to Nikola's court is now a studio for art students. When I put my nose round the door and asked to look around, they welcomed me with Montenegrin hospitality. I spent the rest of the day with them, and the evening too – my last in Cetinje. They work long hours, because everyone is hard up and this town makes no concessions to the under-fifties.

The next day Nebojša gave me a lift to Titograd in his aged Mini Cooper. His girlfriend is a student here, so he drives up each weekend. His own subject is philosophy, and he dabbles in politics. As we rattled down to the plain, he told me about his Party for Moderate Progress Within the Limits of Law. He founded it with five friends, and registered it for the elections. He borrowed the idea and title from Jaroslav Hašek, and like its Czech namesake seventy years before, the PMPWLL's manifesto started with a promise to improve the quality of beer.* Democracy includes the right to be flippant about politics. In an environment like Montenegro, awash with macho solemnity and nationalist mysticism, stunts like the PMPWLL had their value.

Nebojša is a bit of a hippy, soft-spoken and anti-political, unnerved by the sight of horizons shrinking all around him. "I never used to identify myself as Montenegrin," he said with a twitch of impatience, "but now it's 'Montenegro' this and 'Montenegro' that every way you turn. It's so narrow."

Narrow indeed. With an area slightly larger than Los Angeles County and less than Northern Ireland, Montenegro was the smallest republic in the federation and the least densely populated. This was one reason why Montenegrins were content with Yugoslavia; sovereignty and independence seemed self-evidently ludicrous to everyone but the deepest-dyed greens. Besides, the bond with Serbia was something genuine; Montenegrins treated their neighbour as an extension of their own home, which other nations never could.

Their contentment rested on more than a vestige of archaic pan-Slavism; it had a solid material basis. No one here complained that federal Yugoslavia had exploited them. Before 1939, Montenegro was poor as rural Albania is poor today. There was no industry; 80 per cent of people were peasants. Then came the war, and Montenegrins were at the forefront again. They played a tremendous part in the partisan victory, thanks to the pre-war popularity of communism, their warrior traditions, and a number of outstanding leaders – figures such as Sava Kovačević, who appeared as reincarnations of the Turk-slaying chieftains of yore, and were commemorated in much the same terms.

In the first Yugoslavia, Montenegrins did not exist; like

---

* For the record, Montenegrin beer was already the best in Yugoslavia: a strong, peppery brew from Nikšić.

Macedonians, they were counted as Serbs. After 1945 they more than made up for lost time. Influence in the new Yugoslavia rewarded warrior-prowess and communist zeal. In 1944 and '45 the Montenegrin leaders demanded and got the bay of Kotor, which had never belonged to Montenegro. They also acquired half of the Sandžak, which had been mooted in 1943 as a separate federal unit. (The other half went to Serbia.) During and after the war, the percentage of League of Communist members was higher among Montenegrins than any other Yugoslavs. They were over-represented at the highest levels of federal government, the military, and throughout the administration.

This political weight was useful for boosting Montenegro's share of the federal budget. Nonetheless it remained the poorest republic until the late 1950s, when massive investment began to show results. When a fund for underdeveloped regions was set up in 1965, Montenegro profited from extra credits. Development was often absurdly doctrinaire; the inevitable iron and steel works were sited at Nikšić, far from any source of ore. Free-thinking economists might worry that profitability did not increase along with productivity, but as far as ordinary people were concerned, life in Montenegro was improving beyond recognition.

When multiparty elections came in 1990, there was a special incentive to back the party in power; and Montenegrin values set such store by loyalty that many older people believed that they *owed* it to the Communists to vote for them.

The League portrayed itself as efficient, dependable, anti-nationalist. Its campaign poster showed hands tapping on a computer keyboard, above the simple legend: "We know how."

"But *what* do they know?" asked my friend Vesko, theatrically, when I visited Titograd shortly before the elections. "How to screw everything up!" Vesko, who backed the Reform Forces coalition, went around the city pasting strips across other parties' posters, with the legend: "It doesn't matter that they're lying. What matters is that you don't believe them."

Two-thirds of the voters did believe the League of Communists; at least, they supported it. The ultra-white People's Party made a lot of noise in the campaign, but flopped. The Reform Forces coalition of opposition parties, including the Liberals, mustered only 16 per cent of the vote.

This doesn't mean the LC stood outside the green-white division; nobody did, except perhaps Nebojša and his PMPWLL. In the peculiar tangled context of Montenegro, the LC managed to be pro- and anti-nationalist. In the sense that it allied itself politically with the Serbia of Slobodan Milošević, the League tapped the white wellsprings of

Serb-Montenegrin nationalism, and benefited from the thrilling populist kudos of that ideology. At the same time, the League could present itself as the party of stability and welfare, because it was pro-Yugoslav, and everyone agreed that Montenegro needed Yugoslavia in some form. It opposed the other, green variety of Montenegrin nationalism. "We are the party of rationality and peace, the party of ordinary and simple people," I was told by a Central Committee member. "We have nothing to do with this national extremism." And who could gainsay him?

Some other communists could, for a start; and they did. One fraction of communists had turned green, split from the League, and become its worst enemies.

The cause is complex and paradoxical, like everything in Montenegrin politics. Between the Cominform crisis of 1948 and the elections of 1990, the key political event in Montenegro was the so-called "anti-bureaucratic revolution" of October 1988 and January 1989, when the republican leadership was ousted by a concerted effort of popular protest, committee-room caballing, and media pressure from Belgrade. It began with a demonstration in Titograd to support the Serbs and Montenegrins in Kosovo. Such rallies had been staged through the summer in Serbia, building up pressure for Milošević's campaign to revoke the autonomy of Kosovo and Vojvodina, the two provinces inside Serbia. The Montenegrin leadership had declined to give these rallies its endorsement, though it did not join the Slovenes and Croats in criticizing them.

The meeting was joined by local contruction engineers, and by steel workers from Nikšić. Schoolkids, students, housewives and everyone else flocked to the scene, until a hundred thousand people were in front of the assembly building – a sixth of the republic's population.

It was the biggest demonstration in post-war Montenegro, and it was no longer just about Kosovo. The crowd demanded the resignation of two leading politicians. The slogans expressed practical fears about the future, and solidarity with Serbia: "We demand bread!", "We want to work and earn our living!", "Long live the Serbian leadership!" People wanted jobs *and* Milošević, and it is worth remembering that, at this stage, the Serbian strongman was widely viewed in the West as a dynamic innovator in the Gorbachev mould, even as a new Tito in the making.

The leadership's unpopularity was proven by the huge turn-out. Yet there was nothing spontaneous about the event's origins. The thousands of workers were not there by accident; neither were the groups of demonstrators who started arriving from Serbia, Kosovo and Macedonia.

Serbia wanted a more compliant crew in power, because Montenegro could be a valuable henchman in the quest to central-ize the Yugoslav state. The tiny republic had less than 3 per cent of the population, and it produced less than 2 per cent of GNP, but in the federal system it carried one eighth of the political muscle. If the autonomous provinces could be reintegrated, Serbia would have three votes in the eight-man federal presidency. A reliable Montenegro would give Serbia control of fully half the votes in this body, the so-called "collective head of state" and the constitutional commander of the JNA.

The stakes were high, and the leadership panicked. Police were turned loose on the demonstrators with batons and tear gas. A scandal was whipped up, with help from the Serbian press. Slovenia, Croatia and Bosnia-Hercegovina pledged support for their Mon-tenegrin comrades. Meanwhile the steelworkers condemned the use of force and issued a list of demands: acceptance of all constitutional amendments (i.e. to cancel the provinces' autonomy), suppression of "counter-revolution" in Kosovo, economic reform, a ban on price rises, and resignation of the leadership. Inside its headquarters the Central Committee stood firm, but three months later a better-organized demonstration succeeded in toppling the chiefs.

In a decomposing one-party state, these mass rallies in Mon-tenegro, Kosovo and Vojvodina were brilliantly effective. In the eyes of people who had no experience of spontaneous, grass-roots politics – not since 1968, or even the partisan war – they bore a convincing resemblance to the democratic process. I met a number of people who joined the rallies in Titograd in the sincere hope of forcing democratic change. The national colouring of the meeting neu-tralized many demonstrators' suspicions.

When the CC denounced the unconstitutional nature of the rally, everyone on the street knew 'they would say that, wouldn't they?' Sceptics found themselves trying not to defend an indefensible status quo, while insisting that political pressure from the streets was not democratic when it operated in a monopoly system without accountable institutions. Because the rallies were directed by workers against the governors of a workers' state, they undermined governors' legitimacy in a way that was unanswerable except by police terror on a scale that was unfeasible in Yugoslavia in the 1980s (except in Kosovo, of course, because Albanians didn't count).

In Nikšić, 30,000 workers gathered in the assembly yard of the iron works as Radivoje Brajović of the republican presidency faced them like a Vladika condemned by tribal law, resolving to die better than he has lived. "As I have to resign," he told them, "I am proud to hand in my resignation before the workers of the Boris Kidrić iron works." As Brajović left, weeping, some workers cheered his courage. Others jeered.

Amid popular hopes for some kind of communist rejuvenation, a new leadership was installed. In the manner of one-party despotisms, it carried the anti-bureaucratic revolution to the provinces. But the leadership in the port of Bar refused to go. They had done well by their town in recent years, and believed they could swing enough popular support to keep themselves in power. In the spring of 1990 the League dissolved its branch in Bar, expelling 3,000 members. This freed the enterprising rebels to write their own party statutes, and to contest the elections at the end of the year as the Independent Organization of Bar Communists.

By chance I ran into an IOBC delegation at the radio station in Titograd. I recognized one of its members: he was the tour-guide from King Nikola's palace in Cetinje. He explained how the new League leadership "accepted Belgrade's orders without question, *that's* the problem. In February [1990], for instance, Slovenian vessels were banned from our port because of Serbia's economic blockade of Slovenia. The IOBC wants equal partnership with other republics. We have 3,000 members in Bar, where the League has just 300."   Come the elections, the rebels retained Bar. The democratically-approved parliament in Titograd retaliated with legislation to curb municipal power – extensive under self-management – so severely that they, along with the Muslim councils that control two other towns in the republic, were effectively helpless. Bar radio station became the League's Trojan horse against the town's elected leaders. The newly appointed editors were physically prevented from entering the building, and the radio now trumpets non-stop propaganda against the renegades.

"And that, I fear," says Vesko bitterly, "is the real face of democracy in Montenegro."

Faced with such a well-entrenched régime, the green opposition pooled its strength under the Reform Forces party of federal prime minister Ante Marković.

Necessity and history produced a strange alignment. In other republics, the Reform Forces were attacked by nationalists for being crypto-communist and pro-federal, and by communists for their programme of economic liberalization. Here, they were attacked by communists and white nationalists for being anti-federal and anti-Serbian (which was true only in the sense that Serbia's communist leaders were the least placable enemies of economic liberalization). And they were endorsed by green nationalists and green communists because these groups all agreed on one thing, at least: that Montenegro should be democratic, economically liberalized, and sovereign within a confederated Yugoslavia, instead of bonding with big brother.

As a consequence the green opposition presented a bizarre, incoherent, but logical array. The Independent Communists of Bar rubbed shoulders with poetic monarchists from the fringes of the Liberal Party. The Muslim and Albanian parties, representing 12 and 6.5 per cent of the population respectively, sided with the radical greens against Great Serbian chauvinism, which was explicit in the People's Party and implicit in the League of Communists.

The far white opposition, in the shape of the People's Party, collapsed. The PP was ideologically anti-communist but, because the post-1989 League catered very nicely for white nationalism, the party ended up looking like the communists' country cousin.

Green monarchists were particularly pleased by the PP's fiasco, because it had stolen the Petrović anthem as its party song. By a typical twist, the sentiments of the anthem are whiter than white – Montenegrins yearning for the bosom of Kosovo, and all that. By 1990, Montenegrin history had become totally ambiguous; there was no detail of it that could not turn green or white in the right selective setting, like a two-tone chameleon.

The upshot of the election was that Montenegro's government entered 1991 with a rock-solid mandate for its stance of Serbia-right-or-wrong. Croatia and Slovenia set their courses for independence; Serbia refused to discuss a looser state arrangement; BiH and Macedonia groped for a non-existent compromise.

Montenegro alone initiated nothing, had nothing to suggest, but perched on Serbia's shoulder, parrotting its denunciations of separatism and confederation. Momir Bulatović, the key beneficiary of the anti-bureaucratic revolution, and now president of the republic, was mocked as "Milošević's coatpeg" – though often by the same people who admitted that, say what you like about Milošević, his father was Montenegrin, so at least he was "a leaf from our forest".

The coup of 1988–89 had not delivered the hoped-for rejuvenation. Montenegro had been bankrupt since 1987, when more than one third of its enterprises were operating at a loss. The new élite had no economic solutions; the federal budget had collapsed (except to pay the JNA); state subsidies had dried up, and with 90 per cent of the economy still unprivatized, what other sources were there? The media were still brazenly manipulated. Democratically-minded and greenish revolutionaries from 1989 resigned. Montenegro was still a party-state.

Traditionalism in this country cuts both ways, for and against the greens. However, no tradition runs deeper than that of pride, and this elemental trait was offended by the kowtowing to Belgrade. Borrowing a metaphor from Mussolini, Milošević had once described Serbia and Montenegro as two eyes in one head. As confrontation became war in 1991, it was obvious that one eye was weaker than the other. Serbia wanted no condominium, only compliance.

When war was launched against Croatia in August, the gulf between both sides in Montenegro deepened. War fever gripped the republic. JNA conscripts and reservists swarmed up the coast to Dubrovnik, killing and looting, fighting each other for whisky and video recorders.

For "*beyond the limits of their country, they are savage barbarians, who destroy everything with fire and sword.*"

Greens opposed the war as a Serbian-federal affair which could bring no good. Life was dangerous for anyone who publicly condemned the aggression; yet the anti-war faction did not disappear. After the first rush of jingoist madness had spent itself, and the adventure palled into months of attrition, there were peace rallies in Cetinje. Nikola Petrović, grandson of King Nikola, publicly regretted his country's part in the conflict.

Montenegrins had grown accustomed to their isolation from non-Serbian opinion. Newsstands were swamped with Serbian publications, and most of the television broadcasts were imported from Belgrade. My own impression is that people were truly startled to learn, as they did from the tidal wave of international commentary which percolated even here, that the rest of the world did not view the separatist Slovenes as ruthless murderers, and did not agree that Croats were fascists who had got their come-uppance.

At the same time, war magnified the options facing Montenegro. If Slovenia and Croatia could be independent, independence for Montenegro was perhaps not so far-fetched – especially if the only alternative was membership of a rump federation that might, in the event, not be organized on truly federal lines at all. What rôle then for the republican government?

Even "Milošević's coatpeg" smelled trouble; on 18 October he broke ranks for the first time, by agreeing to the European Community's proposed blueprint for a confederal Yugoslavia of sovereign states. Milošević and General Kadijević, the federal minister of defence, rejected the blueprint, which historians may come to see as the very last "last chance" for Yugoslavia.

The gesture was timely; by the end of 1991 voices in Belgrade, not just from the nationalist opposition but among well-known advisers to the ruling Serbian Socialist Party, were saying for the first time that Yugoslavia should be scrapped once and for all. Decoded, this meant that federalism should not be the basis of whatever Serbian-dominated state emerged from the war.

Bulatović reacted to these omens with further reminders. Montenegro quietly absented itself from the Convention on Yugoslavia.* Then a date was set for a referendum, along the lines of those held in Slovenia in 1990 and in Croatia and Macedonia in 1991, on the question of Montenegro's status in Yugoslavia.

With the future of Bosnia-Hercegovina still undecided, Milošević needed Montenegro safely onside. In the first days of February he convened a top-level meeting to agree a plan for eventual federal union between the two republics.

The referendum repeated the pattern of the election result. Even if the idea of independence were a lot more popular in Montenegro than it is, the two republics are integrated in so many ways that it cannot hope to chart its own course. Come what may, Montenegro is hitched to Serbia, for better, for worse. The balance of power inside this marriage will hinge on Montenegro's skill at hoarding its few advantages, and exploiting Belgrade's need for an ally.

Most likely the green opposition faces a long haul, but an interesting and even a promising one. The present alliance with Serbia is strong but not happy: edged with coercion, archaic and triumphalist. If the greens can harness their democrats, monarchists, autonomists, rebels and romantics to a rational programme of national self-determination, the future will be green.

But does the opposition have the wit to stop grumbling about Belgrade and equip itself for a new start? Will it, for instance, take its message to the football stadium? To young people in Titograd, white is grey: Serbism means authority, not glorious myths about Kosovo. The teenage fans of *Budućnost* (Future), Titograd's football team, call themselves "the barbarians"; during the winter of war, they took to chanting anti-Serbian songs at away games in Serbia. These budding greens should be welcomed into a rainbow coalition.

But a radical democratic movement here is as likely as a feminist president in Serbia. Montenegro is monochrome, not a land of rainbows. It does not spawn innovative ideas, least of all in the field of politics, where players change sides, the teams remains the same, and every match is a replay. The thin parched air preserves

* A lacklustre event staged in Belgrade on 3 January 1992, to advertise the popularity of Serbia's stance towards the other republics and their Serb minorities. As a happening, it was Stalinism, pure and ludicrous. As a political indicator, it proved the unpopularity of the said stance.

everything too well, so there seems no room for anything fresh – as if history fills this tiny land to the brim.

Any foreigner is enthralled by this history, and by the incredible landscape that partners it. Montenegro is exhilarating, physically. My blood tingled when I crossed the watershed to Budva, looking into the Mediterranean basin from this outpost of Slavic Orthodoxy. Montenegro should be a gateway between civilizations. Instead it looks and feels like a barrier. For the most part, Montenegrins seem more enclosed than enlarged by their freedom-fighting history and their tradition of *humanitas heroica*. Montenegrin values are vertical; the middle range between heroism and villainy, loyalty and betrayal, is uninhabited because it is alien and, at bottom, despised. The extremism and moralism of Montenegro drive many of its creative spirits away – often to Belgrade, where they go as students and turn into staunch Serbophiles, homesick for their mountains on condition that they don't have to live in them.

What's absent is the average, the plain carbohydrate of social life, with its ordinary randomness, experimentation, and tolerance of doubt. A diet of blood and bone may make a man of you, but it does nothing for mental flexibility.

Reduced to domestic proportions, *humanitas heroica* in the 1990s is hard to tell apart from tight-minded conventionality. Trust in great leaders becomes a terrible weakness for posturing autocrats. Deprived of ancestral glamour, warriors turn out to be patriarchs, liable to make life very tedious for women with different ideas of self-respect.

What isn't lacking, though, is laughter. Montenegrin humour is something special; it warms what would otherwise be a bleak environment. Daily events are told and retold in fantastic anecdotes, spun out and embellished. Montenegro can seem surreal, yet the humour is not at all so; it reminded me of English public school clowning, where the fun lies in taunting authority without disturbing it. (Once in old Montenegro, the story goes, 157 Turkish prisoners were ransomed for an equal number of pigs.) The humour is merciless, like the workers jeering the politician in Nikšić; for its mode is burlesque, not irony; it mocks personalities by savaging their pretensions, rather than turning things inside out by a deft switch of perspective. When people launch into a story, they become look-at-me performers, stagey in a childlike way, playing to the audience of grown ups. It is oddly endearing.

*

Whenever I told Yugoslavs not from Titograd that I liked the place, they assumed I was either sarcastic or in love. Devastated in the

Second World War, it was rebuilt on a grid plan as a model of socialist urbanism. In autumn, when I first visited, it is gauntly beautiful: not a city at all, rather a series of facades, or a frontier town with the rawness burnt away by sun and frost. The streets were never crowded, and no one walked faster than a stroll. The level light gleamed on the glass, and blanched the weathering concrete. Silence and the empty *karst* wait ten minutes' walk from the Central Committee headquarters, snazzy aluminium and smoked glass on stilts. When I passed by, goats were stripping berries from the pettisporum bushes around the stilts. The chauffered black Zastavas took care not to bump them.

Titograd's rivers give its newness away. Close beneath the traffic, the little Ribnica swirls in a cleft of sand and ferns. The air currents on the footbridge high above the Morača are chilly, for the Morača is a mountain torrent, plucking at its steep banks and seething along the centre of its course.

Pomegranates grow in the park above the river. They grow everywhere in Montenegro, glowing biblically on leafless bushes, spilling out of wicker baskets in roadside stalls. When I checked into the Hotel Crnagora the receptionist was eating one hungrily, ignoring the phone that shrilled at her elbow.

With more than 130,000 people, Titograd is the only city in Montenegro. High-rise apartment blocks stand on ground where, within the lifespan of senior citizens, warrior-peasants lived, tending their sheep, cleaning their rifles, feasting on nettles and sour milk. Though the only national dress I saw was worn by someone advertising a benefit concert for UNESCO, the life encased by these apartments is still partitioned along tribal lines. The poverty of consumer choice in Titograd's drab shop windows mirrors the ascetic conservatism of its social codes.

A little proof of this colossal conservatism is the nickname of an apartment block on Hercegovina Street. The block is still known around Titograd as "Goli Otok", after the Adriatic island of that name, where political prisoners were kept in the late 1940s and 1950s.

The crime that bore people to the so-called Yugoslav gulag was "Cominformism": loyalty to the Communist Information Bureau, the Soviet-led front of Communist Parties that was created in 1947 as a successor to the Communist International (Comintern).

The Cominform was an aid for Stalin's control of international communism, and nothing more. The CPs of Yugoslavia, Bulgaria, Rumania, Hungary, Poland, the USSR, Czechoslovakia, France and Italy all belonged, and the headquarters were in Belgrade. Given that it ceased to meet after 1949, and was wound up soon after Khrushchev made peace with Tito in 1955, the Cominform probably, as Kardelj wrote, "came into existence only as a part of Stalin's plan to attack Yugoslavia". That attack was not long in coming. Within months the Cominform expelled Yugoslavia, so placing it "outside the united Communist front".

These words come from the famous Resolution on the Situation in the Communist Party of Yugoslavia, issued by the Cominform on 28 June 1948. It came as a profound shock to the Yugoslav leaders, but not quite as a surprise. Tensions between the Kremlin and the partisan leadership began in 1941, and had worsened ever since. In the spring of 1948 matters came swiftly to a head. Stalin berated the Yugoslavs for not consulting him before moving troops into Albania, as part of the plan (approved by Stalin) to assimilate the smaller state into the federation. Then the Soviet Union refused to sign a trade agreement with Yugoslavia, and withdrew its military advisors and "economic experts".

The Soviet side set out its dissatisfaction with the CPY, drawing an ominous parallel with "the political career of Trotsky". The Yugoslavs responded in kind, spelling out their own "reasons for discontent", principally the recruitment of "our citizens" as Soviet spies, and the paucity of assistance "in the reconstruction of our country".

The Soviet reply withered and incriminated the Belgrade leadership with a sophistical skill that suggests Stalin's own hand. "The Yugoslav comrades do not accept criticism in a Marxist manner but in the manner of small middle-class people; that is to say, they receive it as an offence which lowers the prestige of the CC of the CPY and which touches the ambitions of the Yugoslav leadership."

By complaining about liberties allegedly taken by Stalin's main man in Belgrade, Tito and Kardelj equated him with "any of the bourgeois ambassadors". "Do they not grasp that such a relationship with the Soviet Ambassador means the same as the denial of friendly relations between the USSR and Yugoslavia? Do they not grasp that the Soviet Ambassador, a responsible Communist, the representative of a friendly country which freed Yugoslavia from the German occupation, has the right, and more so the duty, of entering from time to time into conversation with Communists in Yugoslavia to discuss with them all sorts of questions which might be of interest to them?"

The Yugoslavs insisted these accusations were "based on distorted information"; "we are tenaciously building socialism and remaining true to the Soviet Union." But Tito refused to attend the next Cominform meeting for a free and frank discussion, wisely suspecting that he might not return alive.

When the excommunication came, CC members were already weighing the chance of a direct military attack. Although only one member, Sreten Žujović, sided with the Cominform, even Tito's closest associates were traumatized. The imperturbable Kardelj underwent "a painful personal crisis"; he paced his room for weeks, playing Beethoven on the record player. On the night of the 28th, Djilas "fell asleep as usual around eleven o'clock but suddenly woke up just after midnight, trembling with anxiety". For these two and almost all the other leaders, Stalin was the great white father, and Moscow was their spiritual home. They had long since internalized their loyalty to the CPSU. Communists who had fought through the war as partisans, and now reaffirmed their loyalty to the CPY, wondered if perhaps Stalin was right: if "unbounded arrogance" and "bourgeois nationalism" had led them astray.

Their mere survival was thrown into question. It was a dogma of Stalinism that there could be no socialism without a socialist camp. This had not, after all, been disproved, and Žujović spoke for many when he asked: "What can come of our stand in international relations? Where is our place, in which camp?" The "imperialists" were hungry to destroy the Yugoslav revolution, which now stood alone.

As if this weren't enough, Stalin himself would be working to bring down Tito and his "clique". The Resolution was clear about this: "The Information Bureau does not doubt that in the bosom of the CPY there is a sufficient number of healthy elements. . . . The task of these healthy members of the CPY is to compel their present leaders to admit their errors openly and honestly and to correct them . . . or – if the present leaders of the CPY prove incapable of this – to remove them and to raise high a new internationalist leadership".

If these were the reactions among the élite who had witnessed every step in the deterioration of "friendly relations", picture the dismay of the CPY rank-and-file, over whom the expulsion burst without warning. To them, as to the West, the announcement only a few months before that the Cominform's headquarters would be in Belgrade had confirmed Yugoslavia's pre-eminence as "Satellite Number One". And the date of expulsion presaged catastrophe: 28 June – anniversary of the battle of Kosovo in 1389, and of Franz Ferdinand's death in Sarajevo in 1914.

Some of the most faithful comrades could not bring themselves to turn against Mother Russia, even if they hadn't a thought of betraying their country. Exactly how many upheld the Resolution was not known until recently. The revised total shows 55,663 registered and 16,288 arrested or sentenced Cominformists. The number of Cominformist émigrés is 4,928.

It is impossible to know what proportion of the CPY these totals represent, because so many members were recruited during these years – more than half a million in 1948–51. Cominformists were not evenly distributed by area or nationality or class. As Ivo Banac shows in his fascinating study of the episode, ex-partisans were over-represented, as were "Montenegrins, Bulgars, Italians and Czechs (in that order). . . . [Cominformists] were under-represented among the Slovenes, Hungarians, Albanians, and Croats (in that order)." The army was heavily infected; estimates range from 4,000 Cominformists at all ranks, to 7,000 officers arrested. The most senior soldier implicated was Colonel General Arso Jovanović, wartime Chief of the Supreme Staff, then Chief of the General Staff. In August 1948 he tried to flee to Romania with two other high-ranking officers, after failing to rally the healthy elements. He was shot dead on the border.

The Yugoslavs did not understand the elementary rule: that a satellite's place was to obey, not to parley. They also failed to grasp that their enthusiasm for full-blown Bolshevism was at odds with Soviet aims. The Yugoslavs were inconveniently dogged about wanting Trieste; in the United Nations in 1947, they had the temerity to disagree with the Soviet-US plan for the partition of Palestine.

When Tito told a biographer, decades later, that the shock of expulsion "was very hard for me, the more so as I had gained the impression during my earlier conversations with Stalin that he had appreciated my integrity," he was shrewdly giving a Western readership what it wanted: an account of 1948 in terms of personalities. The split cannot be explained away as bad chemistry or bad faith. Kardelj told the Central Committee meeting convened to respond to Stalin's First Letter, that "we" had consistently "supported the Soviet Union in a creative way." This creativity was the issue. Did "the Belgrade clique of hired spies and murderers" – to quote another Cominform resolution, from 1949 – truly believe it could chart its own course, while remaining part of "the united Communist front"?

The Yugoslavs were convinced that right was on their side, morally and doctrinally. They knew they had mass support throughout the country. In addition to forging their own victory, Party members had achieved their own revolution, which Djilas was not alone in ranking beside the French and Russian Revolutions.

Stalin's intention was to split the Party and the country, whereas he united them as never before – or since. It was a bad miscalculation to claim that the Red Army was the real liberator of Yugoslavia. He blundered too when he accused the leadership of pursuing a "nationalist" path. In Yugoslavia, everyone knew that Tito's Party was relentlessly anti-nationalist.

Stalin failed for another reason. Apart from blockading Yugoslavia, economically and militarily, he had no thought-out plan. His misjudgement of the leadership's strength and popularity stemmed from ignorance. "I shall shake my finger and there will be no more Tito," he told Khrushchev; but it was Khrushchev who later described the atmosphere of insane paranoia and sycophancy which surrounded Stalin in his dotage. By 1948 the great white father rarely ventured outside the Kremlin, and "learned about Russia and the world from films which were made specially for him".

"It was enough for the Yugoslavs to show some disagreement with Stalin for him to accuse them of treason," Khrushchev recalled in the portion of his memoirs released in 1989. "Because of Stalin the Yugoslavs became enemies of the Soviet Union . . . Stalin would not tolerate Yugoslavia's innovations and orginality. The [Soviet] leadership did not really understand what Stalin had against Tito, but that did not matter because ever since Kirov's death there was no democracy in the Politburo. [Kirov, First Secretary of the CPSU in Leningrad, had been murdered in 1934.] Stalin forced the situation with Yugoslavia close to open warfare."

Although Khrushchev, by his own account, never heard of any strategy for invasion, the Hungarian general who was supposed to lead the assault came to believe that "what saved Tito . . . was the Korean War. America stood up. Consequently, [Stalin] assumed that if they invaded Yugoslavia, American will stand up again."

The Hungarians were to be joined by Soviet and Romanian forces, with the occupation of Belgrade reserved for the aggrieved Red Army. The Yugoslavs prepared for full-scale guerrilla defence. The assault never materialized beyond a host of minor incidents on the border.

Stalin resorted to sending agents to assassinate Tito; they were all caught.

Sponsored by the USSR and its satellites, the Cominformist émigrés got busy. They published propaganda. They founded the superbly-titled League of Yugoslav Patriots for the Liberation of the Peoples of Yugoslavia from the Yoke of the Tito-Ranković Clique and Imperialist Slavery. They supported cells inside Yugoslavia, to infiltrate organizations and sabotage installations.

Yet this activity, though occasionally dramatic, as when a number of Yugoslav airforce pilots winged their way to sanctuary in Romania in 1951, was piecemeal. Cominformism was no match for the Yugoslav Party or Army, which, as the inheritors of underground struggle, partisan war, and revolution, offered few footholds to instigators of coups. Now the Party honed itself still further, turning its teeth on the Cominformists themselves.

The long-term effects of expulsion were immense. Before the Resolution, in April, Tito had warned his CC that "revolution does not devour its children. The children of this revolution are honest. We must do everything to render harmless those who would seek to destroy the unity of our party." The hopeful promise in the first sentence of these remarks was contradicted by the third. Honesty was not the issue. Cominformists were enemies within, and the security services had *carte blanche* to deal with the "healthy elements". Agents were "expelled" and even "sentenced", to win the trust of real Cominformists.

Soon after that April meeting, the CC expelled its lone dissenter, Žujović. He was arrested and detained along with Andrija Hebrang, the first post-war minister of industry and something of an odd-man-out in the CC. Hebrang was in digrace with Tito and the Leftists for moderation in his economic policy, and for alleged Croat-nationalist tendencies. Already under investigation for suspected links with the USSR, he was barred from the April meeting. According to the official version, Hebrang and Žujović were Soviet agents. Žujović had kept the Soviet ambassador abreast of CC debates. Hebrang's complicity, on the other hand, is unproven; it seems the opportunity was now seized to blacken his name irrevocably. (Perhaps, too, Tito wanted him persecuted as a counter-balance to Žujović, a Serb.) Ranković prepared a damning *curriculum vitae* for Hebrang. During his six-months' imprisonment by the ustaše in 1942, the Croat partisan leader had, it now emerged, agreed to spy for them in exchange for release. He had been subverting the CPY ever since. While the case against him was still being elaborated, he died in prison, supposedly by his own hand. Žujović remained in solitary confinement for two years, until Djilas and Ranković persuaded him to recant.

Djilas maintains that Žujović was brought to see the error of his ways by reading a book about the then recent trial of László Rajk in Hungary. If true, there is an apt irony in this, for Rajk was a prime victim in the wave of show-trials against "Titoists" that swept Eastern Europe in the years after 1948. Koçi Xoxe was executed in Albania in 1949, the same year as Rajk in Budapest and Trajčo Kostov in Sofia. Purged Polish and Romanian leaders' lives were spared.

Except for Xoxe, whose crime was to be Belgrade's spokesman in the Albanian élite, these men had no special connection with Yugoslavia. It was obvious at the time that "Titoism" was a pretext.

The intention and effect of this cycle of purges and show-trials was to subjugate those states absolutely to Stalin's will.

Zujović's treatment was, of course, no less "Stalinist" than that of Slansky or Rajk. Expert persecution of wayward children of the revolution was conducted at all levels of the CPY, by agents who had staffed Stalin's Comintern and were on the most intimate terms with the mentality of their enemy. The reaction to the Resolution was a tightening of party discipline and control, and a strengthening of state security.

The Yugoslavs proved that a socialist régime could survive outside the "family". Was this responsible for unleashing Stalin's terror upon satellite Parties? Or was the Soviet pressure that they resisted through the winter and spring of 1948 itself the first sign of that terror? Judging from the way that "Titoism" was exploited as an alibi for purges within the Soviet bloc, the second alternative is more likely. Show-trials were no new procedure against internal enemies; they had their ghastly precedent in the witch-hunting of Trotskyists and Bukharinists in the 1930s. The Yugoslavs' survival merely intensified the paranoia that had always been a feature of Stalinism.

After two years of attempting to disprove the Cominform's accusations by hardening its own bureaucratic, centralizing policies, the CPY began to cast about for an orthodoxy of its own. Without the Cominform Resolution there would have been no influx of Western credits, no self-management, no non-alignment, therefore no decentralization of economic and political power.

Pursuing this speculation, I suggest there would still have been civil war in 1991. The void left by Soviet withdrawal from Yugoslavia in 1989 or 1990 would have been filled by half a dozen far-Right nationalist governments in the republics. These would have taken up where the četniks, ustaše, domobrani, domobranci, IMRO, Balli kombëtar and the rest left off in 1945 – slaughtering with more abandon, on a bigger scale even than happened.

1948 was an earthquake in Montenegro. With more than 5,000 *ibeovci*, no less than 1.32 per cent of the population was implicated – almost four times the Yugoslav average. More than one-fifth of all arrested or convicted Cominformists were Montenegrin. Many lives were ruined, and many families today carry the stigma of persecution like a private grief that everybody knows. ("She's had a difficult life," I was told about one young woman, "her father was an *ibeovac*.") Hence the Goli Otok apartment block in Titograd, named after its elderly residents who survived the Adriatic gulag.

The reason was not hostility to Tito or the rest of the leadership, but an extraordinary fidelity to Stalin and the Soviet Union. This was transmitted through Montenegro's patriarchal structures, with their ethos of heroism and endurance (in which *inconsistency* was a flaw of character). Its roots, though, lay in a connection with Russia that went back more than two centuries, when Metropolitans Danilo and Vasilije Petrović forged links with the Russia of Peter the Great. Vasilije implored the Czar to accept Montenegro as a protectorate.

Metropolitans sent their nephews, who by nepotistic tradition would succeed them, to be educated in Petersburg, whither they returned for consecration. It was a Russian envoy who helped Njegoš with his reforms, and Russia which kept Nikola solvent. The Russians were seen as protecting Montenegro with their might. They were a diplomatic counterweight to Venice, Austria and Turkey, and if their patronage hardly helped in the daily struggle against the Turks, spiritual support from the home of Slavdom and mother of Orthodoxy was uniquely prized. Devotion to the Czar translated into veneration for Stalin.

The other factor was the nature of Montenegrin communism. Communism was strong here from the start. In the 1920 elections, the CPY won nearly 38 per cent of Montenegrin votes: 10 per cent more than any other region.

The reasons had little to do with ideology and a lot to do with love of Russia and resentment at Belgrade's heavy-handed abolition of Montenegrin independence. Montenegro was pre-industrial and pre-proletarian. Led in these unpropitious (and after 1921, illegal) conditions by intellectuals and students, supported by groups of peasants and artisans here and there, and shaped by the unearthly Montenegrin environment, communism was blazingly ideal and abstract, like Montenegrin pan-Slavism of old, and like the Marxism of Third World liberation movements in the 1960s.

At the same time the Party was fractured and ineffectual, weakened by opportunism. War gave the young radicals their chance to take control, and in 1942 Montenegro was proclaimed an "integral part of the Soviet Union". This act, bizarrely echoing Vasilije's request two centuries before, was one of the so-called "Leftist errors" of Montenegrin partisans in the first years of the war, when they tried to collectivize the pastures and set up workers' councils, there and then.

One of the Leftest of the radicals was the young Milovan Djilas. Unlike others, he had no doubt where his loyalty lay in 1948, despite his confessed "idolatry" of Stalin. His famous *Conversations with Stalin* gives the true flavour of sentimental Montenegrin Stalinism. During his third and last official visit to the Kremlin, a matter of months before the expulsion, Djilas was driven to Stalin's dacha one night, with Zhdanov, Molotov and Stalin himself. He caught sight of the leader's "already hunched back and the bony grey nape of his neck with its wrinkled skin above the stiff marshal's collar . . . With a sad affection, I saw in Stalin a little old grandfather who, all his life, and still now, looked after the success and happiness of the whole communist race."

*

"There *is* an affinity," Slobodan agreed, "I can't quite say why. Solzhenitysn counts here, and people read Tolstoy more easily than modern European fiction. I expect Russia to figure here a great deal in the next twenty years. Russian nationalism, including Orthodoxy, is reviving, and that will be a backdrop for Serbian nationalism. The October Revolution deprived Serbia of its great pan-Slavic context. It may be about to recover some of that."

Slobodan heads the Democratic Party in Montenegro, a minuscule set-up even by local standards; it contested the election with a membership of 500-odd. We were driving to a monastery above the Zeta valley, north of Titograd. "Orthodox after a fashion", he is friendly with the priest and it was time to pay a visit. Hugging the wheel of his car, he negotiated the ribbon of road – mostly on the wrong side – as it curled around grey ribs of the valley's eastern flank, and dipped into hollows where low stone farmhouses were hutched against the elements.

When I asked people about Slobodan, they usually flapped their hands and tutted about his appearance (unkempt), his posture (round-shouldered), his voice (mumbling). All very un-Montenegrin. Where I come from, he might be any polytechnic teacher, a disaffected Labour Party activist. My friends told me he's not to be trusted, he has a bad character, but I couldn't be a judge of that. Anyway, I did not trust the Montenegrin idea of "trust" in politics, and Bobo's point of view intrigued me – chiefly because he saw principles as part of the problem in local politics, not a source of solutions.

"The Montenegrin tradition is very *thin*," he said. "All that happened here for centuries was veneration of Russia and fighting the Turks. Somehow it forced a habit of soldierly submission to an absolute ruler and to Serbia, and then to Yugoslavia. Everyone was either in the Party or very close to it. Which is one reason why there were no dissidents.

"Nationalism exacts a price everywhere in Yugoslavia, but Montenegro is so poor that the price isn't perceptible. Otherwise we'd finish with this nationalism, or curb it as the Slovenes do. In Slovenia they have civil society; in Serbia somehow they don't."

And here?

"There is no conception of society here, only principles. Or rather, declarations of principles – which is not completely bad. Take the division between greens and whites. This resurfaced during the Second World War, then the Communists suppressed it again. Until a year or so ago, anyone would have told you, 'Greens and whites? That's history!'

"Now it's back: the fundamental division in Montenegro. But it is a question whether the division is still truly alive. We are self-sufficient only in mountains, beer and pride. What would sovereignty mean for half a million people? As for the whites, they are naïve. As if our economic misery could be allieviated by the other republics through a new federal contract!

"This is ground for hope, because it must become clear that the white–green division is rhetorical, and consensus could be found on basic priorities. For the same reason the duality of Montenegrin nationalism is actually promising. Nationalism here elicits radical disagreement. In the past families were split down the middle, by the Cominform crisis as well as the Serbian Question. Not now, though; there's a recognition that it's become a quarrel about nothing, not worth fighting over."

We rounded the last corner and the monastery came into view: three low blocks of building on the edge of an escarpment, as grey as the hillside from which they were hewn. The church identified itself by a tiny dome, no more than an arms' span in diameter. Behind, a sparse orchard of apple trees on a rare shelf of level ground. A panorama of the whole Njeguši range, in rumpled black profile against the early evening sky, filled the view.

Father Lazar and his half-dozen monks and nuns have weathered the years of ideological pressure; their problem now is financial. The community has raised enough money to build a new dormitory, and the priest proudly showed us the roof beams and scaffolding. As we sipped coffee and rakia in the kitchen, afterwards, he asked for news from the city. His only comment about politics was a quiet remark that, although he didn't vote communist himself, he wanted them to do well, because the nationalist parties were stirring up trouble.

"Don't you want autocephaly for the Church in Montenegro?" I asked.

He shrugged. Autocephaly was against the wishes of the clergy, he said, tugging shyly at ringlets of his thick grey beard. The clergy considered themselves part of the Orthodox Church, that was quite sufficient for them.

Father Lazar's views were clearly unbudgeable. If the priests, the communists, and two-thirds of the electorate agreed, however sincerely or not, that sovereignty for Montenegro would open the floodgates of nationalism, what chance did the greens have?

The man whose answers I wanted to hear was the poet Jevrem Brković. I visited him one evening with Saša and Nebojša, two friends who knew something about the poet, as everyone does in Montenegro, and were curious to meet him.

He wasn't at home when we arrived. His wife Kaća showed us into his reception room. The walls were lined with bookshelves and sombre oil paintings. Pomegranates lay broken open on the dining table. Soon I heard Jevrem's rolling baritone, and glimpsed him in the corridor, checking his coiffure in a mirror. There was no need; he looked magnificent as he entered with five or six people in tow. Not far short of two metres tall, with a mane of greying shoulder-length hair and an almost Chinese beard sprouting from his noble jaw, apparelled in Levi jeans, a faded tee-shirt, an ample cardigan, and carpet slippers, the poet greeted us warmly and made the introductions while Kaća poured rakia. Then he settled his big frame into an armchair, beaming at everyone, and made hostly conversation with Saša.

It took an effort to pay attention to the others. They were, it emerged, all far-out Liberals, like the poet himself: convinced believers in the "Montenegro option". Two thick-set young men brought up the rear. Looking rather out of place in this salon, they took seats at the back.

Jevrem raised his glass in my direction, bowed his head a little, and rumbled a ceremonious welcome. Then he stretched out his arm, as if to part the Red Sea. Silence. He rested his hands on a silver-topped cane, poised upright between his knees, and nodded benignly at me. Every head turned to watch.

I began by citing one of Saša's friends. "You have Slovene friends?" this woman had said. "Slovenia imported its culture from Vienna. Montenegro had a culture all of its own." "Where can I see this culture now?" I asked. She shook her head briskly. "Nowhere. Montenegro only exists in history, it has no culture of its own. And you know why? Because Serbia colonized Montenegro." Other young Montenegrins had told me much the same.

"I think you must have come across young people who don't know much about it because they don't feel this culture as an everyday need," Jevrem said, when I reported these sceptical remarks. "Unfortunately centuries of Montenegrin culture are now in glass cases, museums, libraries. But any nation with a university, an Academy of Sciences, a national theatre, painters of European repute, and writers recognized not only in Yugoslavia but far beyond, can hardly be said not to have its own culture. Montenegro was the first state in the Balkans and the oldest South Slav state. Its names have been Duklja, Zeta and Montenegro, but it was always the same state and nation, and the young people you meet are themselves products of centuries of that culture, which is ingrained in their very being.

"About contemporary culture they are partly right, because the communists paid more attention to institutions of culture than to culture itself. The Serbian atittude to Yugoslavia and to Montenegro as a part of Yugoslavia has undoubtedly prevented the culture of Monenegro from gaining the proportions it would otherwise have; there has been a diaspora of Montenegrin artists for seventy years, throughout Yugoslavia and Europe.

"At this moment Montenegro is truly an occupied country. You probably don't believe it because everything appears all right in the streets. There are no tanks or police. But in fact there *are* tanks and police in every cultural institution, pro-Serb prejudices, pro-Serb agents impersonating writers, politicians and bureaucrats, and at their head, agent number one: Amfilohije Radović, the Metropolitan of Montenegro . . . or rather the Serb Metropolitan *in* Montenegro. Ours is the only state in the world without its own Church," he declared absurdly. "I mean Orthodox Church, because Orthodoxy is always national.

"The Serbs annexed our Church in 1920. In Broz-Yugoslavia we regained our centuries-old state, but thanks to communism our Church remained part of the Serbian Church, and this is one of the biggest problems of Montenegro and its culture today. We are a nation without a soul. Our soul was taken from us and now we're struggling to get it back. For another of Montenegro's peculiarities is that it was a theocratic state: the spiritual leader was the head of state.

"All the same," I persisted, "aren't you upholding something that the youth of the country say doesn't exist?"

"Montenegro *has* its culture." Jevrem was imperturbable. "But living culture has been killed off by the communist system. In this respect every nation in Yugoslavia lacks culture. Everywhere in the communist realm, from Montenegro to Beijing, physical culture [gymnastics] had priority over real culture!

"A Montenegrin state and culture and nation exist, and now we are struggling to regain our Church too. We are ready. Do you see these young men?"

He pointed at the silent heavies in the corner. "They are members of the 'Guardians of Lovčen', an organization to defend Lovčen and Meštrović's mausoleum from the barbarians. It is a non-violent organization, but it will take to arms if the need arises."

One of the youths growled, "We're Jevrem's bodyguards too."

"Yes indeed," the poet said, "they're threatening to kill me all the time."

"Who are?" I wanted to know.

"For two years now, and these young men are here to protect me. I have received quite a few death threats."

"Because of what you say about Serbia?"

"Yes, and because of my opposition to Milošević, and because I fought for the rights of the Albanians in Kosovo. In my opinion it's inevitable that Kosovo must in the near future become a republic, meaning one of the sovereign Yugoslav states."

His support for the Kosovars was on record, and almost unique among greens. Now, though, I wanted to ask about Lovčen and the ugly mausoleum. At this point Kaća, a watchful presence at the edge of the company, replenished the flask of rakia. Jevrem watched contentedly. "Here you are, Mr Mark," he commented. "According to the old Montenegrin tradition I as host should pour your first drink, then you do it yourself. I'll show you. Before I pour the rakia I do this." He tipped the open flask against his cheek, so that the liquor touched his skin. "Then I take a sip, so. Why? Because I'm guaranteeing with my cheek [*obraz*] that the rakia is pure, and I prove that it isn't poisoned. Every host did thus until communism took over," he concluded. "Communism has even destroyed our traditions." He paused, and a respectful silence fell.

I seized my chance. "About Lovčen: isn't the mausoleum too . . ." I suddenly hesitated to speak my mind, but Jevrem understood at once. "That is a question of aesthetics," he said. "We merely insist the mausoleum stays as it is, where it is. It is a symbol of our resistance, and undeniably Meštrović is one of the greatest sculptors in the world. He made three monuments in Belgrade – to the Unknown Soldier, the Victor, and Thanksgiving to France – and that doesn't bother the Serbs.* But they do mind about the Njegoš mausoleum; for them it means a Croat on top of Lovčen."

"Apart from keeping the mausoleum, what does Montenegro need now?" I asked. "What does it need *most*?"

"Montenegro has had enough of passion, enough of 'epic', both the false and genuine sorts. Enough 'big history'. Its mentality today is utterly submerged in the past. Despite that, all means of technology are available to us, the media and all that, we are still a typical archaic nation. The cult of Njegoš bears a great deal of blame for this. And the cults of our saints, poets, rulers and martyrs as well. If

---

* It does: in 1991, nationalists in Belgrade were demanding the demolition of The Victor.

we want to exist as a modern nation, if we want to *think*, we must reject our historical emotions and face the dreaded present with its computers and microchips and even its prostitution – another aspect of contemporary life which we lack, though the Italians established five whorehouses straightaway, when they invaded in 1941. The Italians played a civilizing rôle in that respect: they introduced sex education to Montenegro!

"Seriously, it's our obsession with history and politics, and communism above all, that has led us where we are. What we need most is a catharsis. We must repudiate our myths, especially the modern ones. The first to go must be the myth of 'Yugoslavism', then the myth of 'Serbism', and then our pathological need in Montenegro to sacrifice ourselves for all the Yugoslav nations, above all for Serbia. Shall we emerge from this catharsis as up-to-date idiots, specialists without souls, or as a historic nation with all our characteristics intact? *That* is the question. But if we don't choose catharsis we shall share the destiny of the Khazars, the ancient nation that became extinct of its own free choice."

Sighs of pleasure arose from the other guests. Someone whispered in my ear, "Even *he* is satisfied with that conclusion."

Saša approved too: "That was really nicely put."

"What did you expect?" intoned Jevrem, folding his arms over his cardigan. "If the interview is over," he said, beaming again, "you shall all stay to eat Dukljan food and drink Dukljan wine." (For the rest of the night, with no explanation, everything was Dukljan.) Kaća ferried trays of goat's cheese, potatoes, salad, and black wine.

My memories now grow dim and patchy. I know we left at half-past three in the morning. I know that one of the company spent half an hour persuading me Homer wrote the *Iliad* about Montenegro. I know I asked Jevrem about the monarchy:

"I hear that Nikola, the Petrović heir, is happy as an architect in France and isn't interested in claiming his throne."

Surprise at my simple-mindedness shadowed Jevrem's brow. "The prince doesn't have to be 'interested' in the throne," he countered. "The throne is *his*. Besides, every Montenegrin wants to be a king."

There seemed no answer to that.

I know Jevrem opened the window for fresh air. Saša shivered and reached for her jacket. "This is how the men of Duklja helped women to put on their garments," Jevrem said, bending low to help. Saša gives as good as she gets: "And I suppose they were even nicer at helping them to remove them?"

"To be sure, to be sure," the poet grinned.

No sounds came through the casement except a blackbird singing and singing in the trees above the Ribnica. We finished the Dukljan food and wine. Kaća brought a handful of keepsakes, which Jevrem handed me solemnly, one by one. There was a postcard of Queen Milena, the wife of Nikola. "Was she really as beautiful as this?" I asked, in the spirit of things. "Much *more* beautiful!" Jevrem said, happily. Then he motioned me to stand. Pinning a "100% Montenegrin" lapel badge on my jacket, he kissed me on both cheeks. "I hereby invest you in the Society of Ancient Dukljans," he said. "When next you come to Montenegro, you will stay in our little house in the country, and we shall hunt the wild beasts together."

I know we walked home, past the tireless blackbird, and Nebojša shook his head in disbelief. "He makes you feel like an aristocrat, doesn't he. Too much. *Too* much."

The best-known fictional Montenegrin is Rex Stout's creation, the detective Nero Wolfe. As a gourmand and orchidist who solves cases without leaving his New York apartment, the elephantine but nimble-witted Wolfe is endowed with suitably prodigious eccentricities. And somewhere at the dark root of his career lies an act of purely Montenegrin deceit; as Stout reveals in *Over My Dead Body* (1940), Wolfe spent World War One fighting with the Montenegrin army *and* spying for the enemy Austrians.

The duplicity of Montenegro is a birthright that burdens its people, nudging them into the strait laces of conformism with one side or the other. Outsize Montenegrins like Jevrem Brković are controversial figures, detested and esteemed in equal measure – if they're lucky. Outside Jevrem's flat, hardly anyone I met in Montenegro had good words for the man. I'm still not sure how much he was pulling my leg, but I like his nationalism the more for being leavened with buffoonery.

As for his faith in Montenegrin culture, well, Jevrem is Montenegrin in the sense that someone else is a nuclear physicist: by years of study and application. There just isn't a call for many nuclear physicists.

He doesn't seek power, so he can afford to let beauty trample on realism; with us, he discussed actual political oppression and his idea for a Dukljan Academy of Arts ("to teach painting, duelling, drama, television, architecture and chivalry") with quite the same twinkling seriousness. Taken literally, he seems quaint, a tower of contradictions: an atavistic modernizer, a patriarchal democrat. As a performer on the Montenegrin stage, he is a true patriot, because his notion of *humanitas heroica* is not nationalist. He was the first person to name the anti-bureaucratic revolution for what it was: a coup. And when Montenegrin troops joined the war in 1991, Jevrem published an apology to the people of Croatia and an ode to

Dubrovnik. Charged with fomenting national hatred, and bringing Montenegrin officials into disrepute, a warrant was issued for his arrest. He fled across the mountains, by night, into Albania, and made his way to Ljubljana; I saw a photo of him there, still smiling, with the silver-topped cane in his hand, as if he knew for sure that the real exile was Montenegro, not himself.

Clear Sky over Serbia

The clouds above the town of Topola moved as calmly as the pace of life below. I crossed the dusty main street into an avenue of bungalow villas, where the only sounds were birdsong and the cackle of a radio through an open window, reporting a distant war.

The avenue led to a wooded hill. On top of the hill stands a marble church with green copper domes. The kings of Serbia and of Yugoslavia lie here. It was built in 1910–30 as a pastiche of late medieval Serbian architecture, ponderously decorated with glossy mosaic copies of frescoes.

Topola is the site of this national monument because it was the home of Karadjordje, "Black George", the pig farmer who led the first Serbian rebellion against the Ottoman Empire in 1804, then ruled the free Serbian territory until the Turks recaptured it in 1813. Karadjordje was murdered in 1817 with the connivance of Miloš Obrenović, one of his own lieutenants who had led a second uprising. The two men's descendants feuded through the rest of the century, until the Karadjordjevići gained the final ascendancy in 1903. King Petar built this church to glorify his family as the rightful successor to the medieval Serbian dynasty. Karadjordje, his grandfather, was buried in the apse, and the crypt was prepared for future generations.

When I visited, Petar's tomb was heaped with wreaths of lilies and evergreen twigs. "The Serbian people of Slavonija, Baranja and Srem" said the message on one wreath. Others were from "The Serbian People of Bosnia and Hercegovina", "The People of Montenegro".

I had an appointment to keep in Kragujevac. The coach rolled south, past ramshackle farms with hurdle fences, haystacks, emerald orchards speckled with goosedown. This is the region of *Šumadija*, "the forest land": immemorial Serbia, a heartland of woods, vineyards, fields, grimy villages and big commercial towns.

Along with my ticket for the marble church, I had been given a calendar of Serbian military commanders. The first illustration was hulking Karadjordje himself, sashed and tunicked. The soldiers wore pistols and daggers stuffed in gilt cummerbunds. Then the khaki marshals of the Balkan Wars and World War One, and finally King Petar and King Aleksandar. Except for prim-mouthed Aleksandar, these could have been portraits of the countrymen getting on and off the coach. In one village, a snowy-haired old man with arthritic joints climbed aboard, and led his apple-cheeked wife to the seats across the aisle from mine. With his superb moustache, deep-set eyes and great rugged nose, he was a ringer for King Petar. When he sat back, clasping his knees with thick hands, he looked more like a khaki hero of 1914. All he lacked was a *képi* and a chestful of medals. He turned to whisper in his wife's ear – something about the relatives they were on their way to see. First she tutted at him, then she had to smile, and when he saw this his own face creased into a grin, and he winked delightedly. I smiled too; it was like being in the presence of Father Serbia, indomitable and golden-hearted.

At Kragujevac the old patriarch ushered his wife out of the coach with dignity, though wincing as he bent to fit with their baggage through the door.

Under Miloš Obrenović, this was Serbia's capital. Then and ever since, it has been a centre of national life, and it has a peculiar air of self-possession, perhaps because its old quarter is still intact. The Second World War brought human destruction, but left the buildings alone. In October 1941, the Germans shot some 5,000 citizens as a reprisal: a crime without parallel in occupied Yugoslavia.

Kragujevac is the biggest industrial town in the Šumadija, and I had come to learn about its economic plight, but my contact – a middle-aged gent who had lived here all his life – didn't want to talk economics. We were meeting on the second day of the coup by hardliners in the Soviet Union, and this man was well satisfied, as if the coup were Mikhail Gorbachev's just desserts for whoring after Europe so shamelessly.

It was a short leap from Gorbachev to Slovenia and Croatia. "It's very simple," he said, putting down his coffee cup and spearing another chunk of Turkish delight with a cocktail stick. "The Slovenes and Croats aren't at war with Yugoslavia – they're at war with themselves. Slovenia has betrayed us, and the Croats have an inferiority complex towards us. They want to go to Europe, but we say Europe is here." He waited patiently for me to nod. "It's simple. We aren't pacifists, we aren't nationalists, we're *Serbs*. And Europe can't threaten us into submission now, because freedom has no price."

This man bore out the reputation that Kragujevac has for hospitality. When we had talked to a standstill, albeit on his terms, he showed me the sights: the handsome *konak* where Prince Miloš lived, the neo-classical school and the courtrooms. Then he walked me to the bus station and waited with me; it was out of his path, it was late, and we were only third-hand acquaintances (he was a colleague of friends of friends), but I had become his guest and his town's, and he would not leave me untended. We parted with warm handshakes and *au revoirs*.

I had a lot to think about on the way back to Belgrade. I came to Topola and Šumadija to clear my head and to find my bearings. Serbia in 1991 was half-crazy, unhinged. It was *Alice Through the Looking Glass* with guns, blood, hatred, and fathomless deceit. Along with the rest of the outside world, I watched Serbia destroy Yugoslavia in the name of Yugoslavia, while storing up disaster for itself, in the name of its own future.

Of course, another construction could be put upon the crisis. Almost all Serbs, like my host in Kragujevac, blamed everything on "the separatists". In the sense that there would have been no war in 1991 had Croatia and Slovenia not defied enemies and well-wishers alike, and walked the plank to independence, this view is true. But it does not amount to a whole truth, or a sufficient one. It was offered to the world, however, with baffling chutzpah, as whole and non-negotiable.

The western republics appeared flexible, to a point. Since the elections of spring 1990, both republics had been pressing for the federation to be confederated. This would have preserved Yugoslavia as a voluntary community of sovereign states, with monetary union, a single market, and separate but co-ordinated armies. On the model of the European Community, the main confederal authority would have been a council of ministers, with a consultative parliament in the background.

Serbia, Montenegro, and of course the federal army (JNA) condemned the confederal option as a warrant to kill Yugoslavia by degrees. They backed instead a proposal to reorganize the state in a way that actually tightened central mechanisms, for instance by weighting certain federal institutions over republican ones. Slovenia and Croatia dismissed this as a "Bolshevik" proposal. Macedonia and Bosnia-Hercegovina hovered somewhere between the two options.

Transcripts of federal presidency discussions on this topic make sorry reading, like schoolboy slanging matches. Each side was convinced that it held a monopoly of truth. As James Gow deftly comments: "Whereas the confederalists identified federation with the old system of Serb-dominated centralism, federalists understood it as the only sense in which Yugoslavia could continue to exist. Conversely, for the federalists, confederation was a code for breaking up Yugoslavia, to the confederalists it could be seen as a way of enabling the Yugoslavs to remain together."

At the end of 1990 and into 1991, the federalists were, by simply refusing to consider confederation, daring the Croatian and Slovenian leaders to act on their electoral promises to secede if confederal reform proved unattainable.

Beyond their economic motives, which were garbled and selfish, but perfectly legitimate, the Croats and Slovenes were driven by political and (in nationalist jargon) national-spiritual motives. Each refusal of confederation strengthened their wish to run their own affairs without reference to the rest of the federation. Why? Because reference meant interference and deference – primarily to Serbia, the biggest republic.

Size, however, was not the main reason why the restless members of the federation felt Serbia's shadow. Serbia was the most influential republic because Serbs were the biggest and most dispersed nation. As the ethnographic map on p. 97 shows, large numbers of Serbs live outside their national republic. With 35 per cent of the federal population, Serbs are 31 per cent of Bosnia-Hercegovina's population, 12.2 per cent of Croatia's and 9 per cent of Montenegro's. The Serbs (along with the Montenegrins) have always been most committed to a unified and centralized Yugoslavia, because unity kept all Serbs in one state; and because centralism of government in a state enclosing such differences was the best way to guarantee unity. Also, a centralized Yugoslavia was bound to be a Yugoslavia in a predominantly Serbian key.

One might suppose, then, that the confederalists were not as flexible as they seemed; for they refused to mollify their challenge to the very principle upon which their opponents could never compromise.

But this skeletal analysis is, again, less than the whole truth. War was the climax of a crisis that had its own dynamic context, of which the main feature was Serbia's drive to re-centralize the state by reversing certain devolutionary reforms of the 1960s and '70s. The first aim of this drive was achieved in 1989 by revoking the autonomy of Kosovo and Vojvodina, the two provinces within Serbia. The second aim was to use Serbia's new muscle to block the confederalists' proposals and impose its alternative.

Devolution had been the outcome of a dialectic dating from the first self-management reforms in 1950. It is a process fraught with problems in any state, and communism always prefers to deal with monoliths, so the process was fitful and incomplete in Yugoslavia; but it went a good long way because economic growth required it.

Growth in the federal units was very unequal, but all units made progress; therefore the totality progressed as well.

This progress was uniquely threatening to those Serbs who insisted upon living in one state; it appeared the thin end of a wedge that would split the federation apart.

Not all Serbs were against decentralization, however. Those whose first and overriding priority was not state unity but something else – prosperity, art, football, democracy, feminism, the future of a community called Yugoslavia, or whatever else – accepted that the dialectic of development brought benefits to outweigh the eclipse of that dream of unity.

Two things happened in the 1980s. The first was the arrival of democracy, knocking timidly at first, but not for long. The reforms of the 1960s and '70s had nothing to do with democracy; they were devised partly to 'buy off' discontent with the one-party system by making it as odourless as possible. Nevertheless, through no fault of their own (from the leaders' points of view), democracy became the big issue, in Yugoslavia and everywhere else in communist Europe.

Add democracy to the dialectic of development, and what you have is an acceleration of the trend for the outstanding reason that the federal units in their existing form were, give or take, natural candidates for autonomy; not in the sense of ethnic homogeneity but as historic and cultural entities. Perhaps Yugoslavia would remain, in altered, looser form; perhaps not.

Now the second thing that happened. The dialectic faced Serbs with a specific challenge. In the other republics, once the communists had accepted that the federal system could not endure much longer, they, along with nationalists and democrats could look to the future, because for the time being they were going in a direction that suited them all – towards greater autonomy.

Serbs, by contrast, were being asked to abandon their own deepest-held national edict: unity in one state. Nationalists swung into action; the view was put about in the early to mid-1980s, and easily gained currency, that decentralization was the crowning achievement of a long post-war conspiracy against the Serbian nation.

As this cultural movement gathered steam, it merged with a second stream of centralists and anti-federalists, coming from a very different source. These were the republican politicians who were hoping to fill the vacuum that Tito's death in 1980 had disclosed at the core of the federal system. These leaders were doubly dismayed at the prospect of the system withering away, because they needed a federation to expand into, and because democracy threatened their own power base.

It was a paradoxical partnership. The authentic Serbian nationalists were anti-communist, because federalism – the foundation of the conspiracy – was a communist affair. As for the politicians, they were anti-nationalist by ideology. Yet they bedded down together, often with elaborate disclaimers, excuses, and much self-deceit. Nor were they alone: the usual quota of opportunists and freeloaders soon jumped in. (The armed forces and the state security services had, of course, been there before any of them.)

In all they mustered a lot of troops: enough to stop the dialectic in its tracks. There was a hideous squealing of brakes. Clouds of stinking smoke covered the scene. When these cleared, behold! The dialectic had been badly bashed and utterly fragmented, but not derailed. A bit of the old federation had sailed ahead regardless. Other bits were bloodsoaked and mixed up with each other, yet creeping on. Others again were stalled, yet their engines still ticked over.

Which is why this chapter's subtitle, if it had one, would be: "How the Serbs turned back the clock but couldn't stop time."

Time can't be stopped and mostly the Serbs knew it, though they kept forcing themselves to suppress this knowledge, deny all the evidence, and believe in their hopeless project.

Croatia was ablaze, Serbia was untouched, and I kept meeting people who insisted the Croats were the aggressors, and they – Serbs and the JNA – were waging a defensive struggle to save themselves and Yugoslavia. They had unleashed the biggest land assault in postwar Europe, and they kept telling me that no nation in history had suffered like their own. Of course they were really telling themselves, but they expected me to listen, and looked reproachful or plain angry if I was impatient with their unawareness and wanted to switch the subject to the actual horrors being perpetrated.

I was moving inside a multi-storeyed labyrinth of deception. The freewheeling pandemonium of events was actually controlled, until almost the end of 1991, by a handful of people who knew just what was happening, and ensured that the rest of the nation was fed an irresistible diet of lies. And the nation guzzled these lies so avidly that it turned into a lie.

But I can't deny it was fascinating, pruriently so, to be in Serbia as the war escalated through late summer. I pictured myself as a doctor in a science fiction film, shrunk to the size of pollen dust and injected into a psychotic patient to observe the exploding synapses, fizzing ganglia, and rogue chemical invasions.

My trip to Topola was meant as a test. I wanted to see if Serbia's part in this war made more sense from this vantage point. If the Serbs truly wanted to reverse time, the logic of their stance would lead them back to this peaceful green hill with its marble church. Karadjordje himself – coarse, fearless, astute, and as brutal as he had to be – was guided in all situations by one passion: Serbia. In some sense he is still the paradigm here of national leadership; and the monarchy was a political factor again in Serbia. As the federation withered, Crown Prince Aleksandar Karadjordjević, sitting in his office in Belgravia, London, had become distinctly impressed by the possibility of taking up where his father had left in 1941.* There was a monarchist movement, and crowds of a few thousand greeted Aleksandar when he visited Belgrade for the first time, in October 1991.

Instead of revelation, Topola offered tranquillity. I breathed the fragrant air, and thought how obscene this peacefulness was. One of the old epic poems about Karadjordje's uprising in 1804 begins with God's saints trying to motivate the Serbs against the Turks. Blood has boiled out of the ground – a portent; the people know their duty, but are scared to rebel. The saints turn the moon black, but still "the Serbs did not dare to rise in arms". So the saints send "bloody banners of war through the unclouded sky". There were no saintly omens in 1991. No banners in the vacant sky. Blood soaked into the ground, not here but a few dozen kilometres away, obeying gravity in the usual way. As for Kragujevac and my middle-aged acquaintance there: too many people were paying too high a price for his blissful certitudes. Months later, in December, when the fighting in Croatia was almost spent, I read about a thirty-five year-old JNA reservist from Kragujevac who returned home after twenty days in eastern Croatia. He refused to go back. "The army will punish me and I will probably lose my job," he said, "but I do not want to fight in this stupid war," which he called "a tragedy, only serving the interests of the people who are in power. What happened in Vukovar is a shame on Serbia. A lot of civilians were killed from army artillery. It was very, very wrong. But because there's a total media blockade, the truth about this war is not getting through to the people." I felt a lift of gratitude to this man who dared not let the reporter print his name.

*

I had come to Serbia from Budva, on the Montenegrin coast. The streets there were lined with Belgrade-registered cars; the coast was

---

* Although he has never lived in Serbia, Aleksandar lacks none of the Serbian aplomb. When a British journalist asked him how important it is that the Karadjordjevići are related to the House of Windsor, he retorted that "they are related to us".

packed with Serb holidaymakers whose favourite resorts in Croatia were out of bounds, and soon to be under fire.

The beaches were grubby and the mood was jovial. A teak-tanned beach bum in flowery bermudas sat beside my friend Saša and smirked: "Hey, shall we go to Knin to protect the Serbs, what about it?" On Montenegro's coast the war was a chat-up line.

July collapsed in vast electric storms. Under a graphite sky I bussed south, past the old royal resort of Miločer, where Serbia's political leaders were recreating themselves and their families: Democrats and Socialists and Renewalists savouring the seafood while Croatia burned.

The grafitti in Bar ranted "THIS IS SERBIA". At Bar I entrained for Belgrade.

The Bar–Belgrade line is an epic railway. From the coast the train climbs to Lake Skadar, pauses in Titograd, then embarks on a spectacular route through the Montenegrin hinterland, or rather above it. The line follows the Morača gorge for a way, breaks across country to Kolašin, and dips into the Tara valley. After Mojkovać it switches to the valley of the Lim and exits to Serbia.

Railways in the Andes must look like this, pinned to the mountain like a curtain-rail, and feel like it too, clanking slowly over the points. Below the carriage windows, crags and scree cascade to tiny meadows and torrents. Montenegro appears a landscape of giant stone dunes, unfarmed, unhomed.

On either side of a viaduct, in the back of beyond, spruce railwaymen stood to attention beside their signal boxes as the train passed. Professional neatness was rare in south Yugoslavia, and here it proved more than local pride in the railway. Since 1878 the leaders of Serbia and Montenegro had wanted a railway connection from Belgrade to the sea. The railway featured in every federal development plan, yet the Latin American section wasn't begun until the mid-1960s, after an unprecedented agreement between Serbia's and Montenegro's Leagues of Communists. Enormous resources were then devoted to the railway despite the consternation of other republics, above all Croatia, whose ports were ailing from under-investment.

The route was completed in 1975. A tremendous feat of engineering, it is also spendthrift and archaic. This is no artery binding the two Orthodox lands, but a rickety railway line. It is often out of service, and the full journey takes anything from six-and-a-half to ten hours. To dream of a railway link in 1878 was one thing: steam locomotion was in its heyday, the gauge of progress the world over. How, though, to justify such labour and investment in the 1960s, when the Ljubljana–Zagreb road was not even a dual carriageway (it still isn't), and the Zagreb—Belgrade road – officially the Highway of Brotherhood and Unity, unofficially "the dead road" – was one of the busiest and most dangerous routes in Europe?*

The railway was patently an expression of pan-Serb solidarity, which for other Yugoslavs was hard to tell apart from Great Serbism. In 1991 this term, always familiar in the Balkans, became famous in the wider world too, chiefly as an accusation flung at the "expansionist" Serbian government by its Yugoslav opponents, and muttered in Western ministries.

Great Serbia is myth, fantasy, history, strategy, taunt, and threat. In no particular order. It is the traditional goal of Serb nationalists. What it isn't any longer, if it ever was, is an achievable goal.

The question of Great Serbia is more than the question of Serbia in Yugoslavia, which is just its most recent form. It originates in eras when the Balkans were a blur of warring medieval states, shrinking and expanding like amoebas under a microscope. It connects each successive Serbia – imperial, Turk-dominated, independent, Yugoslav, war-torn, or socialist – to the platonic Serbia whose image seems to shine like Camelot in the collective imagination.

Stripped of polemic and ideology, Great Serbia is a geographical term. Its maximal meaning is the territory encompassed by the Serbian state at its greatest extent. This was the medieval state founded by Stefan Nemanja in 1169 and consolidated by his son.

Beginning from their clan base at Raška, in what is now the Sandžak, father and son won the support of other chieftains and expanded eastward to the Morava river and westward to the sea. They challenged the Byzantine empire, enfeebled by the Crusades and a Bulgar uprising. Under Stefan Uroš II Milutin (ruled 1282–1321), Nemanjić control reached south to Macedonia and north to the Danube. When Milutin married the daughter of the Byzantine emperor, the "Byzantinization" of the Serbian court began. Its panoply still gleams in the gorgeous frescoes of Dečani and Gračanica churches.

Under Stefan Dušan (1331–55) the kingdom became an empire. Using force only when negotiation failed, Dušan doubled Serbia's territory at Byzantium's expense. Eventually he commanded all the lands from the Neretva and the Danube to the Aegean and western Thrace. Dušan moved the capital to Skopje, the empire's midpoint, and then to Ohrid. He had himself crowned as "Emperor of the Serbs

---

* This hasn't changed: part of the section in Slavonia is still, incredibly, single-lane. A cynic at the Federal Office of Statistics told me that the war, which stopped all Belgrade-Zagreb traffic except JNA tanks and lorries, had obviously been devised as a stratagem to cut mortality on "the dead road".

and Greeks", and issued his Code, the South Slavs' first legal charter. His gold and silver mines enriched the court and paid for his large mercenary army. His near-monopoly of Balkan trade routes was lucrative, and all that stood between his state and mastery of south-eastern Europe was Byzantium, now declining before a new threat from the east: Ottoman Turkey.

The Byzantine emperor tried to use the Turks against the Serbs, unsuccessfully at first, for Dušan saw off Turkish incursions in 1345 and 1349.

Dušan died preparing a final assault on Constantinople. Within thirty years his empire had vanished under Ottoman assault, abetted by quarrels among the Serbian nobles. The empire could not achieve the stability promised by the static splendour of its rituals and artefacts. Its expansion was only possible because Constantinople was beset on all sides. It swelled like a golden balloon until, stretched to membrane thinness, it burst at the first touch.

The Nemanjić dynasty ended in 1371 with the death of Dušan's son. His successor Lazar Hrebeljanović, ruling over a much smaller territory, could not reverse the disintegration of his state, yet he staved off defeat by improvising alliances with surrounding powers – Bosnia, Hungary, Croatia, Ragusa (Dubrovnik), Venice. He beat back the first Ottoman raiders, but when Sultan Murad invaded in earnest, there could be no doubt of the outcome. On 28 June 1389, the Serbian and Ottoman armies clashed at Kosovo.

Serbia ceased to exist in 1458 when its final citadel, the fortress at Smederevo, fell. It only reappeared with Karadjordje in 1804. The last part of Byzantium to fall to the Turks was the first part of the Balkans to rid itself of them.

The other geographical meaning of Great Serbia emerged in the mid-nineteenth century. The principality of Serbia, secure at last from Turkish re-occupation, began to feel its strength. At this point Serbia was a fraction of its present size, smaller even than the territory shown on the map on p. 199. (Niš and the triangle of territory south of Niš stayed Turkish until 1878.) The first programme for uniting the Serbs was drawn up by a minister called Ilija Garašanin in 1844. His criterion of Serbdom was linguistic, not religious or historical. He didn't expect to extend Serbia's borders back to the Aegean. His sights were chiefly focused upon Bosnia-Hercegovina.

The envisaged state would be some sort of successor to Dušan's empire, yet his blueprint – which became a fixed principle of Serbian policy – was also libertarian. As the only free land of Yugoslavs, except tiny Montenegro, Serbia saw itself as the Piedmont of the Balkans, unifying and liberating its enslaved neighbours. There could be no liberty without unity, and who could lead this effort but the Serbs? Expansionism and the cause of Yugoslav liberty appeared to be one and the same.

The current conception of Great Serbia is very different. The modern equivalent of Garašanin's plan is the Memorandum produced in 1986 by a working group of the Serbian Academy of Sciences and Arts. This vengeful document spoke of an anti-Serb coalition by Croat and Slovene leaders in postwar Yugoslavia, of "Serbophobia", of "genocide" against Serbs in Croatia, of Albanian "separatists" forcing Serbs out of Kosovo. Bewailing the three-way partition of Serbia by the 1974 constitution, it appealed to Serbs to look to their national interests. Its entire tone and argument were morbidly, bitterly retrospective.

Doubtless these ageing Academicians took no direct part in the fighting of 1991, but it is fair to say their spirit was faithfully represented by the Serbian Radical Party and its leader, "Duke" Šešelj, a mentally unstable ex-dissident who demanded that Serbia must extend, in the north, from Karlobag on the coast, to Karlovac, south of Zagreb, and on to Virovitica, by the Hungarian border. In the south, this Great Serbia would reach to the border with Greece.

Šešelj's gangs of "četnik" fighters, who boasted of their atrocities against Croats, were loyal servants of the Academicians' vision, as were local guerrilla commanders like Mile Dakić of Petrova Gora, who bragged that the Croats "can secede as much as they want, but they will be able to survey their whole state from Zagreb cathedral".

This conception of Great Serbia is not defined by language or culture. Nobody talks of redeeming the vestigial Serb communities in Romania and Hungary. The spraycan artists in Bar and elsewhere, especially in Bosnia-Hercegovina, who appropriate public buildings with the signature: "THIS IS SERBIA", are no scholars of medieval Serbia, nor do they care where its limits lay; they want to upset the non-Serb locals.* Yet the image of an insatiable Serbia hungry to engulf any territory within reach, was not created in the streets; these spraycan messages merely summarize the incessant demands since the mid 1980s of politicians, intellectuals and media.

Take Serbia's much reiterated "claim" to Dubrovnik. The city-state of Ragusa never submitted to Serbia in the hazy medieval past. The city's cultural heritage is not Serbian, nor is there a large Serb minority; according to the 1991 census only 6.7 per cent of the city's 70,672 people are Serbs, compared to 82.5 per cent Croats. (When a

---

* The best answer can be read on Sarajevo's main post office. Below the crass slogan, a Bosnian sage has replied: "WRONG, DIMWIT, IT'S A POST OFFICE."

spokesman for the self-styled Autonomous Region of Krajina, the Serb rebel zone in Croatia, repeated this claim to me, I protested. He was adamant: the persistence of Orthodox customs around the city proved, he said, its essentially Serbian identity. "But," he nodded ruefully, as if demonstrating his moderation, "Serbia has lost Dubrovnik, that's the truth.")

By 1991 the limits of Great Serbia were fixed by the standing international borders of Yugoslavia. Within those limits, it included the Republic of Serbia plus any other regions where Serbs live or lived or might have lived. Because Serbian history is one of mass migrations up, down, and across the space now occupied by all or part of Serbia, Montenegro, Macedonia, Croatia and Bosnia-Hercegovina, Serb communities live or lived or might have lived just about everywhere except Slovenia and north-western Croatia.

In 1991, "Duke" Šešelj's views were not extreme in Serbia. He was elected to parliament in 1991, and when he told his fellow members that, for instance, Zagreb might need to be napalmed very soon, he was not ejected or even censured. His territorial views seemed widely acceptable too. The Serbian government did not admit that expansion of the Serbian republic was a war-aim, but its agents and proxies had no doubts. Goran Hadžić, for example, the leader of the Serbs in eastern Croatia, said in October that "we are establishing the western border of Serbia, and how far it extends depends on how strong we are." Quite.

*

My status on the train from Bar changed from passenger to guest. Serb largesse enveloped me. My seat was only reserved as far as Prijepolje, but the new occupant wouldn't hear of me standing; he and his wife wedged up and insisted I make myself comfortable again. Opposite us a strapping widow poured coffee for everyone from an urn-sized flask. Beside her, a sleeping girl nestled in her boyfriend's arms.

The window seats were taken by a couple of engineers riding home to Valjevo. We talked about football for a bit; then I said how confused we were in Britain about the war in Croatia. They frowned unhappily and nodded that, yes, it was complicated for outsiders, but the things was, the Croat fascists had to be stopped. The Serbs in Croatia were suffering genocide, as under the ustaše in the Second World War.

But the ustaše killed hundreds of thousands of people, I said. In 1991 a few dozen Serbs and Croats were killed before the war began for real, in August. Now the war was killing far more Croats than Serbs. How could they say the situation was like 1941?

They frowned again, and looked more unhappy. As usual at this point of a discussion, I was downcast by a sense of futility, but it was too late now to go back to football. I tried to look disarming, and their good nature overcame their bristling distrust, like a hedgehog uncurling after a false alarm. They began to talk about Serbs' sacrifices for the Croats and Slovenes since 1914, and how they were paid back with separatism. About the Albanians, separatists too. About the Macedonians, who were freed from the Turks by the Serbs in the Balkan Wars, and now wanted to separate.

So it continued. You would think these young engineers had lost at the battle of Kosovo in 1389, rebelled with Karadjordje in 1804, beaten the Austrians in 1914, risen against the Axis in 1941, been terrorised in Kosovo in the 1980s. In Serbs' speech the people are conjured as one person, who is also Serbia; every generation becomes one generation, which is Serbia too. "Serbia has had enough," they warn you, like a lawyer whose client's Jobish patience is finally drained.

This speech compacts all Serbs into a 'we' that creates 'they', who are forever doing all manner of evil things to Serbia: bad-mouthing and subverting it, hating it, sapping its strength, killing its children.

Homogenizing rhetoric was not exclusive to Serbs, of course; Croats and Albanians bind themselves just as passionately to their ancestors. What was unique to Serbs, as Yugoslavia died on its feet, was the stunning contrast between their self-image as projected in this piteous narrative, and the facts that were there for everyone else to see. There is no understanding Serbia without fathoming its wounded self-righteousness, its perception of itself as more sinned against than sinning.

The sense of grievance comes with a ready-made interpretation of Serbia's part in making and preserving Yugoslavia.

The story begins uncontroversially. Serbs lived for four hundred years and more under the Ottoman heel. Only a handful of churches survived as witnesses of lost glory and covenants of resurrection. (In their remoteness, scale, and design, these wonderful buildings do seem hunched against the rage of centuries, the glacial drag of time.) Subject to every kind of military and fiscal oppression, the Serbs only preserved their identity by never yielding their faith or forgetting their empire.

With liberation and statehood in the nineteenth century, matters became more complicated. For a Serbian perspective, I had asked Borislav Mihailović, a venerable nationalist of unquestioned integrity. "Serbia accepted the rôle of leader, so to speak, among

The constituent parts of the Kingdom of Serbs, Croats and Slovenes

liberated Slav states in the Balkans," he told me. "That rôle has become something which other states condemn Serbia for. Serbia sacrificed itself for the liberation of the Balkans from two empires, the Turkish and the Austro-Hungarian, but now in retrospect it is regarded as imperialistic.

"By the beginning of the twentieth century the Kingdom of Serbia, though very small, was an absolutely democratic state, fit for comparison with any other European country. It was a typical constitutional monarchy with very few rights for the crown. All parties were permitted, including an Anarchist Party. The press law had one article: 'The press is free.'

"Democracy," Mihailović summarized at this point, with infinite dignity, "is not unknown to the Serbs.

"With her relatively well equipped and effective army, Serbia fought three wars. In 1912 Serbia conquered the Turks. As a result Turkey was removed from these territories, from Skopje to its present borders. In 1913 she led a war against Bulgaria, which was also victorious. Then, very unfortunately and to her disaster, she fought a third war, when Austria-Hungary attacked her in 1914. After these three wars, she invested her victory in the liberation of other Slav nations, especially Croats and Slovenes."

To grasp the significance of all this, one needs to know what a holocaust the First World War was for Serbia. A quarter of its population died – an inconceivable loss. After the Serbs' astounding victory over Austria-Hungary in 1914, the best part of a year elapsed before the Austrians launched a massive assault on Belgrade. Meanwhile the high command had been refused arms and support by Britain and France to attack Bulgarian forces massing on the southern border. Seeing their chance, the Bulgarians attacked. Within weeks Serbia was cut in two. Its army made a last stand on the plain of Kosovo – where else? – waiting for Entente aid that never came. The government moved from Niš to Kraljevo to Peć to Prizren, as the Serbian court had moved six centuries before. King Petar, Regent Aleksandar, the government, the chiefs of staff and the remnants of the army fled in dead of winter across Albania to the Adriatic. Of 200,000 troops who began the retreat, 70,000 died on the way.

Throughout the century when Serbs were rebelling and getting their independence, the Croats and the Slovenes were part of Austria-Hungary. In the First World War, they fought for their masters – against Serbia, among other enemies.

In Mr Mihailović's view, "the consequence was that the Serbs developed a great love toward the new state of Yugoslavia, whereas the Croats and Slovenes, having been always in a foreign state, transferred their hatred for Austria-Hungary to the new state of Yugoslavia. Their hatred for Vienna and Budapest was transferred to Belgrade.

"This is what the three nations brought, psychologically and emotionally, to Yugoslavia. All three nations have lived through both Yugoslavias under this misunderstanding. The Serbs really became Yugoslavs, whereas the Croats and Slovenes never committed themselves to the state of Yugoslavia. After the Second World War, the Serbs kept Yugoslavia as their ideal. They overcame the legacy of the war and said 'Let's forget about the genocide against us by the ustaše, for the sake of Yugoslavia.' But the Croats and Slovenes continued to regard Yugoslavia as a great evil.

"In the Tito régime all the animosities among Yugoslav nations were reprojected within the Communist Party. When the Serbian Party differentiated itself, it did so on a political basis; for instance, the hardline faction with Ranković, the liberalisers with Djilas. When the Croatian or Slovenian communists wanted to declare themselves, they did so as nationalists, not liberals or hardliners. It was a perpetuation of the pre-war situation. Although today the Serbs are protrayed as big nationalists compared to the Slovenes and Croats, it is generally just the other way around."

There is nothing chic about Borislav Mihailović; the flame of his nationalism has burned steadily for decades. But his tale of sacrifice and injustice has become highly fashionable; and it won't wash.

Even without checking the facts, one is suspicious of an emotional interpretation of a state's history, as if all can be explained by love and hatred. In his meticulous account of the Serb point of view, Mihailović never mentioned power relations in the first Yugoslavia; as if it doesn't matter that the monarchy was the Serbian dynasty, that the army and police were basically the old Serbian army and police (the army didn't even change its uniform), that the state was centralized and Serb-dominated.

The first Yugoslavia lasted for 268 months. Serbs were prime ministers for 264 of those months; they were ministers of the army and navy for all 268, ministers of the interior for 240, ministers of foreign affairs for 247, ministers of justice for 237 months. And so on – in a state that was some 60 per cent non-Serb.

Serbs delude themselves if they think that Croat and Slovene experience under Austria-Hungary resembled their own under the Ottomans. And when they complain that others did not commit themselves to the new state, they overlook that the new state was constructed so that Serbs could commit themselves to it without compromising their nationality. No such option was open to non-Serbs. Worse: the latter were liable to high-handed treatment *because* they were not Serbs.

Whatever Slovene and Croat revisionists now like to claim, the new state was formed by all three Yugoslav nations, not foisted on any of them, except in the sense that all were hurried along by the tide of international circumstances in 1918. And Serbia never intended to enter the new state on terms of equality. It had brought its victory and statehood to Yugoslavia. Equality was unthinkable; it would have betrayed the hecatombs of dead, who fell in the Balkan Wars and the First World War for Serbia and Serbdom, not some vision of pan-Slavic fraternity.

There is nothing contentious about this, yet one encounters hardly any Serbs who accept it. The entire nation seems blind to the fact and significance of Serb dominance in pre-war Yugoslavia. Therefore it has been able to adopt, almost without noticing, its nationalists' deepest grievance against post-war Yugoslavia: to wit, that federalism – involving equality among the units and nations of Yugoslavia – was a travesty, a ghastly historical accident. Serbs' oblivion to their original hegemony, and hence intolerance of other nations' anxieties when a drive to reassert that primacy resurfaced in the 1980s, follows from the assumption that a Serb-dominated Yugoslavia is right and proper, in which Serb national right is ungainsayable, the arbitrating principle in national disputes.

In 1991 the "separatist" republics acted as if they could wash their hands of Yugoslavia and just walk away, ending their association with Serbia *on their own terms*. Very well; the Slovenian ingrates could depart. Croatia, though, was another matter. If the Croats wanted out, they would have to pay the price first.

Serbs who cast the past seventy years of their history in woebegone terms, secretly exonerate themselves on two accounts. They shrug off the mere reality of Yugoslav national relations, and Serbia's specially responsible place in them. And they excuse their violence toward Croatia in 1991. Any psychologist knows what to make of a parent who stifles his children with hugs, then lashes them with his fists, amid tearful protests that "I did so much for them, I love them so, and now they want to go away!"

*

Belgrade at last. The train station makes no distinction between goods and passenger trains. Some travellers have to make their way between pens of sheep on the platform; others are left where there's no platform at all. Old ladies and crisply-suited businessmen lower themselves to track-level and exit across the sleepers, slippery with merds and oil.

If the station in Ljubljana mocks that town's gentility, this terminus epitomizes its city. The building is a huge, half-wrecked wedding cake, never finished; at one end it peters out as a left-luggage office that specializes in discouraging foreigners from leaving luggage.

At every hour the same mix is swilling through. Always a family cramming a warehouse's worth of highly-strung boxes into a compartment. Always, in summer, a tight circle of backpackers, squatting around their campfire of orange rucksacks. Curly-haired, watchful Albanians in the queue for tickets, clutching wads of dinars. Taxi drivers at the northern portal, with Zastavas and ancient Mercedes. Gypsies rinsing their feet in the forecourt trough.

Grizzled men with laceless shoes and no socks, buffing the walls with their shoulders.

Or are these time-killers supervising the human tide, checking each newcomer against some secret list of credentials? For the marginal types are the city's real mainstream, if it has one. Belgrade is moving all the time, churning like a pebble beach in a storm. It has no ring roads or by-passes: every route breaches the core. Laid open to allcomers like a wall-less house, its population has quadrupled since 1940. Now it stands at 1.2 million. The influx continues unabated, and the city can't keep up; Belgrade is Serbia's abyss of consumption.

"The whole place is made by the crossing of straight lines; I never saw a curve," an English visitor noted in 1903. The main streets are channels, hostile to anything that can't survive without pause or shelter, welcoming everything that moves, from boys on skateboards to armies, those armies that conquered the city three times this century. The trinket stalls under the trees on Revolution Boulevard are limpets, resisting the wash of vehicles and bodies; it takes tough Bosnians or Macedonians to do business here, under the walls of high blank buildings that were built eighty years ago or last year, and seem all designed to depress pedestrians and feed bureaucrats' fantasies of control.

It comes as a surprise to look at the foot of these rusticated cliffs and see the little ironmongers and stationery businesses behind the stalls. Those sheep-pens at the station are no anomaly. Belgrade hasn't moved far from its origins: the garrison and the village. Its focus remains the Ottoman fortress of Kalemegdan. Researchers in the 1970s found that nobody they questioned was more than three generations from the village.

New Belgrade, on the other hand, across the Sava river, is a monument to perfectibility, a hologram city, beautiful from a distance when the sunset flares in its million windows. Work started on this socialist conurbation in the late 1940s, against expert advice. Buildings duly sank into the alluvium. Still incomplete and uncompletable, New Belgrade has dated as only yesterday's futurism can.

Apart from the fine pastel-toned buildings on Knez Mihailova, a human scale is mainly kept in Belgrade by a few surviving Turkish buildings, and by the life subsisting in the crannies. At the side of granite banks and ministries, a plank gate gaily painted blue or red frames a path no wider than the line of bricks that paves it, leading past sweet-peas to a whitewashed single-storey house with a rainwater barrel under the gutters and a television aerial tethered to the chimney.

It is nice to charm your eyes with these oases, but they exist despite

Belgrade, not because of it. Belgrade's only beauty is that it never says no. What you see is what it is, and no one, these days, seems more at home here than anyone else. Big enough to generate differences just by existing, it is a world-city as comely Zagreb and Ljubljana will never be. Its raucous multiplicity reflects the full frame of Yugoslav reality. It doesn't overcome the ugliness, untidiness and sheer poverty of the Balkans because it's bankrupt and anyway it doesn't care. It affronted Slovenes and Croats because it is so Serbian, and because it housed every institution of federal Yugoslavia. They were fed up with a state that had Belgrade as its capital, and any visitor can see why.

The architect Le Corbusier arrived here as a romantic youth, hoping to find "a door to the East, swarming with colourful life". Instead, "for two entire days, we rid ourselves of our illusions". In 1991, illusions were all Belgrade had.

The place was badly out of sorts. It wasn't the shanty suburbs, potholes and broken tramlines. It wasn't that citizens had stopped paying domestic bills, except the telephone (which can be cut off). It wasn't their air of distraction, the shabbiness of their clothes, or the boom in astrological pamphlets. It wasn't the unspeakable press, raving about the Fourth Reich, Kurdish mercenaries paid by Zagreb gold, genocide in Kninska Krajina . . .

The giveaway symptom was the lack of differences, the solidarity behind the government's policy. Consensus is rare in Belgrade at any time; to find it in late summer 1991 was positively freakish. Serbs were dying in a futile war; world opinion, bar the USSR, Romania, and Greece had lined up against Serbia, and international sanctions were in the offing. Serbia was doing everything wrong, yet all but a handful of people agreed there was no other way than the one chosen.

There was dissent in 1991, but it was long past by the time I arrived. In February, 13,000 Belgrade industrial workers had struck. In March, an opposition rally protesting at state control of media had rocked the government. The rally was banned but happened anyway; 30,000 to 100,000 people, mainly students, marched on parliament and TV Beograd. The latter, known as "the Bastille", was protected by cordons of armoured cars and water cannons. "Slobo-Saddam!" cried the students, "Slobo-Stalin!", "Serbia has arisen!", "Red bandits!" Riot police charged and rubber-bulleted the crowds, who tore up tramlines and paving stones. Two dead, a teenage demonstrator and a policeman. Seventy-six injured. Belgrade had not seen such scenes since 1945.

President Milošević went on television to demand an end to "the destructive march of chaos and violence" before threatening: "We will use every means possible to contain the disturbances." He told an emergency session of parliament that "a new seed of evil" had been planted. The "anti-Serb coalition" abroad wanted to turn Serbia into "a vassal-state under foreign domination . . . Internecine conflict can only help those wanting to subjugate us."

Surely the strongman was panicking! President Tudjman of Croatia licked his lips and presented terms to settle insurgents in Krajina once and for all. Oppositionists of every stripe foresaw Milošević toppling at last. The students started an open-air parliament on the Terazije. Sixty-eighters flew in from Paris and London, imagining the years peeling back.

Then . . . nothing. The students didn't know what to demand. Milošević made one or two concessions, sacking a minister and a few editors, and that was that – until April, when 700,000 workers struck across the republic: almost a third of Serbia's workforce. It was the biggest industrial action in Yugoslav history. Many had not been paid for five months – since just before the December elections.

Again, the protest collapsed. When summer and the war came, workers still weren't paid. At least half Yugoslavia's 1.2 million registered unemployed were in Serbia, and almost all the press and television were still state-controlled. Yet no strikes, no political opposition of any significance, burst the unanimity. The leading anti-communist politician, Vuk Drašković of the Right-wing nationalist SPO (Serbian Movement for Renewal), changed tack and spoke of peace. No one paid a jot of attention. The other wing of political opposition, the feckless Democratic Party, appeared paralysed by the contortions required to avoid acting on the knowledge that unity in one state had become imcompatible with democracy and progress.

Almost everyone agreed tacitly to shelve discontent with Milošević while they joined the crusade against Croatia. Peace activists, damned as "traitors to the nation", were brave and hard to find. One of the few, a doctor, diagnosed his country as suffering from advanced necrophilia. "The past has been imposed in Serbia as reality; the present is masked and all visions of the future are blocked. It's textbook necrophilia to react with violence, not discussion, because discussion *evolves*, and violence just kills a living action."

This man took me to a meeting convened in a hospital by a tiny group called Physicians Against War. Its idea was to mobilize their profession in Serbia and Croatia on the basis of shared Hippocratic principles. The background to the event was interesting; the governing Serbian Socialist Party happened to have fifty doctors among its MPs, recruited in the centre and south of the republic when the Party realized that it had next to nil representation among professionals. These MPs were all invited; fewer than half turned up, along with two television crews, a JNA spokesman, and me. When the organizers had had their gentle say about needing to resist the psychology of militarism, the platform was thrown open. I wasn't surprised that only one speaker in the next two hours supported the call to stop fighting, while others said that war must go on because Croats hated Serbs. What was striking was the stark anger vented at anyone who queried the necessity of killing. The imperative of patriotic war had the nation in an armlock.

On my way out of the hospital, I noticed a stained glass window in the hall; it showed a syrupy image of the Kosovo Girl, ministering to Lazar's shattered army. So much for shared Hippocratic principles.

*

The exploits that turned Slobodan Milošević into a demon were the same that made him a saviour. Since 1987, half of Yugoslavia has viewed him as more responsible than any other person for making Yugoslavia uninhabitable. By the summer of 1991 the world had caught up. Milošević was widely seen as "arguably the most dangerous man in Europe, more than any other single person responsible for Europe's first land war since 1945" (the *Guardian*, 28 September 1991). His supporters, on the other hand, who remain legion, acclaim him for reviving and uniting the Serbian nation; like Churchill and Cavour rolled into one double-breasted pinstripe suit.

He is never seen outside that suit, and it is a sounder guide to his identity than his drop-forge rhetoric or his purposeful gait and Schwarzenegger frown. Milošević, the avatar of Serbdom and inheritor of Dušan's mantle, is a bureaucrat, an ex-apparatchik whose natural habitat is not a battlefield, nor a mass rally, but a committee room.

His rise to power belongs in context, along with the Serbian League of Communists' success in bucking the collapse of communism. The powder-trail of responsibility for both these phenomena leads back to the 1960s, when the young Milošević (b. 1941) was working his way up the ladder, and in every republic except Montenegro and Bosnia-Hercegovina, liberal reformists came to gain the upper hand over conservatives. This they achieved because they had Tito's reluctant and, it turned out, temporary blessing. The watershed year was 1966, when Aleksandar Ranković was relieved of all duties. It was a sensational banishment, a triumph for the reformists. As the organizing secretary of the LCY, and security chief for more than twenty years, Ranković had vetted the midde-rank party officials and functionaries throughout the federation. After his fall, the republics appointed their own people. From now on power, and careers, lay in the republics.

Belgrade became a hardship posting for ambitious politicians, who scampered back to base when their stint was up. The crucial federating step of giving equal representation at the top of the LCY to each republic, regardless of its size, was taken.

In Serbia, the political initiative passed to a reform-minded élite led by Marko Nikezić and Latinka Perović. Belgrade bloomed as the avant-garde capital of Europe.

There was, however, a half-concealed difference of motive among the purgers. The reformists knew the all-powerful security apparatus would always obstruct their plans, and had to be broken. Tito, on the other hand, was convinced that Ranković and the security apparatus were usurping his own authority; he resolved to reform the LCY so that it could never again offer a foothold for insubordinates. Also he was persuaded that, by a Yugoslav paradox, Ranković and the unitarists had to be purged for the sake of unity; the federalists were too entrenched to be beaten, so they had to be joined – provisionally.

The policy-making and administrative functions of the LCY were separated. If this weakened the LCY, it was a regrettable side-effect; Tito's support for the liberals was tactical; as always, he was balancing factions and nations against each other. He did not drop his insistence on the LCY's "leading role", and already by 1969 he tried to stem the republicanization of the LCY by creating an Executive Bureau, based in Belgrade. This new body was meant to comprise the republican League presidents and secretaries, so putting them where Tito could keep an eye on them. Most republics found excuses to send others instead, and by May 1971 the leading Macedonian liberal, Krsto Crvenkovski, felt able to claim that "We have evolved to a stage at which it is no longer thinkable that a republican Party leadership could be removed by the federal Party centre."

The following eighteen months proved Crvenkovski wrong four times over. Tito was always astute and powerful enough to remove whomever he wished. The LCY was *his* base, and however much authority it shed, it could not be less authoritative than Tito himself.

This last round of interventions, breaking the reform movements, was widely regarded in the West as a stabilizing move, proving the President's undiminished flair for smacking down the nationalists. Actually it was his nadir. Yugoslavia's best chance of reform turned out to be its last chance, if only because the squads of mediocrities who replaced the liberals were certain to outlive the Old Man and so become immovable.

Of all imaginary retrospective scenarios for Yugoslavia, my favourite begins with Tito's death in 1969 or '70. Barred from aborting the polycentric Left-reformism that he had allowed to flourish, Tito would be seen to have capped his achievements with the greatest feat for any autocrat, namely the most enlightened choice of successors. The SFRY would have continued as a self-reforming socialist state in the middle of a continent retrenching in Cold War after the invasion of Czechoslovakia in 1968. The creativity of the "third way" would have been vindicated, the republican Leagues would have kept attracting the best and the brightest, and there would have been no void (ideological, spiritual, political) for nationalism to fill.

But death withheld its favour. Persuaded that the reformists were moving too far too fast, Tito set about reuniting and redisciplining the LCY, with Stane Dolanc, a Slovene, as his special henchman. The "incorrect", "anarcho-liberal", "technocratic" leaderships were sacked or obliged to resign. Though the long-term consequences varied in the republics according to local factors, the overall result was ruinous. The number of purgees was small except in Croatia, but the effect was to reassure conservatives, who were legion in the political and administrative structures, that nothing had to change.

In Serbia, where the old guard of hardliners expelled with Ranković was joined in oblivion by the liberals, the League was doubly stricken. In this sense Slobodan Milošević is a child of 1966 and 1972.

What could young apparatchiks be expected to conclude except that the League of Communists was a power-machine ready to devour anyone naïve enough to believe otherwise? That safety and success lay in the cynical pursuit of bureaucratic control? Across Yugoslavia, a generation of careerists drew the lessons from the very purges that shoved them higher up the ladder.

Judging by its record, this generation possessed no ideas beyond the principle of keeping its own supreme privileges. Insofar as this called for more than tinkering with the existing system – called, in other words, for an ideological programme, however threadbare – it discovered that nationalism was increasingly apt to fit the bill.

There were exceptions: individuals in Slovenia, Croatia, Bosnia and Macedonia who fought and lost the free elections of 1990 as Communists or with the Reform Forces party. Then they joined the new social-democratic parties, or quit politics for teaching, business, or the law. The point, though, is that the leagues lost power – everywhere except Serbia and Montenegro. Here too, momentum lay with the nationalists, whose complexion differed from republic to republic. But whereas, in other republics, nationalism defined itself against communism, here it was co-opted by the communists.

What's more, they outmanoeuvred their rivals, whom they had already trounced in the late 1980s, when their monopoly of power gave them a head-start in the race to don the garb of national interest and national emotion. Those garments had been lying in a neglected heap on the ground, begging for someone in power to claim ownership. Which brings us back to Milošević, for he it was who noticed the clothes and realized their potential.

Serb nationalists were always convinced that the purge of 1966 was motivated by anti-Serbism. Not only were Ranković and his circle in the security apparatus largely Serbian; their pro-centralism was Serbian too. And had not the scheming *eminences grises* been those canny grandees from Croatia and Slovenia, Bakarić and Kardelj?

Among the nations of Yugoslavia, the majority of Serbs – joined by Serbophile Montenegrins – always favoured centralism versus federalism, which was always preferred by Croats and Slovenes. As the republics and their nationalisms waxed more quarrelsome and assertive through the 1980s, the very idea of a united Yugoslavia decomposed. This faced Serbian communists with a unique dilemma. In other republics, the end of Yugoslavia offered a foothold for intelligent communists to climb out of the pit into which the collapse of communism had dumped them. They too could present themselves as guardians of national interest against an overweening federation, especially if, like Gligorov of Macedonia and Kučan of Slovenia, they genuinely had taken that rôle before it became *de rigueur*, in other words when centralism was still a living force.

The Serbian communists couldn't redefine themselves in this way because there was no space in Serbia for an amalgam of communism and anti-federalism. What defined communism here, after all, was its devotion to a federal, united Yugoslavia. With both communism and the federation itself under mortal attack, and with nationalism resurgent in Serbia as elsewhere, communists had nothing to stand for and nowhere to hide.

Milošević was outstanding in nothing until he made his move in 1987. He sat out the 1970s and early '80s in Belgrade, at the Tehnogas enterprise and then on the board of Beobanka. One of his American banking contacts recalled in 1991: "He was a charming guy, very pleasant. I didn't think he was that powerful at the time. I was surprised to see him rise as a politician." He wasn't that powerful at the time, nor did he rise "as a politician" in the sense intended by the banker. Milošević was a creature of one-party socialism, who stumbled on his mission to integrate the Serbs much as the Argentine junta discovered its vocation to reclaim the Falkland Islands in 1982.

He did not invent the national project that he was to use so efficiently; Serbia's intelligentsia had furnished it ready-made. All he did was turn it into bellicose slogans. It was the notorious Memorandum of the Academy of Sciences and Arts that revealed the potency of this project. Specifically it showed the usefulness of Kosovo as a tool. The "only appropriate" response to the "neo-fascist aggression" in Kosovo was "a resolute defence of the nation and its territory". As a first step the republic had to be reunited. Eventually Serbia should be enlarged to encompass parts of Bosnia and Croatia.

At the Central Committee meeting that discussed and condemned the Memorandum, Milošević spoke only to insist that the condemnation be kept secret.

The Academicians' ideas had not sprung from the blue. Since Tito's death the Serbian Communists had pressed to recentralize the federation. Their efforts were repulsed by the federal assembly and presidency. If the federal structures could not be used, Milošević concluded, they would have to be forced or ignored. He was the first leader to realize that Tito was dead and Titoism was piety.

Meanwhile the power struggle inside the Serbian League that rumbled on through the 1970s, following the purge of reformists, had never been resolved. The League still contained hardliners and liberals with Yugoslavist loyalties. They would have to go, and the occasion of their purge was the Eighth Session of the Serbian League of Communists, late in 1987.

Milošević prepared for this event through the year with inflammatory speeches harping on the crimes in Kosovo and Serbia's need for unity. Some commentators think the key appearance of his entire career was at Kosovo Polje, near Prishtinë, that April. Ordering the police not to restrain the crowd of Serbs and Montenegrins, he shouted: "No one will beat you again!" The crowd swooned. Slobo had found his first catchphrase.

It became one of his best-known lines. He has never claimed to be sophisticated; as a true demagogue he formed a primal, erotic relationship with his crowds. Husbanding his appearances, he barked simple martial speeches to rapturous masses who waved banners, cried "Serbia has risen!", sang "Who says Serbia is small?" and so forth. He turned Serbs everywhere into his constituents. Famed for hardly ever granting interviews — for his magic doesn't survive in print – he lets his senior lackeys in the SSP (currently Borislav Jović and Budimir Košutić) do the public relations work. Cresting a wave of hysterical support in the League's rank and file, Milošević led an "anti-bureaucratic" putsch against the old guard and the liberals.

At this stage he was seen in the West as the front-runner of a confident younger generation, clearing away the has-beens and bureaucrats. This wasn't altogether wrong; the decks were being cleared – not, however, for a revival of Yugoslav socialism.

Mass support was mobilized through a hate-campaign against Albanians. Lazar's bones were dug up for a come-back tour of Serbia. Milošević knew to perfection how to use the street against the committee-room. He, the communist leader, profited by all manner of anti-communist grievances. The crowds howling for "justice" in Kosovo were venting inarticulate fury at the whole stagnation of Yugoslavia, escaping from their fear of rampant unemployment, Brazilian-style inflation, and food shortages.

Vojvodina's leadership was putsched in October 1988; Montenegro's soon went the same way. Kosovo was trickier, but in due course it too was purged. With the other republics cynically yielding to Serbia when they weren't weakly protesting at its methods, constitutional revisions were achieved.

So far, so good. The next goal, to re-establish Serbia's rightful dominance in Yugoslavia, was already half-achieved.

The world, though, had not stood still. Gorbachev's reforms and international gambits had pulled the Cold War's teeth before they put it to sleep. European communism was on its last legs. The Leagues of Communists were wilting, faster in some republics than others, and not least in Serbia, where a pro-Orthodox, monarchical movement was growing apace, feeding on the same atavistic fears that Milošević had ridden so thrillingly, and with one advantage: it could point the anti-communist finger.

He was smart enough not to lose the initiative to this movement; but, of course, he was the last person in Yugoslavia who could stem the erosion of communist credibility. For his crusade had accelerated the growth of pluralism. Early in 1990 the federal League broke under its multiple strains. This left Milošević with nothing but his republican base, and even that was looking shaky.

He had taken out insurance, in the form of getting himself elected president of the republic. This gave him a non-League rôle when he relaunched the LCS as the Serbian Socialist Party, a few months before the December 1990 elections.

The SSP made good use of the interval; it promulgated a new constitution granting authoritarian powers to the president. A date was then set for free presidential and parliamentary elections. Milošević and the SSP won a peculiar ballot. Less than half the electorate voted; the SSP garnered 52 per cent of these votes, and 194 seats in parliament. The other parties have 56 seats among them. Again he had prevailed.

"With Us There Is No Uncertainty," ran the SSP election slogan. As the winter dragged on, there was nothing but uncertainty, despite continuing state control of the economy.

Unity had buttered no one's bread; a quarter of Serbian GNP was expended in pacifying and colonizing Kosovo. By March 1991 the outlook was again bleak for Slobo. Thanks to Croatia's ineffable nationalist government, a pot that had been simmering nicely for almost a year now came to the boil. Its name? As we shall see in the next chapter, it was the Serbs of Croatia – in particular, those from Knin and its environs.

And what of the cultural movement that first revived the revanchist project of national expansion?

Its origins were complex. Serbs seem always to have considered their Christly myth of an empire lost but never forgotten, and one day to be resurrected, as the cornerstone of their identity. In the nineteenth century, this myth became an official cult. As independent Serbia grew in territory and strength, so the cult grew.

Vuk Karadžić (1787–1864), who wrote down and published the epics of the battle of Kosovo, which caused a fashionable stir in salons across Europe, was the same man who reformed the Serbian language. He enthroned the vernacular as the basis for a literary standard. Folklore gained a privileged place in the culture of Serbia. In the modern world, folklore – as a canon of stories, songs, traditions and values – has either been contrived by intellectuals for the rest of the nation; or the intellectuals siphoned it up from the peasantry, to disseminate through their own channels (books, newspapers, and sheet music). In reality, of course, it was a mixture of both; but always the intellectuals controlled the form in which the folklore was disseminated.

A national culture that explicitly draws its myths from folklore, as Serbia's has always done, grants priestly status to its intellectuals; for it trusts them to safeguard the sacred heritage in perpetuity. At the same time, by banishing absolute values in the name of national values, such a culture gives itself no protection from intellectuals who abuse this trust. For there is no court of appeal beyond the nation, and these self-same intellectuals are the nation's appointed judge and jury.

This cultural structure bears an intriguing resemblance to the

Bolshevik or Leninist structure of relations between intellectuals and the people. The linking term is *vanguardism*. In Leninist theory, the proletariat needed a vanguard to explain the aims, mould policy, and generally keep the masses disciplined and eager. In practice, the consequence was "intellectuals on the road to class power".

In Serbia, therefore, intellectuals who grew disenchanted with federal Yugoslavia found it remarkably easy to switch horses from communism to nationalism without losing ground "on the road to class power". Some doubtless did so in good faith; others realized a main chance when they saw one. Dogmatic Yugoslavists, like the Academician and novelist Dobrica Ćosić or the ex-dissident Marxist Mihailo Marković, became the torch-bearers of Serbism.

Non-Serbs watched these transformations with the cold satisfaction of seeing their suspicions justified; for they had always claimed that Yugoslavism was usually a smokescreen for pan-Serbism. Serbs that I met were not bothered by such accusations, because their intellectuals were confirming everything that they felt themselves – or was it the other way round? While I was in Belgrade, the leading daily *Politika* published a long interview with Ćosić on its front page; in it, he exhorted the Serbs not to become apathetic, to stay closely involved with politics, now more than ever. At the same time, Belgraders were telling me that Ćosić was the man who could explain the real truth about the crisis – as if he were a shaman.

The tail was wagging the dog, and the dog didn't know it. Belgrade was an echo-chamber, the capital of a country without a head – a nation that had forgotten the difficult art of insight, and cursed anyone who reminded it.

*

The pity is that Belgrade wasn't and shouldn't be an echo-chamber. I paid a visit to Bogdan Bogdanović and his wife, to ask them what went wrong. Both are old Belgraders, from families resident here since Turkish times. An architect by profession, now retired, Bogdan was mayor of the city in the 1980s, before the Eighth Session. He opposed the new trend in Serbian communism as vociferously as he could – and has been *persona non grata* ever since.

"What's happening is worse than irrational," he said, above the noise of traffic belting past their flat. "It's occult. Our intellectuals at the time of the First World War were much more educated than today. National programmes at that time were drawn up by people from bourgeois families who had been educated abroad. Even their nationalism had articulate forms. Nationalism today is absolutely crazy, with a senseless, unrealizeable programme, but everybody thinks we have a serious programme to achieve Great Serbia. Look at the 'gains' so far: a dozen Slavonian villages, and Krajina, which can't survive without subsidies because it can't even feed itself.

"I feel like a stranger here. There was big rural immigration between the wars, and again when Belgrade was liberated, an armed immigration from all over the country. We old Belgraders were a small minority by the 1970s. Now the best part of Belgrade has gone to Europe or the United States. The city can't keep its urbane mentality because its population changes from day to day, so new Belgrades keep proliferating. In this pattern you can probably find the sources of the occult power that has changed everything . . .

"Serbia needed Yugoslavia, but one differently conceived: multi-national, multiconfessional, multicultural. Such a Yugoslavia could probably have survived. It's quite clear that the Serbian factor is the most destructive in the disintegration of this Yugoslavia.

"I too have a national programme," he said wryly. "For a wise, rich, educated Serbia, even if it is 'small'! Unfortunately very few people think in this way." Few indeed: Bogdan said he could count on no more than two political allies in the city. As I left, I noticed fresh grafitti in the stairwell: "U" – for ustaša.

Nationalism has swallowed the space where subcultures thrive. The biggest Yugoslav rock singer of the 1970s and '80s was a Serb, Bora Djordjević, a Dylanish countercultural hero. Since he declared himself for the Milošević movement, he lost a large slice of his audience – and his music went stale.

Two decades ago, Serbian cinema was one of the liveliest in Europe. No Yugoslav films were showing at Belgrade's cinemas when I was here in 1991. The video rental shop, near where I stayed, did a brisk trade hiring fuzzy prints of movies that had opened in London a month before, but couldn't supply any of Dušan Makavejev's films. The one I wanted to see was *WR: Mysteries of the Organism*. One of its sexy libertarian images kept recurring to me: the heroine Milena posing in her flowery knickers and vest, and breaking the frame around her head with a clenched-fist salute: "Death to male fascism! Freedom for female people!"*

The national resurgence, which even Milošević's critics were unwilling to criticize, has been a sterile, macho affair. The cultural emblem of Serbia today is Sveti Sava, the largest Orthodox church in Europe. Planned for decades, building did not start in earnest until the mid-1980s. The great dome was hoisted aloft in 1990 amid great

* After "brotherhood and unity", the most famous partisan slogan was "Death to fascism, freedom to the people!"

festivity. Money then ran out, and the grey concrete still lacks the intended black and white marble cladding. It commands the skyline: colossal, ugly, unusable.

Made in 1971, Makavejev's *WR* sums up everything Serbia now lacked. It has a hard clarity that Belgrade, mushy with atavism and resentment, could not possibly produce. It operates at a level of psychological awareness far too demanding for the 1990s, when non-national knowledge has been banished, and so many people have been persuaded that force will create solutions, or is better than solutions, or is a solution in itself.

The film's gaiety could have originated nowhere except Belgrade, where Makavejev was born, lived and worked until 1973. That clarity, creating wit by surreal montage, mirrored the raw angularity of Belgrade when its concrete and alloy buildings were springing up and before New Belgrade had lost its utopian gleam. The film's buoyancy reflects the liberal moment when Yugoslav socialism was at its apogee, the economic reforms of the mid-1960s had not failed, and credits were flowing from the West.

The film recounts the American career of Wilhelm Reich, the psychoanalyst who pioneered "bioenergetic" (sexual) therapies for neurosis. He linked neurosis and hence sexuality to fascism, by locating the latter in psychological inadequacy. Altogether *WR* sandwiches eight kinds of film, from Reich's home-movies to Chinese newsreels. Spliced into the documentary material is a fictional story about Milena, a young Belgrade communist with Reichian ideas. "Free love", she says, will solve social problems, reduce crime, and hasten the victory of socialism. "Communism without free love is nothing but a graveyard," she proclaims from the balcony of her apartment to the crowd below. "Abstention is repressive, unhealthy, unjust, *and* counter-revolutionary! Comrades, socialism must not exclude pleasure from its programme!"

The plot involves Milena with a Soviet skating champion, a square-jawed blond who aspires to the iconic perfection of those worker-heroes on old Soviet posters. His name is Vladimir Ilyich, as in V. I. Lenin – a risky piece of humour, for Lenin was not disgraced in Yugoslavia (Tito kept two busts of him in his study). The skater eventually yields to Milena; they have sex, then he kills her. As she recognizes too late, "he's romantic, ascetic, a genuine Red Fascist".

Her death changes everything. The audience hasn't been prepared for it by any of the usual signals. Suddenly the figure who was the film's emotional battery, fusing the fractured narrative with her vitality, is murdered. It is hard, in retrospect, not to interpret this climax as an epitaph for the illusion of "the sixties" that "free love" could create human realms untainted by power; as a premonition of the end of Serbian liberalism, killed in 1972 by Tito; and even of the hope that Yugo-socialism offered a "third way" between capitalism and communism. Makavejev's montage constructs, again and again, sly comparisons of East and West, and until her death, Milena had taken the best from both sides, merging hedonism with social hope, and all with a laughing sophistication that is entirely Makavejevesque, wholly Yugoslav.

One sultry afternoon, I was walking along Knez Miloš Street from the intersection with the motorway, where Belgrade briefly turns into Los Angeles, with smog and flyovers and a city skyline in the middle distance. I passed the German embassy, with its queue of visa-applicants, the American embassy (ditto), the Romanian embassy (no queue there). Then I passed the Ministry of Defence, built in the late 1950s. It is a handsome enough pile, suitably secretive and imposing, though whether "the plasticity of the stone masses" really "reminds one of the Sutjeska river gorge and the heroic battle fought there against the occupier in the Second World War", and thus of "the moral force and bravery of the Yugoslav peoples",* I beg to doubt. It stands opposite the Federal Office of Statistics, still stoically processing data from the six corners of a federation which, thanks in no small part to the uniformed dinosaurs across the road, led by the minister himself, General Veljko Kadijević, had ceased to exist except nominally; and the name was drenched with civilian blood and the blood of teenage conscripts.

Belgrade cried out for terminal satire, although it was perhaps beyond satire. Fascism needed analysing more urgently now than in 1971; but where were the analysts?

Then I saw Makavejev, at a concert of "Artists for Peace". There was no mistaking the round, pallid face, darting eyes and close cropped, salt-and-pepper beard. The concert was rather shambolic and unfocused, as any such event was bound to be. The audience of a couple of hundred well-dressed Belgraders clapped politely and dispersed into the rain.

Makavejev was free to meet the next day. "Where?" he asked. "Somewhere you like," I said. He considered a moment. "The Slavija Hotel. There was a shoot-out in the lobby today, so it should be quiet tomorrow, on the probability principle."

The slab-grey Slavija is a bizarre place to like – unless, like the director, you spent your boyhood hereabouts and anyway you love Belgrade for its cycles of destruction and renewal. It stands on a dingy roundabout above the railway station, rimmed by tramlines

---

* The solemn assertion of fellow architect Mihajlo Mitrović in his *Modern Belgrade Architecture* (Beograd, 1975).

and half surrounded by building sites. One of these had been a flea-pit cinema where young Dušan's uncle brought him to see movies in the 1940s. It was demolished in 1990 to make way for Beobanka, the bank where Milošević, who runs the city like a fiefdom, got his first foothold on the ladder.

Before the cinema a Methodist chapel stood here, built by a Scotsman a few years after the first Slavija Hotel opened in 1882, the year that Serbia became a kingdom. The second version was erected in 1962: a towerblock, with that familiar gritty pigeon-shit tone and texture. A third Slavija, the De Luxe, complete with an executive work-out gym in the basement, had recently opened next door. This is where we met.

Makavejev sat down, slapping a sheaf of newspapers on the café table. "So where did you see *WR*?" he soon asked. I explained that Belgrade had set it running again in my head, and asked: "Where did the film's hardness come from, its modernist energy?"

He grinned. "There was a group of us in the university film society. Half moved into television and another part became film-makers, experimenting with editing. Then we realized we *live* like that, we have several realities, and I put them side by side in a dialectical counterpoint, sometimes expressive, poetic, shocking. Sometimes you fall down the gap, sometimes you create a new metaphor and feel good about it. It was always my idea to be experimental *and* accessible. It was important to be funny. Don't forget we had a strong surrealist movement here before the war, mainly poets, a few painters. We drew on all that, learning to put moustaches on Mona Lisa.

"We were all growing up, learning what is the most avant garde in the world, plus what was avant garde in the 1920s, which was not known in London, New York and Paris. We could see old Russian films that Russians themselves hadn't seen. We knew how to use these resources because we understood its background, we didn't watch it as a museum piece, it was about *us*, about Balkan society. We remembered all kinds of old monuments being taken away after the war. First they took the horseman from a statue, later they took the horse. Things like that.

"In '67 and '68 we were free to be both avant garde and popular, *that's* the quality Belgrade gave to the world. We knew how to turn our wounds into pearls, into poetry."

Makavejev talks very rapidly in mid-Atlantic idiom. Half ruminating and half responding, sometimes he shepherded himself back on track when a question seemed lost forever; sometimes he didn't.

"In WR, I was trying to think through what it meant to be a communist. You fight for the highest ideals and you find blood on your hands, but you don't know where it's from – like the skater at the end, staring in horror at his hands.

"It's like Christianity: when you get a huge number of people willing to sacrifice for something better and it turns into an inquisition, you still have a problem with the initial ideals. How do you reconcile the reality of movement with its programme? Communism is so idealistic that it can't stop, it has no brakes, it has to solve everything so it's doomed. Practically, yes, it would stop when people start screaming, but just to wait for a while and then start up again.

"So where did it go, in Yugoslavia? First they crushed the opposition, not many, a dozen or so MPs in 1946. Then they nationalized everything, down to the smallest pubs. The owners were kept to run the places, but they had to employ more people, and make it an organization, so everything productive was turned into something heavy. For years private cake shops could have only twelve square metres, no more; so bakers divided up their properties, and of course produced better cakes than government could do. Government cakes – horrible.

"I was fifteen in 1947, and I remember going into a flower shop where a woman was counting roses and crying, and she told me 'we're closed, get out'. They had nationalized flower shops!

"At the time, development was quite big, a lot of people were studying, and it was all moving.

"They would publish Russian classics, Tolstoy, Chekhov, but they killed everything to do with religion, astrology, numerology, bioenergy, anything that wasn't Marxistic science. Mathematics and medicine were very big, of course. Social science was high bourgeois, genetics was absolutely no-no.

"Why? Because the communist idea was that you can change anything. And at that time I believed, I joined the Party in '49 to fight the Russians, and when you're active and young, you are part of it all. So we were fighting and they were constantly punishing us, accusing us of anarchism."

Makavejev broke off to sip his coffee. I grasped the chance to finish my first question: how WR had come to mind because Belgrade was so grey now, and . . .

"Don't jump to conclusions," he rebuked. "It's a very lively city in spite of everything, even in the worst moments. It's a city half-destroyed, not quite chaotic. I was born two streets from here. You've seen this square? Before the war it was beautiful, all little shops, there was a fantastic old cinema, another one nearby, both torn down. The square was destroyed by Nazi bombs in 1941, then in '44 by British and American bombardments, very heavy. Four-fifths of the buildings were gone and for fifty years they didn't know what to do with it.

"The city was kept disorganized. Communism was incapable of being organic, and the city was always resisting the communist kind of uniformity. Belgrade always has an incredible influx of new-comers, and this new blood is vulgarizing everything, watering down whatever Belgrade can produce. On the other hand it brings a lot of very interesting people, because in a flood . . ." He shrugged and reached for the cup again.

I wanted to know how *WR* came to be censored, and what had driven Makavejev into exile.

"On a political level they were killing liberal politicians in Serbia in 1971, but publicly they were fighting 'black' movies. We weren't connected, but now I understand we were expressing the politicians' concept.

"The politicians were offended by what we did, but were tolerant. When *WR* was banned, I went for help to Latinka Perović at the Central Committee. 'We are so happy for your success,' she told me. 'But the film's banned,' I said. 'It plays everywhere else in the world,' she said, 'and everywhere is praised. And you know we aren't the ones who banned it here. It's not *us*,' she said, pointing her finger up, 'it's *them*' – meaning Tito. For the first time I realized there were two levels in the party. 'I'd like you to see the film and help me,' I said. 'No,' she said, 'I want to see the film in a cinema. The Party mustn't judge art, art should be criticized by the public.'

"By refusing to see the film, the Serbian leadership refused to judge it. This saved me for a while. Still the film was blocked formally, by Tito's order, using the public prosecutor, who didn't want to be involved in something wrong so he made an 'administrative error'. He used the wrong paragraph to ban the film, so when we appealed he said: 'The paragraphs don't match, your appeal's invalid.' 'Then can we show the film?' we asked. 'Show it if you can,' he said. We tried, and sixty policemen stopped the screening.

"The only way to appeal was through some commission that met once a year. It took us like two years to get there. Meanwhile censorship was established in the region where *WR* was produced, so the commission referred us to this new censorship board, which refused to discuss the film because it hadn't been submitted: the production company said the film was 'incomplete' – though it was playing all over the world!

"The film was *destroyed backwards*, placed in a blind spot so I couldn't fight for it. It was killed without legal procedure because legally it didn't exist. They made the film non-existent, by a joint decision of the trade union and the Party cell in the production company, signed by a colleague of mine. What was grotesque is that fifteen years later, *WR* got a new licence, and who showed the film on television but the man who signed the original decision that it doesn't exist? Because he's film editor at TV Novi Sad, and getting praised for showing banned films!

"After '71 it got worse and worse. At end of '72 they arrested Lazar Stojanović [director of *Plastic Jesus*, another banned film], who stayed three years in jail. Danilo Udovički, architect, writer, also a Leftie, got three years, and other student leaders. In November they purged the liberals, Nikezić and Perović. By '73 I was *persona non grata*. I left in February."

As Makavejev gathered his papers I put my last question. Did he agree that Milena's failure to humanize her Soviet lover was a prophecy of the failure of a "third way" between West and East?

His eyes popped. "But I believed there *is* a third way, and the third way is Yugoslavia!"

As Makavejev said, there was a surrealist movement in Belgrade. Surrealism wove a rainbow thread through the darkness of twentieth-century Serbia, and its best-known exponent is Koča Popović. A legend in Yugoslavia, "Koča" is the most eminent among the handful of Serbian public figures to criticize the Milošević movement. Soon after the Eighth Session, he broke a long silence to remark that, because of current developments, he was no longer Serbian. Perhaps the ensuing rage and threats surprised him; anyway he relapsed into silence. His silence, though, was audible, somehow passing judgement on the nationalist frenzy.

His mere *curriculum vitae* beggars belief. The son of a Belgrade millionaire, by 1930 Koča was writing and translating surrealist poetry, and co-authoring an *Outline of a Phenomenology of the Irrational*. He gravitated to communism, fought in the Spanish Civil War as a battery sergeant in the International Brigades, then was interned in France. He made his way back to Belgrade in 1940, and entered the Serbian Committee of the CPY. Involved with the partisans from the outset, he became commander of the First Proletarian Division – Tito's crack troops. After the war he was army chief of staff until 1953, then foreign minister until 1965. He was a member of the federal and party presidency until 1972, when he mystified everyone by resigning in reaction to the purge. He has spent his Argosine retirement playing tennis by the sea.

He drank to brotherhood with Stalin and Molotov. He taught Tito how to do handstands in the sea. He was the first to translate

Wilhelm Reich into Serbo-Croatian. In the 1960s he drove around Belgrade in a little Citroën, shunning the apanage of his rank. Then he walked away from power. He was the person I most wanted to meet in Yugoslavia; but he was chary. "I am an old man and I want some peace and quiet for a while," he wrote on a postcard. "Besides, I don't like to boast."

I tried again. "I don't think I shall change my decision," he replied. "Circumstances here won't change in the near future. Unfortunately. Also I am old, I am eighty-three now, and there isn't much hope that I shall live to see the desired changes. Almost all our leading politicians are incurable, dull nationalists of the worst sort. Many journalists want to talk to me, and my usual answer is: 'If I tell you stupidities, there will be a scandal, and if I speak intelligently, only a few will understand.' " The last news I heard of Koča was in November 1991; apparently he was safe in a military hospital near Dubrovnik, while the army – the army he once commanded – was pounding the medieval port.

Bogdan Bodanović told me that when his open letter denouncing the Eighth Session was published, there was an orchestrated outcry. "Koča was one of the first to call me," Bogdan said. "He told me: 'As one of the old surrealists, I appeal to you not to back down but to go on.' "

It is a moving anecdote, linking the avant-garde Left of the late 1920s and '30s, which had had to fight for survival in King Aleksandar's dictatorship, to the eclipse of enlightenment in the 1980s. Beacon winking to beacon along the inky *via dolorosa*. "The enemies of surrealism," Bogdan remarked, "were today's Academicians."

The next time I met my Slovene friend Ervin, he asked what Makavejev had said about Slovenia. I told him he had praised the Ljubljana scene of the 1980s as "the first expressive thing ever to come out of Slovenia, and the only recent phenomenon in Yugoslavia with any connection to what we were doing in Belgrade."

"You know the difference?" Ervin said. "They lost and we didn't."

The other difference is that the art from Belgrade was head and shoulders above *Neue Slowenische Kunst*. But Ervin was right. Although some Serbian liberals and sixty-eighters are still influential in cultural circles and opposition politics, developments in the late 1980s cut them adrift. I visited Milan Nikolić and Sonja Liht, classical sixty-eighters, and acquaintances of mine from the anti-nuclear movement. Working round the clock to organize anti-war actions (including the concert where I saw Makavejev) in the teeth of every obstacle that Belgrade could throw at them, losing old friends, weathering telephone threats, keeping contacts in New York, New Delhi and London abreast of the crisis, they were exhausted and depressed.

Milan sighed massively. "These nationalists are creatures of nightmare, all of them, četniks, ustaše, Albanian and Slovene nationalists just as much. We can only wait and hope people will see that *they* are the nightmare, not other nations."

Like Makavejev, Milan and Sonja are Yugoslavists. "People must see that Kučan, Milošević and Tudjman are the guilty men," Makavejev had told me, anticipating Milan word for word. No wonder they were nonplussed. Not only did they have to resist the hysteria: they were committed not to a peaceful dismantling of the federation, but to restoring it in some utopian form. They belong to a defeated tradition of Serbian socialism. "Everything is shades of Right," the film director had said. "People are so fucked up by Left rhetoric that there's nothing Left-liberal, social democratic or anarchistic."

The Slavija had been a fitting rendezvous for another reason than Makavejev's memories. The roundabout in front of the hotel is named after Dimitrije Tucović (1881–1914), who in a life cut very short by war managed to found the Serbian Social Democratic Party and to write a little book denouncing Serb chauvinism towards the Albanians. "The historic task of Serbia is a big lie," he insisted. Like his predecessor Svetozar Marković, and almost like his successors Milan and Sonja (whose party today bears the same honourable name), Tucović argued for a federation of free and equal South Slavs. This was not achieved then and it isn't achievable now – even *less* so if, as Milan and Sonja propose, the franchise of this equality is extended to non-Slavs too.

The defeated tradition endures as a resource for the future, like surrealism.

*

New Belgrade doesn't have an urban focus; perhaps the Sava Centre is its closest approximation. The Centre is a prestige venue for everything from trade fairs to discothèques. It isn't bad-looking, perhaps the best example of Yugo-Socialist Futurism, a style of public architecture whose glory cannot survive the first blades of grass sprouting between concrete paving, dents in the stainless steel cladding, cracks in the smoked glass. The grass could be weeded out, but this rarely happens; lack of maintenance is an essential facet of the style, which looks blandly international but is actually true to context, here. True to Balkan hospitality, which holds nothing in reserve, and Balkan power, which flaunts itself to prove how impregnable it is. True, too, to an ideology that banked so heavily on promises of a radiant future.

By January 1990, when I visited the Sava Centre for the first time, those promises had bounced, like dud cheques. Federal Yugoslavia was a scaffolding that threatened to shiver apart.

No matter how much one republic or another edged towards political pluralism, the reformists could neither be sure of their gains nor hope to renegotiate Yugoslavia without involving the League of Communists. It possessed too much power to be bypassed, so it had to be reformed itself – or finished off.

The LCY was the state inside the state. The elaborate contraptions of federal government were never meant to function without it. Its two basic "structural principles" were that it "acts as a single organization of all members and organizations within the SFRY, on the basis of their uniform ideological and political orientation"; and its "equal status, independence and responsibility in the republics and provinces". Whatever differences arose among members of the federation, whether inside the republican Leagues or outside, could in theory be resolved by the LCY, with its monolithic discipline.

For the centralists, the LCY was still potentially the broadsword that Tito had swung when the liberals got out of hand. Their problem was that, ten years after Tito, it might be too decayed to serve as a weapon. Counting heavily in their favour, though, was its institutional identity; more than ever, it harboured the reactionaries and dogmatists who could be relied upon to resist all reforms that subverted their own power – as could the army, with its own large presence in the LCY and its instinctive hatred of decentralization.

When the LCY's Fourteenth Congress was held at the Sava Centre in January 1990, within weeks of Eastern Europe's democratic revolutions, the ostensible purpose was to show a changing world that Yugoslav communists would swim with the European tide by renouncing their monopoly of power. Privately, it was to be a showdown. The Slovene communists had already committed themselves to open elections; the Serbian League had not.

"This you shouldn't miss," said Ervin, down the phone. "Make or break! Shoot out at the OK Corrall! It'll be the last Communist Congress, you wait."

The weekend kicked off with a press conference by the federal government, in the shape of its deputy premier, Živko Pregl. He smiled a lot and spoke suavely of economic liberalization and government strategy. This involved striking from the constitution all guarantees for the LCY, the Socialist Alliance and trade unions. "Practically speaking, we're opening the way to a multiparty system." Of course they were doing nothing of the kind; practically there could be no party pluralism over the head of the LCY.

The first speech of the congress sounded a very different note. LCY presidents were appointed on the rotor system, and the outgoing president was Mr Pančevski, a relic from Macedonia. He stoked the reformists' worst fears by demanding a return to "the authentic essence of socialism", meaning "the achievements and values of the national liberation struggle and the revolution". "Anti-socialist and anti-communist forces" and "bourgeois ideological dogmatism" had to be resisted, and self-management must be "reasserted under new economic conditions". And so forth.

Western journalists had not expected to hear this stuff again outside Havana or Pyong-Yang. Even so, they were apathetic. They yawned and wished they were back in Bucharest, or anywhere but here, where everyone waited for a showdown between the Slovenes and Serbs, and the showdown kept not happening. As the hours passed it seemed ever more likely that, in the best Yugoslav tradition of brinkmanship, the crisis would never materialize.

At the eleventh hour, almost to the surprise of the participants themselves, it did. What happened was this. At a tumultuous opening session, including demands from the floor for the (Slovene) chairman to be sacked for incompetence, a Slovene delegate staked out his republic's position by asking for its call for human rights in Kosovo to be included in the congress resolution. He also called for congress to operate in full plenary session instead of splitting into commissions.

Other speakers supported him; others denounced it. The chairman took a vote, and the proposal was accepted. Then, bewilderingly, the chairman mooted "a compromise". The Slovenes' crucial clauses on Kosovo, along with their other amendments, should not be discussed in plenary session; instead they should take priority in the commissions. Congress supported the "compromise", and restored the original agenda.

Later I found the delegate who made the original proposal, and said how surprised I was that a Slovene chairman wanted to wreck the Slovenes' initiative. "Me too," he said wanly. Yet he was encouraged by the first vote: "It's the first time in ages that the conservatives have lost. Bosnia and Macedonia supported us. Now it is possible that congress will accept our amendments and change the LCY into a 'league of leagues'. Otherwise we'll have to withdraw, because we can't belong to a totalitarian organization."

More than Kosovo, and more than their espousals of human

rights, the Slovenes' concern was the LCY's structure and procedure. The League, they said, should be composed of "freely associated republican organizations" – a league of leagues. Decisions should not continue to be reached by majority voting; consensus was the only way, because it was unacceptable for entire republics to be outvoted and rejected.

What the chairman's backtracking revealed was a crisis of nerves. The Slovenes were hovering on the edge of an abyss. Momentum for democracy was unstoppable in Slovenia now; the Slovene communists had opted not to obstruct it, and they knew that capitulation at the Sava Centre would mean damnation at the polls. If congress threw their amendments out, they would have to leave. But no republic had ever abandoned an LCY congress, and no one knew what would ensue. Yugoslavia might be unseamed altogether, or shackled by a military coup.

The Slovenes hummed and haaed and trembled at their own audacity. They held a press conference and looked much less assured than the journalists. Were they as anxious when they negotiated with Milošević? I wondered, and went in search of a Serbian delegate, to hear the other side.

None of them wanted to talk. After I had given up hope, I ran into my friend Eva, who joined me for a drink. A Hungarian journalist from Novi Sad, Eva was surpassingly elegant among the grey suits propping up the bar. Soon a power-dressed young man noticed her and swerved towards us. "Tahir Hasanović," whispered Eva. As he threw an arm about her shoulder and started flirting ebulliently, I looked at him closely. Hasanović . . . A rising star on the Serbian Central Committee, under thirty, a fast talker, a limber, likeable fellow, eyes restless with ambition. A Muslim, which made him a valuable asset to his chiefs.

Thanks to Eva, young Tahir yielded to temptation and agreed to talk. Serbia's objections, he explained, derived from sincere concern for the fate of Yugoslavia – unlike the selfish Slovenes. As for free, secret, multiparty elections, of course the Serbs were in favour, but the precondition was a proper legal and constitutional basis. "We must change the 1974 federal constitution, but the Slovenes keep blocking our initiatives, because they don't care about rebuilding Yugoslavia. Like they attack the LCY's statutory principle of democratic centralism,* and we consent to this: democratic

---

* "Democratic centralism" is a sacred tenet of Leninist organization. In theory, it means that policy is freely discussed until a decision is reached. The party hierarchy then implements, unquestioningly, this decision. In practice, it ensures that the party centre retains all decisive power.

centralism can be dropped from the new statutes. But the LCY should be unified, every party needs discipline, and what do the Slovenes propose instead? Nothing, my friend, nothing!"

He was already shifting on his bar-stool, looking around. I pressed to the point. "This talk about a 'proper basis' is stalling, isn't it? The real reason for the fracas with Slovenia is that you don't want to risk losing your party-state power sooner than you are ready, whereas the Slovenes – because of the strength of the democratic movement in Slovenia – are taking that risk."

Tahir smiled. "And it's not smart, is it? Every political actor wants to stay on the scene. In Serbia we were lucky that Slobodan Milošević and other comrades raised the problem of Kosovo in Yugoslavia and the world. Kosovo is the main issue for many Serbs."

It was nice to hear Milošević's opportunism commended so frankly.

"By the way," he finished, rising to go, "you ought to know this congress is really a theatrical event, not a historic one, as some people say, because the future of the LCY isn't the future of Yugoslavia." He patted my knee friendlily, tried to pay for our drinks, and went his way.

The moment of truth arrived, very early on the morning of 23 January (a red-letter date in the ending of Yugoslavia). Repeatedly outvoted at the closing plenary, which rejected all but one of their eight amendments, the Slovenes walked out, led by Milan Kučan, who had been busy behind the scenes arranging reinsurance with the Croats: they had agreed to suspend participation in the congress if the Slovenes left.

Across the country, televisions flickered in the midnight blackness, showing the depleted ranks of delegates in the hushed conference hall, some visibly shocked, others slumped and apparently dozing. Outside, Kučan told a panicky journalist that "the destiny of Yugoslavia no longer depends on the League of Communists."

Milošević and his Montenegrin ally Bulatović, who happened to be in the chair, called for the congress to continue. Ivica Račan, the Croatian leader, then came to the rostrum, leaned over the microphone and said: "The League of Communists of Yugoslavia no longer exists."

Lacking two delegations, the congress could only agree to reconvene a month later. Next day, federal premier Ante Marković famously remarked that the LCY might be finished, but Yugoslavia went on. And so it did, in a fashion, for a while.

Ervin had been right. Tito had been right too, in the turbulent days of 1972, that the LCY was "the connective tissue which binds Socialist Yugoslavia together". Marković, on the other hand, was wrong. Tahir Hasanović was wrong too, twice over; if this could not qualify as a historic event, what could?

Yet somehow, despite dramatic headlines and an adrenalin rush when Kučan and his troops got to their feet, despite a portentous soundtrack (Bach organ fugues droned from the PA speakers for much of the congress), it didn't feel historic. There was no oratory, no passion, no argument worth the name. The decisions that finished Yugoslavia happened banally, in conference halls, like this: by default, by mutual challenge and escalation.

During this long weekend the rest of the world vanished, as if the Sava Centre had fulfilled its architect's dream, turned into a space station, and slipped into orbit. From my perch on an upper staircase, I could look over the heads of delegates trudging in and out of plenaries and commissions, at the frieze of silent city beyond the smoked glass. Distant cars and trams glided by, like back-projections for a drama played out far too late, by actors so self-absorbed that they hadn't noticed the auditorium was empty. As for Račan's warning that stalling the reforms might split the LCY into communist and social democratic factions – Milovan Djilas had been purged for proposing such a split as long ago as 1954, back in the dark ages.

*

Back across the river in old Belgrade, Milovan Djilas was still going strong. *Persona grata* in his own land after three and a half decades, he was a public resource: a panellist in television discussions, a magazine columnist, and still an oracle for foreign journalists.

Except for Tito, Djilas was the only Yugoslav name widely known abroad, until 1991. He was born in Montenegro in 1911, before the Balkan Wars, when King Nikola reigned in Cetinje – seven years before the Kingdom of Serbs, Croats and Slovenes was launched. He remembers announcing his conversion to communism at the age of seven; so his political life is coeval with Yugoslavia's.

A budding writer and revolutionary during the '30s, he became one of Tito's most trusted comrades in the partisan war, despite occasional "Leftist errors" (see p. 177). For even by local standards, Djilas was a fanatical communist.

Tito knew his man; after the war he appointed him as head of agitprop, where he gave free rein to his veneration of the USSR and loathing of the capitalist West.

As one of Tito's two closest advisers, he was at the forefront of the political reforms begun in 1950, when the impact of the Cominform expulsion had worn off. This impact had been great on Djilas. With his simple faith in Stalin shattered, he began to analyse why Soviet communism had erred so far that it wanted to exterminate its most successful admirers. He was not alone in his anguished revaluation, or the conclusion he reached: that the Yugoslavs must carry their revolution forward into post-revolutionary times by abandoning dogma and "bureaucracy", permitting more democracy within as well as outside their own ranks. But unlike Kardelj, Bakarić and other reformists, Djilas refused to draw the line. Defying caution and personal safety, he was soon insisting that the Party had to shed its leading rôle. The Bolshevik who a few years before had explained, about a Serbian democrat who was elected to parliament in 1946, then sentenced to hard labour on trumped-up charges, that "we had to silence him", was now advocating a multi-, or at least a twin-party system.

The League of Communists reacted by expelling and later jailing him, for nine years altogether – in the prison where he spent three years in the 1930s as a communist in royal Yugoslavia.

He became the original dissident, testifying by his own persecution to the dictatorial essence of the self-management system, yet never losing faith in socialism. Officially a non-person long after Tito's death, he was a rallying-point for opposition politics, though never as a leader. He only started to be published again in Yugoslavia in 1989.

Unlike later dissidents, such as Václav Havel in Czechoslovakia or Andrei Sakharov in the USSR, he is not much honoured in his own land. Reformists criticize his egoism, democrats don't forgive his former Bolshevism, Croats and Montenegrin greens despise his Serbophilism, Serbs condemn his anti-nationalism. Historians hint darkly at the numbers he may have killed in the partisan war. In his own recent, so proud words: "I am one of the most defamed men in history."

But solidarity with this man can never have been simple. One reason for his monumental isolation in 1954 is that he consulted no one, canvassed no one's support. Reformists have held this against him; by barging ahead, they say, he provoked a reaction that need never have happened.

Yet, as my Slovene friend Slavko says, somehow Djilas is Yugoslavia. He could not have happened anywhere else, or survived, let alone travelled widely and published his books abroad. "Like all our so-called liberals," Slavko told me, "Djilas isn't a liberal in the Western sense at all: he's a Balkan fatalist. He often sounds like a democrat, but can a democrat believe in the mystique of Kosovo? Like all our individualists, he only understands collectivist emotion, collectivist politics. His anti-Stalinism was utterly genuine, but he can't respect political individualism or believe in individual rights, because everything in his experience tells him that rights are only won by physical commitment in every vein and sinew."

His epoch-making decision four decades ago was visceral, existential, not a matter of judgement or analysis. Subsequently he has made too many errors both of judgement and analysis to qualify for the sagehood which he appeared to covet. Back in 1957 he believed that communist régimes were "succeeding in solving the nationality problem." In the 1960s he proposed that Eastern European states would adopt Yugoslavia's self-management – which, as Soviet satellites, they could never have done. He claimed in 1969 that the Cold War was "a spiritual blood feud"; which was charming but daft.

Djilas admitted twenty years ago that "the idea of Yugoslavia is evaporating before our eyes". Now that the evaporation was complete, he – who terms himself "a Serb-Montenegrin" – persisted in lofty Yugoslavism, the Serbian brand of Yugoslavism which arrogates the right to define the essence, meaning and future of Yugoslavia.

As late as 1990 he hoped that Ante Marković's economic reforms would foster a new spirit of Yugoslavism. In 1991 he took to opining that there was nothing to choose between the governments of Ljubljana, Zagreb and Belgrade: all were nationalist and authoritarian. This won't do; the differences only become insignificant from a perspective so Olympian that no differences matter, and the authoritarianism inherent in any Yugoslav state becomes invisible.

Between and during his prison terms, he penned – on lavatory paper when all else was refused him – a shelf of essays, autobiographies, fictions, and a translation. The essays, especially *The New Class*, were pathbreaking critiques of really existing socialism; their day has passed and won't recur. The novels are overblown and too sententious for western taste: death-laden epics of clan warfare in old Montenegro.

It is the four autobiographies that clinch Djilas's place as one of the supreme witnesses and apostates of the age. These books, plus the *Conversations with Stalin*, will keep his name upon the lips of "generations yet unborn".* At extravagant length, Djilas relates his experience, from childhood – when males in his family were dying in blood-feuds – through his revolutionary apprenticeship as a student and prisoner, when "the world was so clear to me that I felt I could influence its destiny"; the war, when he secretly negotiated for Tito

---

* "To stick with one's idea, one's creativity – however insanely – in sacrifice and self-criticism means to survive, if only for generations yet unborn." (*Rise and Fall*, p. 346.)

with the Nazis; the years in power, when Tito dispatched him to the Kremlin; and the Luciferian fall. (The translation, by the way, was of *Paradise Lost*, Milton's epic of an archangel's hubris, "who durst defy th'Omnipotent . . .")

Massively though not completely candid, sometimes catty, Djilas records his own dogmatism without apology, defending the leadership he shared, missing no chance to cite his own influence, even on trifling matters. But he records too the whole phenomenal talent of the Yugoslav communists in their creative phase.

In some sense these books are politics by other means. I recall two definitions in Djilas's writing: politics is "the struggle for life", and it means "determining the life of a nation and a society". *Determining*, note. With such conceptions, no wonder he describes politics as "the fullest and highest form of human activity". No wonder, either, the reader can feel the deprivation of power driving Djilas's pen like a turbine.

Beneath the panorama of politics and war, the gallery of portraits and rehearsal of fusty polemics, these books reveal a drama of selfhood – the agon of an embattled Montenegrin temperament. Caught between love and duty, literature and politics, conscience and freedom, Djilas relished every contradiction, prized no peace except the stillness at the hurricane's eye.

Despite his ironclad ego, the first-person singular does not come naturally when the subject is his own emotional life. A sentimental education is half-concealed from the writer himself within these books. "Overburdened with moral scruples" in his youth, he became the worst kind of communist puritan, one of those Red Fascists that Makavejev's Milena speaks of, more shocked by adultery among comrades than by the murder of class enemies. "I tried to convince her that as a good communist, she couldn't possibly have trouble with her nerves," runs a typical remark in *Memoir of a Revolutionary*. He continued to preach "communist morality" through the darkest days of war.

His marriage, approved by the Party as "exemplary", was fraught with difficulties. Then he met Štefica, who was to become his second wife and the muse of his dissidence. She is a shadowy presence in Djilas's writing; one's impression is of a self-abnegating woman who prefers it that way. "I discerned an air of devotion," he recalls. "Here might be the woman for me, with whom I could have a family, perhaps three children. That was the first time I had wanted children, and a wife who would be not just a friend but also a devoted being inseparable from me." Their love affair coincided with Djilas's "transition from one intellectual world to another" – his inklings of doubt about Stalinism.

＊

Djilas was at home and willing to meet. I splashed through another late summer thunderstorm to his flat and pressed the bell. The opening door revealed a silvery-haired man in jeans and rough-knit sweater. His face sagged a little, the thin mouth had broadened with age into something like a smile. His gaze was beady as an old forest animal's. He led the way into a penumbral study. Rain streaked the window. I noticed a portrait of Njegoš on the wall. A woman – not Štefica – brought coffee.

He had recently told the *New Statesman & Society* that a wholly new arrangement was needed in Yugoslavia, with fully independent republics and a strong centre – whatever that might amount to. But it followed logically that he had also gone on record as approving the JNA's action against Slovenia. When I raised this, he equivocated in a slow gravelly voice: "In as much as the army is still Yugoslav in tendency, I approved. To date, it still is Yugoslav, but the facts of political life are transforming it into a Serbian army. In Slovenia the JNA had nobody to support, it was a conflict between the army and the Slovenian Territorials. Of course the problem of Croatian separatism is quite different . . ." Without fuss, the subject had shifted.

About Croatia he spoke sense. "The essential mistake of the Croatian leaders is that they didn't understand *the Serbian problem*. They treated it schematically, from the point of view of a centralized Croatian state, which is a sacrosanct dogma for them. Dogma is dogma, whether nationalist or Marxist! Because they didn't understand the Serbs, they treated this conflict as made by terrorists – so-called 'četniks'. Some četniks are there, but now this is a people's rebellion, that's the fact. And the Croats cannot resolve this by force."

I turned our talk to Djilas's literary work, where his aphoristic power gets free rein. His richest book is a study of Njegoš, which includes this striking phrase: "Serbian misfortune, Balkan evil, and the Yugoslav dream." When I quoted this, Djilas perked up. "The Balkans are *full* of evil," he said warmly, "of conflict and passion and irrationality. Perhaps Montenegrin folklore expresses it most fully; there is a proverb, 'Better their evil than my good.' That means, hatred to the point of self-destruction. It is the weakness of the Balkans, but at the same time it inspires their free spirit, *humanitas heroica*, the heroic will to fight."

This was home ground for Djilas, and it seemed best to linger here. "Your autobiographies convinced me," I said, "that Tito was right to remove you from power, because you would never have been dependable. You would always have followed your own convictions. You broke with the Party because it was becoming administrative, Machiavellian instead of visionary. Obsessed with revolutionary purity, you found this too banal, too . . ."

"Vulgar," he prompted, appraisingly.

" . . . and compromised. Too normal."

"Your conclusion is correct," he growled. "From the point of view of power, Tito was right. In the long term, I was right." Now he smiled a genuine smile. "Tito was more pragmatic, but I was not much interested in pragmatism. Even when I was in power I despised power, and it was after they expelled me from the Central Committee that I began to understand the importance of power for the realization of ideas.

"I *believed* in communism. For me, it meant freedom – even absolute freedom. That was my mistake. Absolute freedom doesn't exist, especially not in communism, but if I hadn't believed this I wouldn't have become a communist. Of course the quest for such freedom leads to revolution, violence, overthrowing the ruling classes, the long transformation of society by education. But I was convinced that in the end . . . *no* end, really. I was convinced this process was moving towards more and more freedom, no end to this freedom." The decades sloughed off, revealing the young Djilas, keen and dangerous as a knifeblade.

When I asked why he is so criticized, he levelled his gaze at me. "I still have many enemies. Many of them think I am a danger for their power struggles. Personally I am no danger, perhaps some of my conceptions are. But there are people who aren't against me, who do esteem me as a writer and intellectual and rebel. And maybe rebellion is my essence."

I gazed back, fascinated by the transformation of man into Dinaric legend, re-enacted before my sceptical English eyes.

"Maybe the essence of me is revolution. I am still revolutionary as a thinking person, a writer. I still criticize them.* I am not for violence, of course, but my mind is still revolutionary, despite my so great age!" He chuckled without warmth, paused, and motioned that my time was up.

Halfway down the street I remembered my umbrella. Back on the doorstep, the door half opened and a woman pushed the stupid brolly into my hand, then shut me back into the stairwell. I recognized her face from photographs: it was beloved Štefica, the woman behind the man, still tidying up and keeping her counsel.

*

* "Them"! In 1953, before his fall, Djilas aroused suspicion by referring to the Party élite as "they", not "we".

Last stop in Belgrade was the Tito Memorial Centre. The only other visitor in the complex of buildings was a middle-aged American who spent his holidays pursuing communist personality-cults. He had sweated happily through an open-air speech by Fidel, stayed in Ceauşescu's Bucharest, and got himself included in the first party of Americans to visit Albania, hot on the Hoxha trail. Now it was Tito's turn.

Conscripts guided us around the shooting lodge, the display of Tito's passport, spectacles and such like, and the showcases of gifts. I was forbidden to take notes, but a few items stuck in my mind: hunting rifles presented by Churchill, Brezhnev and Marshal Zhukov, Nasser's diamond-studded ashtray, the coffee service from Saddam Hussein, a buttery gold dagger "given by Mr Walter Keller, Director General of the Damascus Sheraton, 1979".

The museum holds the batons from *Dan mladosti*, the Day of Youth – 25 May, Tito's official birthday. Every year from 1945, this day was marked with a rally in the JNA stadium in Belgrade. Tito was presented with a ceremonial baton that had been carried all around Yugoslavia by relays of young people, organized by the republican Youth Leagues. It was one of the best-known rituals of socialist Yugoslavia, and it was continued after the Old Man's death. By 1987 the Slovene League made no secret of its impatience with the rally. That year, doubtless hoping to provoke, they commissioned a poster for the event from *Neue Slowenische Kunst*. The poster was warmly approved until someone noticed that the artists had plagiarized a Nazi propaganda poster. Other Youth Leagues suspected the Slovenes of sabotage, and Dan mladosti never recovered from the scandal.

In the event the relay and the rally, complete with massed gymnasts and choirs, passed off smoothly – for the last time. To see the batons gathered here, with none for the years since 1987, is to realize how tenuous Yugoslavism had become. The end of *Dan mladosti* did more real damage to the SFRY than any number of discontented nationalists or dissident pamphlets.

The American knew his business; when we reached Tito's study he checked to see if the President used a cushion to raise his stature. He had: a thick one. Apparently he dyed his hair, his teeth were false, and that famous tan came from a sun-lamp. So what? He had to appear what he was: the chief of his peoples.

And behind him, always, was the army. The guard of four, framing his white sarcophagus in the House of Flowers, still changes every fifteen minutes, as it has done since his funeral, "attended by 209 delegations from 128 countries, including thirty-one presidents of republics, four kings, eight vice-presidents of republics, eleven prime ministers, twelve deputy prime ministers, and forty-seven ministers of foreign affairs." Perhaps it should not have been surprising that in 1991 the Chiefs of Staff couldn't accept that Yugoslavia didn't exist.

Behind the Curtain

'Inner' Serbia reaches to the lateral line of the Sava and Danube rivers. The bluff of Kalemegdan, in whose shadow the two rivers merge, is the last ripple of Balkan highland. From its northern terraces you look towards another country: the plains of Vojvodina, extending unbroken from the wooded hills of Fruška Gora, an hour's drive from Belgrade, to the borders with Hungary and Romania and beyond.

Vojvodina looks like nowhere else in Yugoslavia. Watery, fertile and flat, under clear skies it is immense, like the American Midwest, and the blue is multiplied in rivers and canals that crisscross the region like the latticing on a dragonfly's wing. These plains were the bed of the prehistoric Pannonian Sea. The Austrians began the first large-scale land drainage scheme in Europe here, in the 1750s. There are still pockets of wild marshland, in remote eastern regions, reminders of pre-Habsburg backwardness. Otherwise, cultivation rules. Vojvodina has long been a granary, first for the owners of feudal estates, who controlled the place under Austria-Hungary; then for Yugoslavia, and now for Serbia. Placid fields of wheat and maize fill the landscape. Great stands of poplars fringe the canals. In autumn, apple and plum trees on the roadsides bend under their burdens.

The old Pannonian sea, though, is never far away. Abandoned cellars in Subotica fill with water, and the villas of Novi Sad, capital of Vojvodina, are less secure than they appear, being built on sand.

In bad weather Vojvodina is claustrophobic as only flatlands can be. Then it seems the most landlocked place in the world. I once spent two wet weeks in Novi Sad; from my seventh-floor room, watching ragged curtains of mist trail over the seaweed-coloured Danube and the fortress of Petrovaradin, as the cars sluiced past below, headlamps haloed by the rain, I yearned like a child for Istra and the Adriatic.

In 1991, I longed for Vojvodina, even for its tedium. If it had gone mad too, Yugoslavia's failure was surely complete. I called my friends Eva and Marta to forewarn them, and boarded the next coach.

*

The Habsburgs had a big reason to drain the Pannonian marshes. The Turkish drive into central Europe in 1683 proved the last. Beaten back by the Austrians and Venetians, the Turks lost southern Hungary – including the territory of Vojvodina. The Austrians advanced even south of Belgrade, but could not secure their gains. In 1699 the treaty signed at Karlowitz (Sremski Karlovci), just south of Novi Sad, gave almost all of Hungary to the Habsburgs.

War soon broke out again, and the Turks were not finally excluded until 1718. Lady Mary Wortley Montagu passed this way in 1717, and saw bones whitening on the battlefield at Karlowitz. "The finest plains in the world," she exclaimed, "as even as if they were paved, and extremely fruitful; but for the most part desert and uncultivated, laid waste by the long wars."

As the southern marches of the empire, the plains had to be repopulated. The Empress Maria Theresa, whose influence here was more decisive than anyone's has been since, imported peasants, farmers and traders to exploit the reclaimed land and secure the frontier. Waves of Croat, Magyar, Ruthene, Slovak, German and Romanian settlers joined the indigenous Magyars and Serbs, as well as the thousands of Serbs who had migrated from Kosovo and Metohija in the 1690s and early 1700s, following the Austrian retreat before the then-resurgent Turks.

The Croat and the Serb settlers had special status as frontier guards; in return for tax privileges and religious freedom, they policed the *vojna granica* or *vojna krajina* (Military Frontier). A spartan tradition of pride and independence was transmitted from father to son, just as in the southern Habsburg borderlands, where Serb communities protected Knin and the Lika. Between 1690 and 1802 these Vojvodina warriors spent ninety years at war.

The region became what it is today: an incredibly intricate patchwork of peoples – some twenty-four of them, with a population of two million. Not that the mixture has remained stable. Before the First World War, Vojvodina was roughly a third Hungarian, a third Serbian and a third German. Now Serbs are 54 per cent, while the number of Hungarians has barely changed, so they are 22 per cent.

Serbs came after World War One to farm abandoned Hungarian estates, and after the Second World War almost all the 360,000-strong German minority was expelled, such of it as had not fled. It was replaced by Serbs, Bosnians, Montenegrins and Macedonians – literally replaced: the newcomers, mostly battle-scarred partisans reaping the rewards of victory, moved straight into the Germans' comfortable farmhouses and villas.

Like Kosovo, Vojvodina became autonomous within Serbia, in

recognition of its special identity, and pragmatically, to prevent Serbian predominance in the federation. Unlike Kosovo, Vojvodina was not a site of systematic oppression of non-Slavs, or not after the wave of partisan reprisals against Hungarians had spent itself. The carve-up of Yugoslavia in 1941 had awarded fascist Hungary its "lost" territory in Vojvodina; the Hungarian occupation was atrocious, reaching its nadir in January 1942, when 2,000 Jews and Serbs were slaughtered in Novi Sad. Their corpses were pushed through the ice on the frozen Danube.

For a while the Hungarians were viewed with deep suspicion. Conditions slowly improved, and in the 1960s and 1970s they benefited, like all minorities, from the reform process. Vodjvodina became a Yugoslav success-story. Officially, there were no "minorities". The province had five official languages and two alphabets; signs outside official buildings gave their information in Cyrillic Serbo-Croatian, Latin Serbo-Croatian, Hungarian, Romanian, Slovak and Ruthenian. Schooling in these languages was available, as were newspapers, magazines and books. Television airspace was proportionate to the nationalities' size; the Ruthenes, for instance, with 1.01 per cent of the population, had two hours per week. The region prospered, with the most productive farmland in Yugoslavia, highly developed communications, and Habsburg habits of hard work.

Such gains were precarious because, within a one-party system, the region's limited sovereignty could always be revoked. And so it was. Between 1988 and 1990 the same three-card trick that worked in Kosovo (an inner-party putsch combined with mob pressure and hysterical press campaigns against the mutilation of Serbia) succeeded in negating Vojvodina's autonomy. In 1990 the average public-sector income in the region had sunk to sixth place below Serbia, Bosnia and Montenegro. And non-Yugoslav peoples (in reality, non-Serbs) became minorities again.

Nenad Čanak, a Serb who heads the Social Democratic League of Vojvodina/Yugoslavia, put the matter simply: "We were robbed. The Serbian régime is nationalist, so has no answer to economic quesions. They need money, and they took it from Vojvodina to subsidize their policies in Serbia. For instance, Vojvodina's power distribution company was merged with those of Serbia and Kosovo, along with the PTT and the railways. These companies' capital was moved to Belgrade, emptying the Vojvodina banks."

*

The coach pulled out of Belgrade toward the rolling vineyards and sunflower fields of Fruška Gora. These hills are scattered with

Orthodox monasteries, most of them built in the sixteenth century by the first refugees from the south.

Two centuries later, with the second great influx of Serbs, Novi Sad became the "Serbian Athens". What Kosovo had been to medieval Serbdom, Vojvodina was to the modern Serbian renaissance. The Serbs here had economic and cultural possibilities that the oppressed peasantry south of the Sava and Danube could only dream of. A merchant class and intelligentsia evolved. Books were printed in Cyrillic. The first governments of independent Serbia were subsidized, armed and staffed by Serbs from north of the Danube. The *Matica srpska* (literally, Serbian Queen Bee: a cultural society), founded in Budapest in 1826, moved to Novi Sad and is still here. In 1848, the springtime of nations, encouraged by the Hungarians' success against Austria, the Serbs here proclaimed the Serbian Vojvodina, meaning "Duchy", as an autonomous region. They were crushed, and Vojvodina stayed Hungarian until 1918.

The monks and nuns of Fruška Gora vegetated amid their green hills until the Second World War. When Basil Davidson arrived in 1943 as a British liaison officer searching for partisan bands, he found the monasteries "empty and in ruins, and the paths overgrown." This part of Vojvodina was directly controlled by the Germans, who raised the dreaded 'Prinz Eugen' ss Division from among the local *Volksdeutch* and used it against the anti-fascist resistance. At the same time a Cossack division was on the loose, killing and freebooting.

Both here and on the plains beyond the Danube, "death was literally everywhere", Davidson recalled. At least the hills gave cover to the partisans; on the plains in winter they had to dig holes in the ground and crouch there during searches, praying that any fascists who walked overhead would not notice the muffled echo beneath their boots.

But the partisans were less at risk than the Jews. Davidson sat at the Café Stolz in Novi Sad "studying German transport", and watched spectral columns of Jews from Serbia and beyond, shepherded by "brisk and cheerful German soldiers" on the way to Szeged death camp in Hungary. My scalp prickled when I read this; for it was at the same café that I first met Eva in Novi Sad, in 1989, and Eva is part Jewish herself (also part Croat and mainly Hungarian: a true Vojvodina cocktail).

Szeged was not the destination of all Vojvodina's Jews. Danilo Kiš's family died in Auschwitz, and Aleksandar Tišma, Vojvodina's best-known living writer, slaved in a Transylvanian camp until the Red Army swept in from the east.

When I met him in 1990, Tišma was presiding at Vojvodina's

Academy of Arts and Sciences, which stands on a cobbled street near the archbishop's palace in the old centre of Novi Sad. Fiction about the last war had a vogue in Yugoslavia in the 1980s, most of it vengeful and grisly. Tišma's work is in a class apart, honest and cliché-free. His novels are commemorative, almost archival, though not elegaic about pre-war Novi Sad, "bypassed by history", or its vanished Jewry.

Living in wartime or present-day Vojvodina, "the crossroads of Pannonia and the Balkans", Tišma's characters try to survive the slaughter or to live with their memories as best they can. One of the latter, Miroslav Blam, was saved by a journalist who was then killed by the partisans for editing a newspaper which had collaborated, tacitly, with the Hungarian fascists. Married to a Christian, Blam is safe but haunted by complicated guilt at his survival, and a sense of double futility at having outlived the faith that he had abandoned to save his skin.

Is Novi Sad is a haunted town? "A little," Tišma conceded. "For instance, I had three friends in Papa Pavle Street. One was a poet who committed suicide rather than turn informer for the fascists. Another became a communist and survived a Soviet labour camp. He's now in New York. The third lived with his mother; they were both killed by the Hungarians. When I go to this street I have a feeling of ghosts, because I see these people's houses, the windows they looked out of.

"Novi Sad had three and a half thousand Jews, and they *all* went to camps. Today there are one hundred or so. The Jewish street, as it was called, simply doesn't exist. A whole community had its spiritual and physical life here, its customs, its physiognomy, and were brushed away like so many crumbs of bread."

I walked down the Jewish street, now Yugoslav People's Army Street. It is still lined with watchmakers and opticians: some proof of continuity. The great synagogue, locked up for years, has been refurbished as a cultural venue. Life goes on. People in Novi Sad aren't fanatical. It has a university, one of the best youth magazines in Yugoslavia, and fine theatre. Hexagonal prefab kiosks sprout overnight like mushrooms on street corners, waste ground, the grass patches between apartment blocks. The minorities' worst fears after the putsch in October 1988 – the so-called "yoghurt revolution" because the crowd pelted the old leadership with dairy produce – were not at first realized. But: "On 26 October, 1991, the Vojvodina provincial government announced major changes to the editorial boards of minority-language newspapers, including the main Hungarian daily, *Magyar Szó*, the Slovak *Hlas Rudu*, and the Ruthenian *Ruske Slovo*, which were all accused of having breached editorial policies laid down by the provincial parliament by expressing "open support for the separatists" in Slovenia and Croatia. Some 150 journalists at *Magyar Szó* staged a protest in early December at the appointment of Miklos Maroti as editor-in-chief, claiming he was not a journalist, was not fluent in Hungarian, and supported the Serbian Socialist Party." (*Index on Censorship*, February 1992.)

In the summer of 1991 Vojvodina had not lost its serenity, its becalmed passivity. Tišma explained this atmosphere as in part a result of the Second World War's sheer ferocity. "It was so terrible that a good majority was ready after to accept any rule which could give them a little optimism. Otherwise they would not have accepted communism, because only five per cent of a people can ever really be communist. The war gave this doctrine a chance to rule over masses because they were exhausted and wanted only peace and to be left alone.

"We are outside the main currents of Yugoslavia. The strongest mentality was the highlanders', they gave the main tone. In that war they saved this country from losing itself completely, and they remained the dominating factor. Since 1945 Vojvodina was always a little behind the curtain. People don't express themselves much. The war was terrible here but it was worse in the mountains. Anyhow, Vojvodina *didn't* win the war – the mountains won the war, not the plain. Because this fascist Germany, and pro-fascist Hungary, were still part of Europe. Hitler had this idea he was defending Europe, and in some way he was right – a terrible, genocidal Europe, but a kind of Europe all the same.

"This mixture of peoples is a very good thing of course, but it's a fact that when you have so many nations you cannot have one centre; you are always aware that there is another and a third and a fourth. If I offer an opinion, then I know that a Hungarian or Slovak or Romanian may think differently, for whatever reason.

"This is also a motive to be discreet, not so open, so sure of one's opinion – that's the 'serenity' you mention. It's the Pannonian way of thinking, not outspoken or vehement, more relativistic. But it's a result of geography too, and climate, and people's occupation with the soil."

A result of the Danube too, I feel, mingling human differences in its ceaseless, turbid flow. Usually Eva spends every weekend at her family summerhouse upriver, near the Hungarian border. This year it was not safe, with gunboats cruising up and down, and snipers on the other shore, so I met her and Marta in Novi Sad.

At bottom they are frankly baffled by the nationalists' armour-plated hatred of irony and proportion. Eva especially has no time for the wheeler-dealers in the Democratic Forum of Hungarians in Vojvodina, which won eight seats in the 1990 Serbian elections. "They're just the same as Milošević," she says, turning up her nose, "calling you a traitor and a 'bad Hungarian' if you disagree with them."

Whether or not this attitude is a Habsburg legacy, it certainly sets Vojvodina apart from the ethos and traditions of the state that has now absorbed it. (This territory belonged neither to Dušan's medieval empire, nor to the independent Serbia born in 1878). The Hungarians seem particularly prone to an advanced form of this scepticism. Once, a year before the 1991 war, I spent an evening with Eva, Marta and their friends, hoping to learn what the Hungarians wanted for themselves and for Vojvodina. A roomful of any other Yugoslavs would have outlined their agendas and listed their demands and, of course, their heart-rending injustices. These people just looked at each other, hoping someone else would pick up the gauntlet.

*

The most obscure nationality, to me, was the Ruthenes. The first time I came to Vojvodina, I knew only that they were a stateless people. Then, by luck, I ran into Mr Mihal Ramać, bearded poet, journalist, ex-novice, and "one hundred per cent Ruthene!"

He explained that the Ruthenes are an East Slavic people who came from Carpathia at the same time as the Slovaks and Germans and Romanians. Their centre is the village of Ruski Krstur, which means Ruthenian Cross. They number 22,000 and have their own weekly magazine, television, and schoolbooks. Some twenty students enrol every year to study Ruthenian language and literature at the university.

In 1990 their magazine began to write about the Ruthenian Church after a forty-year silence; and in May the first independent political association, the Union of Ruthenians and Ukrainians of Yugoslavia, was established. Its president was one Julijan Tamaš, who, in the tradition of central European nation-building, is also the university's professor of Ruthenian and the community's foremost intellectual. He was the man to meet, Mihal said.

Professor Tamaš settled back in a wicker chair on the terrace of the Serbian Theatre in Novi Sad, ordered a whisky, folded his hands across his embonpoint, and fielded questions like a veteran, though not before delivering the usual short-course. The Ruthenians never had their own state, he began, but always had their language, schools and intellectuals. "Ruthenian is the oldest Slavic language. In the fourteenth century Ruthenes taught in Serbian monasteries, and Serb historians concede as much. Now they put our school at risk, yet we taught them how to read!"

When a minority speaks in Vojvodina, "they" are Serbs. It was largely fear for their rights after the 1988 putsch that launched the new Union. The other factor was a Ruthene revival across Eastern Europe – one of the lesser known effects of the revolutions of 1989 and 1990. For the first time the communities in Ukraine, Poland, Czechoslovakia and Yugoslavia, amounting to some one and a quarter million people, could communicate freely. A world congress of Ruthenes was organized in March 1991.

What of the Union's larger aims? Was it a prototype for an Academy? "We want to create the conditions for an epic of Gilgamesh for the Ruthenes," the professor said. I tried not to gape, while he eyed me shrewdly and sipped his whisky, sure of his effect.

Meanwhile, bizarrely, two dozen long-legged contestants for "Miss Novi Sad" were swanning past in tights and leotards, practising their catwalk style on the sunny terrace behind the professor. "The strongest doesn't always win," he proceeded imperturbably. "The loser still has the word and the freedom to create. For minorities, culture is the basis of identity – working and creating, not fighting and dominating. And the Ruthenian Question is *the* question of central Europe."

According to Ukrainian nationalists, "the oldest Slavic language" is a hotchpotch of dialects, not a separate language at all. Vojvodina's Ruthenes have done the most to develop a literary standard, partly because they are, in the words of one Western analyst, an "outstanding example of what can be done when a government allows a minority its head", and partly because Ruski Krstur was the birthplace of Havrjil Kosteljnik.

A Slovenian scholar, Rado Lenček, wrote recently that "there are three supreme cultural events in the history of a philological nationality: the translation of the Bible into a language; the creation of the grammar of this language; and the appearance of a national poet". If the Ruthenes are still waiting for a poet to pen their Gilgamesh, their grammar appeared back in 1923, and they now have the word as well – the Ruthenian Bible was completed in 1990.

The grammarian was Kosteljnik, born in 1886. Photographs show a grave, priestly man. Not only was Kosteljnik obscure, as he inevitably was; in the spectrum of European culture of his day, he was self-obscuring, burrowing into untimely causes with the instinct of a mole fleeing the sun. Perhaps intellectuals from small nations always face this choice: Enlightenment or Antaeus, river or stone. If they opt for the river, they may be ignored for imitating the bigger fish – if they don't drown. If they stay on the bank, they won't drown but can still be ignored, however beautifully they sit there intensifying their stoniness. Kosteljnik lacked even this choice; there was no river within reach of the Ruthenes. Abhorring the atheistic, cosmopolitan spirit of his age, he opposed it in poetry, philosophy and polemics.

Stone's virtue is endurance; it outlasts every fashion. Even his far-out philosophical projects are not irredeemable, and one of Kosteljnik's political causes, a Ukrainian national state, is now safely achieved. Ruthenian statehood still seems pie-in-the-sky, but anything can happen before the current East European and Balkan convulsions have run their course.

Describing Kosteljnik as "living and dying oppressed by the cultural, ecclesiastical and ideological controversies between East and West", his biographer concludes: "It is difficult to live in the world feeling that you belong to no one. The home of a poet is his language, no matter how many people speak it – and even if no one speaks it at all." The biographer is, of course, Julijan Tamaš. I asked him if the Ruthenes had yet produced a political leader to match their cultural champion. "If Kosteljnik was our Karadžić," he said, referring to Serbia's great philologist, and smiling for the first and only time, "perhaps I am our Masaryk. Who knows?"

Mihal took me to Ruski Krstur, a tidy village between Novi Sad and Sombor. The first few hundred Ruthenes arrived here in the 1740s. The church was completed in 1784, its glowing iconostasis was finished a few years later, and mass is celebrated every Sunday with a bible presented by Maria Theresa. Wars that sucked in the Germans, Hungarians, Jews and Serbs of Vojvodina never scarred this village, and it is a peaceful, orderly place still. Bricklayers at work greeted Mihal as we walked by. The fountain by the crossroads gurgled amid rose bushes. Storks on their shaggy chimney-top nests threw back their heads and rattled the mating-song.

The portly priest was at home. He ushered us into his library for rakia and coffee. This rakia, he explained as he pushed a cigarette into the bowl of a curling, painted holder, was made from the last pressing of grapes that produce the communion wine. Did I find it good?

"Very, but it makes my throat smart. We English, you know . . ."

"Ah," he sighed, "pity the priest! I must bless each new house, and at Christmas, every household: a glass in every one."

Mihal wanted me to see his school – the one Professor Tamaš had mentioned as under threat. There are 500 children in the junior school, and 180 in the secondary school. All teaching is in the

Ruthenian language. Changes in Vojvodina's education system mean that classes in a "minority" language must have at least twenty pupils. This imperils many of the 200-plus Hungarian schools, but poses no threat to this, the only Ruthenian school in the country. So good is its reputation that Serbian, Montenegrin and Hungarian parents want their children to come here, despite the language. Morale is high.

As we left I asked Mihal if there weren't any communists in Ruski Krstur. He grinned. "Of course. The headmaster for one, but he's a *real* communist, never dogmatic or corrupt. Everyone in the village respects him, including the priest. He encouraged me to train for the priesthood in Rome, because he knew my heart was set on that." He looked at his watch. "It's too late for lunch. Let's catch the train to Kisać and have supper at my home."

Kisać lies a few kilometres north of Novi Sad. The station is a depot for a nearby timber mill; the train slid between head-high stacks of planks, so we had to climb down sideways and breathe in as the train hauled away, leaving the place to wasps and evening swallows.

Mihal's home is a whitewashed bungalow squeezed like an afterthought between the tracks and the last brick farmhouse. Inside, Mihal's study is white too, with images of Gorbachev, the Virgin enthroned, and a smiling Lech Walesa pinned above the bookshelves. Outside are a vegetable garden, a few yards of lawn, a little trellis of vines, and a terrapin in a metal bucket. The Belgrade–Budapest express makes the air quake, but Mihal, his wife and their daughter have lived here ten years and paid no attention to this hullabaloo or the archaic clatter of the goods trains.

In summer they live mostly outdoors, and we found Mihal's wife preparing *kotlić*, a goulasch of pig's trotter, rabbit and scrag end, simmered all afternoon in onions and peppery stock, over a wood fire. "This mustn't be hurried," Mihal explained, easing the bubbling mixture round the pot with a wooden spoon.

I went for a walk. Kisać was laid out on a grid pattern 250 years ago to accommodate Slovak immigrants. Now there are 70,000 Slovaks in Vojvodina, and Kisać is still largely a Slovak village. House facades and walls are painted powder blue or duck-egg blue with the ridges and scrolled patterns highlighted in navy. Even the star on top of the war memorial is blue. The streets were spotless, the cherry trees on the verges were speckled with fruit. Dwellings stand end-on to the road, their windows veiled: the discretion of Vojvodina. The long sides of the houses open onto their farmyards, like a gallery. In the older houses – dates are moulded on their gable ends: '1912', '1909', '1969' – these galleries are decorated with a frieze of bright posies, and flower baskets hang from the eaves. Broad-beamed grannies leaned against the walls, chatting or mending brooms in the fading light. Only the old market place and the empty flour mill were neglected. There are five video rental shops – one per thousand inhabitants – and twice that number of Protestant churches. Mihal invited his Slovak neighbours for dinner. They all talked a Pannonian argot of Slovak mixed with Serbian and Ruthenian. Would they mind if their children don't marry Slovaks? No, though (the husband cradled his fingers) "Slovak with Slovak: it's normal." Anyway, they feel Yugoslav: their families have lived here for 200 years, this is their home, not Slovakia.

As for the future, they shrugged. "We hope there won't be civil war, and . . ." At this point little Maia, Mihal's twelve year-old daughter, finally got the better of her shyness: "*I* hope everything just continues the same, and that Jason Donovan comes to Novi Sad!"

*

I told Nenad Čanak of the Social Democratic League what Eva, the Slovaks and the Ruthenes had told me. They are content to be Yugoslavs, as long as they aren't pushed around. "Of course," he said. "Vojvodina means one cosmopolitan way of thinking. There's a big difference between Hungarians here and Hungarians in Hungary, Slovaks here and in Slovakia, Croats here and in Croatia, Serbs here and in Serbia. I'm a Serb myself, and I'm trusted by the other nationalities, which makes me a rare bird; but I'm not the only Serb who fights this government. Vojvodina was never part of Serbia. After 1945 the communists attached it to Serbia because there were no četniks here and Vojvodina's Serbs were meant to dilute the royalism that was still strong in Serbia. Serbs are obsessed with 'united Serbia', but united Serbia doesn't exist, or only in the sense that the Third Reich existed in 1944, because you have tanks and police in Kosovo, and you have a tough régime in Vojvodina. We can be three in one, but we cannot be just one."

"Serbs must think you're a terrible secessionist."

"They have a word for that: *autonomaš*. They even call me a 'Vojvodina nationalist', whatever that may mean. What they don't grasp is that the question of autonomy is the question of Serbia, because the options are either full autonomy for Kosovo and Vojvodina with strong connections to Serbia, or no Vojvodina in Serbia and no Kosovo in Serbia. If they ignore the differences, they will destroy Serbia. Vojvodina must have its own police, courts and laws. It must be a province of Serbia *and* Yugoslavia. If Yugoslavia is destroyed, all options are open."

Mettlesome but implausible talk. More than half of Vojvodina's people are Serbs, the rest is mixed. What's more, in area Vojvodina represents a full quarter of Serbia – the richest and most developed quarter. The non-Serb 46 per cent faces a very Serbian future.

Čanak's Social Democratic League fared badly in the elections. Of course, the times were against any multinational party, but I wonder if he relied too heavily on Vojvodina's favourite self-image: that it is "Little Europe" where everyone lives in harmony, and trouble is imported by "colonists". A likeable and benign myth, it is a myth all the same. When I told Ervin that Vojvodina seemed a Yugoslav success story, he retorted: "That's only true in the sense that even Yugoslavia could not screw up Vojvodina's well-weathered, bedded-down pluralism."

I said that mutual tolerance was more than enough to be going on with, certainly better than the only alternative.

But was violence the only alternative to quietism? At least one man scoffed at that bleak wisdom. His name is Ljubiša Ristić and he directs the National Theatre in Subotica. I had heard plenty about him: how he is Yugoslavia's Kantor, Stein, or Brook; how he started a lawsuit against the theatre critic of *Magyar Szó*; how arrogant and brilliant he is; how he ripped out the seats from Subotica's venerable theatre and sold them; how – and this was unique in my experience –nobody could tell me his nationality.

What caught my imagination were Ristić's experiments. When he arrived in 1985 he upset everybody by merging the Hungarians and Serbians in the company and staging mixed-language versions of national classic dramas. Multinational provincialism is still provincialism; the cultural watchdogs of both nations howled at Ristić's insensitivity. He was a positive embarrassment in the 1980s, when the élites of all republics and regions were vying in narrowness and stupidity, harping on national differences to shore up their own power.

Artists joined him from Slovenia, Macedonia, Belgrade, the best from everywhere, and they staged everything from Aeschylus, Shakespeare and Molière to works by local dramatists, always with this mixed company. Ristić laid Vojvodina's plurality on the line, put it to the test, and exported it every summer to the rest of Yugoslavia and beyond, to Australia and Mexico and who knows where, as "Yu-fest", a travelling theatre festival.

Even Eva and Marta were sniffy: "Maybe he means well, but it doesn't work, it's form and no essence. He ignores what people want, which isn't all this radicalism."

The director was at his theatre and invited me to visit. As the train pulled into Subotica, Eva's parting remark came damply to mind:

"That town used to be too far from Budapest, and now it's too far from Belgrade, you'll see." The low sheds and rusty rolling stock weren't an encouraging sight. Subotica is the last stop before Hungary and the station milled with conscripts, backpackers, and other border flotsam. Sixty years ago Graham Greene set the climax of *Stamboul Train* here. "There was no platform", he wrote; nor is there now. One of his characters, a communist, is taken off the train, court martialled and shot on the spot. Another, a Jew musing on "the nightmare of Subotica", thinks: "It was in some such barren quarter of the world, among frozen fields and thin cattle, that one might expect to find old hatreds the world was outgrowing still alive."

I hoped Ristić would counterbalance that grimness, and he did. A few hours later, at two in the morning, we drove to Subotica's synagogue. It was built between the turn of the century and the First World War – Subotica's heyday, when it was the third city in Hungary, and abloom with art nouveau. The synagogue is even more theatrical than the town hall, Subotica's other glory. With its lavish swirls and curves, plastered in pale pinks and creams, the effect is of iced gingerbread. I was stumped for comparisons until Ristić mentioned Gaudi, the magician of Barcelona.

Bolts slammed and a bleary watchman opened up. The director trotted up the steps and threw the light switches. "Here – this is my theatre."

When the town leaders invited Ristić to direct their theatre, he made it a precondition to have use of the empty synagogue. The Jewish community, reduced since 1945 to a few dozen, came to trust him. Designed for religious ritual, nothing in the building needed changing; it became an alternative venue.

Ristić put it to use straightaway in a four-hour production called *Madách Commentaries*. Updating a classic Hungarian drama about Adam, Eve and the Fall, the action started in the theatre, moved into the main square, where the audience watched the kidnapping of Aldo Moro and other scenes, then inside the town hall for more, while a live orchestra played the soundtrack. As the earnest, 180-page programme put it, "spectators are free not only to choose the beginning of the show but to construct their own ideas of continuity and succession." Finally to the synagogue for the Last Supper, where anti-Christ, surrounded by revolutionaries from Garibaldi to Dany Cohn-Bendit, sat "as a permanent challenge to divine order, and to Adam in his path through history". For the first time in forty years, a packed synagogue witnessed the Passover ritual – with a reading from *Das Kapital* as well as the Haggadah.

Ristić and his team wanted to rouse Subotica from its lethargy and put it where it had never been: in the high-cultural limelight. Between the world wars the town had declined; after 1948, because it lay a stone's throw from the Warsaw Pact, Subotica's industry was relocated in the south. Its population sank to 60,000, half its present number. Now its art nouveau has been restored; it has become the best place between Belgrade and Budapest to buy clothes; its chic bars stay open till the early hours.

Back in the office, Ristić squatted on his chair, elflike. I had half imagined a von Sternberg figure in jodhpurs, marshalling his minions. With his jeans and shaggy moustache and bandy walk, he looks more like a Macedonian shepherd. A sort of ferment seemed to follow the man around, a vapour trail of whims and connections. He is no Vojvodina regionalist. On the contrary: "Čanak's so-called 'Vojvodina option' is old hat, it counts for nothing in the sum of Yugoslav politics." A sixty-eighter who left the Party in '72, Ristić remains a convinced Yugoslav.

"For someone who has been dreaming for many years of a 'unified Yugoslav cultural space' for collaboration and co-operation, Subotica is ideal. National complications are visible here, which makes it easier to try and overcome the tensions and latent confrontations. And no question is more important for the future of the Yugoslav idea than this cultural dimension, because Yugoslavia is mostly a cultural idea, only *later* political, and least of all economic.

"You see, the decades which followed 1918 were supposed to produce a special civilization which would be a fruitful mixture of different peoples and their languages, traditions, religions. It never happened, and Yugoslavia now seems a very old and tired idea. This feeling that we're living in a very *ageing* world is hard to bear.

"It was clear to a few people, fifteen years ago, that this would happen. These few repeatedly warned that Yugoslavia is not forever and people who like the idea and the life which is a consequence of the idea will have to fight for them.

"Today's strategy of nationalizing cultures, of dividing people, doesn't look very real to me. The divisions are no more real than the amalgamation was real seventy years ago, and this paradox is the paradox of Yugoslavia. The same trouble which started seventy years ago, merging all these different peoples, traditions, cultures, is persisting in the impractical and not very secure divisions which started a few years ago."

"Where does this leave the unified Yugoslav cultural space?"

"That's reality. For thinking people Yugoslavia is not only a state, a market and a political superstructure. It's a way of life. It doesn't matter if Yugoslavia exists as a state or not as long as Yugoslavs and Yugoslav culture exists. Not as a 'new' culture to amalgamate the differences, we don't need that – we need a space in which all the cultures can communicate and influence each other. If the country splits up, there would be no change for me personally. I would continue working on the unified Yugoslav cultural space in different states.

"To be Yugoslav is not to claim a nationality, it's a statement about one's position in the world and in history. It's not like being Serb or Slovene or English. To be Yugoslav means 'I want to be at home in Slovenia and in Serbia. I like Macedonian rhythms, I like Slovenian melancholy, I belong to the Mediterranean'; that's what Yugoslavia means, a cultural feeling that one belongs to a civilization of some kind. Of course, there are a lot of people around who prefer the sweet sensation of belonging to very narrow communities, whether regional or national, but I feel like many other people in this country."

"But are there enough of you?"

"Definitely. More people think this way than like Croatians or Slovenes or Albanians or Macedonians. And a lot of people identify themselves as Serb or Croat nationals, and so on, but *also* feel like Yugoslavs.

"There's something else, very specific to Yugoslavia. Taboos were attacked in the theatre first. Anyone who wants to turn the theatre into an instrument of national revival or of a party, will usually be rejected. Theatre is the last cultural area of pan-Yugoslav contact and communication. Too many people are used to working together, and there's no way to stop theatre people from travelling from Ljubljana to Subotica, from Subotica to Skopje. No way to stop that."

No way except the war that broke out six months after our talk. In the autumn of 1991, Nenad Čanak was arrested and sent to fight the Croats in Slavonia. Thousands of Hungarians resisted the draft, and Vojvodina became the main base of anti-war campaigns in Serbia.

It was a superb gesture, bringing post-modernism to an area that was never quite modern, making Subotica an outpost of true Yugoslavism. Yet Ristić never sounded more Yugoslav than when he said the end of Yugoslavia would change nothing.

He and his company were hanging onto Yugoslavia by their fingernails, because the actual offstage Yugoslavia no longer knew what to do with such ideas. Theatre was a last refuge of reason because theatre deals in multiple identity; in this sense Yugoslavia was a drama school without walls. To be *a Yugoslav* rather than an inhabitant of Yugoslavia was a vocation, not a given identity. For theatre people, such a vocation was second nature. But most others had enough to do making money, finding an apartment, pleasing their husbands, getting the harvest in. What use did they have for a spare-time vocation?

A telefax message is framed on the wall behind Ljubiša Ristić's desk. It was sent by the writer Danilo Kiš, euphoric on the day the doctors said his cancer was in remission. It killed him six months later, in October 1989. The original fax has faded to illegibility; Ristić keeps it behind a photocopy, which is bleaching in the electric light.

Kiš was born in Subotica in 1935, to a Hungarian Jewish father and a Montenegrin mother, who had him christened in the Orthodox faith in 1939 to protect him from new anti-Jewish legislation in Hungary. His father and almost all his family were murdered in Auschwitz. After the war his mother took him to live in Cetinje.

Ristić collaborated with Kiš and honoured him in 1991 with a season of plays by him or adapted from his fiction. Otherwise there is no evidence of Subotica's connection with this great artist. When I asked a municipal official if a monument of some kind is planned, she said with a hint of reproach, "Yes, a bust. But he didn't come back here, you know."

This lady wasn't the first; Kiš specialized in offending local sensitivities – national ones too, once with such severe results that he was driven to emigrate. For Kiš, cosmopolitanism was a matter of moral and aesthetic principle.

In the madness of 1991, Kiš kept occurring to me as a touchstone of lucidity, a reminder of essential virtues. I came to value him as my Yugoslav friends value him. The baroque verve and bite of his sentences still thrilled me; likewise the scope of his ambition, to write truthfully of the Jewish genocide and gulag-Bolshevism in fiction of superlative artistry. What I appreciated more, amid the clamour of parliamentsful of "poets" and "essayists", was his conviction that a writer's responsibility is to language and art, never to authorities or nation.

Kiš loved Rabelais best of all and exulted, as the other had, in magnifying the oddity of the world. Unlike Rabelais, he selects and burnishes his themes with a perfectionist's stubbornness. His art dances despite its burden of melancholy: the melancholy of its own precision and of the inclusive spontaneity that it can't possess. For – unlike Rabelais again, maybe unlike anyone before the twentieth century – history had denied Kiš the chance of belief in innocent creation. He was cursed instead, with the twofold guilt of a survivor who made literature.

The present is no age for fantasy, he believed; mere happenings should be enough for any artist. More than this, it seemed to him wrong – sinful – to make things up. When he allowed himself, Kiš invented unforgettably. One of his last stories tells of an encyclopaedia compiled by a "religious organization or sect whose democratic programme stresses an egalitarian vision of the world of the dead ... and aims at redressing injustices and granting all God's creatures an equal place in eternity." The sole criterion for inclusion: no name which appears in any other encyclopaedia may be entered. The sole principle of compilation: "there is nothing insignificant in a human life, no hierarchy of events." Its tireless contributors "believe in the miracle of biblical resurrection, and they compile their vast catalogue in preparation for that moment. So that everyone will be able to find not only his fellow men but also – and more important – his own forgotten past. When the time comes, this compendium will serve as a unique proof of resurrection."

Kiš's narrator reads the entry for her father, dead from a sarcoma two months before. She finds that "nothing is missing": "an affair with a Bosnian woman, a waitress, in Sombor; a bicycle accident near Čantavir ... a night ride in a cattle wagon on the Senta–Subotica line ... a ride in a crowded truck over the muddy road between Zrenjanin and Elemir". These are the toponyms of Vojvodina, Kiš's own childhood landscape. It isn't true that he didn't come back.

Kiš later said that by writing "The Encyclopaedia of the Dead", he had competed with God, and his cancer was punishment. For his doctors had told him that his malignancy commenced at the time he was composing the story. One imagines from his photographs that Kiš always bore within himself, Lazarus-like, the knowledge of a death evaded and owed. He saw art as a fight with death, and one's satisfaction that Kiš's art hasn't lost the struggle doesn't lessen the regret that he is no longer here. In every sense, he straddled Yugoslavia; his phenomenal parentage linked him to the marshes of central Europe and the Dinaric heights around Lovćen. "The ethnographic rarity which I represent," he remarked drily, "will die out with me."

The Drunken Geese of Croatia

Begin with the shape: two sides of a triangle, reaching eastwards into central Europe and southwards down the Adriatic coast, with the vertex at Karlovac and the Istran peninsula as an afterthought in the north-west. Was ever a state so bizarrely formed? And its ungainliness is emblematic. This improbable geography limns a tormented history and forecasts a future just as difficult.

True to its appearance, Croatia is an aggregate of regions. While these regions don't combine as a natural unit, they do amount to a national entity, but not one can be homogenized as a model nation-state. This is partly because the regions have their separate histories and patterns of development; and partly because 21 per cent of Croatia's population is not Croat.* As Croat nationalists' traditional mission is to achieve model nation-statehood, they are committed to a false totality – which then, needless to say, must be defended "by all necessary means" against external and internal enemies.

Croatia's ratio of border to land-area is far too high in a part of the world where political units had better be compact, bunched as in military formation, not splayed so vulnerably, all frontiers and underbelly. When war came, in 1991, the aggressors moved easily to seal off Vukovar and Dubrovnik, at Croatia's eastern and southern extremities. Far away in Zagreb, the government might as well have been in another country for all the support it gave its besieged citizens. This neglect was in part calculated – a cynical political choice, not merely fated by shape. But that's another story, and my own experience of Croatia started in a different era, in 1989, when Eastern Europe was still, by the skin of its teeth, the Soviet bloc, Yugoslavia was shaky but intact, multi-party elections flickered like a mirage on the horizon, and the JNA stayed in its barracks.

It was high summer in Dalmatia, but my first sight was of grey, not the dazzling blue and white promised by the brochures. The ferry

---

* Unless specified, all such figures in this chapter refer to the status quo before the 1991 war.

had departed Rijeka at nightfall; I awoke in my saloon-bar chair at dawn, as we slid into Split. Peering at the grubby harbour, breathing the petrol fumes, moved not a whit by the dim outline of Diocletian's palace beyond the palm trees, I suspected the coast of Illyria had been oversold.

By late afternoon the sun had abolished any doubts. Lying on the eastern shore of Hvar island, where limestone cliffs tumble into the sea, I listened to cicadas in the pines, sniffed the resin and lavender on the breeze, and squinted at the coastline of Biokovo shimmering almost touchably across the sound. My father had died a month before, and I was scoured, screened off from the friends who had invited me here. The sunlight, sea, and breezes were healing, and my reaction to the word Dalmatia is still one of gratitude. Now this reaction is a subliminal shutter-click, crushed a split second later by enduring shock at what has happened, not on Hvar or the other islands but along that superb littoral, from Molunat near Montenegro to Rijeka in the north. More than four-fifths of Yugoslavia's coast lay within Croatia, almost 1,800 kilometres. Most of it, in the second half of 1991, was liable to bombardment from land, sea and air.

Since that week on Hvar, I travelled every inch of the coast road at different seasons, always postponing a closer look at the towns for one mundane reason or another, never suspecting it might become impossible to return – or too late. Twice I approached Dubrovnik from the south; the road climbs from Kupari to a crest and suddenly Dubrovnik is revealed, cradled in its walls like the dream of a perfect city. As I wrote this chapter, those renaissance battlements were called into service again. The mayor begged in vain for Western help. Day after day for two months, tanks and artillery of the JNA unloaded their shells on the 55,000 refugees crammed in its cellars along with the 5,000 inhabitants of the old town.

At Ston, half an hour's drive to the north, napalm was reportedly used, cremating hamlets and swathes of farmland.

There is a typically savage and regressive irony – typical of the logic of the federation's terminal crisis – in the fact that the attacks on Dubrovnik and Dalmatia seemed to clinch the Western states' reluctant conclusion that Yugoslavia was finished. For it was here, along this coast, that Yugoslavia was conceived and named. The word itself was first published in a Dalmatian periodical in 1848, in a poem.

Like Istra, Dalmatia was a compound of Slavic and Italian (Roman, Venetian) elements fixed in a Byzantine, then a Venetian, then an Austrian mould. It lived and developed separately from the other Croatian lands to the north and east, which, from 1102 until the collapse of Austria-Hungary, were under Hungarian domination.

Together, these three territories – Dalmatia, plus the old provinces of Croatia and Slavonia – constitute the republic's fateful dog-leg shape. They represent most though not all of the medieval Croatian kingdom, which also reached deep into what became Bosnia. Southern Dalmatia and eastern Slavonia were separated by the Ottoman invaders, pressing northwards, driving much of the Croat population before it, with its nobility. Radical nationalists still dream of reversing this displacement, by incorporating parts or all of Bosnia and Hercegovina into a Great Croatian state.

By the end of the seventeenth century, the frontier between the Habsburg and Turkish Empires had stabilized. This zone became the Croatian–Bosnian border, approximately following the curve of the river Una. As the Military Frontier, it was a corridor where the communities were freed from feudal bonds and answerable directly to the Habsburg War Council, bypassing the authorities in Zagreb, in return for vigilance against the Ottomans.

Dalmatia's population was Croat, overlaid by an Italian-speaking stratum, and with a Serb minority concentrated in the north, around the Military Frontier. Communication among the Slavs was relatively free, away from Turkish and Hungarian rule. Austria provided both Croats and Serbs with a common foe, not too repressive. Encouraged to national self-assertion by their experience within Napoleon's Illyrian Provinces, and inspired by the rise of nationalism across the sea in Italy, a cultural movement burgeoned in the 1830s and '40s: this was Illyrianism, calling for Yugoslav unity based on linguistic commonality, but without amalgamating national differences.

As surely then as later, the notion of Yugoslav unity-in-diversity fascinated the intellectual élite, and proved a political contradiction in terms. Even the linguistic commonality was contentious; championing one Serbo-Croatian dialect as the standard for all Yugoslavs, Illyrianism did not beguile the Slovenes or Bulgars, who had languages of their own. Nor did it evoke much interest in Serbia, where the Serbs were busy fashioning a canonical folklore and a linguistic standard of their own, as the very criterion of Serbdom.

Illyrianism incubated a romantic, almost abstract strain of feeling, which would later become, scarcely altered, the lofty essence of the "Yugoslav idea'. When in the 1840s it was put to the test as a political project for the integration of Dalmatia, Croatia-Slavonia, and the Military Frontier, Illyrianism failed. This failure was a minor intellectual event, obscured after 1848 by sterner conceptions of nationality and statehood. Still, it closely prefigured the failure in our time of its offspring, Yugoslavism. In each case, an appellation was contrived by an élite to advance a project of multinational freedom and mutual aid. In each case, too, this high-minded idealism was so helpless to deal with real contingencies – whether interference from outside or bad faith inside – that it nurtured its opposite: distrust and hatred. Disillusion with the failure of Illyrianism helped to engender Croatian radical nationalism in the 1860s. Thus started the venerable Yugoslav tradition of idealists converting overnight (or in prison) into national extremists.

In 1848 the Hungarians rebelled against the Habsburg dynastic state, and declared that Croatia, as a unit within the empire, was abolished. The Croatian *Sabor* (assembly) promptly cancelled its ties to Budapest. The Dalmatians thought the opportunity for union with their co-nationals in Croatia and Slavonia had arrived; they demanded reincorporation of the Military Frontier.

Exploiting this national sentiment, the emperor offered Croatia unity and autonomy within the empire in return for help to crush the Hungarians. Jelačić, the governor of Croatia, duly led his troops forth.* Once victory was achieved, the emperor broke his side of the bargain: a united Croatian entity was too likely to unbalance his multinational empire. The *Ausgleich* (Compromise) of 1867 returned Croatia and Slavonia to Hungary, which revoked its abolition, recognized the Croat nation, and granted limited self-government under the Sabor. It also promised to unify the Croatian lands at some future date. This never happened; Dalmatia stayed Austrian to the end.

Instead the Hungarians incorporated the Military Frontier into Croatia. This appeared a concession; actually it was a stratagem to distract the Croats from their pursuit of integration by setting them against the Serb minority, whose numbers were swelled and suspicions roused by the ending of the Frontier's autonomy.

It was an astute move. Croat feeling had altered since its Illyrian spring; the hopes dashed in 1848 and again in 1867 had spawned a radical movement whose ideology has recurrently plagued Croatia ever since, like political malaria.

Spokesman of the new ideology was Ante Starčević, leader of the

* Jelačić's reputation is a neat instance of nationalist revisionism, and of the Croats' ambiguous ties to Austria-Hungary. Although he preferred to rescue the dynastic state than to support the Croatian revolution, and although he was distinctly pro-Yugoslav, Jelačić has been sanctified by Croat separatists.

Stranka prava, or Party of Right, founded in reaction to the influx of
Frontier Serbs into Croatia. Unlike the Illyrianists and their successors, Starčević set no store by the Habsburgs as a source of
enlightened protection against Hungary and its feudal landlords; or
as anything else. His party's ultimate goal was a Great Croatia
stretching from the Alps to Bulgaria, and south to Albania. The only
political subjects in this vast territory would be Croats; the rest
would either be Croats by another name, or sects that counted for
nothing.

The Right nominated by Starčević's party was the inviolable right
of the Croats to reconstitute their national state in the historic
Croatian lands. Underpinning this imperative was a theory of the
state as an unextinguished legacy from the medieval kingdom.
Because the Croats had agreed on union with Hungary in 1102,
transferring the throne legally to the Magyar king, they had not been
defeated or annexed; their link with Hungary was contractual, and
Croatian sovereignty was compromised but intact. The symbol of
state continuity was the Sabor in Zagreb. Until the eighteenth
century this institution had retained its old powers, albeit over a
much smaller territory than the kingdom of yore. By Starčević's day
it was reduced to a provincial assembly, answerable to Budapest.

Hungary's increasingly dictatorial attitude gave the Croats
motives to support Starčević's preposterous claims. Yet Croatia was
a complex political space, never one-dimensional; parallel with
Starčević's rejection of Illyrianism, another man was building and
completing it. Josip Juraj Strossmayer from Osijek, capital of
Slavonia, was a prophet of liberal and humane Yugoslavism, a
Catholic bishop who abhorred bigotry against the Orthodox
Church. For he was moved by a tremendous ecumenical dream: to
overcome the schism between Catholic and Orthodox Christianity.
Using his episcopal revenue to found a Yugoslav Academy and a
university in Zagreb, Strossmayer wanted a Yugoslav federation
within the Habsburg Empire. While his programme did assume a
Croatian privilege to lead the effort for Yugoslav unity, it looked
forward to eventual equality of nations.

After Starčević's death the Party of Right fragmented; his primitive notion of right was overtaken by a new generation of Croat
students and leaders who came, thanks to Hungary's plainly
incorrigible repression, and partly to changes of stance by the
Kingdom of Serbia, to see Yugoslav unity *outside* Austria-Hungary
as the best option for Croats. In 1905 a Croatian-Serbian Coalition
was launched in Zagreb, melding the liberal separatist and federalist
streams in Croatia Slavonia. Backed too by Habsburg-Serb politicians, the Coalition triumphed in elections to the Sabor.

The Coalition with its Yugoslav programme held the promise, to many, of a solution to the Croatian conundrum. Saddled with an unworkable and divisive theory of political nationhood, the separatists (Starčević et al) had aspired to an emancipation that Croatia-Slavonia was powerless to achieve. By contrast, the federalists were realistic about the Dual Monarchy's power, but their goal was unattainable because the Monarchy and its estate-owners were too hidebound to trust any policy toward their Croats and Serbs except *divide et impera*.

By the Balkan Wars (1912–13) it was clear that Croats were making almost all the running towards union. Serbia did not need to show enthusiasm or adapt to Croat sensibilities; it would inevitably and rightly predominate in any Yugoslav state – on its terms.

In short, the conundrum was not solved but modified. Unsupported by other Yugoslavs, meaning above all Serbia, the Croats could not exert enough leverage against the surrounding powers to stand a chance of keeping their independence, even if Austria-Hungary should hand it to them without a murmur. Yet if they embraced Yugoslav unitarism, how could they escape domination by Serbia, which already had an independent state with an army, and a revolutionary movement seething in Bosnia?

Croat politicians were circling this dilemma in 1914, when the First World War supervened and presented them, soon enough, with an immense opportunity – and a risk on the same scale.

War set the Habsburg Yugoslavs against the independent Yugoslav states; Croats, Slovenes, and Habsburg Serbs too, were among the troops invading Serbia and Montenegro.* Political contacts survived, and as the bloody stalemate turned to impending defeat for the Central Powers, three-way negotiations started among the Serbian government, on Corfu; those Yugoslav politicians from the Dual Monarchy who were agitating with the Yugoslav Committee in Britain and France; and those who had stayed behind.

From the beginning all three factions foresaw some kind of Yugoslav state or states emerging from an Austro-Hungarian defeat. And from the beginning there was unremitting controversy about the shape this state would take. Serbia wanted to extend its boundaries around Croatia-Slavonia, Dalmatia, Vojvodina and Bosnia-Hercegovina, where almost as many Serbs lived as in the Kingdom of Serbia itself (some 1.9 million as against 2.26 million). It did not,

---

* When the 25th Domobran regiment moved at the outbreak of war to a reserve position near Belgrade, its youngest non-commissioned officer was the twenty-two year-old Josip Broz.

however, seek a new kind of state. Federalism of any sort was out of the question; ideally, Serbian government would be extended to embrace the gains. The very name "Yugoslavia" was frowned on because it was implicitly federalist, and would veil Serbia's leading part in guiding the Yugoslav peoples to freedom.

For Croat politicians, on the other hand, a federal arrangement came to appear the only safe bet. Even convinced unitarists grew suspicious of Great Serbian designs; some tried to win guarantees for Croatian prerogatives in any future state. The Croats were, as ever, trapped by the weakness of their position. Although Serbia had lost the war, militarily, by 1915, its statehood, dynasty, and army would be the institutional kernel of any new union.

When revolution in Russia robbed the Serbs of their strongest backing, Prime Minister Nikola Pašić was forced to compromise. The Corfu Declaration was drawn up by his government and the Yugoslav Committee. It announced the intention of Serbs, Croats and Slovenes to found a constitutional, democratic, parliamentary monarchy under the Karadjordjević dynasty. In this kingdom the historic territories would not exist, and the equality of the three "tribes" (as the nations were called in the terminology of the day), their flags, religions and alphabets would be guaranteed. The status and prerogatives of the monarch remained ominously vague.

The Yugoslav parties in Zagreb and Ljubljana had been encouraged by Entente successes and the death of Emperor Franz Josef to keep pushing for full autonomy within the Dual Monarchy. Events in 1918 overtook such plans. The disintegration of Austria-Hungary was not an Entente war aim until very late in the day: perhaps not until June 1918, when the go-ahead was given to the formation of Polish and Czechoslovak states, which in turn made a Yugoslavia inevitable.

In October, pro-Yugoslav parties from the collapsing Dual Monarchy formed a National Council of Slovenes, Croats and Serbs. The Sabor promptly announced that Croatia, Slavonia and Dalmatia were "a completely independent state", which joined the National Council to make a sovereign State of the Slovenes, Croats and Serbs. The Sabor transferred its powers to the Council, which in turn declared its willingness to "enter into a common state with Serbia and Montenegro".

Outside the debating chambers of Zagreb, however, the Croatian lands were in chaos. One reason for the galloping speed of developments was the fear of Italian expansion, and the Italian army was already helping itself to Istrian and Dalmatian territory secretly promised by the Allies in 1915. At the same time, Serb communities across Croatia and Slavonia were vowing their loyalty to King Petar

Karadjordjević, while Croatian towns declared for the young Habsburg Emperor, Karl. The peasantry was helping itself to the vanished Hungarian landlords' estates. The National Council had to beg Serbian military help to quell the turmoil. Help was forthcoming, more in the spirit of annexation than of assistance.

Thanks in part to sharp practice by Serb leaders in Zagreb, in part to pragmatic acceptance of the *fait accompli*, the National Council became malleable to Belgrade's designs. Come the end of November, only one member of its central committee voted against direct unification, roughly on the terms of the Corfu Declaration. The dissenter was Stjepan Radić, founder of the Croat People's Peasant Party. Unlike his colleagues, Radić took his bearings from the peasantry rather than the urban classes. On the eve of their departure for Belgrade, where unification was declared on 1 December 1918, he warned them that the Croats did not want this unification. The Councillors, he said, were acting "like drunken geese in a fog".

When the fog lifted, the Croat "tribe" found itself less autonomous and culturally less empowered than when it was divided under Austria-Hungary.

Radić's farmyard simile tolls down the years. When the Croats finally opted out of Yugoslavia in 1991, their chosen geese were just as drunken, wandering in a fog no less dense. In Subotica, Ljubiša Ristić had told me: "Croats are always unhappy and frustrated with politics, politicians and ordinary people alike, because they are very stubborn about their political ideas but these ideas are too complicated to be realized." In fact the complication arises from context. For a century and a half, each great opportunity for the Croats to achieve the standard national goals of unity and self-determination has been so fraught with provisos that time soon exposed it for a mirage. Disillusion bred vengeful savagery among the worst, intellectualism and passivity among the best. Twice Croatia has been led by men who insisted that the mirage is the genuine article – as if the complications that deny nationalist fulfilment do not exist because they must not. The ustaše fascists did this in the Second World War. In 1990 and 1991 Croatia's first democratically elected government did it too, led by an ex-partisan general who had fought those same fascists in the name of a socialist federal Yugoslavia.

*

Croatia's new president in 1990 and his government (very much his government) saw themselves from the outset in messianic terms. The political task before them was a sacred duty. True to history,

Croatian nationalists again pretended that complexities could be annulled by dogma. Again they wanted to carve a bigger portion from the joint than they could swallow, or than their neighbours would let them keep without a fight.

In other words, the bloody sequel to Croatia's bid for independence in 1991 hinged not on its elected representatives, nor on the 77.9 per cent of its people who registered as Croats in the spring census, but on its Serb population. More precisely it hinged on a fraction of that population: the communities of Krajina, a self-constituted territory of communities with Serb majorities, named after the *vojna krajina* (Military Frontier), between the north Dalmatian coast and the Bosnian border. The actions of these communities hinged, in turn, on a core of extremists sponsored by Serbia's government in Belgrade.

Trouble was being stirred in Krajina before the April 1990 elections, with hate campaigns in Serbian media against the "fascist", "ustaše" Croats. When Dr Tudjman spoke at a pre-election HDZ rally in Benkovac, one of Krajina's larger towns, he was threatened by a simple-minded Serb wielding, apparently, a toy pistol. Much was made by both sides of this incident. A month after the elections the president of the Serb Democratic Party in the same town was allegedly attacked. Uproar ensued. The SDP leader claimed to see "all the elements of ustaše aggression" in this assault, and he used it as a pretext to "suspend all relations with the parliament of the Socialist Republic of Croatia and all Croatocentric parties". No discussion, no bargaining. To make matters worse, the SDP was then the only Serb political party in Croatia. Democracy had crashed before the race was underway.

Tudjman's government dug in, amending the constitution to deny the Croatian Serbs any kind of political autonomy, and vowing never to cede "as much as a millimetre" of the republic to any rebels. Serbs were purged from the republican police; guns were retrieved from the army reserve arsenals in Serb zones. Signs in Cyrillic and Latin alphabets – common in mixed Serb-Croat areas – were replaced with Latin-only signs.

The Serbs of Krajina announced a referendum in August 1990 to settle the issue of autonomy in Croatia. Given that Serbs were a majority in these districts, that no outside authority vetted the procedure, and that Croats were doubtless intimidated from using their vote, the result was a foregone conclusion. The "historic terrritories of the Vojna Krajina" were proclaimed autonomous. If Croatia opted to leave the federation, this territory would annex itself to Serbia proper – with which it shared no border.

In Serbia, meanwhile, President Milošević was playing the Krajina card to coax patriotic support away from the opposition in the months before Serbia's December election. He had other motives, too, to encourage the Croatian Serbs; they were stalking horses to test the nerve of the government in Zagreb, and, later, to justify drawing the JNA into the conflict.

It was now that serious disruption began. Through late summer and autumn, the rebels blocked the roads and railway; which did much damage, for Knin lies on the direct routes from Zagreb to Split, Yugoslavia's second port and the second city of Croatia. The effect on Dalmatia's tourism may be imagined.

The rebels broke into police stations to seize weapons; the Croats responded by laying siege to rebel villages. The Sabor raged, and swore to reimpose its authority, but baulked at seizing back the lost zone. Meanwhile the JNA stepped in, impartially so it claimed, to stop the conflict from escalating.

The rebel centre was at Knin. During the winter of 1990–91, other communities in the vicinity followed Knin's lead and opted into Krajina, which spread north along the frontier with Bosnia, around the armpit of Croatia, towards Slavonia, until it covered a fifth of Croatia's area – though under 4 per cent of its population, so poor and barren is Krajina.

Spring brought massive strikes across Serbia and student protests in Belgrade. The six presidents of the republics began a series of high-profile summits. Krajina was a key obstacle to progress at these summits. On 1 April the Independent and Autonomous Region of Krajina, as it now termed itself, requested the parliament in Belgrade to annex it to the territory of the Republic of Serbia. Next day the Serbian parliament pledged support for Serbs in Croatia and asked the JNA to patrol areas where they were fearful.

Rather late in the day, I realized that Krajina was much more than a symptom of general crisis; it was the fulcrum, as Kosovo had been in the late 1980s. The rebels meant to go the distance, by forcing Croatia to postpone its declaration of independence beyond the end of June, or making a mockery of that independence. And the government would not compromise: Tudjman and his besotted entourage viewed Knin as holy Croatian land, where the medieval kings were crowned, etcetera.

My photographer friend Crispin wanted to see Krajina too, and we agreed to rendezvous in Zadar at the end of April. Beyond Šibenik, northbound traffic on the coast road dwindled. Groups of men with rifles loitered under clumps of roadside trees. News kiosks in Biograd had been overturned; youths perched on low walls around the main square, muted and alert.

Tension rose higher as the coach rolled north. More overturned kiosks. The windows in Zadar's smart new bus station had been smashed. The atmosphere was frantic and unnaturally quiet at the same moment. People streamed away from the old town centre, walking fast and barely speaking to each other. Crispin arrived from Ljubljana, and we went straight to the centre.

A gang of teenage boys wielding table legs and iron bars filed purposefully through the maze of Venetian alleys, gutting one Serb-owned property after another: a shoe shop, a gents' outfitters, a café, a grocers' store. As the gang moved on, a policeman sauntered into view, crunching shattered glass under his boots as he glanced indifferently at the damage. Other boys pushed through the on-lookers, not bothering to conceal the stacks of looted video tapes bulging inside their jumpers. The air was fragrant with coffee beans, spilt on the flagstones. Passers-by searched for familiar faces and whispered excitedly, breaking off to look up and down the street, as if retribution might arrive at any minute.

Crispin asked a posse of wreckers relaxing at a bar if he could photograph them, and they posed obligingly with a brace of nearby policemen. Then they bought us a beer. A heavy-lidded youth with a crowbar beside his chair contemplated me as I drank. "What's your religion?" he asked dully.

"None. What's yours?" — as if there were any doubt.

"Catholic."

Antemurale christianitatis! Praise the Lord and pass the ammunition!

We had arrived at the very hour when Zadar joined the strife between Croats and the Serb minority. A policeman had been killed that day near Benkovac, trying to stop a band of Krajina men hoisting the Yugoslav flag on a hilltop. (Was any Croat life laid down, in 1991, so futilely?) The street gang wanted revenge, and not just for the dead man. All Croats were fed up with the Serbs and with the JNA's specious neutrality — none more than those who lived on the coast that suffered most from the rebellion. Like other Dalmatian towns, Zadar is overwhelmingly Croat; more than 83 per cent of its 130,000 people. Politically, however, Zadar is unlike the other littoral towns; for historical reasons (it was an Italian possession between the world wars) it is strongly nationalist, and voted for Tudjman's HDZ in the elections. The Serbs in Knin claimed the HDZ's policies had forced them to defend themselves by rebelling. So Zadar's involvement was dismally inevitable.

Later that night one of the wreckers gave us a tour. We inspected the gutted JAT office (non-Serbs everywhere saw the Yugoslav airline as a Serbian operation), then a shoe shop. Andrija compared the goods strewn around the premises with his own footwear: "Italian," he explained coolly. "Expensive, but one really can't wear this 'Borovo' stuff."

Then into his car to visit the roadblocks, detouring (not at our request) to glimpse the sublime pre-romanesque church of St Donatus, floodlit for the tourists who had already stopped coming. "What kind of music d'you like?" he asked, accelerating through the empty streets. "New Age?" He slotted something spacey into the tape machine. "I know this is not good," he shouted, waving with his free hand at the violated properties. "But . . . it has to be."

The roadblocks were manned by civilians in their twenties and thirties armed with hunting rifles and table-legs. The first group we met included a marine engineer, a basketball player, and a pop singer. "I've fought the [communist] star with the cross all my life," said the engineer ardently. "This is the end of Yugoslavia. This is war. We've waited a thousand years for this, and the moment is now very close. We must be free, not an occupied country any longer."

Closer than they knew. By the end of November, seven months later, Zadar was a prime target in the war waged by Serbia and the federal forces against Croatia. With no water or electricity supply, blockaded by the navy on one side and bombarded by the army on the other, Zadar was under dreadful siege. Who knows if Andrija or the gun-toting HDZ activists we met that April night, when nothing stirred and not a light shone in the JNA barracks, are still alive? Everybody spoke of war, yet few believed the logic would be allowed to roll to its conclusion. For my part, I wanted to see Andrija's fashionable shoes and music as tokens that a sense of proportion, grounded in healthy materialist values, would prevent the violent stand-off in Croatia from escalating much further. Instead I should have taken his attitude, blending communal violence, fatalism, and sightseeing, as an omen of how smoothly the momentum for war was gathering.

Besides, both Crispin and I were too struck by the boorishness of the local HDZ to try and forecast. Not by choice, we visited the party headquarters at two in the morning; a roadblocker who had posed for a photo now revoked his permission and wanted the film. Crispin was reluctant, so we were escorted to a Venetian palazzo. Our guides (guards?) dumped their weapons, with a clonk, on the heap of knives and revolvers outside the party chief's room. Inside, a dozen men ranged around the walls regarded us sullenly. The chief was on the phone, wiping his sallow neck and face with a handkerchief. No one could shine at such a moment; still, this pint-sized character was instantly dislikeable. "Who organized the gangs of boys tonight?" I asked the nearest unscowling face. "HDZ," it said, confirming the obvious.

Of course the chief had his way, Crispin yielded his film, and we went to bed. A police reservist was patrolling the road outside our hotel. Like all Croats old enough to have finished their conscription in the JNA, he was liable to be called up as a reservist for the republican police. In real life he was a waiter, before the collapse of tourism drove him abroad; but he was too sensible to be vengeful. He was a Dalmatian moderate. "These empty-headed boys are spoiling everything," he said about the gangs. "I didn't vote HDZ and I don't care for Tudjman, though he's a positive figure for Croatia. But you see, I can't keep my Serb friends these days. They call us ustaše, which is nonsense, and we call them četniks, which isn't true either. Those are Second World War names, not for today. The Serbs in Knin don't believe it anyway, not most of them; they are manipulated."

Manipulated by whom? By Belgrade, of course, as every Croat could tell you. When the triumphant HDZ committed Croatia to claim its sovereignty within a confederation of republics or, failing that, to seek total independence, the Serbian government – which refused a confederal settlement point blank, and had its own reasons for wanting a diversion – was bound to stir up the Serbs of Croatia. Instead of handling its Serbs with kid gloves, the Croat leaders provoked them.

"Like drunken geese in a fog."

Croatia's recklessness in 1990 and 1991 has its source at the ceremony of unification on 1 December 1918, when Prince Regent Aleksandar explained that the three Yugoslav peoples in the new kingdom were one nation under three tribal names. (Three only, note: Montenegrins and Macedonians were accounted Serbs, and Bosnian Muslims were nationally "uncommitted".)

One tribe was first among equals. It could not have been otherwise; the disposition of forces and influence stood all in Serbia's favour. Croat hopes were blighted, as centralizing measures were imposed by the king and his largely Serbian ministers. Education, taxation, the Orthodox Church, the army and police, civil and diplomatic services were all expanded and reorganized to enhance Serbia's power and status in the kingdom. Throughout the interwar period, few federalist Croats were permitted access to power.

From the start Stjepan Radić, dubbed the uncrowned king of Croatia, and his Peasant Party, which as a mass movement claimed the support of 90 per cent of Croats, were the biggest political obstacle to the centralists, though it won fewer seats in the

November 1920 elections than the Communist Party. Both were harassed by the government, which jailed Radić and soon outlawed the CPY.

The CPY led Slovene and Muslim opposition to the draft constitution presented in 1921 and backed by the two strongest Serbian parties. They failed; the constitution was adopted on Vidovdan (St Vitus' Day, 28 June) by just over half the assembly — less than the two-thirds majority demanded by those parties from the ex-Habsburg territories.

Royal Yugoslavia never recovered from the rift and bitterness caused by foisting the Vidovdan Constitution — which spoke of "the Serbo-Croat-Slovene nationality" and "the Serbo-Croat and Slovene language" — on the anti-centralists. The parliamentary system lurched from crisis to deadlock, until 1928, when Radić and four other Croat deputies were shot in the assembly by a Montenegrin deputy. Two died instantly, Radić six weeks later. The CPP and its allies withdrew to Zagreb. The prime minister resigned, and the king stepped in. Proclaiming a royal dictatorship, he abolished all political parties, changed the state's name to the Kingdom of Yugoslavia, and abolished the historic territories by reorganizing the Kingdom into provinces named after rivers.

Aleksandar was a sincere man who intervened for the sake of "national unity". He was assassinated in 1934 at the hands of a terrorist organization that came into existence when parliament was abolished. This was the ustaša organization of Croat extremists, led by Dr Ante Pavelić, collaborating on this occasion with Macedonian nationalists. Operating from Italy and Hungary, the ustaše were convinced that nothing short of Yugoslavia's destruction could liberate Croatia. Their revolutionism was a marginal position; federalism was still the Peasant Party's demand.

The threat of fascism on Yugoslavia's borders combined with a worsening economic crisis inherited from Aleksandar's dictatorship to weaken the unitarist argument; meanwhile the Western powers pressured Prince Regent Pavle to tackle the Croat question more constructively. Pavle manoeuvred to appoint a more flexible Serb as premier, who negotiated with the CPP. They came up with a measure to create an automous province of Croatia, under a governor appointed by and responsible to the crown, that shared legislative power in the province with the Sabor, reconstituted and freely elected. (This Croatian territory is shown on the map overleaf.) Belgrade would keep control of defence, foreign affairs and trade.

This attempt to federate Croatia's status was pushed through by decree in 1939. Probably it would not have succeeded; Croat discontent was allayed, though extremists weren't satisfied. Serbian

The administrative units of the Kingdom of Yugoslavia, 1929–1941

dismay was loud. Slovenes and Muslims, and Serbs too, mooted the idea of identical provinces for themselves.

The next phase of Serb-Croat relations opened on 10 April 1941, when Belgrade was suffering its fourth day of *Blitzkrieg* and the German army swept into Serbia from the north. On that date the *Nezavisna Država Hrvatska* (NDH: Independent Croatian State) was proclaimed. A quisling pseudo-state, NDH was run by Pavelić's ustaše as a protectorate of the Axis. Pavelić and his terrorists had enjoyed Italian and Hungarian hospitality for a decade; now they seized their chance to wrest a free Croatia from the wreckage of Yugoslavia. It suited their patrons to let them. But Axis exploitation of extremist Croatian grievances soon backfired. So insanely murderous was NDH's treatment of its Serbian, Jewish and romany subjects, and of anti-ustaša Croats, that thousands flocked to the resistance forces, especially the partisans.

The ideology of NDH drove the traditional Right-wing ideas of Croatian nationhood to an unfettered logical extreme. Only Croats were political subjects of NDH; the remainder had no legal existence. This remainder was enormous, because NDH encompassed all of Bosnia and Hercegovina, as well as Bačka and Srem, up to the doorstep of Belgrade. One third of the inhabitants of this area were Orthodox Serbs: almost two million. Upwards of a million were Muslim too, but Pavelić had no quarrel with them; they were blandished in propaganda as long-lost Croat brothers.

Pavelić's formula to purify the territory (and settle scores with the pre-war enemy) by converting one third of Serbs to Catholicism, expelling a third to Serbia proper, and exterminating the remainder, does reek with the authentic Nazi stench. Unlike the Final Solution of Jews, however, this genocide was not attempted methodically, with science. Ustaše slaughter was done with axe blades, ropes, and blunt instruments, even inside the concentration camps. Only a few thousand Serbs were expelled, and an uncertain number converted.

But how many were killed? This became the most intensely disputed statistic in post-war Yugoslavia. The true figure will never be known; data is too scanty. Since 1946 the official estimate was that some 700,000 Serbs, Jews and romanies were killed in NDH. Scholarship has revised the figure to 350,000–450,000. Of these, as many as 150,000 may have died at Jasenovac, the main concentration camp: 100,000 Serbs, 30,000 romanies and 20,000 Jews.

Serbs tend to react to any querying of the received figure as an attack on Serbdom and all its values. (Their own historians' revisions go the other way: up to a million.) Croats, on the other hand, when NDH and Jasenovac are mentioned, tend to become miserable, angry or evasive, sometimes all at once.

There is a very widespread belief among Croats that the scale of ustaša slaughter was exaggerated in Tito's Yugoslavia, so that all Croat national sentiment would be blackened by fascism. Most likely this suspicion is well founded. Titoism operated by setting Yugoslav nationalisms against each other, and the ustaša record was too convenient not to use, discreetly, especially in the post-war years when Tito's régime needed urgently to reconcile the Serbs to the new federal system.

Croat nationalists, spying an even more sinister Serb-led conspiracy behind the exaggerations, went further. Croatia, they said, has been deliberately saddled with an eternal debt of guilt to all Serbs. The fact that Serbia's own equivalent of the ustaše – the cětniks – murdered Croats and Muslims with no less savagery was overlooked. Croats had nothing to be ashamed of, these nationalists said: by contrast with the Serbs, they had been over-represented among the partisans. And anyway, the NDH was a direct result of Great Serbian tyranny in the first Yugoslavia.

It says much about the central place of these matters to Croat nationalism in its current, anti-communist shape that the best-known exponent of this conspiracy theory is the country's president. In the 1960s Tudjman came to the conclusion that no more than 70,000 people died in Jasenovac, and larger figures had been publicized with "the obvious aim of making the Croatian nation odious in the eyes of the world and itself."

He scores several points. The fate of Jews in Serbia was no better than in NDH; proportionally, the Muslims of Bosnia suffered a worse genocide than the Serbs; Serbs do exploit their wartime sufferings to monopolize the moral heights while cultivating their self-image as the greatest martyr among nations and smearing the Croats, most effectively, with a reputation as a somehow innately fascistic people.

The trouble is that Tudjman serves the truth no more impartially than such opponents as Radomir Bulatović, who maintains that 1.1 million Serbs were exterminated at Jasenovac. The president's estimate of slaughter at Jasenovac keeps plummeting. He tries to apologise for the Croatian and Bosnian Catholic clergy which, with too few exceptions, equivocated with NDH when they did not endorse it. He also wants to separate NDH from the ustaše, as if the former promised genuine statehood until the latter betrayed it; which is nonsense.

Worst of all, Tudjman emerged in the 1980s as a pundit of anti-Semitism – as if the imperative of exculpating the Croats left him no choice but to blame their other victims. Any Croat nationalist must be free-thinking and quick witted to avoid anti-Semitism, which has a high-class pedigree in Croatian political tradition, and in the Catholic Habsburg prejudices which lurk within the current propaganda about Croatia being "European" and not "Balkan", unlike the Byzantine, backward Serbs. Tudjman appears to lack both the freethinking and the wits. So warped is he by resentment at the alleged Serbo-communist conspiracy to demoralize Croatia that he treats that plot as more momentous than the primary fact of ustaše killing.

Nor is Tudjman's obtuseness on this issue particularly extreme. The best that Croatia's political parties could come up with in 1990, as the Serbian media conjured an ustaše spirit stalking the land, was a unanimous proposal that all the victims of the Second World War in Croatia should be commemorated "with equal dignity and tenderness".

Given the sheer political dividend of disowning NDH as a travesty and admitting that the ustaše were enemies of humanity, and given that only a maniac fringe admires either, why don't Croatian politicians do so? For a purely nationalist reason; it would concede too much of the other side's indictment, and the NDH was at least part of 'our' history, so *ipso facto* it cannot be all bad.* Far from breaking with NDH, Croatia's first democratic government seemed bent on reviving its symbols in a blaze of glory, without any effort to cleanse these medieval insignia of their twentieth-century taint.

The result was wretchedly predictable. Serb extremists had the political ammunition they needed against Zagreb. Serb moderates in Croatia were made to look implausible. Croatia's wartime atrocities clung to it like the old man of the sea, which no amount of counter-accusations can ever shake off.

The rest of the sad story is soon told. Until the 1960s, nationalism was taboo in Croatia as everywhere. Titoism operated by privileging the Serbs there beyond their numbers; though only 12 to 14 per cent of the population, the percentage of Serbs in Croatia's League of Communists was usually double that number. Hence Serbs were over-represented in the administration and leadership; likewise in the police. Thus the Serbs were compensated for having to live in a federation, and Croat nationalism was kept in check.

Frustration erupted in 1967 (a few months after the fall of Ranković) in the form of a Language Declaration signed by eighteen cultural institutions and 140 intellectuals, including Croatia's greatest writer, Miroslav Krleža. Their key demand was full constitutional and practical equality for four instead of three Yugoslav languages, with Croatian and Serbian as separate tongues. Croatian should be used in schools and media throughout the republic instead of Serbo-Croatian, which was presented as an oppressive unitarist invention.

There was an uproar of condemnation in Belgrade. But the Croatian Spring was not to be easily halted. A mass movement for cultural and economic autonomy was led by the *Matica hrvatska*, Croatia's most venerable institution after the Sabor, and taken up by the students of Zagreb. In the LC of Croatia, meanwhile, a number of

---

* A further motive for silence was that Tudjman and his party had milked Croat émigré communities in Germany, Canada, Latin America and Australia for an estimated US \$8.2 million to boost the HDZ campaign funds. These communities have links to NDH. However, there is no reason to suppose that, without these subventions, Tudjman would have confronted more intelligently the recent history of Croatian independence.

popular, youngish reformists rose to the leadership, assuring their critics that the mass movement was socialist in spirit, not nationalist.

It took Tito's personal intervention, requested by the JNA and the old guard of the LC, to freeze the Spring. Hurling accusations of counter-revolution – sin of sins – at the leadership, he began a purge whose effects on the country were even more destructive than the purge of liberals in Serbia. The *Matica hrvatska* was banned. Hundreds of politicians resigned. Intellectuals, including Dr Franjo Tudjman, were jailed.

*

Crispin wanted to photograph tanks, so I drove the ninety kilometres to Knin, capital of Krajina. The empty road curled upwards through limestone villages. Clouds cleared above grey and tawny hills, desolately beautiful like the Scottish Cairngorms. Thin sheep grazed thin grass among boulders and maquis. Pylons strode to the interior, breaking the horizontal vistas.

We were in a jaunty mood, glad that every second put more distance between ourselves and the Papish bootboys of Zadar. Except for bullet holes puncturing the road signs, and the flags – mostly Croatian, sporting the red-and-white chequerboard motif that so outraged Serbs – fluttering above villages and rocky hilltops, nothing suggested a political crisis. Then we rounded a corner near Kistanje to see a JNA tank parked neatly at the roadside. Two armed soldiers motioned us to pull over, cast a bored eye at our passports, and waved us on.

When I passed through Knin in 1989, a year before the trouble started, it had a backwoods atmosphere of bristling bad temper. It felt the same now: ignorant and obsessive – a town with room for one idea in its head, and God help anyone who disagreed.

Lazar Macura explained the rebels' point of view. An ebullient, big-framed man who used to be an English teacher, Mr Macura had become the press attaché for Krajina chiefly because its political bosses, Milan Babić and Milan Martić, did not care to deal with any journalists except the Serb media. Babić, a dentist by profession, was the "prime minister" of Krajina. Martić was the police chief in Knin until the new Croatian government dismissed him as part of its drive to cut the number of Serbs in its police force. Then he led the uprising, in August 1990.

The government had not been willing, or able, to commit enough forces to regain control of the region. Every week brought news of more roadblocks and shoot-outs; Croats/Serbs complained of being terrorized by armed Serbs/Croats; each side took hostages, and each viewed the other's military support as a national militia. The JNA condemned the Croatian National Guard as an illegal formation. Serbs echoed this accusation, and praised the JNA as their saviour. Croats raged at the neutrality of an allegedly federal army that treated the elected government and the insurgents even-handedly.

"We want to be people in Croatia," Macura told us, pouring thimble glasses of *Kosovska loza*, "as we always were until now. The new constitution has eliminated us as people. Then we told the government to remove the chessboard from the Croatian emblems because it was the ustaša symbol. But they didn't want to listen."

Every Serb we met in Krajina cited the status of Serbs in the Croatian constitution of December 1990 as a gross and ominous affront. The constitution of socialist Croatia had defined the republic's Croat and Serb inhabitants as equal; whereas the preamble to the new constitution decreed that "the Republic of Croatia is hereby established as the national state of the Croatian nation and the state of the members of the other nations and minorities who are its citizens: Serbs, Muslims, Slovenes, Czechs, Slovaks, Italians, Hungarians, Jews and others, who are guaranteed equality with citizens of Croatian nationality."

At issue was the Croatian Serbs' status as a part of the Serbian nation. To be sure, the preamble mentioned "other nations", but far from being placated, the Serbs bridled at this condescension. As for being listed alongside Muslims, Slovaks, Italians, etcetera, and equated with them constitutionally . . . ! For Serbs, above all for the Serbs of Krajina, to be ranked among "other nations" anywhere in the Yugoslav lands would be hard to swallow in any circumstances. That this should happen in "the national state of the Croatian nation" was intolerable. Anything less than *majority* rights have never been worth having in Krajina. Others might have to put up with minority rights; but not Serbs, not here.

All this historical, emotional background was condensed in Macura's violent expression, "eliminated us as *people*" – as a nation. Zagreb could have promised its Serbs heaven and earth as individuals, and they would still have reacted hostilely to any hint that their collective status would be downgraded. The Croatian Ministry of Information protested in vain that although "the Serbs as a *collective* did definitely lose" in post-war Croatia, because their national institutions were suppressed, along with Cyrillic script "and the marginalization of their church and culture", many Serbs gained as *individuals*. The circle of winners was much wider than what is called the political élite." Vain, too, to continue: "It is then extremely important to insist on the existence for Serbs of both a *collective* and an *individual* choice." It was hypocritical to present the Croatian Serbs as rejecting the progressive liberal option when the Croatian state had constituted itself, regressively, as a national state in which non-Croats would more than likely be second-class persons.

This is why the European Community's talk of guaranteeing minority rights in Croatia, as it attempted to broker a ceasefire in the autumn of 1991, did not impress the Krajina rebels. Here, minority rights are an irrelevant concept, and so they will remain until enough people feel secure enough not to be governed by national solidarity when they cast their vote. Until liberal democracy dawns, a fig for minority rights! In Yugoslavia as socialism withered, the only rights that counted were national, the kind that in the past – in the history canonized by nationalism – were won by main force, held by vigilance and ruthlessness, lost by weakness or incaution.

Such was the Krajina Serbs' point of view. Since the Military Frontier was removed from Croatian control in 1578 until it was reunited with "civil Croatia" in 1881, these Serbs – some of whom had been settled here by the Turks themselves, who learned very early how best to set Orthodox and Catholic Slavs against each other – were immune from feudal obligations to the Habsburg landlords, on condition that they guarded the frontier. Armed autonomy became a birthright for the penurious communities of peasant-soldiers in the Dalmatian interior.

Mr Macura was a likeable chauvinist. When he finished telling us that "Croats speak Serbian", exaggerating the number of Serbs in Croatia,* and complaining how Zagreb exploited the natural resources of Knin, he commended the decency of the Serbs. "Only 8.6 per cent of people in Knin are Croat. We could do whatever we want to them, but they are completely safe. We won't do anything to them unless they provoke us."

(*That's* what minority rights in Krajina meant. Three months later the mere fact of being a Croat in, or near, Krajina amounted to mortal provocation of Serb paramilitaries and federal tanks and aeroplanes. To be a Serb in majority-Croat areas of southern Croatia was almost identically perilous.)

Back, then, to his favourite topic: the HDZ government. "They want to separate from Yugoslavia. Very well. I still hope for a compromise, so we can be an autonomous region in Croatia. Otherwise . . . Well, if they have the right to leave Yugoslavia, then *we* have the right to stay. They are so stupid," Lazar grinned. "They

---

* Serbs commonly insist that 15 to 20 per cent of Croatia's 4,760,344 were Serbian. According to the census of spring 1991, whose results are undisputed, the figure was 12.2 per cent: 579,542 persons.

just aren't clever enough. If they only said that Serbs exist as people and Cyrillic is an official alphabet, no one would use Cyrillic.* But they don't know *how* to achieve what they *want* to achieve."

"If the Serbs in Croatia have the right you're claiming," I said, "why don't the Albanians of Kosovo possess the same right in Serbia?"

"Because they are a nationality in Yugoslavia, not a nation," Lazar said, invoking the constitutional difference between the Yugoslav nations, with the nominal right to secede, and nationalities (Albanians, Hungarians, Slovaks, Romanians and so on), which did not have this right.

"But that's verbalism, isn't it, just playing with definitions. The reality is that 90 per cent of people in Kosovo are Albanian and they have as much right to autonomy and self-administration as you or any other national group in Yugoslavia."

Interestingly, he lost a grip on his argument. No rational defence exists of Serbs' refusal to admit parallels between their own dispersed nationals, and others. The world must accept, apparently, that Kosovo is an internal Serbian matter, whereas the fate of Serbs outside Serbia is rightful ground for rebellion and interference. So Lazar resorted to the usual conspiracy-mongering: how Albanians from Albania had flooded into Kosovo since 1945, how Tito split the Serbs into četniks and partisans to make them kill each other. . .

We were getting nowhere. "How do you see the future?" I butted in.

"I *don't* see it," he said, on his feet now and striding round his desk. "It's impossible to predict anything here. I'm very sorry to live in such a crazy country, but I can't go to Zanzibar!"

The front line, Lazar told us, was near Benkovac, a community of 33,000 souls, 40 per cent Croat, 57 per cent Serb. So to Benkovac we went, retracing our route past the lonely flags, pylons and tanks.

Lazar had alerted a three-man reception committee in the Serb hotel. ("There is a Croat hotel too, but don't go there," he cautioned with a twinkle, "the HDZ might arrest you.") The local member of parliament, a gaunt, restless character, was eager to talk at one moment, guarded and morose the next. He had stopped attending the Sabor months ago, along with the other Serb MPs. An electrician called Krste was keen to describe how the police beat him up and

---

* Article 12 of the new constitution: "The Croatian language and the Latin alphabet shall be in official use in the Republic of Croatia." Under protest, the government conceded that Cyrillic could be used in districts where Serbs were the majority.

chased him and his family out of their home on the edge of town. Crispin scrutinized the man for photographable signs of assault – in vain. Mental trauma, though, radiated from his startled eyes and agitated movements. Something had happened, but what? The next hours brought no clear answer.

Last of the trio was Miloš, a strange impish character, kept at a partly respectful, partly bemused distance by others we met. He suffers from a disability – mild cerebral palsy, perhaps – which twists his broad leonine head onto his shoulder, and hinders his speech until words overflow in a torrent. He talks a lot but rarely what the others, or we, expected to hear. Fond of helping strays, he invited us to stay. Alone of anyone we met in Krajina, his ability to laugh was intact. In bygone times he might have been a holy fool.

The committee wanted to show us a nearby (Serb) village that had been emptied by Croat terrorism. Men milled around the crossroads there, muttering about the snipers on a nearby hilltop. It emerged that only one road was abandoned, and after much conferring, three men – including Miloš and excluding the MP – agreed to take us a few hundred metres down the road. The half-dozen farms looked empty enough, except for one old woman feeding her chickens. Crispin wanted to investigate further, but our escort wagged a finger: "Don't go past the next bend in the road. The snipers have it in their sights." Miloš grinned and backed away, as if to say, "Believe it if you choose, I don't know, it's up to you." We peered beyond the bend and saw nothing, heard nothing but wind in the branches and a farmhouse door creaking somewhere. So we retreated – but from what? We wondered if our legs weren't being pulled.

Next stop should have been a crisis meeting at the village school where the community was airing its grievances. But they refused to let us in. Miloš shook his head at this, and as he pondered what to do with us, a passing farmer recognized him and invited us home.

The next half hour epitomized the cussedness and monomania of Krajina. We sat in Dušan the farmer's damp front room, bare but for a wooden table, chairs, grimy nylon half-curtains, and a framed poster of Njegoš on the wall. Dusaň rested his thick forearms on the table and answered our questions, willingly at first. This end of the village had not been threatened, so he stayed. Bad things happened up the road, but not here. – What things? – Threats, some shooting . . . It put him in mind of the war, he said, when he was a boy and only the Italians stood between the village and the ustaše.

While Crispin circled around taking photos, Dušan's magnificent brow gradually puckered. He told Miloš in a stage whisper that he thought we were spies, and now we had his photograph as well as his opinions . . . Without telling us to leave he made it clear we must go.

He stood by his front gate as we drove away. He felt bad because he had been inhospitable; we felt bad because he didn't believe us. His jaw jutted unhappily: a bull beset by picadors.

As we returned the few kilometres to Benkovac the stony fields and barren flag-capped hills seemed all too true a measure of people's poverty of outlook. Crispin still hoped something remarkable would happen in front of his lens, and we had promised to stay with Miloš, so we couldn't leave yet, though I wished we could. Miloš, in the passenger seat, looked at my scowling profile and twitched with mirth. "Oh how silly their suspicions are," he gasped. "Think of it! In Yugoslavia we all need to work together, we need people who can think for the whole country, and we don't have anyone who can think for fifty kilometres around." He slapped his leg and grinned hugely at me. "Come, don't be miserable. Let's eat."

Eat we did, in Benkovac's best restaurant. Just as we finished our excellent schnitzels, the lugubrious MP appeared again, wringing his hands. He had dragged himself here to justify his reluctance to accompany us along the abandoned road. His shame was embarrassing, and seemed irritatingly beside the point; though we were glad to be assured that some sort of danger really did, maybe, lurk down that quiet lane.

Next morning Crispin roamed the market with his camera while Miloš took me to meet a friend of his, a schoolteacher. "People are *shocked* by all this," she said. "For forty-five years we've lived in peace. I'm Macedonian myself, and I never asked myself who is Serb and who Croat. Now parents keep their children from school because 'something might happen today'. And yesterday we had a call from Zagreb: we can't count on our wages any more, because Benkovac is in the rebel zone. More than half the factories in town have shut down this year, but nobody talks about the economy, not a word."

We were interrupted by Crispin with the MP in tow. "Enough's enough," my friend said, "let's go. More of them think I'm a spy." The MP wrung his hands again: "You must understand how difficult . . ." Embarrassment and relief tussled on his face. Then inspiration braced him. "Wait," he exclaimed, "you can't go without souvenirs." Half an hour later he was back with two coopered wine cups of fragrant juniper wood, and a group of men we hadn't seen before. "How beautiful," we said. "Whom can we thank? Who are they from?" The MP conquered his dejection at last. "The people," he said sweetly. The ad hoc leaving committee nodded and smiled. "They're from the people."

We went to Krajina to see a crisis and found symptoms and circum-

stances, never the thing itself. Or so we thought. Later I understood
that what we witnessed was the crisis: the Yugoslav doomsday
machine ticking down to civil war. By the time we arrived in Zadar
and Krajina, actual incidents of violence had been swallowed by the
atmosphere of mutual antagonism and distrust; as if the atmosphere
spawned the incidents rather than vice-versa.

Given that the crisis in Krajina had been painstakingly prepared by
media and political campaigns to convince Serbs that they were in
mortal danger, this impression was accurate enough. The killing had
hardly started but a war-psychosis was fully developed. Antagonism
and distrust was felt and transmitted by everyone we met – of whom
only one had direct experience of violence. The atmosphere bred
violence and the expectation of violence; at best, it bred resignation
to the worst that might befall.

The Croats in Zadar had painted the rebels of Krajina as villains.
Villains there were, no doubt, and not only on one side. The Serbs we
met, however – except for Mr Macura – looked and behaved like
victims; not nice victims with beseeching eyes, but victims all the
same. Mountain bandits waging patriotic struggle should enjoy
themselves a bit more than those poor muddled people were doing.
What was more, their dejection and helplessness revealed a half-
awareness that they were fall-guys, instruments of an adventure
undertaken by the élite in Belgrade.

There were no brakes to halt the slide to further violence. To judge
by their spiralling demands, the rebels did not care for practical
solutions to their grievances at all, but only for the maximal solution
– annexation to Serbia – which was no solution at all.

Reality was excluded; positive approaches from the other side
were discounted in advance. Contact between the antagonists had
shrunk to a chicken-game of provocation.

The provocation is a staple ingredient in nationalist conflict
everywhere, and Krajina was a laboratory of provocations. Objectively, a provocation is an act – be it word or deed – which
wounds another nation, whether intentionally or not. Actually, the
context of a provocation is never objective; if it were, there would be
no place or need for provocations. Thus an act becomes a provocation when it is named as such. In conditions of crisis, the term is
thrown around like mud and whitewash, used to present one's own
aggression as self-defence or legitimate retaliation. (Mr Macura gave
the game away when he told us, contentedly, that "Tudjman can be
provoked very easily.") When a friendly Serb in a village near
Benkovac told me, "What happened in Zadar yesterday was total
genocide", he was interpreting the hooliganism there – itself a

response to the *provocative* killing of the Croat policemen – as a *provocation*. This excused the next Serb act of violence, whatever that might be.

Every charge of provocation contains a promise of reprisal which, to be adequate, pays the other side back *with interest*. This escalation is justified in advance by magnifying the offence. In this example, the destruction of property was "total genocide"; and what reprisal is not justified by genocide?

Some militiamen in Krajina once stopped my friend Ervin's car and told him, among coarser home truths, that: "You aren't a human being, you're a provocation!" They spoke more truly than they knew, for the second half of their accusation verified the first. There was "nothing personal" in their verbal attack; any Slovene on that road, at that time, would have fitted their bill equally well; and if they had carried out their threat to beat him up or kill him, he would have deserved it by provoking them.

Krajina was a microcosm of Croat-Serb relations. Each side had become a cipher to the other, and everyone felt more or less disempowered. However much they disliked what was happening or the direction it was taking, nobody we met considered that they might even try to avert the worst. At ground level, *choicelessness* weighed on everyone, though unequally; more sensitive, flexible people suffered most from the absence of alternatives, while the more belligerent ones welcomed it because it confirmed their behaviour: "*We* have no choice because *they* are doing these things to us and we must defend ourselves," etc. Also, I believe, because choicelessness was apparently a democratic national condition, shared by the whole tribe from Milošević to a roadmender in Krajina. Yet this was another deception; apart from the existential difference that the roadmender was exposed to all the risks of living and fighting on the front line, his choicelessness was imposed by a chain of local, regional and national leaders who had chosen – freely chosen, at the higher levels – to "have no choice", by foreclosing the alternatives to violence. On both sides, nationalism had created the illusion of a common fate shared by all.

Serbs who were opposed to national polarization, to the leaders' refusal to negotiate, were powerless to articulate their objections – and not only because "traitors" were liable to be treated accordingly. The explanation lies in the nature of communism and its collapse. By definition, one-party rule cannot permit independent social institutions and practices. When that rule disintegrates, its own institutions and practices disintegrate with it – especially if they are damned as responsible for society's problems. In Yugoslavia, not only were the communists no longer around to bang heads together; they left behind nothing that could be used to oppose the dissension sowed by nationalists. Decades of brotherhood and unity vanished without a trace. Communism had sealed the wartime wounds without suturing them. After half a century, no healthy tissue had grown under the scabs; underneath were only atoms of national blood and flesh. It emerged, to most people's bewilderment, that no social fabric whatsoever linked the peoples. Only voluntary, individual connections such as friendships and mixed marriages, and certain professional traditions of collective all-Yugoslav endeavour (in science and theatre, for instance) survived the end of communism to span, tenuously, the chasms between nations; and these proved helpless to stem the general regression to tribal identity and solidarity. The result, in Krajina, was armed autonomy and Great Serbism on one side, just as the other side grabbed the chance to clamp its control upon the irksome Serbs of the Frontier at last.

*

As Croatia's spring crisis ripened to a summer of war, Zagreb seemed out of touch with the regions in the way that capitals often are. A few days after leaving Krajina I stood in front of the president's palace in Zagreb, at noon, watching the changing of the guard. Robed in scarlet and gleaming with braid, the soldiers performed a prancing, balletic ritual in the space between the palace sentry boxes and Saint Mark's church. A band beat time: rackety tackety tack, rackety tackety tackety tack! The little crowd of spectators clapped.

Easy to mock this operetta ceremonial when soldiers were really using their guns in Krajina, and really dying. But it was not so foolish. No one insists, as I had expected, that the spectacle draws on native military traditions. A choreographer was commissioned to examine these rites in other countries and invent something suitable for new, democratic Croatia. New states need their voodoo more than old ones, after all, and this was a harmless way to meet the need.

If only Croatia's leaders had been as sensible in more important respects. The preamble to the new constitution, quite apart from that sentence which so offended the Serbs, announced all too clearly the government's intentions. Kicking off with an exultant clause about the "millennial national identity of the Croatian nation and the continuity of its statehood confirmed by the course of its entire historical experience", this text spells nothing but trouble. Its swagger betrays a hazardous level of anxiety about that very identity and experience; from this macho stance the nation's history can only be extolled or defended tooth and nail, not understood. Any parliament that enshrines such a text in the state constitution has so much to prove that it won't be capable of calculation. When the experience of statehood is as problematic and, for that four-year period of 1941–45, catastrophic as Croatia's has been, the parliament should be sacked forthwith, before it plunges the country into a new variation upon old patterns of disaster.

That gratuitous "entire" gives the game away. No people in the Balkans has a seamless history of statehood, so the rest of the preamble is obliged to make factious claims, such as that the Sabor never "sanctioned" Croatia's absorbtion into Yugoslavia in 1918. This sulky revisionism had nothing to do with scholarship; by delegitimating Croatia's original participation in Yugoslavia, the government wanted to recast the seventy-plus intervening years in its own image – to purify the past, with whitewash if necessary.

As for the future, needless to say that would be purified too. The Sabor's first action at the end of May 1990 was to revoke the constitutional clause that had given every nationality in socialist Croatia the right to reject any measure that threatened its rights, if it could muster a two-thirds majority. Rubbing salt in the wound, the clause was revoked with less than a two-thirds majority. The Sabor became a Croat club. Serb MPs were outnumbered and, when the rebellion began in Krajina, shouted down. They were searched for weapons at the entrance, while the Croat members entered untouched.

When I met President Tudjman's foreign policy advisor, Mario Nobilo, I asked what the government had thought it was doing, after its election in May. Those crucial last seven months of 1990, when the republic might have been laying a solid groundwork for independence by winning the support of all its inhabitants, appeared to have dissipated in a haze of gestures which encouraged vainglory and false hopes among Croats, while antagonizing Serbs. When, for example, the Square of the Victims of Fascism, in Zagreb, was renamed the Square of the Rulers of Croatia, what signals were sent to non-nationalist Croats and to Serbs? And when the Museum of the Revolution of the Peoples of Croatia, in the same square, was replaced by the Museum of Croatian History?

Mr Nobilo's reply was defensive. "There *might* be fewer Serbs manning the barricades if we had taken better account of their reactions to our emotional explosion when we won the elections. This wasn't directed against anyone, it was just an explosion, which the Serbs took as being directed against them. If we had celebrated for three months less we would have less . . ." he shrugged, then squared his shoulders. "But in my opinion it wouldn't change the problem because Belgrade's policy would be the same.'

In my opinion, too. But did Zagreb have to help Belgrade so sedulously? As for the rest of his answer, Mr Nobilo's plea was disingenuous. The explosion was directed against someone; nor could it have been otherwise. Croat self-assertion was against Yugoslavia, and, in concrete terms, this meant against Serbia – above all the Serbs within Croatian borders.

It is difficult for Westerners, especially those who wanted to believe in Yugoslavia, to appreciate that for many Croats, Yugoslavia as a state of equal nations simply never happened. In royal Yugoslavia the prime victims of centralism were bound to be the Croats, because, as the second largest and the most Westernized nation, with an identity as developed as the Serbs', their aspirations were higher, so had further to fall.

The world did not want to know about their gripes, because it wanted all the Yugoslavs to buckle down and make their state work, and (since the Second World War) because it was partly convinced that Croatian national sentiment was incorrigibly fascistic. Thus the world was blind to the significance of the 1971–72 purge in Croatia. For nationalists, "Karadjordjevo" – where Tito carpeted the republican leaders – represented a tragedy for which socialist Yugoslavia could never be forgiven.

Thereafter Croatian autonomism, let alone nationalism, was blocked on two fronts: by the federation, collectively (like all other autonomisms), and by Croatia's own Serb community. This had no equivalent in other republics. The 1970s and '80s are known as the "Croatian silence". National consciousness could not percolate into the institutions of the republic, making friends and influencing people as socialism retreated, because of the number of hardline Serbs in key positions. Unsurprisingly, the Croatian revival, when it came, was strident and choleric.

By the late 1980s, when the ebb of federal power had weakened the grip of those hardliners, Milošević's movement in Serbia had already welded Serbian communism and nationalism into a single bloc. Belgrade and the JNA appeared ready to use the Serbs in Croatia as a Trojan horse, to achieve a putsch along the lines of the "anti-bureaucratic revolutions" in Vojvodina, Kosovo, and Montenegro. This fortified the dogmatists among the Serb minority, which was anyway nervous – for its own indisputable reasons – at the rise of Croatian nationalism. True to the bitter dialectic of Croatian experience, radicalism abetted radicalism on both sides. Among Croats, the result was a mood of passionate revisionism. Huge numbers of people became convinced that they had been forbidden to utter their country's name for twenty years, and suchlike nonsense. This mood ensured success for Tudjman and his party, facilitated by the disarray of Left and other democratic opposition. By the time the sclerotic League of Communists reacted to events by appointing a liberal Croat as leader, it was too late to redeem its record. Nevertheless, with 90 out of the 349 seats in the Sabor, the Party of Democratic Change (PDC) – its new designation – is the largest opposition party. So the political invisibility of the Left since the elections is baffling, except in the light of 1971 and, more especially, as a symptom of the ever-escalating crisis, which forced out the PDC's Serb supporters. Almost 70 per cent of Croatian Serbs had voted PDC, not for the Serbian Democratic Party, their self-appointed guardians. When Serb MPs abandoned the Sabor, they decimated the anti-nationalist opposition – which suited the radicals on both sides very well.

As an anti-communist, anti-federalist, therefore anti-Serb coalition of Right-wing liberals and armour-plated nationalists, fronted by victims of Karadjordjevo, the HDZ seized the initiative early in the election campaign, and never looked back. Unashamedly identifying itself with renascent Croatia, adopting national symbols as party insignia, the HDZ encouraged Croats to walk tall.

Compromise and calculation were no part of the electoral remit to Tudjman and his government, who have since proved themselves devoid of those talents. Something has been said about Tudjman already; a bit more is in order, because he symbolises much about newly democratic Croatia. I only saw him once, at a press conference after one of the summits in spring 1991, bringing together the presidents of all six republics. Admittedly the Serb and Montenegrin journalists were baiting him – the location was Cetinje: enemy territory for any Croat nationalist, let alone the anointed successor to King Tomislav and Stjepan Radić. Even so, he cut a memorably repellent figure. Pompous, tight-mouthed, he spoke awkwardly and with unconcealed impatience. When the hacks kept poking him with questions about his bullet-proofed BMW, he stormed out. Remarkably, he had made his Serbian rival appear reasonable; for Milošević treated all questions sympathetically, so that you only noticed his contempt for truth a moment later.

Press conferences bring out the worst in Tudjman; he is too dogmatic and naïve to handle them. As the youngest partisan general at the end of the Second World War, he became a career soldier and then a historian. In time, he started researching the NDH. Publication of his revisionist findings led to official disgrace in 1967; prominent in the Croatian Spring, he was jailed after Karadjordjevo. Significantly, he still admires Tito, and aspires to the same style of authority: majestic but populist, trusted implicitly, obeyed without question, beyond reach of the indignities inflicted by a free press.

(When a Catholic Albanian couple asked Tudjman to be godfather of their ninth child, as Tito would have been, he could not resist.) He has exploited every power and prerogative within his reach to turn Croatia into a presidential state.

However, he vexed his more radical supporters – especially among the émigrés – by soft-pedalling the election promise to seek independence if Yugoslavia could not be confederated. Despite his messianism, he is, like Kučan of Slovenia, an old Yugoslav who had to be forced by Belgrade's scheming and intransigence into abandoning Tito's creation.

Like other dissidents, this Titoist ex-general passed directly from communism to nationalism. He isn't anti-democratic; simply, democratic values have never occurred to him, and the crisis that he partly made but mainly inherited gave him no chance to learn on the job.

Nothing, however, excuses his sheer lack of judgement. He is reportedly deaf to advice except in emergency, and it shows. His rigid centralism, ignoring wise advice from Istra and Dalmatia, has been mentioned. His attempts to manipulate Milošević early in 1991 were woeful. After the March demonstrations in Belgrade, Tudjman hurried with unseemly speed to meet his opponent (at Karadjordjevo!) and exploit his weakness. When Tudjman then acknowledged for the first time that Kosovo was an internal Serbian matter, it was supposed that the dividend would be Milošević's admission that Krajina was an internal Croatian matter. No quid pro quo was forthcoming; Tudjman was left with nothing but a deep-dyed stain of opportunism and, far worse, ineptitude.

Likewise with the incendiary question of Bosnia-Hercegovina. In January 1991, and again in July, he was dumb enough to raise the issue of dividing BiH between Croatia and Serbia, hoping to cut a deal with Milošević at the Muslims' expense. What Tudjman overlooked was that his opposite number had never mentioned partitioning BiH. Again Milošević kept silent; again the Croatian president had, in the words of a former advisor, made the error of believing that political enemies could become friends without the loss of natural allies.

Whether the decision to opt out of Yugoslavia in June 1991 was a misjudgement, is not for outsiders to say. Only Croats can know if the price they have paid for independence was worth the prize. What is certain is that, by this stage, Croatia was locked in a cycle of reactions which left no option but to opt out.

Whatever analysis one makes of the transition to democracy in this republic, Tudjman and his party were what Croatia wanted, and it is doubtless fitting that 30 May, the date when the HDZ government was sworn in, became a public holiday: the Day of Croatian Statehood. For outsiders, of course, the intoxication was tiresome. After a week in Zagreb I would have been glad never to see or hear the nation's name or its cognates again. The words were everywhere, from the CROATIA AIRLINES banner across one of the busiest shopping streets, to the propaganda about Dubrovnik in a new tourist booklet as "an oasis of Croatian sovereignty for a thousand years" (that millenarianism again) – as if the entire point about Dubrovnik were not that it melds, uniquely, Italo-Venetian with South Slav traditions.

So I had to remind myself, as I baulked at the anti-abortion posters wailing that EVEN A FOETUS IS A LITTLE CROAT, the kiosks flogging mantelpiece busts of Tudjman and laminated maps of Great Croatia, and the ubiquitous flag with its chequerboard, that this is what a glut of national pride looks like after famine and under pressure. None of it was meant for outsiders; this was a private function.

But I was still irritated, especially by the airs and graces, the heavy odour of Mitteleuropean snobbery. Walking away from the Habsburgish changing of the guard, I wondered how many of the spectators believed that the Habsburg Austrians and Hungarians had disdained the bumpkin Croats as peasant labour and cannon fodder, and surely regarded their statehood as a legal fiction, convenient for allaying middle-class conceit.

Tudjman was not adequate, perhaps no one would have been, to the mission of extricating Croatia from Yugoslavia at minimum cost. And there is no evidence that Croatia can produce a democratic alternative. Quite the contrary: a few weeks into the war, as neo-fascist paramilitaries, clad in ustaša black and using ustaše salutes, rallied to defend areas that the National Guard wouldn't or couldn't hold, it was clear that the political price of the war will be horribly high.

But perhaps Zagreb's dandified centre augurs a better future. Smart boutiques and cafés line the cobbled lanes near the cathedral – reminders that German and Austrian investment is poised at the border, waiting only for a modicum of peace. It is charming, and no more melancholy than Habsburg cities should be; Trieste, Prague, Budapest, Vienna all retain this air of reassuring worldliness, faded but adaptable, humanly scaled. And its population is mixed; more Serbs live in Zagreb than in Krajina. Known, sometimes sneeringly by their militant co-nationals, as urban Serbs, they stayed in the city through the war, keeping a low profile and vulnerable to neo-fascist terrorism. Croatia needs them to stay.

Perhaps Zagreb will find the rôle it seeks, and enter the next millennium as a missing link between Italy and central Europe. Meanwhile the street-sweepers use twig brooms, the city outskirts are still "the hideous blockhouse, soul-destroying buildings" that Orson Welles (exaggerating in the American way) noticed thirty years ago, and the trams made in Czechoslovakia still break down in the rain. I like these reminders of socialism and the Balkans, and Croats should cherish them as heirlooms, proof of needed continuity. They need to stop treating their past – history itself – as a provocation.

Arriving in Zagreb from Belgrade in the summer of war, I had been conditioned to expect anyone I met – be they officials, doctors, soldiers, whoever – to lie about the war. And I was startled when they didn't, not to me, nor to themselves. (False expectations were another matter.) We inhabited the same dimension of reality. Our definitions of aggression, defence and violence, of grievance and *casus belli*, of good and bad, bad and worse, appeared to coincide.

The coach that plied stoically along the deserted Highway of Brotherhood and Unity had returned me to planet earth; and I was glad. The war had attenuated Zagreb's manifold intellectual life, not yet obliterated it. The media were disgraceful, but at least people knew it. Mario Nobilo's admission, quoted above, was disingenuous in part; still, it would have been inconceivable from his counterpart in Belgrade, where the official line remained that Serbia was not even at war, and the Serbs of Croatia were merely defending themselves from genocide.

It was a relief to meet people whose analysis of their government and whose insight into the war was more acute than anything I encountered among foreign commentators, whether in London or Ljubljana. One figure who freely criticized the Croatian coverage of the conflict was Dr Slobodan Lang, once a minister of health in socialist Croatia, now a teacher of public health. In his spare time, Lang is a peace activist who specialises in solitary acts of witness, both to publicize specific wrongs and to prove the possibility of individual action.

When I visited him, he had just returned from Dalj, a Danubian village at the eastern limit of Croatia, twice as far from Zagreb as from Belgrade. He was part of a joint Croatian-Serbian commission to investigate an alleged massacre by JNA bombardment on 1 August.

As so often in this war, forensic proof of atrocity could not be found. "What we discovered," Lang explained, "is that we cannot answer the question of the dead without answering the question of the living. Only 150 people are left in Dalj from 2,500. We have to find what happened to the rest, but this is not easy; those who aren't dead are refugees in Serbia, or in the autonomous zone the Serbs have created in Slavonia [a second Krajina], or in Croatia proper. Some on the Croatian side wanted to make the number killed as great as possible, in order to legalize hate. Others wished us to make it much smaller. Whatever happened in Dalj, the atmosphere of massacre exists. There is a collective psychosis. Television does not broadcast a single peace message. You are not allowed to have debates on peace, and people are quite unaware of the absence of such ideas."

As for the Serb minority's complaints, Lang's limpid comment was unanswerable: "Croatia made a very serious mistake in not being able, when proposing a Croatian state, to propose a modern European state. The government could have shown that freedom for Croatia would create more freedom for Serbs [in Croatia] because a more modern state will bring faster economic development, more human rights, more ecological protection. That Serbs will have better communication with their own nation, and, since free Croatia would be more advanced than Serbia, they will be able to help their own nation. Instead the government played around with ridiculous flags and petty behaviour."

Lang's perspective is in no way typical – or in no way but one. It was poignant to see how his perspicacity became clouded with idealism as soon as I asked about Europe's role in the crisis. He shares with so many of his compatriots an unnerving zeal for the concept and potential of Europe. "Nobody in Yugoslavia desires a state in the nineteenth-century European sense," he exhorted, not quite convincingly given the Croatian government's posturing. "What these countries are fighting for is to be a European region in which their own cultural dignity can be preserved." With the Cold War over, "for the first time ever, all the regions and nations and cultures of Europe can be recognized at the same time. The rainbow of Europe can be realized."

"Who else has the responsibility to preserve their own differences if not the cultural groups themselves?" he demanded rhetorically, and his answer gave the most civilized case for dismantling the federation that I heard. "Through dissolving Yugoslavia, at the same time you can integrate it. The movement towards smaller and bigger are identical. Nobody can explain to me why I should feel more strongly about Slovenes than Slovaks, or Macedonians than Bulgarians. The point is, how can I treat all as equal? If I treat myself as Croat and want to have a relationship with everybody else, I have to get rid of Yugoslavia to be able both to respect myself and everybody else.

"No matter how much one respects Yugoslavia's history, in its current form it is an instrument of hate and people will live more harmoniously if it breaks down. For me, personally, Yugoslavia in recent times is a symbol of killing Albanians. Now it is killing everybody. To get rid of Yugoslavia is to stop the killing."

This Europhoria needed pondering. An ice-cream parlour near the CROATIA AIRLINES banner sold a flavour I hadn't seen before: "Europa '92". I ordered a bowl of the stuff – palely citric, with a saccharine aftertaste – and tried to disentangle the needs and strategies knotted together and tagged with the continent's name.

Political strategy wove the coarsest strand. The government's pragmatic aim from the outset of fighting was to internationalize the conflict, because Croatia could not achieve independence against Serbia and the JNA without outside backing. This was likeliest to come from the European Community, where Croatia had a powerful friend in united Germany. Short-term benefits of EC support would be the deterrent value, and later, perhaps, practical aid. The long-term reasoning was valid too; as Dr Vladimir Veselica, one of the dissident class of '71 and now a minister in Tudjman's cabinet, told me: "By entering the EC as separate states, we [the Yugoslav republics] could solve our Balkan problems, which we cannot do with Balkan methods."

Yet this strategy was devised, then endured the disasters of war, because it responded to felt needs. The Catholic strand is visibly important as a shaping influence; yet I don't believe – despite my interrogation in Zadar, and one or two creepy encounters with unctuous patriotic priests – that faith figures in many Croats' minds as a motive for "going to Europe". As an element in the national identity, though, absorbed during the centuries under Venice and Austria-Hungary, on the edge of the Orthodox and Muslim abyss, Catholicism and its Latin ritual haven't been outdated as a factor in the Croats' sense of being outposts of a culture centred far away. Their Europhilia is ardent and romantic, like the patriotism of expat Englishmen, toasting the Queen's birthday as the sun sinks below the baobab trees. It signals a yearning for home which isn't like that any more and probably never was. In 1991 Croats who have no personal experience of Western Europe, nor any conception of the dynamics shaping its integration, invoked the name of Europe as a charm – white magic against the encroaching Eastern darkness. Sometimes they were aware that their starry-eyed affiliation to Europe was powered by chauvinism toward the Balkans, and even anti-Serb racism, but usually, they weren't.

The Western orientation of Croatian culture is indestructible, as real as the Balkan undertow forever dragging the country south-eastwards. The best exponents of this culture don't deny its duplicity, or rather multiplicity, for all the contradictory elements of Yugoslavia live in Croatia too, organically, not as parasites upon some pure Western essence. Miroslav Krleža, the colossus of modern Croatian literature, straddled the hubris and despair òf Croatian destiny. His art sounded the chasm between national dreams – second-hand fantasies anyway, he implied, of banal fulfilment – and narrow-reality, always controlled by distant powers, that mocked and confounded the dreams' periodic resurgence. He wrote whereof he knew; disillusion and resurgence were inside his skin; did he not sign the Language Declaration in 1967, his seventy-fifth year?

Zagreb's intellectuals – of any nationality – tend to be Europhiles and polyglots, picking up new ideas and putting them together in marginal mosaics. Among writers today, Dubravka Ugrešić writes fiction replete with erudition and barbed irony. She is a literary scholar, much travelled on both sides of the Atlantic. Perhaps this is why her view of Croatian Europhoria is unusually sober, not to say gloomy. Explaining the peculiar "cultural shame" that she experiences in the West, she said: "We don't know *anything* about culture in the West, and people's interest, when I am in London for example, reminds me how closed we are in Yugoslavia, how culturally egocentric, how arrogant, not interested in anything these days except in our own problems."

There is a "complex of provinciality" among Yugoslav intellectuals, she said, taking one of her fictional characters as a typical case: "He's certainly excluded because he wants to be in Europe or America or whatever it is, and we are not there, you know? We are not there."

"Not in Europe?" I asked.

"Not yet, or not ever. You can declare anything you want, but you can still see that border. All the walls are destroyed, of course, but the border still exists. More, I think, because of our side than yours."

Once upon a time the Yugoslav idea offered refuge and even solutions to Croats who saw the best future in a free and equal community of peoples. From Strossmayer the founding father, to Meštrović the sculptor, Josip Broz the communist-federalist, and Ante Marković the last federal premier, the truest Yugoslavs were Croats. Yugoslavism was an alternative national tradition here, and its murder in 1991 will be mourned for a long time as an elementary deprivation. This helps to account for the eclipse of Croat Leftists and democrats: their Yugoslavist defence against nationalism had been torn from them by a war waged against their nation in the name of Yugoslavia. They were crippled twice over.

I wanted to see the Yugoslav Academy, founded by Strossmayer in 1867, before it closed or changed its name. Too late. The paintings had been removed in case of air raids, and the name was changed a month before I came knocking on the door.

"Strossmayer would be sad," I said idiotically, just to say something.

"Hah!" grunted the custodian, but he was patient with me. "We can't help that. We had to do it. We can't have this word 'Yugoslav' because Yugoslavia doesn't exist any more. Because of the fighting."

*

The war in Croatia began in Slovenia. In comparison with what soon followed, the ten-day war at the end of June and beginning of July appeared almost civilized and friendly – "a Mickey Mouse war", as a Croatian official put it to me, with forgivable sarcasm. At the time, however, it had horrified almost everyone in Yugoslavia, and shocked the wider world. And whatever the casualty figures, it was a battle for the future of two states; its outcome determined much that happened next. For the army had blundered, and someone would have to pay. By acting against Slovenia, it went much too far; then it failed by not going far enough. It showed the rigid but irresolute single-mindedness of an institution that had stopped thinking some time since.

Imagine if the JNA had succeeded in taking back the border points. Slovenia's bid for independence would have folded, and Croatia's too, because the international community would have been relieved to have every reason not to consider recognizing them. So the war against Croatia would not have happened.

Hindsight shows what an impossible scenario this is. (Not that hindsight is needed; one reason why foreigners were shocked by the ten-day war is surely that independence appeared a reasonable step for Slovenia to make.) The question is, why did the JNA high command believe, presumably in the teeth of its own intelligence reports, that a quick show of force would persuade the rebel republic to back down?

Believe it the high command did. The Slovenes had taken over the international borders as part of their unilateral secession. The JNA's stated objective was to restore federal control of the border crossings, the international airport at Brnik, and the port facilities of Koper. Early on 27 June 1991, while the last carousers from the independence celebrations were still on the streets of Ljubljana, columns of tanks were despatched from barracks inside Slovenia to the Italian and Austrian borders. The tanks were unprotected by infantry, unsupplied and unprovisioned – as if the expedition would meet no resistance. Border points were seized, but could not be secured, because the Slovenes treated the JNA as invaders, and kept fighting. The chiefs of staff and federal government were rapidly faced with a dilemma: to escalate the action against Slovenia, or to climb down.

The government wanted the borders secured but had no stomach for a war; on the afternoon of the second day of hostilities, it demanded a ceasefire. Judging by their speeches, some of the top brass wanted escalation; General Negovanović, chief of army intelligence (hence one of those most responsible for the fiasco) interrupted the Belgrade television schedule to denounce the "filthy, brutal and nasty war being waged on the territory of the republic of Slovenia against JNA units". General Adžić, the chief of staff, went on television a few days later: "We have to accept war because the alternatives – surrender or treason – do not exist for us." Slovene fighters "hiding in their caves" would be tracked down. The federal government had "placed every obstacle in our path", and the Slovenes were "brutal and unscrupulous back-stabbers", but "we shall achieve control and carry things through to the end".

By the time this hair-raising message was broadcast, Europe had become decisively involved. The troika of European Community foreign ministers had flown in. A ceasefire was being brokered. Things could not be carried through to the end. Under the terms of the Brioni Declaration signed on 7 July, the JNA returned to barracks.

Both sides knew which had won and lost. By agreeing a fortnight later to withdraw all its forces from Slovenia, the JNA admitted to everyone except its own, more obtuse officers – who believed Adžić's assurance that the withdrawal was tactical and temporary – that Slovenia was gone, never to return.

What must the JNA have concluded from this débâcle? It was clear that future actions against "the separatists" had to be concerted, large-scale, and ruthless. It was equally clear that the European Community could not be trusted as an ally in the JNA's mission to preserve the federation; it would have accepted the limited action against Slovenia, had this succeeded, but concerted, large-scale action against Croatia would rapidly alienate the EC.

What was more, perennial Western attitudes on the matter of Yugoslav integrity were shifting at last. At the start of the ten-day war, EC leaders assumed that "the first prize" was "to keep Yugoslavia together" (British Prime Minister Major's words). Within days, however, there were signs of flexibility. In part, these were displayed to put pressure on the JNA and federal government. Presumably, too, contact with such men as Adžić and with Slovenia's leaders persuaded EC foreign ministers that a state with such primitive guardians, and such determined opponents, had slim chances of survival.

Yet the German conversion to Slovenian independence, and softening of British, French and Dutch resistance, was surely related to the transparency of the issues. The ten-day war was not a civil or an ethnic war; it was a war of national independence – of state power. As my friend Miha Kovač wrote at the time: "When we resolved to defend our political decisions with a gun in our hands, the stakes became much higher. We suddenly realized that we were struggling – to paraphrase [Slovenia's President] Milan Kučan – for a different life from the one we have had. If Slovenia does not become a sovereign state, it will mean that we shall no longer be masters of our own lives."

Not just Slovenes and foreign governments realized that the stakes were this clear, and this high. The 136,000 personnel of the JNA were one part officer corps to two parts conscripts – 18 to 24 year-olds from every part of the federation. The conscripts were in the firing line, of course (half of the JNA's casualties were born in 1970 or later), and they were not convinced that Slovenes were their enemies. This was a further reason why hardline generals' hopes were dashed: morale and motivation were too low to prosecute war against the breakaway republic. As a dejected colonel told *Mladina*, the army found itself "ideologically unequipped to fight the Slovenes".

This was the army's situation in early July. But what of the army as a Yugoslav institution? The JNA hasn't loomed large in this book, although I was often aware of it as I travelled. Conscripts hanging around railway stations. Officers strap-hanging on a Belgrade tram, slim wallets of documents tucked under their arms like newspapers. The JNA House in every town, displaying the red stars and the cases of monochrome photographs, showing conscripts on exercise. The barracks above Sarajevo with a slogan over the archway entrance: "Our future lies on Tito's path".

I kept hearing about it, too. I have described its paradoxical rôle in the Slovenian Spring. The "army option" was a phrase on many people's lips in Bosnia-Hercegovina, before the elections; but the army kept a watchful distance. (In Serbia, on the other hand, senior army figures endorsed the Serbian Socialist Party of Slobodan Milošević.) Its part in Krajina, in the build-up to war, has been mentioned.

As pluralism was installed across Yugoslavia, the JNA was very trickily placed. Although the reforms of the 1960s and '70s had affected the armed forces too, they remained a unitary institution, and, unlike the League of Communists, could not be republicanized unless the high command took the initiative to encourage reform. This never happened, because the Chiefs of Staff stayed loyal to "Tito's path". They saw the JNA as the last guarantor of the SFRY's integrity. It was represented in the republican assemblies, and the secretary of defence – a professional military man – was entitled to a seat on the federal presidency, a body which was, since Tito's death, the collective head of state and commander-in-chief.

Historically and politically, the JNA was Tito's army. Tito, the commander-in-chief for life, had looked after his armed forces, ensuring their prestige, their budget, and their officers' high standards of living. In exchange, he used it to bring pressure on republican leaders.

By the late 1980s the armed forces were left high and dry on "Tito's path". Their budget had been progressively reduced. Their political leverage depended on having a unified League of Communists as their partner. Like everything else in Yugoslavia, they had to choose between the Slovenian and the Serbian options for the future: either devolution toward republican sovereignty, or a Serb-dominated federation.

They yearned for the certainties of Tito's Yugoslavia. They didn't want to take over and run the show, like some Latin American junta, but neither did they want to see their power and privileges dwindle away. So they took the Serbian side, because anything was better than the unknown hazards of confederation.

There were other reasons why the armed forces made this choice. As a federal bureaucracy in their own right, they were bound to be centralist. Slovenes were viewed by the JNA as outsiders. (My friend Iztok remembers when an officer told him and his fellow conscripts – young men from all over the federation – that "Slovenes and Albanians are the enemy".) The Slovenian Spring had a pronounced anti-militarist slant; the campaigns against military corruption and for the right to conscientious objection had infuriated the officer corps, in part because the corps was predominantly Serb and Montenegrin: about 70 per cent, as of April 1991.

So the army cheated. It overlooked Serbian transgressions against Kosovo and in Krajina, while claiming still to be the impartial servant of the federation and drawing, of course, its hefty portion of the federal budget. But the more it interfered in the political process, in order to keep its authority, the more tattered its Yugoslav legitimacy became, and the more unpopular it grew. Already marginalized by the same dialectic that made confederation the only future for Yugoslavia, the JNA aligned itself with one republic and its nationalism. Defeat in the ten-day war turned alignment into blood-brotherhood.

*

Rather than licking its wounds, the army redoubled its activities against Croatia, which had declared independence on the same day as Slovenia. Everything was in place for a conflagration, and after their defeat, the chiefs of staff set a match to the tinder.

In the spring of 1991, the JNA had made trouble in Slovenia and Croatia, but more by far in Croatia. Slovenia had always been dispensable, but neither the JNA nor the Serbian government could let Croatia leave the federation without a fight. Since the Croatian elections in April 1990, Belgrade and the JNA had been obstructing and provoking Tudjman and his government. Krajina, in the west, was primed. The JNA worked with radicals in Serb communities. As communal relations between Serbs and Croats deteriorated, guerrilla activity started in parts of Slavonia where Serbs were concentrated. Train lines were blown up. Roadblocks were erected around Serb villages, which became no-go areas, protected – as in Krajina – by the army. Hostages were taken. Sniper fire was exchanged across the corn fields. Mounds of sandbags became a feature of street-corners in the placid market towns.

As Croatia made its own bid for independence in Slovenia's wake, the Serb-JNA brotherhood moved into action. Propaganda about the ustašoid, neo-nazi, fascistic, genocidal Croats had been running for more than a year, since the Croatian election campaign. It was now intensified, and bolstered with anti-German sentiment. Within the JNA, the allegation that united Germany and Austria wanted, perhaps in combination with NATO, to smash Yugoslavia, finishing once and for all what they had attempted in 1914 and 1941, was dinned into soldiers' skulls, where it would have met little resistance, for the army had been nourishing itself on such delusions for decades.

The thesis was circulated that the existing republican borders were "administrative" and communist, not historic or ethnic, therefore no basis for eventual international borders. "If *anyone* has the right to choose where to live," people kept telling me in Belgrade, as if uttering a noble and self-evident principle, "*everyone* has the right." It emerged that everybody except the Serbs in Croatia and Bosnia was an exception to the rule; but so what? The pseudo-logic, chanted like a mantra by Serbian media and leaders, did the trick of convincing the aggressors that they were defenders.

In short, *it worked*. Serbs, Montenegrins, and others too in the JNA and the paramilitary forces believed, at least for the first few weeks, that they were saving Yugoslavia, not destroying it; that they were fighting sub-human fascists, not people. The JNA was the successor to an anti-fascist army, born in the partisan war, maintained to defend the achievements of the socialist revolution. The ustaše had been fascists, and Croats; they had specialized in killing Serbs, and they were German proxies. Propaganda laboured to persuade all Serbs and Montenegrins and anyone else who would listen that once again they lay in mortal danger, that Serbdom and Yugoslavia needed them.

When General Adžić growled that Germany was intent again upon her historic drive "to the warm seas", he very likely meant it. Milorad Pavić, Serbia's best-known novelist, stated that "the Serbian people were forced into war, and the only dilemma was whether more Serbs would die if they succumbed to fascist genocide as in 1941, or if they put up resistance"; and doubtless he believed it. Radovan Novačić, a Croat commander of Serbian volunteers in western Slavonia, explained that he did not suffer from divided loyalties because "I'm not fighting the Croats, I'm fighting the ustaše and blackshirts who are slaughtering old men and women". A JNA major, commanding the ammunition dump at Bjelovar, north of Zagreb, blew up himself and fifteen soldiers rather than surrender to the National Guard.* Who can judge at what point propaganda merged in these brains with wishful thinking, and became belief?

At the level of psychology, the message worked by imposing two kinds of choicelessness. One kind appeared in the epic, belligerent guise of "the supreme choice": the call, so seductive and coercive in Serbian society, to risk life and limb for your people by attacking other people. The other kind was the choicelessness of the victim: the peasants and labourers who were told their lives were in danger, and who panicked – as they were meant to do. What Dr Lang had called the "atmosphere of massacre" spread across the plains of Slavonia like fire before the wind.

Using Serb villages and JNA barracks as their bases, the aggressors' method was to consolidate control of an area by using villages as stepping stones. Serbs would arrive in Serb communities, warning people that they were about to be killed and should leave at once. Large numbers would flee in fear and confusion. Then the JNA moved in, with paramilitaries in support, ostensibly to protect property and remaining Serbs. Croats and Muslims would flee, carrying fear into the next settlement. Meanwhile the army and guerrillas cleaned up the pockets of resistance.

Krajina expanded northwards into Banija and Kordun. It was a

---

* Was the example of the old *hajduk* Stefan Sindelić shining like a remote pool of sunlight in the major's darkling mind? Sindelić, who detonated his gunpowder in 1809, killed himself and his warriors rather than be captured by the Turks.

perfect base for raids into Dalmatia too, where the navy helped by bombarding National Guard headquarters and radio transmitters from the sea. The southern rim of Slavonia, bordering Bosnia, was soon taken, because the army's bases in Bosnia were safe even from the preventive blockades that the National Guard mounted, when it could, in Croatia. Srem and Baranja, abutting Serbia, Vojvodina and Hungary at the eastern end of the republic, were sitting ducks.

Nowhere was untouched, except Zagorje (the northernmost part of Croatia) and Istra. Within two months of retreating from Slovenia, the JNA – in partnership with Serb paramilitaries – controlled one-third of Croatian territory and rampaged over another third. There was resistance everywhere from the National Guard and, increasingly, from the neo-Nazi militia mustered by the Party of Right, an extreme nationalist grouping that claimed to have 15,000 men under arms.

When panic-mongering was not effective, the army did what armies do: mined, mortared, and blasted, invariably claiming that it had not fired first. Schools were targeted, hospitals were razed, churches were gutted – always, when tiresome journalists or the famous white-clad EC observers pestered for motives, in self-defence. (General Milan Pujić did not deny that the JNA had shelled Osijek hospital *because* the Croats were using it as a machine gun nest.) Meanwhile the paramilitaries – a mixture of local Serbs up in arms, and volunteers from the motherland – looted, raped, murdered with insouciance.

This berserk destructiveness defined the war for anyone trying to follow events from a distance. And the medieval atrocities – children mutilated, old people disembowelled, victors' insignia carved into the flesh of prisoners – were the essence of this war, not a side effect. In part, they were a substitute for achieveable war aims, which the aggressors never had. Partly they were a war aim in themselves. Partly they were the natural expression of tribal passions and native warrior tradition. Partly they were the work of criminal elements, for Serbia's jails were trawled for recruits to bundle off to the front. Gangsters and murderers only had to don a četnik cap, grab a gun, and they had *carte blanche* in Croatia. Perhaps they were the least deluded members of the Serb-JNA brotherhood.

These statements may seem excessive. Granted that the goal of preserving all of ex-Yugoslavia receded with every shot fired, did not the JNA still possess the achieveable aims of, at best, toppling Croatia's separatist government, and, at least, keeping as much of the federation intact as possible? As for the paramilitaries, they had a range of demands; minimally, they wanted to stop the Croats from keeping Krajina; maximally, they wanted to carve Great Serbia out of the five republics. Were not these compatible demands more flexible than they appeared, and achievable in some form, some degree?

The answer to the first question is that Croatia's government could only be toppled and its secession reversed in the imaginations of officers so out of touch with reality, and immune to the lessons of recent experience, that it was no wonder the JNA found itself in this impasse. As for the rest of the federation, Yugoslavia's unravelling could not be stopped at Slovenia, or, then, at Croatia. By attacking these republics, under any pretext, the JNA shot itself into a corner. Its morale collapsed. Its intake of conscripts dwindled. Croats who had disliked their government's jingoism and centralist policies – for instance, Dalmatians and Istrans who were no supporters of the HDZ – came to hate the JNA and the federation that it claimed to represent. The Macedonians destroyed the call-up lists, to obstruct the annual draft. The presidency of Bosnia-Hercegovina instructed people to ignore the draft.

Only two factions resisted the process of osmosis that was submerging the JNA in Serbian political interests. One was the armed forces' own diehards (perhaps including General Kadijević, the federal minister of defence). The other was radical nationalists in Serbia itself, who by the end of the year were protesting angrily that the army was not pursuing Serb expansionist goals ardently enough.

The JNA's time was up. When it stood still, it was eroded on every side by developments beyond its control. When it acted, it accelerated the erosion. As more and more bits of the federal body dropped off, the skeleton of a Serbian army stood revealed. Regional commanders aligned themselves with local (Serb) leaders – around Dubrovnik, in Krajina, Slavonia, and Bosnia. Kadijević resigned on the last day of the year, signalling the death of military Yugoslavism. International recognition of the breakaway republics, in mid-January, confirmed that the JNA's best, indeed only, hope was a compromise with the leaders of Bosnia-Hercegovina; an entente, allowing the army to regroup and gather the resources pulled back from Slovenia, Croatia and Macedonia too.

This is why the JNA had no war aim beyond punishing the enemy, and surviving in a different and diminished form. It was unleashed without a strategic goal, and guided by little more than hatred of Croats and fear of the future. When General Rašeta of the Fifth Army District (encompassing Slovenia and part of Croatia) told reporters, in October, that "We are aware we may lose our lives, but we are sure the republic of Croatia will not triumph," he summarized the entire strategic wisdom of his Chiefs of Staff.

In the case of the paramilitaries – the so-called četniks and other guerrillas – the motives for aimless destructiveness were not even checked by a disintegrating habit of discipline. They were swayed directly by the spirit reigning in Serbia and its sidekick Montenegro, not at all by the JNA's ghostly Titoism.

I say spirit rather than policy or strategy. It was a necrophile spirit of refusal and revenge. At ground level, there had been no articulated, realistic sense of purpose in Serbia for several years – nothing beyond reconquering Kosovo and attacking the "separatists" in other republics. Whatever the ugly excesses and miscalulations of Croatian nationalism, it gave the republic a forward-looking project. Independence was its ultimate, though not unconditional goal. Despite Tudjman's crass threats, his government was not about to try and wrest chunks of Bosnia-Hercegovina into Great Croatia; nor was it agitating the Croat minority in Vojvodina.

An equivalent timely project for Serbia would have been democracy and modernization. The leaders of the republic could not afford to be projectless, but democracy was not an option. Territorial gain, though it gladdened the heart, paid no wages. On the contrary: the occupation of Kosovo drained the exchequer like a nuclear weapons programme.

So they offered their nation a different project, a negative one in keeping with the atavism and violence latent in their rule. This project boiled down to the refusal of change. Milošević began earnestly to provoke conflict in Krajina a few days after the March demonstrations rattled his windows in Belgrade. After that – right through the war – he extemporized. If his people clamoured for Great Serbia, and fought for it, then well and good. For his part, he was not trying to carve out a Great Serbia, or to preserve the old federation; he knew too well that the first was impossible and the second was finished. War brought sweet relief to him and his beleaguered régime; so they kept it going as long as they were gaining territory and not falling too far behind in world opinion. For the Belgrade government knew as well as everyone else that no settlement could be achieved in the teeth of international opinion. As for the future, when war started to bring diminishing returns, he would think of something else to stay on top.

It was risky, but as long as the opposition was dazzled and divided by the charms of a patriotic war, it was less risky than the alternative. It left Serbia friendless, bankrupt, besotted with illusions, and confused about itself to the point of schizophrenia. And of course it was murderous – rather, slaughterous. But the leaders could not *make* Serbs kill Croats, after all; they could only exhort them to believe it was the proper thing to do.

Consciously, the paramilitaries, like the JNA, were fighting a war against enemies that deserved no quarter. (And why not bombard schools and hospitals? Ustaše children and patients are ustaše too.) Pre-consciously, or half-consciously, they were avenging a sense of loss and despair. The Croats and Slovenes were being punished for possessing what Serbia and the JNA lacked: hopes for the future.

In this sense, every confrontation signified as much as any other; cornering a farmer in his barn and slitting his throat was as real a contribution to the war effort as occupying ("liberating") a town. Perhaps more real; the farmer-fascist was dead for ever, but who knew how long the forces of liberty could hold the town?

This isn't to deny the territorial motive, but it ran second as the priority for the Chiefs of Staff, the Serbian leadership, and ultimately for the soldiers too. The battle for Vukovar became the climax of the war because the massive forces of attack – as many as 50,000 JNA and paramilitaries – clashed there with an incredibly dogged resistance. Lying on the Serbian border, very far from Zagreb and in easy range of gunboats on the Danube, Vukovar begged to be "liberated". The more it resisted, the more it had to be taken – as revenge for resisting. When it fell on 18 November 1991, Vukovar looked like Stalingrad in 1943. The ninety-day siege was not prosecuted to this dreadful end because Vukovar hindered the advance of the JNA-Serbs, who could move freely around and beyond the town. The point is, destruction *was* victory.

Similarly with Dubrovnik. When the army started bombarding the famous old seaport at the end of October, capture was indeed the aim; in this sense, the battle came to a climax in the first week of December, when the aggressors almost took the Imperial Fort. But they didn't try all that hard. If liberation was the stated purpose, punishment was the deeper motive, and it could be achieved with howitzers. Either way, long-term possession was neither here not there. "We are going to force the ustaše to surrender because that is the only way to protect this city," explained Colonel Koprivica, commander of the bombardiers, in a sentence that would have impressed Orwell.

Fortunately Dubrovnik repelled its Orwellian protectors, at the cost of some 150 dead, 900 wounded, and very extensive destruction of the town's monuments and treasures. We can be sure that, had they broken in, the liberators would have expressed very vigorously their hurt at the town's prolonged and ungrateful defiance.

In truth, of course, the aggressors' loss and despair was not Croatia's or Slovenia's fault. Responsibility lay with history, with their own political class, and with the intellectual handmaidens of that class, who wanted to convince them that classes do not exist, only blood, soil, and nations. For, as Brecht wrote in the late 1930s, trying to alert the Germans:

WHEN IT COMES TO MARCHING MANY DO NOT KNOW
That their enemy is marching at their head.
The voice which gives them their orders
Is their enemy's voice and
The man who speaks of the enemy
Is the enemy himself.

*

The Yugoslav crisis could not have been better timed to ensure concerted attention from the rest of Europe. At the end of June 1991, the European Community was in the final stages of preparing its long-awaited treaty on political union. Issues of federalism were at the centre of political and public attention – for the first time ever, in the case of Britain. The United States decided to leave Yugoslavia to the Europeans.*

So, partly by default, the EC became the third player in the conflict. At the outset, it was too divided on the matter of Yugoslavia's future to attempt to be more than a well-intentioned moderator. It is a rule of modern history that when war happens in the Balkans, the rest of Europe immediately demands that nothing change, however unstable the *status quo ante*. In October 1912, the great powers warned that, should war "break out between the Balkan states and the Ottoman Empire, they will tolerate at the end of the conflict no modifications of the territorial status quo of Turkey in Europe". Ten days later Montenegro, Serbia, Bulgaria and Greece were at war with Turkey, and soon expelled it from the peninsula. The great powers bowed to the result; what else could they do? Whatever Europe says, it accepts Balkan transformations if these are decisively achieved and trenchantly upheld. Tito knew this, in the Second World War; so did the Slovenian leaders in 1991.

The difference in 1991 was that Yugoslavia no longer filled a key strategic junction of the continent. The end of the Cold War had removed the "Soviet threat" to the Adriatic. In the era of Helsinki Accords and the European Community, Yugoslavia's neighbours were not about to pounce on its territory, even if their own nationalists coveted a portion of it. The "Fourth Reich" conspiracy was a threadbare effort by the aggressors to provoke Pavlovian reactions among Serbs and in the JNA, on the alluring premise that empires still competed for Yugoslavia.

---

* The United States' quiet hostility to Slovenian and Croatian independence was important in encouraging the JNA. It will be interesting to learn what rôle US Ambassador Zimmerman played behind the scenes, during the autumn.

What the EC wanted to protect, back in June, was the Helsinki order in Europe. Presumably it believed that the Brioni Declaration guaranteed a cooling-off period, for it was then that the EC blundered – by turning its back once the Declaration was in place, although Croatia had been smouldering since April, and was now likely to blaze up. Would a strong show of concern for Croatia, including a firmer willingness to recognize its independence promptly if it were attacked, have deterred the aggressors? Perhaps. But such a show was not possible, because, as diplomats repeatedly assured us, "international recognition does not work like that". (But it did a few months later, although Croatia was still not in control of its territory or borders, and still at war with a neighbour.) Yugoslavia's status as an international subject, and the JNA's status as its army, were unquestioned; only Germany and Denmark were keen to break protocol by interfering in its internal affairs, and use recognition as a stick against JNA-Serbia.

A further ingredient in the EC's early passivity was the success of Belgrade's propaganda. The Community tended to treat the question of the Serbs in Croatia even-handedly with the plight of Croatia in the federation. By making minority rights the principle of its peace-brokering, it seemed to have been persuaded that the fears of "genocide" were the real *casus belli*. This caused despair in Croatia, as people were strafed and cluster-bombed in the name of a state that "the Europeans" insisted was more legitimate than their own wish for independence. Thousands were killed, and scores of thousands uprooted and made homeless.*

The government in Zagreb made the best political use it could of their suffering and vulnerability. It knew that the only positive selling-point of Croatian independence, in the eyes of all but Germany and Austria, was that it might put an end to this incomprehensible and destabilizing war. Tudjman's strategy was to soak up the assault, blockading JNA barracks and installations while complaining bitterly and imploring recognition as the only cure. Then he could sue for help from sympathetic countries. (The arms embargo against Yugoslavia, in place since July, was hurting the victims far worse than the aggressors, who had ammunition stockpiled throughout the country.)

I am not injecting the element of cynicism; it was there in Tudjman's calculations. Of course, in one sense there was no

---

* It appears that the war had claimed upward of 10,000 lives, by February 1992. As many as a million people were displaced, including an estimated 100,000 Croats and 150,000 Serbs who fled ex-Yugoslavia.

alternative. As there was never any question of the president, his government and army capitulating *in toto* – presumably the only measure that would have satisfied the aggressors – and as Croat forces were massively outnumbered and outgunned, what choice did they have but to soak up the assault?

True, the poor bloody infantry had no choice. However, the government distorted the war into appearing a purely national matter; it shares responsibility with Belgrade for mystifying the war as a blood-feud, when it was a complicated struggle for power and survival. Croatia's leaders seemed too dull to grasp that this mystification served the aggressors' cause much better than their own.

In Vukovar, to take the best-known case, as much as a third of the 1,800 resistance fighters were Serbs, Ruthenes, Hungarians, and so on. Slavonia is a mixture, and Vukovar was a special sort of community; its citizens didn't want to be "liberated" by anyone. Zagreb, though, presented Vukovar as a pure-bred martyr for the Croat cause. More gravely still, it persistently denied military support to Vukovar, either for party-political reasons, or because it estimated that the vindictive siege brought good publicity.

Meanwhile, the war was radicalizing Croatian politics along all too predictable lines. The president, secret police, and military arrogated sweeping powers. There was a surge of support for the Party of Right. Jittery about Croatia's image, the government clamped down on the neo-fascists, but it could hardly refute their bitter charge that Croatia had been led into war ill-prepared, and was now ill-defended. Atrocities and war-crimes were committed by the victims of the war too, as became clear when the Helsinki Watch organization released a report about a massacre at Gospić. The full account of horrors perpetrated is yet to be compiled, and it never will be, without international pressure.

While Tudjman sued for recognition, and signed every piece of paper that the European Community brokers at the conference in the Hague pushed in his direction, the activity of Serbia's Milošević was more complex. He was the key figure; EC and United Nations mediators flew first to Belgrade, then Zagreb. Only Milošević could deliver the second-best thing to unity, namely a smaller version of Yugoslavia. By the same token, he could prolong the war indefinitely – for instance, by taking it into Bosnia.

Through the autumn, he played a Hitlerian double game. It was extraordinarily simple and effective, like all his best adventures. He negotiated with the Westerners, putting his name to more than a dozen EC ceasefires, each time emerging to tell the massed ranks of media microphones that prospects for peace were better than ever. (Officially, Serbia was not at war: a legal fiction designed to prolong the JNA's credibility as a federal army, and Yugoslavia's credibility as a state.)

Back home, he would tell the natives that "the spectre of fascism is knocking on our door . . . Circumstances have led us . . . into battling with forces which are *breaking up Serbia and Yugoslavia* and are restoring a long-gone world . . . They are dark, conservative forces which we believed had left the historical stage. That is why we have no choice, just as we had none half a century ago, but to stop them." (My italics. Of course, nobody was threatening Serbia; only Great Serbia was jeopardised by Croatian independence. As for dark, conservative forces, no one incarnated these better than Milošević himself.)

As the charade of ceasefires continued through the autumn months, the EC seemed at times worse than useless, as if it could not grasp that ceasefires offered the aggressors no motive to cease discovering what they could get away with. In fact, Serbia's position was fluid and constantly shifting; and thanks to German initiative, the EC was slowly applying pressure where it would count.

The army was weakening with every passing day; there were mass desertions, officers shooting their men, the Hungarian reservists from Vojvodina refused the call up. Even Serbs and Montenegrins who went to the front as gung-ho warriors were returning in shame. This disaffection spilled into civilian and political life in Serbia; Belgrade was brimming with refugees – 150,000 by early November. These strains were not unmanageable, but Milošević needed to show better results than a handful of "liberated" towns.

At the same time, Milošević's proxies in Krajina were proving troublesome. His demands on their behalf were tactical, hence negotiable. Krajina was a bargaining chip. In mid-October, he was demanding international recognition for Serb enclaves in Croatia as a separate state. A month later, Serbia accepted Croatian independence in its present borders, with international guarantees for Krajina. The hajduks of Knin felt, understandably, betrayed.

Why the turnaround?

The second half of October and first week of November were the turning point of the war. Milošević had less and less room for manoeuvre. Neither the EC nor the UN would contemplate border changes between the republics by force, and Serbia's pleas that it sought only rights of self-determination for Serbs had ceased to convince anyone. Milošević's efforts to interest the Bosnians and Montenegrins in a mini-federation had come to nought. The Serb-Montenegrin coup within the federal presidency had further discredited the aggressors.

The EC had begun by wanting Yugoslavia to stay the same. Then it wanted a total solution to the crisis; in practice, this meant dusting down and endorsing the familiar confederal option of a loose association of sovereign states, with special guarantees for minorities. When Milošević, alone of the republican leaders, refused this, the Community bit the bullet. Backed by the USA and USSR, selective sanctions were applied against Serbia and Montenegro on 8 November.

Milošević's stated reason for rejecting the Carrington Plan – as the confederal blueprint was known, after the chairman of the Hague conference – was that, by restoring Vojvodina's and Kosovo's autonomy, it interfered in Serbia's internal affairs. This was self-evident common sense to Serbs, of course, but not others. The Community seemed finally to accept that national and minority rights did not account for Serbia's instigation of the war or its behaviour in the peace process. Henceforth, Serbia was treated almost unceremoniously as the obstacle to peace. Recognition of Croatia within its borders was imminent – even the reluctant Brits admitted it.

Meanwhile the United Nations had become involved, at the behest of the Germans and French, who had their sights set on a UN peacekeeping force. As war became a stalemate, with the JNA incapable of advancing and the National Guard too ill-equipped to retrieve lost land, the focus of international concern moved to Bosnia-Hercegovina. The UN special envoy made it his mission to prevent an explosion in BiH. This gave Milošević some badly-needed leverage in negotiations.

On 16 December, the European Community made a last attempt to end the war. Bulldozed by German pressure, and frustrated by its failure to date, the EC announced a schedule to recognize the independence of any republic which applied for it. Provided the republic met certain criteria (human and minority rights, acceptance of international borders, and co-operation with EC and UN peace initiatives), it would be recognized a month hence.

It was the most momentous international decision about Yugoslavia since 1941. Serbia threatened that the war would escalate; many British commentators agreed. They were wrong. In effect, an ultimatum had been delivered to Serbia. Putting it another way, Milošević's bluff had been called. When the UN came up with a plan to install its peace-keepers within the disputed zones of Croatia, Milošević accepted. Krajina objected to being sacrificed, but the Serbian government succeeded in carrying public opinion (which was sick of war), the JNA (what choice did it have?), the paramilitaries and their warlords.

15 January came. Croatia and Slovenia got their recognition. Tudjman and his entourage were jubilant; they had lost every battle but won the war. Now the work of reconstruction begins. The UN peacekeeping forces to be deployed in the three Serb enclaves will make it harder for Belgrade to interfere, and give the Croatian president and his government an interval to find a more productive approach to the largest minority. Will they take the chance to recast the question of Krajina as a matter of regional rather than national policy?

For Milošević and his régime, to wage the war was victory enough; but how to survive the peace? The dissolution of the USSR had seemed to remove his main backer; as things turned out, it offered a rôle-model. The EC states did not cease to recognize Yugoslavia, and Milošević angled to inherit the state assets, as Russia had done in the USSR. There remains the matter of the name; a minimal Yugoslavia would consist of Serbia plus Montenegro, and this prize might not suffice to disarm Milošević's critics, including the swelling chorus of nationalists who want Serbia itself to be released from Yugoslav bondage. The earliest indications, though, are that as long as anti-nationalist opposition remains so weak, Slobo the survivor can pass himself off as the only man able to bring peace to his tormented country, etcetera. If so, neither Serbia nor its neighbour republics will have stable peace. The unravelling of Yugoslavia needs to run its course.

Yearning for the South

Macedonia was not the last republic that I visited, but it felt at the time like journey's end. Memory and maps remove it still farther until it blurs and shimmers, a levantine *ultima Thule*.

Yugoslavia always hinged on the Belgrade-Zagreb axis, with Sarajevo as man in the middle. In the 1980s, Ljubljana and Prishtinë joined these cities at the forefront. But Skopje? No, the influence of Macedonia was no greater as the federation ended than in earlier times.

As for its part in the terminal catastrophe, that was symbolised by the killing of a Macedonian conscript, early in May 1991, at the hands of a mob in Split, infuriated by the JNA's pro-Serb stance in Croatia. He was one of the first victims of the war, but who cared where he was from? An angry crowd demonstrated in Skopje, and nobody outside Macedonia paid the blindest bit of notice.

In Skopje I stayed with my friend Goce, who lives in a suburb donated by Denmark as part of the international aid after the earthquake of 1963. Wooden and single-storey, with big picture-windows, the houses have an oriental look, perhaps because the apple blossom was out, a million tiny flags in the cold breeze.

When Goce was busy, I chatted with his mother, a poet and amateur telepathist. Macedonian spirituality is something distinct, a compound of mythological roots and Orthodox faith, stained by modern catastrophe and sometimes livened by New Age notions; for Macedonians are worldly people, travellers by need and now by choice. Goce's mother was soon rebuking me for my lack of belief, and tracing it in my family background. A bit of this was more than enough, and I turned the questions around. "I was born in 1932," she said, "and brought up in Vojvodina."

"Although your parents were Macedonian?"

"Yes." She rocked back on her chair, flapping her cigarette hand. "They moved because here in Macedonia it was blood, blood, blood."

Except for Alexander the Great, bloodshed is what Macedonia means to foreigners: blood spilled limitlessly for a cause that no outsider understands.

Except in the minds of Greek nationalists, the brazen Hellenic ring of Macedonia's name has nothing to do with the Macedonian Question, which was and is a particularly overwrought version of the usual nineteenth-century scenario. Macedonian national consciousness was born, rather late by Balkan standards, where four powers overlapped and competed for territory. One of these was the Ottoman Empire. The remaining three were in process of consolidating their statehoods and identities, so were proselytizing more or less aggressively wherever they got the chance; and the territory now occupied by the republic of Macedonia was mainly where they got the chance.

It is an intricate story, triply contested in structure and detail. Going back to the beginning: the ancient state of Macedonia encompassed the territory of the present-day republic. This territory became Roman, then Byzantine. Byzantium lost it to the Bulgars, who lost it to medieval Serbia, until the Serbs were conquered by the Ottomans. It remained Turkish for 500 years, until the Russians advanced to Istanbul, and forced the Turks to abandon most of their Balkan lands to the new state of Bulgaria. This Great Bulgaria endured only a few months in 1878; the western powers would not accept a Russian ally on such a scale, straddling the peninsula. Turkish rule was reinstated in the area of present-day Macedonia, creating a vacuum that Bulgaria (smarting over its lost gains), Serbia (keen to expand, and blocked every way but south), and Greece each wanted to fill, preparatory to land-claims when the Turks finally were kicked out.

As for the inhabitants, the dirt-poor artisans and tenant farmers who lived in these malarious plains and stony uplands, many were none too sure of their nationality. In the south, nearer the Aegean, they spoke Greek. In the east their dialect was more or less Bulgarian, and in the north, beyond Skopje, the vernacular was a kind of Serbian. In the central zone, which was definitely Slav, the independence movement was emphatically pro-Bulgarian, because of language, because Bulgaria offered the best sponsorship against Turkey, and because of nationalist evangelism by the Bulgarian Church.

In the 1890s, the movement sprouted two wings. The Macedonian Revolutionary Organization (later prefixed by Internal, to become the IMRO) was set up secretly by students. Its goal was political autonomy, not against Bulgaria but because the students judged that no border revisions would ever give Bulgaria all of Macedonia, so autonomy was the only way to ensure that Macedonia stayed Bulgarian in spirit and culture.

The Supreme Macedonian Committee, based across the border in Bulgaria, wanted to incorporate a liberated Macedonia into Bulgaria. It used terrorism against Serbian and Greek clergy and teachers – tactics that IMRO at first condemned. In time, IMRO itself split into pro-Bulgarian and autonomist factions.

Autonomy for Macedonia was on no agenda when Bulgaria, Serbia, Greece and Montenegro combined against Turkey in 1912. Victory was followed by land-grabbing. Discontented with its haul, and still hankering for 1878, Bulgaria rounded on its allies, and was rapidly beaten. The result was the three-way division that persists today, into Vardar Macedonia, held by Serbia, then Yugoslavia; Pirin Macedonia, held by Bulgaria; and Aegean Macedonia, held by Greece.

"Regardless of how long they last," wrote the war correspondent Leon Trotsky, "the new boundary lines have been drawn across the living bodies of nations that have been lacerated, bled white, and exhausted. The Balkan states breathe mutual hatred, and hatred no less acute fills the fragments of nations caught within the separate states. Suspended owing to utter exhaustion, the war will be resumed as soon as fresh blood is flowing in the arteries."

As for Macedonia, it had indeed been liberated from the Turk; but "to speak of the 'liberation' of Macedonia, laid waste, ravaged, infected with disease from end to end, means either to mock reality or to mock oneself."

Though war was resumed two years later, when Bulgaria invaded Serbia, Trotsky was in one particular too gloomy; the new boundary lines in Macedonia have endured almost unchanged. In another respect he was too sanguine; for he believed the Balkan Wars had made Macedonian terrorism obsolete. Not so. In the new state of Yugoslavia, Vardar Macedonia was called South Serbia. Autonomist Macedonianism and pro-Bulgarian Macedonianism were alike anathema to Belgrade, which persecuted both while devising grand schemes, as in Kosovo, to import thousands of Serb settlers. In Pirin Macedonia the IMRO grew in power until it was a parallel state administration, a sort of semi-legal mafia that launched terrorist expeditions into South Serbia. It was a Macedonian who murdered King Aleksandar in Marseilles in 1934.

Blood, blood, blood.

In the Second World War, the occupying Bulgarians outwore their initial welcome in South Serbia. Anti-fascist resistance divided along the conventional lines: either pro-Bulgarian, or favouring autonomy in a federalized Balkans. The Communist Party of Yugoslavia now recognized Macedonian autonomy and nationality, yet solely in a Yugoslav context – as one of the five constituent nations of a socialist federation. To many, and not only Bulgarophiles, this looked like a ploy. Local experience had blackened Yugoslavia's name in South Serbia, and the CPY had great difficulty mustering a partisan force. When it succeeded, in 1943, it was by dint of leading the struggle against the Italians in the western margin of Vardar Macedonia.

Tito's policy was flexible. His minimum aim was to keep Vardar Macedonia. Maximally, he would have liked to add the Pirin and Aegean segments to it. Partisan victory secured the minimum, and the Yugoslavs hoped to get more at the negotiating table. Like Albania, Bulgaria managed to stall their bullish pressure to join the federation until 1948, when the Cominform expulsion ended all hope of uniting Macedonia.

As for the Aegean portion, the Greek communists smelled a rat in the CPY's line on Macedonia (that all Macedonians had the right to be united in their own state, i.e. the Yugoslav republic of Macedonia). Nor was there any question of them yielding a metre of territory, however grateful they were for aid in their war against the government in Athens.

The Greek government has always dismissed Macedonian nationality and language as Titoist fabrications. Historically, Macedonia means Greece; politically, it means a Greek province; and that's that. Greece's own Slav Macedonians have no minority rights, and are referred to as "Slavophone Greeks". In the 1950s, Bulgaria reversed its wartime recognition of a separate Macedonian nationality. From that time on, the line has remained that Macedonians are Bulgarians with local differences, and their language is not a language at all but a dialect of Bulgarian.

Federal Yugoslavia, meanwhile, shored up its southern bulwark with all the cultural agencies at its disposal. Institutes of Macedonian history and language proliferated. The Orthodox Church was permitted to become autocephalic, with its own archbishop and hierarchy. To date, only the Vatican has recognized the Macedonian Church; the Ecumenical Patriarch of Constantinople wants nothing to do with it, and Macedonians wonder if the Serbian Church is yet reconciled to its loss.

The Macedonian Question was a national problem that communism could not even pretend to solve. Scowls were frozen on the faces of the three protagonists. Yet every passing year made it less likely that the hostile gestures expressed real irredentism.

The end of communism promised much. Bulgaria, for almost the first time in its modern history, was neither fascist nor Russian-aligned. Greece had no ideological excuse for its intransigence. Also, its membership of the European Community gave it political leverage against its neighbours, yet harnessed it against revanchist adventures. Yugoslavia was democratizing; when free elections were held in the Republic of Macedonia in 1990, the nationalist parties won encouragingly few seats – under a third.

The opportunity was there to let realism into the Macedonian Question, and the foremost reality was a process that was complete long before the fall of communism. For Yugoslav Macedonians born since the Second World War, the Question was academic. Whether or not they believe the Yugoslav propaganda that backdates Macedonian nationalism by several centuries, and claims medieval figures like King Samuilo (d.1014) as prototype Macedonians, they have no doubt who and what they are, and it isn't Bulgarian, Greek, or Serbian. The origins of Macedonian nation-building may be wrapped in controversy, but the result stands for all to see – all who have eyes . . .

Yet this young nation with the ancient name has lost its key sponsor. Its northern neighbour is no longer Yugoslavia but Serbia, a country destined for a turbulent reckoning with democracy and its own recent past. As a result the Macedonian Question is now, for the first time, explicitly about regional power, not ethnology or language or folklore.

When the European Community agreed, at that historic meeting on 16 December, to recognize the independence of any Yugoslav republic, provided it guaranteed internal democracy, minority rights, and existing frontiers, Macedonia seemed low on everybody's list of priorities. In fact, Greece had inserted a spoiler clause against Macedonia. Aspirants to recognition had to prove they harboured no territorial claims "towards a neighbouring Community state".

A referendum in September had given the government in Skopje a mandate to seek independence. In December and January it worked hard to qualify for EC recognition, for example by dropping a constitutional clause that called for all Macedonians to be united. Meanwhile Greek Prime Minister Mitsotakis toured western capitals, persuading Germany and Italy not to recognize Macedonia.

When the EC inspectors duly judged that Macedonia and Slovenia were the only republics fit for recognition, the Greeks dug their heels in, insisting that the very name Macedonia implied claims against them. On 15 January, when Slovenia and Croatia were recognized, Macedonia was left out in the cold.

The Greeks' given reason was that independence for "the so-called 'Republic of Macedonia' " would rekindle territorial disputes. This seems implausible. There is nothing that can be called a separatist movement among Slavs in Greece; Bulgaria appears to have outgrown revanchism at last; nationalist parties in Skopje show no sign either of winning a parliamentary majority, or of attempting suicide by crusading for *terra irredenta*.

In reality, the government in Athens is trying to forestall a Slavic-Islamic bloc from Ankara to the Adriatic. Non-recognition, on the other hand, is sure to generate instability; and partial recognition may be equally dangerous. The first states to recognize the republic's independence were Bulgaria and Turkey, but until Greece, Serbia and Albania follow suit, and its neutrality is guaranteed, Macedonia will be little more than a fistful of loose change in regional wheeler-dealing. With Albania distracted by poverty and isolated Serbia grateful for Greek cordiality, the Greeks rightly judge that theirs is the biggest fist. But for how long?

"Macedonia has one of the languages and cultures of the world," Goce said, "both small but both genuine. I want them to exist. That's why I voted for independence in the referendum. Before the [1991] war, most of us wanted a confederation – because we didn't trust Serbia. Now that Yugoslavia is finished, we must have independence."

"Can Macedonia survive without Yugoslavia?"

"No. Yes. I mean, it's too soon to say."

We were walking around Skopje. Goce was born in 1959, so the city has been a building site almost all his life. After the earthquake, which killed a thousand people and made a hundred thousand homeless, aid poured in from all sides, partly because of Tito's teasing non-aligned diplomacy. Skopje's modern quarters reflect federal Yugoslavia's prestige in the Cold War, as well as the credit-based boom that died with Tito in 1980. The theatre and the television centre would grace any western capital. The plate glass windows in the giant shopping centre display grey pyramids of stuff that people don't want or can't afford.

Although Macedonia was the poorest republic, it had its share of mad doctrinaire planning. Goce was helping me to look for information about the FENI ferro-nickel plant, a notorious disaster. The bureau of statistics shrugged and pointed us to the chamber of commerce. The chamber of commerce pursed its lips and suggested the ministry of information. The porter at the ministry directed us to the ninth floor. Before we knew it, a secretary had ushered us into the ministerial presence.

He was shuffling papers on his desk, and listening to a tape of The Animals on a ghetto blaster. "Come in, come in!" he said warmly, stepping round his desk with hand extended. "Drink? We're out of whisky, but . . ." Then he cocked an ear: " 'The House of the Rising Sun'. Not bad, huh!"

He wasn't surprised by the evasiveness. FENI embarrassed everyone, even though it was a communist fiasco, not the new government's. His ministry would furnish whatever I needed.* Now we could talk about nicer things. Was I aware that our romantic movement had created problems for them? But of course! Lord Byron persuaded so many people that Macedonia was Greek. And was I perhaps able to explain why the BBC World Service carries no programmes in Macedonian? "I shall be grateful if you convey our interest in having this," the minister said gravely, refilling our glasses with rakia.

"Aren't you used to such courteous ministers?" Goce asked me afterwards, tickled by my bemusement. "We aren't *all* terrorists, you see."

*

From Skopje I travelled south-east, through the Albanian regions. The towns here are sullen and impoverished, a jumble of muddy breezeblocks straggling over the hillsides.

More than 95 per cent of Yugoslav Macedonians live in their own republic – a concentration exceeded only by the Slovenes. Yet Macedonia's population of 2.1 million is nowhere near homogenous; a third is non-Macedonian, and most of that portion is Albanian. Before Kosovo's autonomy was cancelled, Albanians fared much worse here than their co-nationals to the north. Fear of Albanian birthrate was nimbly exploited by the nationalist parties in the elections, and there was no softening of policy by the new government. Macedonians say Albanians must use Macedonian as the state language; Albanians want equal language rights. It's a bad situation: a nation and a large minority both beleaguered and neither respectful of the other's fears.

But I was on holiday from politics, heading for Ohrid, one of the world's magical lakes.

Fifteen kilometres wide and twice as long, the lake is flanked by mountains that rise a thousand metres. The western ranges lie in Albania. From where I stood, in the town of Ohrid on the eastern shore, they were forbidding: black, powdered with snow.

Ohrid and its partner town, Struga, have high places in Macedonia's brief national history. Struga was the birthplace of the Miladinov brothers. Dimitar was a teacher; he undertook the first

* No, it wouldn't; the minister's juniors flatly refused.

grammar of the Macedonian language. Konstantin was a poet. Together they made the first anthology of folk songs. They died in an Istanbul prison in 1862.

The brothers drew inspiration from Ohrid's earlier history, which connects the town to the taproots of Slavic literature and Christianity. When Simeon of Bulgaria wrested these lands from Byzantium, in 893, he installed two monks, Kliment and Naum, at Ohrid. These men, both Slavs from Macedonia, had been taught by a Byzantine Greek from Salonika called Methodius. This great scholar, with his brother Cyril, invented two Slavic alphabets, one of which became Cyrillic. Methodius was invited to Moravia because its prince wanted to counter German Catholic power. After Methodius's death, Moravia fell under Catholic sway; his pupils fled – including Kliment and Naum.

In Ohrid, the two monks taught the Slavonic scriptures and their master's alphabet. Their pupils became priests and teachers throughout the Slavic Byzantine lands. Ohrid's glory as a theological and cultural centre lasted until the Turks captured it in 1395.

The town spreads around a natural amphitheatre of hills, and every new vista along its twisting, dipping streets seems to reveal another set of ruddy brick cupolas. One of these churches – I couldn't find which – holds Kliment's remains. His brother's tomb lies at the southern tip of the lake. At dawn the next day I took a bus there. The only other passengers were a few soldiers, who walked past the monastery to their border garrison in the forest beyond.

Sveti Naum is the last stop before Albania. The monastery and its church stand surrounded by forest on a knoll of rock above the lake. A little river runs through meadows behind the knoll, and merges with the lake. This is the Black Drim, rippling glassily over tresses of weed. Two swans slept on the bank, wreathed in their whiteness.

The river that exits from the lake at Struga, thirty kilometres away, has the same name. "And it's the same river," Goce had assured me.

"You mean the same water?"

"That's what I mean."

I imagined braids of Drim water weaving darkly through the lake, like translucent eels – like the eels of Ohrid that swim, in the autumn, downriver to the Adriatic and then, so it's said, across the Atlantic to the Sargasso Sea where they spawn at fathomless depths. Then they return, all the way.

Did Konstantin Miladinov know about the homing eels when he wrote "Yearning for the South"? It became the best known poem in the language, treasured especially by drinkers and emigrants.

> If I had an eagle's wings
> I would raise myself and fly on them
> To our shores . . .
> Here I am in a circle of darkness.
> Fog covers everything . . .
> Give me the wings and I'll wear them;
> I'll fly to our shores,
> I'll come again to our places,
> To Ohrid and to Struga,
> Where the sun can warm the soul . . .

The poet wrote these verses in Moscow, where he hoped to interest a publisher in the Miladinov collection of folklore, but had no success. So he brought the material back with him in 1860, and published it in Zagreb, thanks to Bishop Strossmayer – Strossmayer, the father of Yugoslavism, who dreamed of overcoming the schism between the Western and Eastern Churches.

It was raining softly. I crossed the Drim and walked up to the monastery. The courtyard around the church was empty but for a pair of peacocks, motionless on the paving stones. Inside the church a bearded priest was busy, coming and going behind the iconostasis.

Only the portal and threshold remain of Naum's original basilica. You wouldn't give them a second look unless you knew. They were carved in the tenth century, when Christendom was divided but before the formal schism. I touched the clammy marble. It seemed translucent, like pale grey jade. Paler reefs and cloudscapes bloomed within it. Who can read these signs, these symmetries? What cycles do they augur of South Slav growth and decay?

Other people arrived: a young couple, carrying their little son. They whispered something to the priest, who bustled with new vigour. He swung a smoky censer around the apse, intoning as he went. A christening was afoot.

I watched for a while, then headed back to the bus stop. Next departure was at two o'clock – six hours away. The kiosks and restaurants were shut for the winter. The rain was very wet. Buttoning every button, I set off. At the edge of the first village, I sheltered under the eaves of a hut and wiped my spectacles. The lake was blurred with rain and low cloud; Albania had vanished.

Two cows clopped along the road from the village, led by a fat old woman in woollen skirts and cardigans. She grinned like a Hallowe'en lantern at the sight of me, bedraggled under my eave, and called a greeting. I smiled back, and dashed the short way to the village. No café was open – it was Sunday – but a kind shopkeeper made me a coffee. I bought souvenirs and loitered by his door, waiting for a northbound car. Then a dozen people came down the road in twos and threes, walking fast, rainwater sluicing past their shoes. Some carried umbrellas, tilted into the wind. Others clutched tulips and plates of pastries. They turned into a field beyond the row of shops. I followed. The field was a churchyard and the people were mourners, huddled over a grave.

Afterword

The Final Solution of Bosnia-Hercegovina and other matters of concern

> *Bosnia, that exotic country*
> *in the heart of Europe . . .*
> *Danilo Kiš*

For nearly six months now – since early April – the Republic of Bosnia-Hercegovina has been assaulted with extreme violence and absolute barbarity. Its people are massacred: perhaps 30,000 have died, perhaps 50,000, perhaps more; no one knows.* Men are herded into prison camps to be executed, beaten, tortured, or if they are lucky, humiliated and starved. Women, children and old people are chased away from their homes at gunpoint, abandoning whatever chattels they cannot carry. Cattle wagons deport thousands of these people northwards, away to Croatia, Slovenia, Italy, Hungary, Austria, Germany – anywhere. Others are allowed to escape in their cars, at least as far as the first guerrilla checkpoint. Most are forced to flee on foot.

The aggressors control three-quarters of the republic, and at least one Bosnian in three is a refugee. Those who stay behind are subject to tyrannical controls of their freedom of association, communication, mobility and employment.

A spokesman for the United Nations High Commission on Refugees (UNHCR) has likened these controls to the Nazi restrictions on Jews. The same organization estimates that Bosnian homes have been destroyed through the spring and summer at an average rate of

---

* As early as 2 June, the vice-president of BiH mentioned the figure of 50,000 dead. In mid August, a US Senate Foreign Relations Committee report put the death toll at 35,000, of whom 20,000 had been killed in the course of "ethnic cleansing".

200 per day. Villages are razed; towns and cities are blockaded, starved, laid waste with phosphorous, napalm and cluster bombs. Bridges are blown. Fields and roads are sown with mines.

It is an attempt to obliterate Bosnia as living entity and idea. One might almost say that, from the point of view of those who mastermind the aggression, so many people have to be killed and so much property must be destroyed to persuade the Bosnians themselves and the onlooking world that BiH is a false or impossible entity, glued together by hatred and communism, that the idea of BiH is anachronistic, sectarian . . . In short, that it is bad so it *deserves* to die. And if it isn't bad, anyway it is definitely finished now, smashed beyond repair. Either way, BiH loses – terminally.

This is what the aggressors want their victims and everyone else to conclude. The victims aren't convinced, of course, but that doesn't matter so much, because the victims have no independent power to restore BiH unaided. The really significant audience at the Bosnian theatre is the outsiders, who fall into two unequal parts. Crammed into the first row or two of seats is the Serbian and Montenegrin public. Behind sits the crowd of Western governments, publics, and institutions – including the United Nations, for the Bosnian conflict has confirmed again that the world body cannot be galvanized to act unless the West, above all the permanent members of the Security Council, and above *all* the USA, wills it.

Mostly the Western publics boo and hiss the ghastly spectacle; sometimes they check their watches, yawn discreetly, tap their feet with impatience. Their governments and institutions riffle through wads of documents on their laps, conferring in low voices, looking up now and then to add a hasty boo, wagging a finger at the stage and devoutly wishing the entire scene to disappear.

The Serbs and Montenegrins down in the front seats, meanwhile, are making a minor pandemonium of their own. Some scramble over the footlights to join in the slaughter, egged on by others with war-whoops and patriotic cries. A smaller number rounds on the enthusiasts, denouncing the assault. Others again have turned to face the larger foreign audience, and stand yelling madly that the aggressors on-stage are really the victims and the victims really the aggressors. The majority, though, scratch their heads, looking confused and very grim, sunk in a stupor of introversion as the corpses pile up before their half-averted gaze.

This caricature is unfair to Western institutions, or rather to the governments which breathe life into them. Or ungenerous, perhaps. A pedantic case can be made that the European Community and the United Nations managed their unprecedented co-operation rather well, under the circumstances, and without their tenuous presence and steady pressure, the devastation would have been even more extensive.

Anyone can concede the last point, and certainly it is hollow to condemn the Community and the UN for practical sloth and moral torpor without considering the sheer political and strategic challenges of Bosnia. On the other hand, these states and organizations not only make a meal of every genuine problem: they concoct false problems and false analyses of the conflict, to dilute the case for military intervention to stop these massacres "in the heart of Europe".

For such apathy, such cynicism, what forgiveness? So I wondered one day in July, listening to a Croatian friend describe her vain attempts to raise funds and support for Bosnian refugees in Trieste, her second home. "And they will pay for this, the Western countries, you wait," Ljiljana predicted direly. "Didn't we Croats pay for ignoring the Albanians in Kosovo when Milošević wanted to hammer them? We paid with interest – with every drop of blood. Now Italy, Britain, America think they can abandon the Bosnian Muslims. And they will pay."

You don't have to believe in cosmic justice to intuit that Ljiljana may be right; faith in common decency and sense is quite enough. The daily news, as I write this, shows that certain people are paying already. George Bush, the do-nothing American president,* has won no credit by his inert altitude to BiH. In Europe, the Community leaders who have bumbled and equivocated during the Yugoslav wars are the same ones who drafted the Maastricht Treaty on European union. Now they are watching their electorates challenge their plan. People smell a rat, and no wonder.

Whatever the future of the Treaty, the zeal for European union has drained away in 1992, as surely as Eastern Europe's euphoria at the fall of communism vanished like morning mist in 1990 and '91. Bush's frailty was plain long before April, and disillusion with the EC might have set in anyway – recession is global. But perhaps it was the Bosnian horrors that, by exposing a moral emptiness within the smooth process of EC integration, pulled the plug.

The continuum of "collective European failure in Yugoslavia" has

---

* "There's been a decision at the highest level that the Yugoslav crisis is a foreign mess ... The US bureaucracy is simply following the will of its superiors on this one": George Kenney, who resigned as deputy chief of Yugoslav affairs at the US State Department on 26 August, in protest at the "ineffective and counterproductive" American policy toward BiH. These remarks were made on British television, 1 September.

been almost seamless, ruptured only by rare bursts of tough-minded realism. The failure over BiH has been more culpable as well as more spectacular than that over Croatia, because the Bosnian government unlike its Croatian counterpart did everything in its power to heed the European leaders and remove causes of conflict; because Europe's dithering has wrenched an even higher price from innocent Bosnians than from innocent Croatians; and because Europe has no excuse for not learning in Croatia how to distinguish the genuine causes of conflict from ostensible causes and pretexts, and framing its policy on that basis.

(The Americans haven't been any better. Miffed, seemingly, at misreading the run-up to conflict in Slovenia and Croatia, the Bush Administration spent the autumn sulking in its tent. Then it barged back into the limelight by taking up the cause of Bosnian independence, only – like the Europeans – to abandon the Bosnians utterly when the assault came.)

In the course of the late summer and autumn, as the Serbs and the JNA signed and ignored ceasefire after ceasefire in Croatia, the European mediators seemed finally to learn that the peril faced by Serbs in an independent Croatia was not the real cause of Serb-Montenegrin-JNA aggression. The turning point, in this respect, was Serbia's rejection in October of the EC's proposal, accepted by the other five republics, to reform Yugoslavia into a loose confederation of sovereign states.

Whether, on the other hand, the Community grasped that the true twin-engined motor of war was the Yugoslav generals' nihilistic drive to preserve as much of the old federation as possible, whatever the cost, plus the Milošević régime's imperative need for national conflict outside Serbia to divert the country from chronic internal discontents (political and economic, in that order) which the régime can't tackle because tackling them would mean ridding Serbia of the incubus régime itself . . . Whether the Community grasped *this* was not clear at the time. The unfinished sequel of mistakes suggests that it didn't and still hasn't.

Consider the crucial matter of recognition. The conclusion begging to be drawn from the chronology of events in November, December and January is that the EC's threat to recognize Croatia imminently as an independent state in its existing borders acted as an unignorable constraint on the aggressors. The level of violence fell; Serbia returned to the negotiating table; the 2 January ceasefire was brokered by Cyrus Vance, the UN special envoy to Yugoslavia. This paved the way to international recognition of Croatia on 15 January, followed by deployment of a UN Protection Force (UNPROFOR).

There were other reasons too for Belgrade's new pliancy: the military stalemate after the fall of Vukovar, the unpopularity of the EC's sanctions, against Serbia and Montenegro, the face-saving possibility of negotiating with the UN instead of 'capitulating' to the "Fourth Reich". But the coercive threat of recognition was indispensable. The Community had insisted for months on preserving the inter-republican borders; but words are words, after all, and recognition was proof positive to the aggressors that a resolute land-grab would not be recognized yet again in Balkan history sooner rather than later by the watching powers.

Even as the lesson was apparently being learned in Croatia, at that country's immense cost, it was ignored in Bosnia-Hercegovina. The EC foreign ministers at their historic 16 December meeting established a mechanism for republics to gain recognition as sovereign and independent states. Candidates had to apply within five days; if they satisfied five criteria concerning human and minority rights and territorial claims against other republics or non-Yugoslav neighbours, they would be recognized in January. The candidates' case would be examined by an Arbitration Commission chaired by Robert Badinter, a French constitutional lawyer.

This mechanism was devised for the benefit of BiH and Macedonia, and it left them both in the lurch. Croatia's and Slovenia's applications were a formality. Serbia and Montenegro would certainly not apply, because their entire stance in the war necessitated their persistence in the fiction that they somehow, mystically, *were* Yugoslavia, however many republics chose to "disassociate" (the judicious term used by Slovenia and Croatia to define their decisions of June '91).

The four republics duly applied. Slovenia, Croatia and Macedonia satisfied the Commission, despite doubts about Croatia's provision for its Serb minority. As for BiH, Badinter reported that it was difficult to know what the people wanted, and suggested a referendum on independence.

Now the EC committed a cardinal error. It recognized Slovenia and Croatia, but not the other two. If this was ominous for Macedonia, for BiH it was a disaster. The Community's collapse of nerve – falling back from the realism of 16 December – can only have encouraged the forces that would shortly unleash their carefully prepared assault.

At the time, no doubt, Badinter's suggestion for a referendum to decide BiH's future looked rather proper and sensible to the EC. But the proper judgment for a constitutional lawyer to reach was not a proper decision for the Community to enact. In the actual conditions of that moment, and in the light of the extremist Bosnian Serb leadership's campaign since before the election of 1990 to pre-empt independence by threats and bullying, the real function of such a procedure – with its utterly predictable outcome – would be to buy time for that leadership and for the Yugoslav People's Army then amassing men and material in the republic, and to hand them a propaganda tool. The referendum was held on 1 March. Sixty-three per cent of the electorate voted; of these, 99 per cent opted for independence. The great majority of Serbs (31 per cent of the republic's population) boycotted the referendum. The leader of the Bosnian Serbs has described the result ever since as Muslims and Croats "ganging up" against Serbs.

Did the Western mediators even anticipate this? The main value of a referendum in their eyes was, one assumes, that it allowed a relapse into verbalism and procrastination.

Looking back, they might plead extenuating circumstances. In mid January they were trying to finalize the so-called Vance Plan, to deploy the UNPROFOR. President Tudjman was being harried to accept terms which barred Croatian authority from extending into the UN Protected Areas (UNPAS): those areas of Croatia, amounting to some quarter of the republic's entire territory, controlled by Serb rebels in tandem with the JNA. At the same time, the most intransigent Serb leaders in these zones were being bullied by Belgrade into accepting the UNPROFOR in their self-proclaimed *krajina*. By the end of February, agreement had been won from all parties. But recognition of BiH in January – so the plea might run – would have risked antagonizing the Serbs there so much that the 2 January ceasefire in Croatia might have collapsed, so aborting the UNPROFOR deployment.

This imaginary plea is the best I can think of, in the mediators' defence. And it doesn't stand up. Not because the situation in Croatia was not finely poised, nor even because the Vance Plan – weighted against Croatia though it is – was not worth implementing. It is inadequate because it does not touch on the deeper European motive and misunderstandings, underlying the negotiators' approach to the conflicts in both Croatia and BiH.

The deeper motive in Croatia was peace as soon as possible. Or something that resembled peace, even at the cost of appeasing the aggressor by freezing his land-grabs as UNPAS. Never mind the causes of conflict: wrap up a deal now! That was the priority, and it maximised the chances of aggression in BiH.

Underlying this cynical and lazy priority were several key mis-understandings. The most significant of these – apart from blindness to causes – was historical and cultural as much as political. It concerned the idea and reality of Bosnia-Hercegovina.

For a start, the Europeans proposed that a sovereign BiH could be divided into "three constituent units, based on national principles and taking into account economic, geographic and other criteria". Such was the crucial wording of the *Statement of Principles for New Constitutional Arrangements for Bosnia and Hercegovina*, drafted by the EC and signed on 18 March by the Bosnian government, the Bosnian Serbs and the Bosnian Croats.

This document, which also upheld the republic's existing borders, was as worthless as the previous autumn's ceasefires: within a month, the assault had begun. The point is, the Western mediators should never have supposed that their fudging *Statement* offered any firm ground for "further negotiations" ("A working group will be established in order to define the territory of the constituent units . . ." Indeed!).

The nations are fairly thoroughly mixed, almost like the colours in a painting by Jackson Pollock, as President Izetbegović recently remarked. Some statistics are in order. "According to the census of April 1991, BiH's population was 4,354,911. Of the 109 munici- palities in the republic, thirty-seven had an absolute Muslim majority, thirty-two a Serbian absolute majority, and thirteen a Croatian absolute majority (the combined population of these eighty-two municipalities was some 2.7 million). A further fifteen municipalities had a simple Muslim majority, five a simple Serbian majority, and seven a simple Croatian majority (the combined population of these twenty-seven municipalities was about 1.7 million)." (*Radio Free Europe/Radio Liberty, Inc. Research Report on Eastern Europe*, 28 February 1992.)

No viable system for the republic can be derived from "national principles", whether that system is to be the infamous *cantonization* (carving-up by a classier name), or a three-way division of political and administrative powers with no territorial carve-up. I am authoritatively advised that the 18 March *Statement* intended the latter as the basis for a settlement. However, I would defy anyone to deny that any division of power along national lines is an invitation to carve the republic up. And any carve-up must leave large numbers of any nation in the 'wrong' units. Unless, of course, coercion is used to purify the units . . . Once admit the principle of national units, and BiH is on the slippery slope. For if nationality is the constitutional basis of these units, members of the 'wrong' nation will be treated as an encumbrance, a danger.

Did the mediators even realize what an unpromising history and pedigree the concept of "units on national principles" had in BiH? It had dominated, indeed paralysed the political agenda since the 1990 elections.

Taking its cue from Belgrade, where almost all political parties demanded the cantonization of BiH, the Serb party in Bosnia – the SDS (*Srpska Demokratska Stranka*, Serbian Democratic Party), led by Radovan Karadžić – wanted a cantonized BiH as a "confederation of three national communities" inside a federal Yugoslavia. In the autumn of '91, when it became clear that the Bosnian Muslims and Croats were, on the contrary, being driven by events towards independence with all its perils, the SDS raised the stakes by forming six "Serb Autonomous Regions" and holding a referendum for Serbs. Ninety-eight per cent of an 85 per cent turnout backed the formation of a Serb republic *inside* BiH, if the republic broke with Yugoslavia. (Ninety-eight per cent! Welcome back, Stalinist statistics!) In an independent BiH, Serbs would be reduced to minority status, and this could not be allowed – especially as the majority Muslims were conspiring to turn BiH into an Islamic theocracy. This has remained the SDS dogma.

Of course, a Serbian republic inside BiH would destroy BiH in all but name, and probably quite soon in name also. But that, Karadžić implied, was the Muslims' and Croats' problem. The Serb leaders weren't offering proposals for discussion; they were delivering an ultimatum.

In December and January, the SDS's manoeuvres to forestall independence became more explicitly threatening. (Parenthetically: it appears a model of the ending of Yugoslavia itself, with the Serb extremists in power saying "Just you dare secede!", while doing everything to intimidate other nations and heighten their insecurity.) According to the Assembly of the Serb People of Bosanska Krajina (largest of the self-proclaimed Autonomous Regions), the "Republic of the Serbian People of Bosnia-Hercegovina" would comprise the six Regions plus other areas and municipalities with a Serb population. The assembly promised rather demurely that "territorial separation ... will be conducted in a peaceful way and by agreement", though didn't explain how this agreement would be gained or what might happen if agreement were unobtainable. In short, this was as close to a charter for "ethnic cleansing" as could be hoped for. It was issued on 9 January, and no Western diplomat should have supposed that the 18 March document supplanted it.

The Croat attitude was ambiguous, and remains so. In Croatia only the extremist nationalist Party of Right was openly opposed to Bosnian integrity and independence – on the grounds that all of BiH rightfully belongs in a Great Croatian state. However, western Hercegovina, where most of the Croats are concentrated, stands to Croatia as Montenegro stands to Serbia: a fountainhead of national spirit. More bluntly, it is a traditional breeding ground of block-headed national zealots. An addiction to fantasies of annexing western Hercegovina is part and parcel of Croat nationalism. Nationalist leaders always tend to believe that they can have everything, achieve *all* their goals, if only they persist. Rationally, Tudjman himself – a textbook nationalist if ever one was – knew that, as the Croatian war dragged on, any tampering with BiH's integrity would set a dangerous precedent: it would greatly strengthen the secessionist and autonomist demands by the Serbs rebels in the Croatian UNPAS. He must also know that cantonization would prolong the travails of Croatia itself, because any Serbian canton must include east Hercegovina, from which artillery will always be able to threaten Dubrovnik and Konavle. In all probability it would also include north-western Bosnia, which would greatly benefit the Serbs of Krajina.

But Tudjman is dim and dogmatic, and he cannot relinquish the dream; hence his secretive summits in '91 with Milošević over the future of BiH. Even now he hasn't learned: being clumsy (as clumsy as Milošević is astute), he keeps saying the wrong thing about BiH, which always triggers Western accusations that Zagreb is in cahoots with Belgrade to carve up Bosnia. It's as if he were at pains to represent Croatia's policy as predatory when it is no worse than scavenging and opportunist. Croatia recognized BiH in April, along with the European Community; and it has provided immensely more practical aid for Bosnia's survival than anyone else. Ambiguous aid, to be sure; the Croats want to break the supply routes to Serb rebel enclaves in Croatia, as well as secure those portions of BiH earmarked for annexation, should the republic either cease to exist or – what would amount to the same – be dragged back into "Yugoslavia". But aid nonetheless, and quite as precious as the West's deliveries of food and medicines, if less wholesome.

In June and July, the West, again understanding nothing or not wanting to understand, threatened Croatia with sanctions for interfering in BiH. Alarmed, Zagreb promptly pulled its forces back from northern Bosnia. More territory fell to the Serbs. More Bosnians died and fled.

Croat attitudes inside BiH are divided too. Soon after the SDS founded the Serb Autonomous Regions, the Bosnian branch of HDZ (the ruling party in Croatia) created two "Croat Communities" in majority-Croat regions. These were less of a challenge to the Sarajevo government than the Serb Regions – more a territorial insurance against future disintegration. But of course, they too eroded Sarajevo's authority and fostered separatist delusions among the Croats themselves.

The hardliners of Hercegovina may dream of joining the national motherland, but many Bosnian Croats have another loyalty (as, to be sure, do many Bosnian Serbs in Sarajevo, Tuzla and other towns). The leader of the Croatian party in 1991 was one such, Stjepan Kljuić. An invincible believer in BiH's integrity and independence, Kljuić resisted Zagreb's pressure in December and January to entertain the cantonal option. He resigned on 2 February, a month before the referendum, telling his party that "many of you who are sitting here and support cantonization will actually be living in a Greater Serbia. I'll leave for Australia . . . and then you'll realize that I was right all along." Wise words. But the pro-cantonizing faction carried the day. Presumably the new leadership then worked out the 18 March formula with the SDS, or more likely agreed when the SDS mooted it, leaving the government isolated and under pressure not to obstruct what Lord Carrington (chair of the EC peace conference on Yugoslavia) and Mr Cutilheiro (responsible for negotiations about BiH) probably liked to think was a respectable interim solution.

As for the Muslims, they always saw cantonization as a disaster. They are bound to lose in any territorial shareout, for two reasons. They are the most dispersed nation, and they lack a neighbouring state to sponsor them politically and militarily. Serbs and Croats cohabit in only a few districts of the republic whereas Muslims live with both, throughout. The Muslims are the cement in BiH, and were bound to suffer most by any dis-integration. The main Muslim party wanted a secular state with protection of national rights but where individual rights were the basis of constitution and law. Izetbegović had insisted in the first half of '91, when rumours abounded in Sarajevo of secret deals among the three national leaders, that he would never negotiate cantonization.

Thus, even in conditions of general peace, it would have been careless of the European mediators to suppose that the 18 March formula could hold for long without very vehement and practical international support for the Bosnian government; and there was no sign of *that* before 18 March, let alone since.

In the light of actual events in Croatia and the predicament of the Serbian régime, and given the sheer quantity of JNA troops and weaponry which had withdrawn into BiH from Slovenia, Croatia and latterly from Macedonia too, the mediators' tactic seems criminally irresponsible. All the more so because the Bosnian government – legitimately elected in 1990 – had done everything to accommodate the mediators, the Serbs and the JNA. The latter it treated with tolerance and generosity. It had only a tiny militia of its own. It had trusted in the strength and honesty of Western diplomacy. It even accepted the absurd *Statement of Principles*, appeasing the Serb and Croat leaderships and the Europeans against its own wishes and better judgement, for the sake of a peace in which it, along with Bosnians and Bosnia's friends everywhere, wanted so desperately to believe.

Perhaps ignorance, inertia and cynicism are playing equal parts in the West's approach to BiH. Perhaps one or two of these vices predominate. Who can be sure, before the transcripts and memoirs are published? But we all know the result.

In January, February and March, as the Bosnian government jumped tamely through the Community's legalistic hoops, the Bosnian Serb leaders and the JNA continued to arm their paramilitary forces and to secure strategic vantage points, ready to act as and when recognition of BiH was imminent – and all in the knowledge that the West was neither equipped to prevent a swift land-grab inside BiH, nor willing to react forcefully when the land-grab came. The record of European involvement in the conflict showed that the Community had never caught up with the pace of events. Back in June '91, when the JNA tanks rolled out of their barracks in Slovenia, the Europeans (and Americans too) insisted straight off on keeping Yugoslavia together – as if the Western strategic imperatives of the Cold War were carved in stone! As if the sight of Slovenian soldiers blowing up Yugoslav tanks were a prelude to terminal crisis in the federation instead of a finale, and proof that the federation could not be kept alive on any terms acceptable to all! And now, six months later, the Europeans seemed to assume that the threat of recognition would be as effective in BiH as in Croatia – as if the outcome in Croatia had not upped the ante for the JNA, the Milošević régime and its puppets in the SDS, giving them more cause to start a war in BiH, not less. Once war had begun, they had no motive to join the peace process except to dissemble their true aims, deny their atrocities and defer intervention, so buying time until they are ready to sue for peace – on their terms. Which is all motive enough, of course.

Clearly, Serbian policy in Croatia and BiH is self-destructive, and one hopes that more Serbs will see this sooner rather than later. The policy isn't, though, destructive to the régime in Belgrade. Quite the reverse; *stopping* the war would be nihilistic for the régime, because it could not survive the release of anger and frustration after a year and more of futile loss and horror. The longer the war goes on and the longer Serbia is quarantined by sanctions, the more the aggressors need something to show for their expenditure of Serbian life and welfare. This vicious circle cannot be broken by "remonstrance after remonstrance, protestation after protestation"; or by sanction upon sanction.

To date, the West has done nothing to puncture the aggressors' confidence that they can do what they wish in BiH with essential impunity. Diplomatic isolation, the bluster of worldwide condemnation, even the economic blockade of Serbia and Montenegro imposed by the Security Council on 30 May: these measures have brought little or no benefit to BiH, because they do not alter by a whit the bedrock truth that the aggressors have more reason to continue their assault than to stop it. Their only serious worry is the chance of Western military intervention to stop the massacre before they are ready. So far, they have been nimble enough to defuse that possibility. Not that much nimbleness is needed: the will to intervene just isn't there, and Western leaders have been doing the Serbs' propaganda work for them by dredging up every argument and pseudo-argument against intervention.

We have learned, for instance, the unlikely news that Prime Minister John Major is haunted by the spectre of Dien Bien Phu, where Vietminh forces defeated the French army in 1954. We are told that intervention might get Western armies embroiled in BiH for decades, like the British in Northern Ireland.

More credibly than Mr Major but no more creditably, the Bush Administration has invoked the precedent of Vietnam as a deterrent. Many people, up to and including "the Lord" himself (as Peter Carrington is wryly known in the Slovene and Croatian press), have warned how many German divisions were tied down in Bosnia during the Second World War. The same people warn that military intervention in BiH would have no clear objective, and remind us how the Bosnian terrain is tailor-made for guerrilla operations, how much "the Yugoslavs" like fighting, etcetera. The most effective of these admonitions is the one about objectives. But no one has yet explained why the objective cannot be to support the legitimate government of BiH and its blueprint for the republic. Once this objective is allowed to steer the diplomatic initiative, some real progress might be made at the negotiating table; most likely it would bring Zagreb and its minions in Hercegovina to their senses straightaway. If military intervention were still required, it could be organized by agreement with the government.

These false analogies and unwarrantedly pessimistic warnings are proffered alongside selective revision of current events. Politicians and commentators opine sagely that panicky, "premature" recognition by the EC was responsible for the explosion of violence in Bosnia, or anyway exacerbated it. Often this is merely a coded attack upon Germany for hustling the other Community states, last December. Perhaps these politicians and commentators realize that this thoroughly unhistorical argument originated in Belgrade and Banja Luka (capital of the Bosnian Serb "Republic"). Perhaps they don't. Anyway it is the opposite of the truth. Recognition of Croatia and Slovenia helped to scale down the war in Croatia. As for BiH, I have presented my view; not only was recognition crucially delayed – when it came, it was halfhearted and brought no commitment to BiH's integrity and sovereignty.

The function of the "prematurity" argument is, in fact, to blacken the most realistic and adequate moment of Western diplomacy. It implies that the fake cause of war was the real cause; if the Bosnian Serbs had not felt threatened by suddenly finding themselves adrift in an independent BiH, they wouldn't – so runs the logic – have taken up arms.

Alternatively, and just as spuriously, the argument implies that recognition aborted the chance of a solution acceptable to all sides. But if so, why had the Serbs signed the 18 March *Statement* which granted the possibility of cantonization? In truth, the Serb-JNA position against Bosnian statehood was non-negotiable. (Karadžić had warned that a referendum would mean war; for once he was telling the truth.)

Another piece of wisdom fast becoming received is that the Community also blundered by insisting from the outset that only peaceful changes to the borders between the republics would be recognized. It is difficult to say whether this opinion is more arrogant than ignorant, or ignorant than arrogant. It takes its cue from Great Serbian propaganda that these borders are merely "administrative", invented by Tito, nationally unjust, no basis for statehood. It assumes that the peoples and republican governments of former Yugoslavia do not themselves know very well that these borders define different national, historic and cultural entities, and would not resist tooth and nail any forced border changes, regardless of the altitude of the European Community.

Both these arguments carry a further implication: that the assault on BiH, like its predecessor on Croatia, can be 'understood' and perhaps to some extent forgiven because the aggressors were provoked. This argument takes the aggressors' own excuse for their genocidal onslaught and drapes it with diplomatic gravitas and a touch of humility (after all, we shouldn't have let German pressure cloud our better judgement).*

---

* Like certain victims of rape, the Bosnian government was plainly asking for trouble. "Contributory negligence" is the judicial term. A tendency to blame the victim, evident in Croatia's case, has become compulsive in the case of BiH. I cannot recall any British politican or pundit who did not view Croatia's plight in 1991 with distaste. Since the fighting has transferred to BiH, the Bosnians have been pitied as victims but their government is rarely

Another lie underpins these arguments. This is the claim, repeated daily by a thousand journalists, that this is an *ethnic war*. This notion originates, like the others, in Belgrade and Banja Luka. It is a misnomer, because the Serb, Croat and Muslim nations are ethnically indistinguishable. (The number of Bosnian Muslims of Turkish descent is minute.) And it is pernicious, because it disguises a consequence as a cause and mystifies the conflict as an orgiastic free-for-all, far removed from political calculation. A spontaneous Balkan combustion – an outbreak of Balkan violence, endemic and insensate, that must be left to burn itself out. Not hard to understand because moderately complex – incomprehensible because irrational. Mr Karadžić never misses a chance to explain in his good English that ceasefires keep being broken because ethnic hatred runs so deep. He knows his audience, and the message he sends is seductive: "Don't intervene! You can't do anything about an ethnic conflict except stand well back. Outsiders would be attacked by everyone, they'd never get out alive." All of which is secret music to the ears of Europeans who don't want to intervene anyway . . .

As well as selective revision, there has been selective suppression. In early August, the first pictures of a Serb concentration camp were broadcast on Western television. The sight of skeletal, half-naked men milling around behind a high barbed-wire fence was deeply shocking. Several days later the shock was compounded by revelations, leaked by Bosnian diplomats in New York, that UN peacekeepers had known in detail *since May* about the full gaumat of "ethnic cleansing", including camps, home burnings, deportations and summary executions. They had taken no action to publicize or investigate these early reports, of which Security Council members swiftly denied all knowledge. Until a full account is published, suspicion of a cover-up at some high level must remain.

What is the upshot of all this? Outrage has been dulled, doped with fake fatalism. Sober appraisal of military options to stop or diminish the horrors has been swamped by trumped-up alarmism. Calls for action have been smothered. The triumphant noise about Western technology delivering air-to-ground missiles down Iraqi chimneypots is nowhere to be heard, and instead we are told solemnly that Britain and America (for instance) will never commit ground troops to Bosnia.

seen as the proponent of the only viable future for the republic *and the region*. There is a correlation between the innocence of an embattled victim and the urgency of an onlooker's need to deny that innocence, if the onlooker wants not only to stay uninvolved but to justify his non-involvement.

As a matter of fact, both these countries and many others have undertaken to send ground troops to protect humanitarian supplies. But ground troops for peace-making action are not the issue; the Sarajevo government isn't even requesting them. What's wanted is a Security Council resolution, reached by consultation with the government of BiH (a UN member state, after all), to forbid further use of the heavy artillery, tanks and strike aircraft which are bombarding Sarajevo, Bihać, Tuzla, Jajce, Mostar and many points in between. Violations by any side should be answered with air strikes against the offending weaponry.

If such action merely interrupted the turkey-shoot of Bosnian cities and citizens, or redressed the drastic military imbalance, it should be taken. In fact, there is good reason to suppose that it would achieve much more, transforming the conflict and so infusing the peace process with new plausibility.

This reason is inherent in the nature and aims of the assault. As in Croatia, the aggressors' strategic goal, insofar as they possess one, is unrealistic on two accounts. It is undermined from within by their own witlessness and cowardice, and it assumes a feeble and short-lived resistance by their victims. (I wish I could add a third account: Western intolerance of massacre and expansionist aggression "in the heart of Europe". But Western tolerance seems inexhaustible.)

The SDS's aim is to occupy and keep as much of BiH as possible. This means controlling the territory which separates Serb strong-holds in eastern Hercegovina, eastern Bosnia and and north-western Bosnia. It won't be enough to seize and dominate these swathes of territory, as in a traditional war of invasion, then hang on for an armistice and try to ratify the *fait accompli* with a peace treaty. The Serb side doesn't carry enough weight, militarily or diplomatically, to impose its own terms for peace; it has to persuade the West that its preferred terms are the only feasible terms. There are too many non-Serb Bosnians in these areas who will never accept to live under occupation in their own homes. Besides, the international community would likely use the non-Serb populations in the occupied areas as a lever to force Serb withdrawal. To have a chance of enduring much beyond the conflict, the national map (as on p. 97) must be redrawn at once. Hence the genocidal onslaught.

All the majority-Muslim cities must be subjugated and "cleansed". Then the great arc of territory from Bihać to Tuzla and Trebinje – maybe three-fifths of the republic – can be annexed to "Yugoslavia" or, as second best, redefined as the Serb canton in Bosnia-Hercegovina: a papery, nominal Bosnia-Hercegovina that might have to be acknowledged if the Europeans and the UN Security Council dig their heels in. The remnant of BiH will be tossed to the Croats and Muslims.

With all the soldiers (54,000 of them) and weaponry donated to the Serbian Republic of Bosnia by the JNA before the latter "withdrew" across the river Drina in mid May, it has been a simple matter for Karadžić's *Einsatzgruppen* to drive hundreds of thousands of people from their homes. By the end of April, some two-thirds of BiH was under Serb control. The Bosnian defenders mustered by the government when the assault was already underway had no artillery, no tanks, no planes, no missiles.

But as before, the Serbo-Yugoslav military machine is not up to the job. As in Croatia, destruction and rapine are the ends as well as the means for too many of its hoodlum soldiers. Killing or expelling unarmed peasants is one thing; taking cities in order to expel non-Serbs is quite another. The aggressors' only method is to blockade a town, set up their artillery on the surrounding hills (there are always hills in BiH), and unload shells on the defenceless citizens day after day, month after month.

This method – the Vukovar Technique – bespeaks an oafish, slovenly army without brains on top, discipline below, or morale anywhere. Apart from its barbarity, the method doesn't even work. Karadžić boasted on 17 May that "we could take Sarajevo any time. We could finish them in five days." Four months later Sarajevo is still untaken. On 14 July, he told UN negotiators that Goražde would fall within two days. At the end of August, the besiegers of Goražde abandoned their artillery emplacements above the town. (Karadžić says he ordered a withdrawal in accordance with promises made at the London Conference. A Reuters journalist reported from the emplacements a few days later that the scene suggested a rout.) Tuzla has not fallen. Nor have Bihać or Mostar.

This is why we may suppose that the limited measures mentioned above might transform the picture. The aggressors have paid no price for their territorial gains; who knows what will happen when the spell of impunity is broken? Who knows what the impact would be on the morale of Bosnian defence forces, on public opinion in Serbia proper and among Bosnia's Serbs, many of whom have never seen the evil Karadžić as their spokesman?

But intervention almost certainly won't happen. After the French president François Mitterand broke the West's peculiar self-imposed quarantine of Sarajevo by his daring visit on 28 June (Vidovdan!), the EC and UN have been more or less eagerly supplying humanitarian relief. This course of action demonstrates to everyone, not least themselves, that something is being done for the victims, if only – as Bosnians grimly joke – to fatten them up so the gunners and snipers have more to aim at. Also, it allows the UN and EC to preserve their neutrality. And without neutrality, these bodies cannot negotiate between the "warring factions" (that wretched phrase!) in BiH.

Relief operations cannot be mixed with military intervention. But relief operations are conducted on the sufferance of the Serb forces, so humanitarian aid furnishes the aggressors with useful leverage for blackmailing. On 14 August, goaded by the Western public outrage that followed the first pictures of Omarska concentration camp, the Security Council reluctantly authorized force ("all measures necessary") in support of humanitarian aid convoys into BiH. The mediators haven't so far availed themselves of this permission, because they rightly fear that military support is the thin end of a wedge, leading to a crisis that would force them to intervene militarily (which they don't want to do) or back off completely, leaving the aggressors free rein (which they cannot do: it would look too bad. Anyway, the West knows that it is embroiled in former Yugoslavia for the duration).

For their part the Serbs won't block the aid, because they know that it serves their turn by substituting for military intervention. Nor, however, can they afford to let aid be funnelled in freely, because it strengthens the Bosnians' resistance; so they plunder the relief convoys and shoot the occasional UN peacekeeper. Hence the stop-start rhythm. And soon the winter weather will do the stopping on the Serbs' behalf.

It is a fantastic situation, a nightmare of make-believe. While Serbia is punished by sanctions, the Bosnian Serb leadership is treated neutrally – as if it is an independent actor in BiH, not implementing Belgrade's wishes. The West pretends that the established process of negotiation does not inherently favour the aggressor, and that the parties to the Bosnian conflict are more or less equally responsible for perpetuating the violence, because none of them will "compromise" – as if the price of compromise were identical for all sides, and the results of compromise would be equally positive in any case! Also, the West pretends that its diplomatic pressure against the aggressor is obtaining results, or will do so imminently. Karadžić, meanwhile, pretends that he is participating in the peace process, and his master Milošević pretends that Serbia has nothing to do with the conflict anyway.

For their part, the Croat forces based in eastern Hercegovina hold some 20 per cent of BiH. They lie fairly low, bolstering the Bosnian defence forces in some areas, undercutting them in others, "cleansing" Serbs where they can while violently restraining the neo-ustaša extremists from engulfing further territory, seizing a percentage of aid from the relief convoys that pass through from the coast to Sarajevo, and waiting for the UN, the EC and the Serbs to settle Bosnia's fate among them.

The make-believe produces some bizarre situations which at least embarrass, one hopes, the Western powers. The UNHCR, for instance, is obliged by the Security Council to negotiate solemnly with Karadžić, the Pol Pot of Bosnia,* for permission to evacuate refugees whom Karadžić's men have expelled; they are, in effect, asking to be allowed to expedite "ethnic cleansing" even as Serb gunners are targetting the UNPROFOR barracks in Sarajevo.

Really, one might almost agree with the conspiracy theory rife among Bosnians themselves that Western leaders are more discomfited by the Sarajevo government's stubborn *and unexpected* endurance than by their own vacillation or the monstrousness of "ethnic cleansing". If Izetbegović were to capitulate, the whole ungodly mess would seem so much clearer; the EC and the UN would be free to do business with the real power-brokers in Belgrade and Zagreb, and the Muslims could be ushered into a canton of their own.

Nothing, of course, would be solved. The Muslims of BiH would become the Palestinians of Europe. "Ethnic cleansing" would continue, at lower intensity, for another generation. Prison camps would become a permanent feature of the landscape. Very soon, Muslim terrorist networks would be active in the Serb and Croat cantons, and vice versa.

And the Serbian régime would still be there, unappeased because unappeasable, needing to assualt Kosova or even Macedonia.

The arguments for integrity and sovereignty become ever more compelling. Because it is a multinational state, in which no people makes an absolute majority, and none is a minority, Bosnia-Hercegovina is not, as the spectating powers seem to suspect, dispensable. On the contrary, it is necessary between the nation-states of Croatia and Serbia. A unified BiH offers the only chance of the three nations getting peace and security across the territory of the whole republic, wherever they live. There are some two million

---

* Not a casual insult. Dr Karadžić is a pathological liar who sees himself as a messiah of national revolution. A Serb from Montenegro, he has no feeling for Bosnia and sees Bosnian integrity as nothing other than an obstacle to the fossilized Great Serb project. Rasim Kadić, whom readers will remember from the political meeting in Pazarić (p. 101), has recalled a meeting with Karadžić in mid April, when the assault and genocide were under way. "I am willing to sacrifice this entire generation," he told Rasim, "if it means that future generations will live better." (*Mladina*, 14 July 1992.) No doubt he is more discreet and amenable with Lord Carrington, Lord Owen and Cyrus Vance, but let no one doubt that given the opportunity, Karadžić will reduce all of BiH to a Passchendaele landscape of smoking rubble and charred tree stumps, if this would guarantee Serbian possession in future.

Bosnian refugees, and the total is rising daily; only if a unified BiH is restored will these people be able to return home. The spectating powers, however, can't even decide that Bosnia-Hercegovina is desirable, let alone necessary and possible. Their policy of backing by agonized degrees toward military action is bad for everyone except for all the worst people.

*

Outside Bosnia-Hercegovina, the critical development in former Yugoslavia since I finished this book has been the deployment of the UN Peacekeeping Force in Croatia, and its vicissitudes there.

Deployment of the 14,000 UNPROFOR personnel began on 16 March, and was completed during the summer. The three UN Protected Areas are shown on the map at the front of this book. Together, they amount to a quarter of the republic's territory. As the fighting reached stalemate in November and December, these were the areas controlled by the Serb rebels and JNA forces. Croat forces were unable to regain this land; the rebels had reached their limit. Zagreb swore that the rebels would be subdued and the checquered flag would soon flap again over Knin and Vukovar. The rebels swore eternal resistance.

According to the terms of the Vance Plan, the "blue helmets" would be stationed throughout the UNPAs to stabilize and demilitarize them, so allowing negotiations for "an overall settlement of the Yugoslav crisis" (*sic*) to proceed. Also, by restoring peace and security to these zones, the conditions would be created for refugees to return. The UNPAs would be demilitarized through the withdrawal of the JNA and Croatian Army, and then through disbanding and disarming the militias. The UNPROFOR was authorized to control access to the UNPAs, to monitor the local police, and to check that no further expulsions or other human rights violations took place.

The Plan was born amid ill omens. President Tudjman didn't want to sign when he discovered rather late in the day, or pretended to discover, that Croatian authority would not apply inside the UNPAs. This wasn't, he said, what had been agreed. On the other side, Milan Babić, the leader in the biggest rebel enclave, Kninska Krajina (see pp. 270ff.), refused to sign unless Croatian writ didn't run in the UNPAs. The Western mediators were so desperate for an agreement that they appeased Babić, despatching the German foreign minister to twist Tudjman's arm.

Babić himself, meanwhile, was summoned to Belgrade and compelled there – by torture, so he alleges – to swallow his other main objection to the Plan: the stipulation that the JNA garrison in Knin must schedule its full withdrawal from Croatia.

Thus there were major stresses hidden within the "full and unconditional acceptance" of the Plan on 21 February by "all parties concerned" (I am quoting the UNPROFOR's own press briefing). Nor have these torsions been smoothed out, during the Plan's stage-by-stage implementation. On the contrary, they have tightened to the point where they constrict the UNPROFOR operation and threaten its viability.

The government in Zagreb does not hide its frustration with UNPROFOR. Nothing, it claims, has been done to expedite the return of the 275,000 Croats displaced from the UNPAS. In fact low-intensity aggression continues. Non-Serbs are still expelled from their homes, vacant properties are plundered and commandeered by Serb settlers, and remaining Croats are still not safe from violence and theft. Militiamen and policemen who are known to have expelled non-Serbs from "UN Sector East" are not sacked by the local Serb rebel authorities, despite UNPROFOR demands.

UN Sector East is known to the rebels as the "Serb Autonomous Region of Slavonia, Baranja and Western Srem". It is the most troubled of the UNPAS, because it is the only one contiguous with Serbia itself, making it easy for reinforcements and supplies to be driven in or ferried across the Danube.

This is another key Croatian grievance. The Serb rebels contravene the Plan by smuggling in arms and supplies from Serbia, beneath the noses of the UNPROFOR. Although the JNA has withdrawn, the local militias don't want to disarm or disband, and the UNPROFOR won't demand compliance with the Vance timetable for demilitarization. All in all, the blue helmets' efforts seem half-hearted or even grudging to Croatia.

While the UNPROFOR concedes that these things all happen, it is frustrated by the Croatian authorities' own perversity. For one thing, they are slow to discipline the self-styled "patriots" who blow up Serb properties all over the republic – as slow as the Serb rebels to sack the culprits on their side. Also, the government appears to feed popular discontent with the UNPROFOR as a distraction from its own failings – which include the fact that the government did, after all, consent to the Vance Plan. Besides, the Croats make their own illegal incursions into the UNPAS, sending guerrilla missions to bomb Knin, and generally making life nasty for the rebels and settlers.

Certainly the Croatian authorities at all levels encourage ill-feeling toward the UNPROFOR, which is easy to achieve because the blue helmets' rôle seems to the great majority of Croats so wrongly passive, so wrongly *impartial*. An average citizen of Croatia may not know the terms of the mandate, but he or she knows for sure that Croatia was assaulted and invaded by wicked četniks, and any peace plan which doesn't send the četniks packing as fast as possible has nothing much to do with justice, and probably can't be trusted. The government, of course, knows the mandate all too well. Resentful of having been obliged to consent to its terms in February, it sees no reason not to exploit popular ignorance and desire for the restitution of stolen and destroyed communities, homes, livelihoods.

The UNPROFOR is spread too thinly to fulfill its mandate efficiently. Its internal communications are fraught with difficulties; besides not speaking the local languages, the blue helmets in different sectors come from different countries, twenty-nine in all, so often cannot even talk to each other. Making matters worse, it appears that some units have been very poorly briefed about the whole background to their mission.

But from Croatia's point of view there is a deeper problem than these: a structural problem of the first order. This is the mandate itself, which does not permit any force to be used against the rebels. In UN peacekeeping terms, the Croatian operation falls under Chapter VI of the Charter ("agreement and co-operation"), not Chapter VII. The blue helmets can only mediate; they need both sides' consent at every stage. They are not there to restore Croatian sovereignty at any price.

The pleasant logic of UNPROFOR deployment is that, by tactfully encouraging the moderates on both sides and cautiously isolating the extremists, and by generally tramelling everyone in the meshes of dull procedure and due process, the terms of the Vance Plan will eventually be fulfilled and the displaced people will be able to return. After all, the Plan is premissed on the principle that Croatia's borders will not change, so the Croats don't have to worry about that. And there are already some indications that moderates in Knin may be gaining an edge over hardliners who insist that the UNPAS will never again belong to Croatia, even if Zagreb can be persuaded by the West to grant them special status.

This logic is long-term, looking beyond the remaining six months of the UNPROFOR's twelve-month deployment. Which doesn't answer the Zagreb government's urgent wish to be able to reassure its traumatized electorate that what was lost in the war will definitely be regained in the peace.

As always in searching for solutions in the arena of former Yugoslavia, one is led ineluctably back to Belgrade. A future for the UNPAS cannot begin to be charted before the rebels accept that Croatia is the only country they have, like it or not. But they won't accept this until the conflict stops in Bosnia-Hercegovina. That won't happen until the Bosnian Serbs drop *their* unrealistic demands. And that, in turn, won't happen until the Serbs of Serbia have kicked out Milošević and his régime, bag and baggage.

*

In Serbia, nothing has happened to raise anyone's hopes. On 27 April the *Savezna Republika Jugoslavia* was proclaimed in Belgrade. It comprises, of course, Serbia and Montenegro. No other state has recognized this contrivance as the successor to the SFRY. Alone among EC states, Greece – which is entangled in dangerous games of its own, in the south Balkans – would like to.

A fortnight later, with pressure mounting from abroad to pull the Yugoslav Army out of BiH, Milošević purges the senior ranks of the JNA. Thirty-eight generals are ousted, and several admirals. The generals include Blagoje Adžić, the neanderthal Minister of Defence. Milutin Kukanjac, the commander in BiH, is replaced by Ratko Mladić, formerly of the Knin garrison, a fanatic who had opposed the withdrawal of the JNA from Krajina. After this night of long knives, the Yugoslav Army is again the Serbian Army in all but name, just as it was when Yugoslavia was born seventy-four years ago.

One is reminded of those nature films which show a plant swell and burgeon beneath a rotating sun; now the film is playing backwards, yet the plant withers slackly as it shrinks, instead of returning to the bud.

Serbia is undoing itself, staggering back to its crib self-blinded, cursing the world. It is the catastrophic nation of our day.

A Serbian-born American millionaire called Milan Panić was invited to be the Prime Minister of "Yugoslavia". Someone was needed to negotiate with the Europeans, who loathe Milošević and can't even claim to believe a word he says. Mr Panić threw himself into the job with gusto; he raced from one Balkan capital to another, contradicting himself from day to day, waving his arms and preening in front of the cameras. A sincere patriot, he wants to rehabilitate Serbia and get the sanctions lifted. Hence, at the London conference on former Yugoslavia, he appeared to discomit Milošević by promising, for instance, that "Yugoslavia" would recognize Croatia in its present borders, if special status is accorded to the Serb enclaves. He also met Ibrahim Rugova – the first top-level contact between the Kosovars and Belgrade.

Back in Belgrade, members of the "Yugoslav" parliament from the Serbian Socialist Party – Milošević's powerbase – proposed a motion of no confidence in Panić and his federal government. It seemed that the puppet was acquiring a will of his own, and needed an admonitory smack. The motion was defeated after the "Yugoslav" president publicly backed Panić's behaviour in London.

Western commentators promptly speculated on the power struggle in Belgrade. As yet, however, there is no struggle; Panić still has no powerbase of his own, and he cannot challenge Milošević – even assuming he wants to – until a substantial proportion of the SSP defects to him. Perhaps there is a rift between the two men; perhaps not. What does it matter? Serbian policy remains unchanged in all essentials. Besides, Panić has said more than once that the Bosnian Serbs are entitled to keep almost all of the territory they have seized.

The president who backed Panić is none other than Dobrica Ćosić, the sombre novelist and Academician who is universally seen as father of the nationalist movement in the mid '80s – the movement which the Serbian League of Communists picked up and wielded as a hammer to smash Kosovo's autonomy, and Vojvodina's, and Montenegro's leadership, with each blow rendering the federation less progressive, less reformable, and less habitable for non-Serbs. It is entirely apt that the dutiful Ćosić should preside over his hideous creation, ready to sink with it beneath the waves.

As for the Serbian opposition, it remains internally divided and radically perplexed by the national war being waged in BiH; Vuk Drašković still wants to be against Milošević and *his* war, without abandoning traditional Serb national goals.

Nor is there yet any sign that the public will either hasten Milošević's long-postponed appointment with democracy, or shake any life into the opposition. Anti-government feeling runs high, seemingly generated more by anger at the prospect of *losing* the war in BiH than by shame or guilt at complicity in massacres. The economic sanctions imposed on Serbia and Montenegro by the United Nations on 30 May appear not to be increasing the citizens' capacity for insight and democratic protest.

*

Macedonia is still non-existent. Greece refuses to moderate its refusal to let the Macedonians attach their name to an independent state. On the contrary, Athens has exploited the disarray over ex-Yugoslavia among the other EC members, winning their agreement not to recognise Macedonia as such. The EC isn't even, apparently, seeking a compromise, preferring instead to await Skopje's capitulation. But no government in Skopje can yield to Athens' insistence that Greece has a political copyright on the name Macedonia. The Macedonian nation in an aggregate, raw and unweathered, if forced to abandon its nominal identity, it may discompose – which would be dangerous for everyone, the Greeks included.

Meanwhile, the price of non-existence is bitter to Macedonians, especially since the UN imposed its sanctions on Serbia. Skopje observes the sanctions – what else can it do – despite the UN's refusal to admit Macedonia's right to statehood under its proper name.

The effect in Greece itself of the official hate-campaign against the northern neighbour is inevitably regressive and illiberal. Critics of the campaign are persecuted and silenced. The small communities of "Slavophone Greeks" are likely to become alientated by the whole wretched business, and discover a novel yearning for contact across the border.

And what of the Slovenes, whose eventual impatience to enter History had brought Yugoslavia crashing down? After the high drama of 1991, an atmosphere of hangover is palpable in Ljubljana. Economic truths are harsh. The old internal Yugoslav and Soviet bloc markets are no more. Privatisation is as problematic as in every post-socialist country. Tourism is a quarter of the pre-war norm. At the same time, 70,000 refugees have arrived from BiH, and more are on the way . . .

With such cheerless prospects, it should not surprise that the government is playing the national-populist card. Foreign Minister Rupel recently announced that Slovenia disputes up to one-third of its border with Croatia, and may offer its case for international arbitration. One must hope that the irony of this absurd claim is not lost upon the Slovene public, and that the government will be roundly mocked into retraction.

Finally, some better news – perhaps the only nice news of the summer. On 2 August, when elections for the president and one chamber of parliament were held in Croatia, Istra enhanced its reputation as the most free-thinking region in the former Yugoslavia. Despite much blather from Tudjman and other of the HDZ elite about the "Croaticity" of Istra, its citizens voted solidly for the Istran Democratic Convention (see p. 74). A pinprick of light in the gloom.

14 September 1992

Appendix

Danilo Kiš on Nationalism

Nationalism is first and foremost *paranoia*. Collective and individual paranoia. As collective paranoia it results from envy and fear, and most of all from the loss of individual consciousness; this collective paranoia is therefore simply an accumulation of individual paranoias at the pitch of paroxysm. If, in the framework of a social order, an individual is not able to 'express himself', because the order in question is not congenial and does not stimulate him as an *individual*, or because it thwarts him as an individual, in other words does not allow him to assume an entity of his own, he is obliged to search for this entity outside identity and outside the so-called social structure. Thus he becomes a member of a pseudo-masonic group which seems to pose problems of epochal importance as its goals and objectives: the survival and prestige of a nation or nations, the preservation of tradition and the nation's sacrosanct values — folkloric, philosophical, ethical, literary, etc. Invested with such a secret, semi-public, or public mission, A. N. Other becomes a man of action, a tribune of the people, a semblance of an individual. Once we have him cut down to size, isolated from the herd, and out of the pseudo-masonic lodge where he had installed himself or been installed by others, we are faced with an individual without individuality, a nationalist, Cousin Jules. This is the Jules that Sartre wrote about, a zero in his family, a man whose only distinction is that he can blanch at the mere mention of a single topic: the English. This pallor, this trembling, this 'secret' — to be able to blanch at the mention of the English — constitute his social being and make him important, existent: do not mention *English* tea in front of him, or the others will start winking and signalling, kicking you under the table, because Jules is touchy about the English, good God, everybody knows that, Jules detests the English (and loves his own folk, the French), in a word, Jules is a personality, becomes a personality, thanks to *English* tea. This kind of profile, which fits all nationalists, can be freely elaborated to its conclusion: the nationalist is, as a rule, equally piffling as a social being and as an individual. Outside the commitment that he has made, he is a nonentity. He neglects his family, his job (usually in an office), literature (if he is a writer), his social responsibilities, since these are all petty compared with his messianism. Needless to say, he is *by choice* an ascetic, a potential fighter biding his time. Paraphrasing Sartre on anti-Semitism, nationalism is *a comprehensive and free choice, a global attitude not only toward other nations but toward people in general, toward history and society; it is at once a passion and a world-view*. The nationalist is by definition an ignoramus. Nationalism is the line of least resistance, the easy way. The nationalist is untroubled, he knows or thinks he knows what his values are, his, that's to say national, that's to say the values of the nations he belongs to, ethical and political; he is not interested in others, *they are no concern of his*, hell – it's other people (other nations, another tribe). They don't even need investigating. The nationalist sees other people in his own image – as nationalists. A comfortable standpoint, as we noted. Fear and envy. A commitment and engagement needing no effort. Not only is hell other people, in a national key of course, but also: whatever is not mine (Serbian, Croatian, French . . .) is alien to me. Nationalism is an ideology of banality. As such, nationalism is a totalitarian ideology. Nationalism is moreover, and not only in the etymological sense, the last remaining ideology and demagogy that addresses itself to *the people*. Writers know this best. That's why every writer who declares that he writes 'about the people and for the people', who claims to surrender his individual voice to the *higher* interests of the nation, should be suspected of nationalism. Nationalism is also kitsch: in its Serbo-Croatian variant it takes the form of squabbling about the national origin of GINGERBREAD HEARTS.* As a rule the nationalist doesn't know a single foreign language or any variant of his own, nor is he familiar with other cultures (they are no concern of his). But there is more to it than this. If he does know foreign languages, which means that as an intellectual he has an insight into the cultural heritage of other nations, great or small, they serve only to let him draw analogies, to the detriment of those others, naturally. Kitsch and folklore, folkloric kitsch if you prefer, are nothing but camouflaged nationalism, a fertile field for nationalist ideology. The upsurge of folklore studies, both in this country and in the world at

---

* Biscuits in the shape of hearts, or people, or things, decorated with coloured sugar, and sold by bakers in Vojvodina, Serbia, and other parts of ex-Yugoslavia. (Translator's note.)

large, is due to nationalism, not anthropology. Insisting on the famous *couleur locale* is likewise, outside an artistic context (i.e. unless in the service of artistic truth), a covert form of nationalism. Nationalism is thus, in the first place, negativity; nationalism is a negative spiritual category because it thrives on denial and by denial. We are not what they are. We are the positive pole, they the negative. Our values, national, nationalist, have no function except in relation to the nationalism of those others: we *are* nationalist, but they are even more so; we slit throats (when we must) but they do too and even more; we are drunkards, they are alcoholics; our history is proper only *in relation* to theirs; our language is pure only *in relation* to theirs. Nationalism lives by relativism. There are no general values – aesthetic, ethical, etc. Only relative ones. And it is principally in this sense that nationalism is reactionary. *All* that matters is to be better than my brother or half-brother, the rest are no concern of mine. To jump not very high but higher than him, the others do not count. This is what we have defined as fear. Others are allowed to catch us up, even to overtake us, that is no concern of ours. The goals of nationalism are always *attainable*, attainable because modest, modest because mean. You don't go jumping or shot-putting to reach *your own* best but to beat the only others who matter, so similar and so different, on whose account you took the field. The nationalist, as we noted, fears no one but his brother. But him he fears with an existential, pathological dread; for the chosen enemy's victory is his own *total* defeat, the annihilation of his very being. As a shirker and a nonentity the nationalist does not aim high. Victory over the *chosen* enemy, the other, is total victory. This is why nationalism is the ideology of hopelessness, the ideology of feasible victory, victory which is guaranteed and defeat which is never final. The nationalist fears no one, 'no one save God', but his God is made to his own measure, it is his double sitting at the next table, his own brother, as impotent as himself, 'the pride of the family', a family entity, the conscious and organized section of the family and the nation – pale Cousin *Jim*. To be a nationalist is therefore to be an individual with no obligations. It is to be 'a coward who will not admit his cowardice; a murderer who represses his murderous proclivities without being able to master them, yet who dares not kill except in effigy, or in the anonymity of a crowd; a malcontent who, fearing the consequences of rebellion, dares not rebel' – the spitting image of Sartre's anti-Semite. Whence, we wonder, such cowardice, such an attitude, such an upsurge of nationalism, in this day and age? Oppressed by ideologies, on the margin of social changes, crammed and lost between antagonistic ideologies, unequal to individual rebellion because it is denied to him, the individual finds himself in a quandary, a vacuum; although he is a social being, he takes no part in social life; although he is an individualist, individuality has been refused him in the name of ideology; what is left but to seek his social being *elsewhere*? The nationalist is a frustrated individualist, nationalism is the frustrated (collective) expression of this kind of individualism, at once ideology and anti-ideology . . .

Translated by Ivana Djordjević, with thanks to Pascale Delpech and M. T.

Note

This glittering polemic first appeared in 1973, and quickly became well known. Kiš himself, relishing the scandal, called the text "notorious".

He reprinted it in *The Anatomy Lesson* (1978), a book-length refutation of certain highly-placed critics of his previous book, the series of linked stories called *A Tomb for Boris Davidović* (1976). These critics (Kiš dubbed them the *Cosa Nostra*: the old-boy network of favoured literati who superintended Belgrade's cultural institutions) had accused Kiš of shameless plagiarism: decanting motley odds and ends into preset narrative moulds.

This moribund anti-modernist scolding bore, in the Yugoslav context, a two-fold political attack. The stories in *Boris Davidović* were blatantly anti-Stalinist, which was acceptable in Tito's "non-aligned" federation; but implicitly they were, perhaps, anti-socialist too. As if this weren't dubious enough, there was the matter of Kiš's poetics. Aesthetically, Stalinism and nationalism are twins under the skin. Cosmopolitanism is a mortal enemy of both, and Danilo Kiš was cosmopolitan to the core. Half Hungarian-Jewish and half Montenegrin, the epic and surrealist traditions of Serbian culture were merged in him with the ironic, urbane reflexes of Mitteleuropa. He was a polyglot; he translated from Russian, Hungarian, French and German into Serbo-Croat. He was much influenced by Russian formalism, and used its methods of montage and "estrangement" in his own fiction.

All this was inherently suspect, if not offensive to the official guardians of Yugoslav (especially Serbian) literature, who thought that *Boris Davidović* furnished their chance for revenge. Despite their not scrupling to invoke anti-Semitism and the "purity of national culture" in their cause, the mafiosi lost the battle for public, professional and legal (sic) support so resoundingly, one easily forgets that the practical outcome was defeat for Kiš: he emigrated from Belgrade to Paris, where he lived for the rest of his life.

Now the "Serbo-Croatian variant" of nationalist antagonism has been exploited to rend Yugoslavia apart, and the prestigious name of Danilo Kiš has been stolen back. For . . .

> Not even the dead succeed in getting away from the national relabelling. Danilo Kiš, the last "Yugoslav" writer, a writer who emphasized his Central European, his Yugoslav identity, who fled to Paris from the local manipulators, not even he could escape. Though they couldn't take him alive, they got him when he was dead, burying him with full Orthodox pomp. Now they wave his name like a national banner, the same ones who had once chased him out.

Dubravka Ugrešić in *The Times Literary Supplement*,
15 May 1992.

Post Script

For reasons of space, this Appendix had to be omitted from the first edition of this book; I had almost forgotten about it when I read a jagged, child's-eye account of recent – wartime – visits to the six republics by the novelist Christopher Hope.

"Is it right for a Christian to live with hatred in his heart?" the novelist asked a gung-ho monk at the Morača monastery in Montenegro. "The urbane, smiling Monk considers the question. 'No. But the other side are much worse.' "

Acknowledgements and Notes

I thank Ervin and Mirjam, my first friends in what used to be Yugoslavia, for everything; and my editor Neil Belton, for his discernment and tireless support. So many other people helped me in so many ways that it would be invidious to try and list them – even if I knew all their names.

*

The epigraphs come from: Ivan V. Lalić, *The Passionate Measure*, translated by Francis R. Jones (Anvil, 1989). Ivo Andrić, *The Bridge on the Drina*, trans Lovett F. Edwards (The University of Chicago Press, 1977). Milovan Djilas, *Njegoš. Poet, Prince, Bishop*, trans Michael B. Petrovich (Harcourt, Brace & World, Inc., 1966). Danilo Kiš, *Gorki talog iskustva* (BIGZ, Belgrade, 1991).

I am generally indebted to the following books about Yugoslavia: Ivo Banac's majestic *The National Question in Yugoslavia: Origins, History, Politics* (Cornell University Press, 1988 edition), and his *With Stalin Against Tito: Cominformist Splits in Yugoslav Communism* (Cornell, 1988). Paul Shoup, *Communism and the Yugoslav National Question* (Columbia University Press, 1968). J. B. Hoptner, *Yugoslavia in Crisis 1934–1941* (Columbia, 1962). Dennison Rusinow, *The Yugoslav Experiment 1948–1974* (Hurst, 1977). Wayne S. Vucinich, ed., *Contemporary Yugoslavia. Twenty Years of Socialist Yugoslavia* (University of California Press, 1969). Stevan K. Pavlowitch *Yugoslavia* (Ernest Benn, 1971). The *Handbook on Yugoslavia* (Federal Secretariat for Information, Belgrade, 1987). I take this chance to thank Branka Magaš for her excellent commentaries on Yugoslavia in *New Left Review* and elsewhere.

Slovenian Spring

'Nationalism is not . . .': from Isaiah Berlin, *The Crooked Timber of Humanity* (Murray, 1990). *Baptism on the Savica* is translated in *Slovene Studies* (1987). Claudio Magris's comment occurs in his *Danube* (Collins Harvill, 1989). I was helped by Carole Rogel's *The Slovenes and Yugoslavism* (East European Monographs/

Columbia University Press, 1977). The English traveller who disparaged Nebotičnik was Bernard Newman in *Albanian Back-Door*. Tito, Djilas and Kardelj discussing self-management are described by Djilas, *The Unperfect Society: Beyond the New Class* (Methuen, 1969). 'It was the . . . in Eastern Europe': from Slavenka Drakulić, *How We Survived Communism And Even Laughed* (Hutchinson, 1992). Quotations of Slavoj Žižek come from his interview in *Radical Philosophy* 58 (Summer 1991). Anne Dacie's *Instead of the Brier* (Harvill, 1949) deserves to be read.

Istran Summer

'A country so bountifully favoured . . .': from T. G. Jackson's superb *Dalmatia, the Quarnero and Istria* (London, 1887). Ligio Zanini's *Martin Muma* appeared as a double issue of *La Battana* (95/96), a quarterly review published at OLGE-NIRO »EDIT«, Boulevard Marx-Engels 20, Fiume-Rijeka, Croatia. The encomia of Istran stone are from Adrian Stokes, *Stones of Rimini* (Faber, 1934). Marisa Madieri's *verde aqua* is published by Einaudi. The 'very strange scene' on Brioni in 1956 was described by Veljko Mićunović in his *Moscow Diary* (Chatto & Windus, 1980). Quotations from Richard Burton's diary are from Melvyn Bragg, *Rich. The Life of Richard Burton* (Hodder & Stoughton, 1988). Non-alignment: I am indebted to Alvin Z. Rubinstein, *Yugoslavia and the Non-Aligned World* (Princeton University Press, 1970); Richard L. Jackson, *The Non-Aligned, the UN, and the Superpowers* (Praeger, 1983); A. W. Singham and S. Hune, *Non-Alignment in an Age of Alignments* (Zed Books, 1986).

Bridges of Bosnia

The Bogomil footnote is from Steven Runciman, *The Mediaeval Manichee* (Cambridge University Press, 1947). On the national liberation war: in addition to the general books cited above, I commend Mark Wheeler, *Britain and the War for Yugoslavia, 1940–1943* (EEM/Columbia, 1980). Fitzroy Maclean's classic account of his adventure with the partisans, *Eastern Approaches,* has been reprinted by Penguin Books (1991). Basil Davidson's *Partisan Picture* (1946) and *Special Operations Europe* (1987), should not be missed. 'The enemy is . . . hands three times': from *The War Diaries of Vladimir Dedijer*, published in three volumes by the University of Michigan Press, (Ann Arbor 1990). The revisionist account of Allied policy toward wartime Yugoslavia is given in Nora Beloff, *Tito's Flawed Legacy* (Gollancz, 1985), and in books by David Martin and Michael Lees. *The Railway – An Adventure in Construction,* edited by E. P. Thompson, was published by the British-Yugoslav Association in 1948. 'The officers of . . . 1945 general election': from Michael McConville, *A Small War in the Balkans* (Macmillan, 1986). Morgan-Giles was writing in the *British-Yugoslav Journal*, 1990/2 'Our people's lives . . . or accept it': quoted by Celia Hawkesworth, *Ivo Andrić: Bridge between East and West* (Athlone, 1984).

The Dark Side of Europe

Edith Durham's *High Albania* (1909) was recently reprinted by Virago Books. *What the Kosovars Say and Demand* ('8 Nëntori' Publishing House. Tirana, 1990) is a valuable collection of articles, polemics, interviews and bulletins by Kosovars about the events of 1988–90. The 'Letter to the World's Public' was published in issue 1/1990 of the *Serbian Literary Quarterly*, published by the Association of Serbian Writers. The Croat journalist who researched Kosovo crime statistics was Darko Hudelist (see *Start* magazine, 31 October 1987). The Belgrade book on the same matter is *Kosovski čvor: drešiti ili seći?* (Kronos, 1990). For background on Kosovo in

Yugoslavia, Arshi Pipa and S. Repishti, eds., *Studies on Kosova* (EEM/Columbia, 1984). There is a facing-page translation of the *kanuni: The Code of Lekë Dukagjini* (Gjonlekaj Publishing Co., New York, 1989). The novel of Kadaré's that I quote is *Chronicle in Stone* (Serpent's Tail, 1987; originally, Tirana, 1971). A fascinating consideration of the battle of Kosovo in history and myth is Thomas A. Emmert, *Serbian Golgotha: Kosovo, 1389* (EEM/Columbia, 1990). Anne Kindersley's *The Mountains of Serbia* (Murray, 1976) can be commended as a companion to the Serbian monasteries. The verses about Lazar's choice are quoted from *Marko the Prince. Serbo-Croat Heroic Songs*, trans Anne Pennington and Peter Levi (Duckworth, 1984). Milošević at Gazimestan: from Ivo Banac, 'Political Change and National Diversity', *Daedalus*, 1989.

Montenegro: 'Favoured Above Millions'

I learned much from Sir Gardner Wilkinson, *Dalmatia and Montenegro* (Murray, 1848). Milovan Djilas, *Montenegro* (Methuen, 1964), and his *Njegoš*, op. cit. Christopher Boehm, *Montenegrin Social Organization and Values: political ethnography of a refugee area tribal adaptation* (AMS Press, New York, 1983). A fusty old translation of *The Mountain Wreath* exists, by J. W. Wiles. Information about Montenegro's overrepresentation in the power structures of federal Yugoslavia can be found in Lenard J. Cohen's exhaustive *The Socialist Pyramid: Elites and Power in Yugoslavia* (Tri-Service Press, 1989). Regarding 1848, Ivo Banac's book is peerless. 'came into existence . . .': from Edvard Kardelj, *Reminiscences* (Blond & Briggs, 1982). 'very hard for me . . .': from Phyllis Auty, *Tito. A Biography* (Penguin, 1980). 'learned about Russia . . .': from Mičunović, op. cit. 'It was enough . . .': from *Khrushchev Remembers: The Glasnost Tapes* (Little, Brown & Company, 1990). Michael Charlton's article in *Encounter*, July-August 1983, quotes the Hungarian general. Djilas's *Conversations with Stalin* was published by Rupert Hart-Davis in 1962.

Clear Sky over Serbia

Aleksandar Karadjordjević's retort: from 'On the road to Ruritania', by R. Tomlinson, *The Independent on Sunday*, 22 December 1991. The epic poem quoted is 'The Beginning of the Revolt against the Dahiyas', from *Marko the Prince*, op. cit. 'a door to the East . . .': from Le Corbusier, *Journey to the East* (The MIT Press, 1987). 'For the federalists . . .': from James Gow, *Legitimacy and the Military: the Yugoslav Crisis* (Pinter, 1992). 'We have evolved . . .': from Rusinow, op. cit. 'Intellectuals on the road to class power' is the title of a book by György Kónrad and Istvan Szélenyi. Bogdan Bogdanović's satirical account of the Eighth Session, and his open letter, are in *Mrtvoužice* (BST/Cesarec, Zagreb, 1988). The eight kinds of film in *WR: Mysteries of the Organism* are enumerated by John Russell Taylor, *Directors and Directions* (1975). Other books by Djilas include *The New Class, Memoir of a Revolutionary, Wartime, Tito: the Story from Inside, Rise and Fall*.

Behind the Curtain

Basil Davidson's books are cited above. The only work of Aleksandar Tišma yet translated is *The Use of Man* (Faber, 1989). The Western analyst quoted is Professor Paul Magosci at the School of Slavonic and East European Studies, London, on 13 May 1991. Kiš's major fiction including *The Encyclopaedia of the Dead* (1989), is published by Faber.

The Drunken Geese of Croatia

Antemurale christianitatis – before the ramparts of Christendom – was the old Vatican description of Catholic Croatia. 'the obvious aim . . .': from F. Tudjman, *Nationalism in Contemporary Europe* (EEM/Columbia, 1981). Virago publish two works by Dubravka Ugrešić: *Fording the Stream of Consciousness* (1991) and *In the Jaws of Life* (1992). 'When we resolved . . .': reprinted in *Deset dni vojne za Slovenijo* (Mladina, 1991). 'WHEN IT COMES TO MARCHING MANY DO NOT KNOW': from Bertolt Brecht, *Poems 1913–1956* (Methuen 1976). The detail about the great powers in 1912: from Barbara Jelavich, *Russia's Balkan Entanglements 1806–1914* (Cambridge, 1991).

Yearning for the South

'Regardless of how . . .': from Leon Trotsky, *The Balkan Wars 1912–13* (Monad Press, New York, 1980). Stoyan Pribichevich describes the eels of Ohrid in his *Macedonia. Its People and History* (Pennsylvania State University Press, 1982). 'Yearning for the South' is quoted in the translation by Milne Holton and G. W. Reid, from their anthology *Reading the Ashes. An Anthology of the Poetry of Modern Macedonia* (University of Pittsburgh Press, 1977).

Epilogue

Peace-making, Peace-keeping: European Security and the Yugoslav Wars by James Gow and James D. D. Smith (Brassey's/CDS, London, 1992) was useful to me, and I recommend it to anyone seeking to unravel the rôle of the European Community in 1991 and early 1992. I am indebted to James Gow and Bojan Bujic for insights offered in conversation. " . . . failure in Yugoslavia": Martin Woollacoot in *The Guardian*, 27 August 1992. " . . . right all along": from the *Radio Free Europe/Radio Liberty Research Report on Eastern Europe*, 28 February 1992. (I also used *RFE/RL Reports* for 5 July 1991, 25 October 1991, and 31 July 1992.) "remonstrance after remonstrance, protestation after protestation": from Gladstone's speech upon the Eastern Question to the House of Commons, 7 May 1877.

In the light of current European treatment of the Bosnian Serb leadership, the relevant passage of Gladstone's superb oration is worth quoting at length: " . . . Necessary guarantees, something beyond mere promises, adequate securities, consisting in something beyond and above the engagements or ostensible proceedings of the Turkish Government constituted indeed the pith of the extracts which were read by the Chancellor of the Exchequer on the first night of the Session from the Instructions to Lord Salisbury. Well, what has now become of those necessary guarantees? They are all gone to the winds. We are told in the despatch published this morning that we are to found our hopes on the fact that the Porte has promised certain things, and that as it has promised we cannot be sure that it will not perform. This is the vital point; it lies at the root of the whole matter. We are now told to rely on those promises. But, for my own part, I would repeat what I said on a former occasion, when we were trying remonstrance after remonstrance, protestation after protestation. Those protestations, and those remonstrances, and those representations which have been lavished in such abundance on the Porte by Her Majesty's Government, are all very well up to a certain point; up to the point at which there remains some semblance of a reasonable hope that they may possibly attain their end. But it is not so, when we have found by long and wide experience that they produce no substantial result whatever . . ."

In 1992, no one expected a Gladstone to arise and castigate the Western governments' timorous appeasing of Bosnia's destroyers. But did we – did the Bosnians – deserve the leaders we got? As their gems of insight risk being lost amid the scarlet torrent of atrocities in BiH, I have rescued three average sparklers for posterity. Prime Minister Major on 26 May: "I have reached the conclusion, not without some consideration, that Serbia bears the greatest responsibility for the present situation." Lord Carrington (formerly a Conservative foreign minister) on 22 June, after talks with Serbian leaders in Belgrade: "I got nowhere, I find this very disappointing." Foreign Minister Douglas Hurd, on returning from a visit to former Yugoslavia and Albania in mid June: "One of the things one learns from actually being [in BiH] is that the fears and hatreds which have been unleashed are absolutely formidable."

Appendix

Permission to translate and publish the text by Danilo Kiš was kindly given by Pascale Delpech. The translator is Ivana Djordjević (with thanks to Pascale Delpech and M. T.). Translation copyright © Pascale Delpech 1992. Christopher Hope's article was published in *The Guardian*, 11 July 1992.

Index